SHANKS' MARE

SHANKS' MARE

Being a translation of the TOKAIDO volumes of

HIZAKURIGE, Japan's great comic novel of travel

& ribaldry by IKKU JIPPENSHA (1765–1831)

Faithfully rendered into English by THOMAS SATCHELL

Published by the CHARLES E. TUTTLE COMPANY of Rutland, Vermont
& Tokyo, Japan: publishers of "Books to Span the East & West"

Representatives

Continental Europe: BOXERBOOKS, INC., Zurich

British Isles: PRENTICE-HALL INTERNATIONAL, INC., London

Australasia: PAUL FLESCH & CO., PTY. LTD., Melbourne

Canada: M. G. HURTIG LTD., Edmonton

Published by the Charles E. Tuttle Company, Inc.
of Rutland, Vermont & Tokyo, Japan
with editorial offices at Suido 1-chome, 2-6
Bunkyo-ku, Tokyo, Japan

© 1960 by Charles E. Tuttle Co., Inc.

Library of Congress Catalog Card No. 60-14370

International Standard Book No. 0-8048-0524-5

First Tuttle edition, 1960
Seventh printing, 1970

PRINTED IN JAPAN

TABLE OF CONTENTS

NOTE TO THE NEW EDITION

THOMAS Satchell's translation of the Tokaido section of *Hizakurige* was published by subscription in Kobe in 1929. It introduced for the first time in English a celebrated comic novel that had entertained generations of Japanese readers. Regrettably, however, the extremely limited number of copies in the first edition (which, by the way, has become a collector's item of considerable value) did not allow the translation to acquire the large audience that it most decidedly deserved. It is thus with great pleasure that the publishers once again introduce this ribald Japanese classic to foreign readers.

Modestly, Mr. Satchell did not permit the appearance of his name on the title page of the first edition. In fact, it was only in the Japanese publisher's notice at the end of the volume that any clue to the translator's identity could be found, and then only in the phonetic characters in which his name was printed. It thus becomes a privilege to identify him at long last and to give him proper credit for his achievement.

Thomas Satchell was born in London in 1867 and first came to Japan in 1899 to join the staff of an English-language newspaper in Kobe. In 1902, he became editor of the Yokohama *Japan Herald*. From then until the outbreak of the Pacific War in 1941, he engaged in newspaper work and in the teaching of English. He was interned during hostilities and was unable to take up active work again at the end of the war. He died in Kobe in 1956, leaving his Japanese wife and two daughters, and was buried there at the Kasugano Foreign Cemetery.

Satchell's deep interest in the language and literature of Japan led to the production of another translation: a privately printed (1935) selection of poems from the *Manyoshu* and the *Hyakunin Isshu*, two of Japan's poetic classics. The book was called *These from the Land of Nippon*. The translations, he explained, were "intended to be read not as translations but as verses inspired by the originals."

Summer, 1960   THE PUBLISHERS

TRANSLATOR'S PREFACE

HIS book is a translation of the Tōkaidō section of 'Hizakurigé' by Ikku Jippensha, and is unabridged, save for certain punning poems, mostly on the names of places through which the travellers passed, and the few sentences joining them to the text. Occasionally, also, some details as to the temples, etc., which are to be found in all guidebooks, have been omitted as superfluous. It has to be remembered that 'Hizakurigé' was intended to be a guidebook, albeit a comic one. 'Hizakurigé' was originally published in parts, each part having a preface reminding the reader of the stage in the journey which had been reached in the previous issue. These prefaces now seem superfluous and they have therefore been omitted in the translation. The general preface to the whole work has been retained, however. One alteration in the order in which the travels are generally issued has been made. In modern editions the part called 'Introductory' is put at the beginning of the work. Inasmuch, however, as it was written twelve years after the issue of the first part and is of the nature of an afterthought, containing many details in the careers of the two heroes which are inconsistent with those related in the body of the book, it has been thought advisable to consign it to an appendix.

The translator feels that some apology is due for the paucity of the notes. 'Hizakurigé' offers an inexhaustible field for the commentator, both from the linguistic and the antiquarian points of view, but details which are of interest to Japanese readers often do not appeal to foreign readers, while on the other hand there is much that the foreign reader would like to know which seems superfluous to the Japanese reader. The native commentaries therefore leave something to be desired in the information they give, and extra information has to be sought elsewhere, at the expense of much time and labour. The best commentary is that issued by Mr. Yonekichi Deguchi in an edition of the Tōkaidō section of the work published by the Isseisha of Tōkyō. Mr. Deguchi's work came to the notice of the translator too late to enable him to take full advantage of its learning, but he has to acknowledge his indebtedness to it for clearing up many doubtful points. The only other edition with a commentary is that issued by the Sanseidō. This is now out of print.

The translator is also greatly indebted to Murray's ' Handbook for Japan,' an inexhaustible mine of learning on Japanese customs and traditions due to the researches of Prof. Basil Hall Chamberlain, and also to the same author's ' Things Japanese.' He has also to express his grateful thanks to Mr. M. G. Mori for directing him to other sources of information and solving many problems, but chiefly his obligations are due to Mr. K. Kubota, who first introduced him to ' Hizakurigé ' and has since devoted many hours to assisting him in the elucidation of the text.

The colloquial side of a language always offers greater difficulties in comprehension and translation than the literary side, and ' Hizakurigé ' is written almost wholly in the colloquial language, the difficulty of which is increased by the extensive use of dialect. The two heroes speak the vulgar Edo dialect, which may be compared to the London Cockney dialect, and the other persons introduced speak in the dialects of their parts of the country. Thus we have a constant variety of dialects throughout the book, adding greatly to the flavour of the original but increasing the difficulty of comprehension. Added to this there is a constant flow of jokes, some so subtle as to be no longer comprehensible to the commentators, and innumerable puns, which are the despair of the translator. Altogether the difficulties of translation are considerable, and although the present translation has been gone through many times to eliminate ' howlers,' the translator feels that he cannot hope to have been successful in avoiding all blunders. They must be attributed entirely to his own inabilities and in no degree to those whose assistance he has sought.

Some difficulty has been experienced in getting suitable illustrations for the text. The original illustrations, some of which were by Ikku himself, were not very good. In later complete editions of 'Hizakurigé' they were replaced by illustrations which had either been redrawn from the originals in the early editions or were entirely new. It is from these illustrations that the cuts in the text have been taken. They are full of humour, the only pity being that the original engraving was badly done.

Finally the translator has to thank all others who have in any way helped to make this translation a success or assisted in its production, including Mr. A. Morgan Young, who has kindly gone through the proofs.

Money.—The metal currency of feudal times in Japan was rather complicated owing to the variation in the standards of value and the private minting of coins. The coin used in everyday life was the **mon,** a copper coin with a hole in the middle so that it could be strung on a cord for convenience in carrying a quantity. The purchasing power of the **mon** was practically that of the modern **sen,** now the lowest coin in the Japanese currency and about equivalent to a farthing in English money. There was a smaller coin than the **mon,** called a **bun,** ten of which were equivalent to a **mon,** and there were a number of larger coins, the value of which in terms of the **mon** varied. The following table gives a rough idea of the value of these coins in terms of the **mon** :—

> Ryō (gold)=1,000 mon
> Mommé or Koban (gold)=1/60 of ryō
> Bu=250 mon
> Kwan or kwammé=1,000 mon
> Shū=62.5 mon
> Bun=1/10 of mon
> Rin=1/10 of bun

Distances.—Distances were measured in **ri** and **chō,** 36 **chō** being equivalent to one **ri,** which equals 2-2/5 miles.

Pronunciation.—In the pronunciation of Japanese names the general rule is for the vowels to be pronounced as in Italian and the consonants as in English. **G** is always hard as in ' good ' ; **j** soft as in ' join ' ; and **ch** soft as in ' chat.'

The approximate vowel-sound equivalents in English are **a** in ' part,' **i** in ' kit,' **e** in ' let,' **o** in ' nor,' **u** as in ' should.' In words of more than one syllable **u** is slurred over (breathed), so that ' Densuké ' sounds like ' Denské.' In the diphthongs each vowel retains its individual value. Thus **ai** is pronounced like the vowels in ' my inn,' **ei** like the vowels in ' may eat,' etc. There are no silent letters and all vowels must be pronounced clearly, especially finally. Thus ' Kita ' must be pronounced more like ' Keetar ' than ' Keeter.'

Double vowels and consonants are pronounced long.

LIFE OF IKKU JIPPENSHA

SADAKAZU Shigeta, better known by his pen-name of Ikku Jippensha,* was born in 1765 in the province of Suruga, now part of Shizuoka Prefecture. His father appears to have been a petty official and thus able to secure admittance for his son to a nobleman's house in Edo, where he was brought up. Later Ikku himself occupied some small official position in Edo till, in 1791, when he was twenty-six years old, he moved to Ōsaka and entered the office of Tosanokami Odagiri, a magistrate of that city. Whether he had started his literary career before he left Edo does not appear, but there is evidence that he wrote for the stage at Ōsaka during his residence there of six or seven years. His first venture in matrimony was at Ōsaka, when he was adopted into the family of a timber-dealer by marriage with the daughter of the house, a procedure still followed when there is no heir to succeed to the headship of the family. The position of adopted son-in-law is always irksome, however, and Ikku found means to get the marriage dissolved before he returned to Edo. Another adventure as an adopted son-in-law also ended in failure, but a third marriage proved more fortunate.

---

* In Japanese these names would be reversed,—Jippensha Ikku, Shigeta Sadakazu,—the family name coming first and the personal name last.

On his return to Edo Ikku seems to have taken to literature for his means of livelihood, a number of humorous sketches appearing from that time over his pseudonym of Ikku Jippensha. It was the custom of the time to take another name on attainment of manhood, and thus Ikku changed his boyhood name of Ichiku to Sadakazu when he reached man's estate. When he began to write, however, he adopted his former name as a pseudonym, shortening it to Ikku, and added to it the name Jippensha, which is supposed to be a punning reading of certain Chinese characters connected with incense, in the sale of which he is said to have been at one time engaged. These books brought him a certain amount of recognition as a humorous writer, but it was not till 1802 that he leapt into fame with the first part of a series of comic adventures on the Tōkaidō, the great road which connected the Shōgun's capital of Edo with the Emperor's capital of Kyōto. The humours of the road had been touched upon before by other writers, but never with such liveliness of characterisation and imagination. 'Hizakurigé,' the name under which the travels were issued, means literally 'knee chestnut-horse,' a term used in the same sense as the English 'Shanks's Pony.' It gives a series of pictures of the characters met on the road, the inn life, and the troubles and adventures of two ne'erdoweels of Edo named Kita-hachi and Yajirobei. Kita and Yaji, as they are called for short, are now as familiar in Japan as Mr. Pickwick and Sam Weller. Indeed, the first part of 'Hizakurigé,' which covered the ground between Edo and Hakoné, brought Ikku into much the same prominence in Japan as Dickens was to achieve in England some thirty-five years later with the 'Posthumous Papers of the Pickwick Club.'

Year after year Ikku continued to issue a portion of the journey till, in 1809, he had taken his two heroes to the end of their adventures in Ōsaka. That such a gold mine as they had proved should henceforward be neglected was an impossible thought. Imitators had appeared, but the public demanded more of the real thing. In 1810 accordingly Ikku accompanied his two adventurers to the great Buddhist shrine of Kompira on the island of Shikoku, and in 1811 he went with them as far as Miyajima. These were short excursions. A longer one was to occupy most of the remainder of his life. This was a journey along the Kisokaidō, the road running from Gifu Prefecture north to Nagano. Begun in 1812 this series was not completed till 1822. In 1814, however,

Ikku turned aside and wrote an introductory portion to the whole series of travels, detailing the life story of Yajirobei and Kitahachi up to the time they left Edo and the circumstances which drove them out of that city. Twelve years had elapsed since he had started the two on their travels, and many of the suggestions as to their past lives that had been given in the course of the narration had evidently slipped Ikku's memory. He forgot that he had taken his heroes to Fuchū in Suruga Province and displayed them as totally ignorant of the topography of that town, since in the ' Introduction ' he assigns them that very town as a birthplace,— in fact makes them not Edoites at all but migrants from the provinces. He forgot also that he had killed Yaji's wife and given him children when he shows him in the ' Introduction ' as divorcing his childless wife. In spite of these glaring errors and others of lesser importance this ' Introduction ' was henceforth printed at the beginning of all collected editions of the travels and has since continued to hold that position.

Ikku had still nine years to live when he finished the adventures of Kita and Yaji on the Kisokaidō, but it was not until his course was almost run that he again introduced them to the public. Probably their resuscitation was due to financial reasons, for in March 1830 Ikku was burnt out of his home by the great fire of that year, which cut a swathe through Edo over two and a half miles long. The new series reverted to the style of the ' Introduction,' inasmuch as it dealt entirely with adventures in Edo. The first part was issued in 1831 and a second part was promised. But this Ikku did not live to complete. He was stricken with paralysis in July of that year, and died on August 7th, in his sixty-seventh year.

The tradition that Ikku was a great practical joker, which obtained even when he was still alive, is not substantiated. Stories were told of how he had once carried home a bathtub on his head, confounding with his ready wit all the persons into whom he blundered on his way ; how he had induced a New Year visitor to take a bath and had then appropriated his clothes and paid a round of New Year calls on his own account ; how he had startled the mourners at his funeral by concealing fireworks in his death-robes, which exploded when the body was burned. This last story, of course, was not told till after his death, but the apocryphal nature of all the stories is shown by the fact that they were well-known jokes in the books of humour before the time of Ikku. As a matter of fact Ikku seems to have been a somewhat saturnine person, a conclusion which is supported by the most authentic picture of him, reproduced above from the 'Gisaku Rokkasen.' It is recorded that a person who once accompanied him on one of his journeys, expecting to be greatly amused and enlivened by his jokes, was disappointed by Ikku's taciturnity.

Judging from hints dropped in 'Hizakurigé' he was a sworn enemy of all shams. He hated priests, whom he evidently regarded as hypocrites, and he was not inclined to take the swaggering samurai at their own valuation. It is stated that he was once in conflict with the authorities owing to the publication of a book entitled 'Bakemono Taiheiki,' which was deemed to infringe an ordinance prohibiting pictures and writings concerning warriors, and that he was chained by the hands for fifty day as a punishment. He was therefore on the official blacklist and had to be careful what he wrote. His coarseness, like Rabelais's, may be considered a screen behind which he fought abuses, but it was more probably an offspring of the moral atmosphere of the time. In any case it is a part of the picture which cannot be omitted if a correct view of the whole is to be obtained.

The ashes of Ikku were buried in the Zenryū Temple at Asakusa, Tōkyō, and a tombstone erected bearing the Buddhist name given him after death of 'Shingetsūin Ikku Nikkokōji.' Three years later his family and friends erected a monument to him in the precincts of the Chōmei Temple, Mukojima. On the face of the monument appears the well-known comic crest or seal (reproduced on the title-page) which Ikku had adopted, in the shape of a bamboo-rake with the first character of his personal name ('Sadakazu') inscribed in a circle, and above this an inscription and a poem, which may be freely rendered :—

However novel and interesting things may appear at first, when they become common they lose their interest; but things of which people never tire are a bright moonlight night and dinner, to which may be added a book and saké.

My allotted span of life has passed. Oh, give me peace and rest at last !

HIZAKURIGÉ

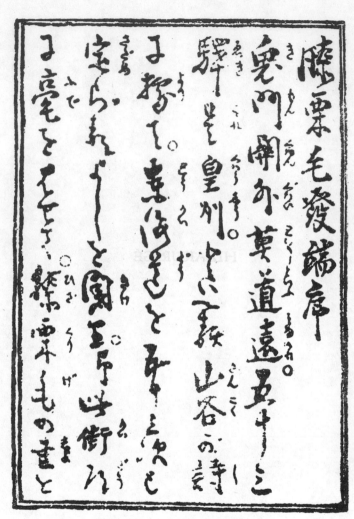

Preface to Original Edition

PREFACE

"IT is not far between the barriers, since fifty-three stages are all our country." Thus wrote Sankoku, the poet, and I have heard that it was from this poem that the stages of the Tōkaidō came to be fixed at fifty-three.

Again, it is the song of the carriers about the Hakoné hills that softens the hearts of the labour-masters, and it is the song of the postboys about the sparrows in the bamboos that awakens pity in the hearts of cut-throats.

Drinking in the virtue of these songs—along with something else—while turning over the leaves of the road-books on the journey to the capital;—using the staves of the carriers as my pen, and inspired by the music of their cries, here have I written a record of the fifty-three stages of the Tōkaidō.

You will find many bad jokes and much that is worthless in the book, which is moreover overburdened with many poems where sound and sense conflict. Along with this there is much of the one-night love-traffic of the roads,—in fact there is as great a variety of objects and everything is as mixed together as the goods in the shop of a general dealer.

This much by way of a preface. Now we will start on our journey.

BOOK ONE

BOOK ONE

HE breeze murmuring through the pines on a beautiful spring day sounds like one singing to the harp of how the pine trees at the gate bring wealth, freedom and happiness. Then truly the highways seem like the hair of the head. Not a single hair is disturbed,—a sign of the glorious times in which we live, when the reputation of our warlike heroes survives only in the pictures of cock-crowing Adzuma;—when our bows and swords—even those made of wood—are hung up as an offering to the god of the thousand swift-brandishing weapons; —when the great exploits of the land rich in harbours,—the deeds of the Golden Age,—seem to pass before our eyes. Now is the time to visit all the celebrated places in the country and fill our heads with what we have seen, so that when we become old and bald we shall have something to talk about over the teacups. Let us accept the invitation of these bosom friends and go with them on their long long journey. Let us join this dissipated Yajirobei and his hanger-on Kitahachi, with their money kept warm in the loin-cloths round their navels; with their light foot-gear and their many shells of ointment, which will keep their feet from getting sore for thousands of miles; and their cotton robes dappled like the flesh of a clam. Let us go with them through foot-worn Yamato, welcomed by the divine wind that blows from the Grand Shrine of Isé, with the flowers of the capital and the plum-blossoms of Naniwa at the end of our journey.

Here they are already at Takinawa, which reminds them of the epigram

> We remember we've forgotten
> When we get to Takinawa.

But they have nothing to forget. Theirs is the easy life of the bachelor. No more than the rats are they required to waste money on rent, and as all the property they have is tied up in a bundle they have no anxiety about that. It is true that they had to make a small offering of rice at the family temple, and besides that pay a hundred coppers to get a travelling permit. Moreover, instead of paying what they owed to the landlord, they had to get their papers to pass the barriers. However, they made some money by selling to a second-hand dealer what they had of value, leaving the rubbish in the house for the next tenant to return thanks for. The stone weight for the pickle tub and the knife for scraping the pots and pans they left next door, and the house opposite got the torn sunshades and the oil jar. Nothing is left, but there is still the difficulty of paying the rice bill and the saké bill. They are very sorry to go away without paying them, but then as the old poem says

> Whether in this life or the next we cheat
> In either case our punishment we'll meet.

This made them burst into laughter; after which Yajirobei began humming,

> It is not right
> To fly by night
> To escape the dun,
> The Edo dun ;
> But what can be done
> Save tuck up your skirts
> And cut and run.
> So get you gone,
> You Edo dun !
> The water is deep and the river wide ;
> You can rave all you like on the other side.

Thus amusing themselves they quickly passed Shinagawa and Suzu-ga-mori, and reached Ōmori.

At Ōmori straw-plaiting is the great industry and each house sells articles made of it.

> 'To get us food please buy our ware'
> The children cry when travellers pass there.

Then they crossed the Rokugō ferry and went into the Mannenya to have a meal.

'Good morning,' said the maid.

'Let us have two trays, please,' said Yaji.

'I say, Yaji,' said Kita. 'Look at that girl. She used to be as slender as a willow and now she's like a mortar. Somebody's been pounding her. And isn't it strange that all the teahouses on the road should have dried up flowers in the alcoves. Look at that scroll. What is it ? '

'That's carp going up a waterfall,' said Yaji.

'Is it ? ' said Kita. 'I thought they were eating vermicelli.'

'You'd better eat your food instead of talking nonsense,' said Yaji. 'The soup's getting cold.'

'Halloa!' cried Kita. 'I never knew they'd brought it.'

They quickly gulped down the beans and rice set before them.

'Well, we've cleaned up that dish,' said Yaji.

'Let's go a bit further and have something tasty,' suggested Kita.

They paid for their meal and were just starting off when they saw a daimyō's procession coming from the opposite direction. The running footmen in front were an old man of sixty and a boy of fourteen or fifteen. Both of them were inn servants.

'Down, down!' cried one of the footmen. 'Off, those with headgear.'

'Those with the head covered don't have to squat down, it seems,' said Kita.

'Why?' asked Yaji.

'Because he said off with them!' answered Kita.

'Postboy, hold that horse's mouth,' called out the footman.

'How's he going to hold the mouth of the horse?' said Kita. 'He-he-he!'

'That man behind is not bending low enough,' went on the footman.

'Does he mean me?' asked Yaji. 'Of course I'm not low enough. You couldn't expect it of one who's as tall as Kumonryō on Atago Hill.'

'Don't make fun of them,' said Kita, 'or you'll get 'em angry.'

'Look,' said Yaji. 'Aren't those fine fellows? See how regularly their clothes are folded and how they keep in line. I know what they're like. They're like an airing of clothes in Yoshichō.'

'Halloa!' said Kita. 'Look at the helmets of those fellows with the bows. They look as though their heads were swollen.'

'And look at the length of their cloaks,' cried Yaji. 'You can see their whatyoumaycallems peeping out.'

'He's a fine fellow—the lord,' said Kita. 'I expect he's a great man with the maids.'

'There you go meddling with things you don't know anything about,' replied Yaji. 'You don't suppose people of that sort would stoop so low, do you?'

'Why not?' said Kita. 'There you are. Look at him. See how erect he is. Come on, we can go on now he's gone.'

They got up and went on, and at the end of the town met two postboys.

'Won't you ride, gentlemen,' they cried. 'We're on our way back.'

'We'll ride if it's cheap,' said Yaji.

'Just for a tip,' cried the postboys. 'Two hundred coppers.'

Having settled the price, Yaji and Kita got on the horses and rode along, the horses' bells ringing shan-shan-shan and the horses whinnying hin-hin-hin.

Then another postboy came past from the opposite direction.

'Halloa, you beast,' he said. 'You are early.'

'Go and eat dirt,' replied the other postboy.

'Ugh!' replied the first. 'Suck it.'

The only salutations of these kind of people when they passed each other seemed to be abuse.

'Here, Iga,' said the postboy of the horse Yaji was riding on, 'that fellow you were drinking with yesterday, that was Bōshū of the upper stage, wasn't it?'

This kind of people never call each other by their names but only by the name of the provinces they come from.

'Last night,' said Kita's postboy, as he spat in the road, 'the wife of that chap Bōshū was doing a job for herself outside the master's back door. The noise of it made me feel quite ill. She don't care where she does it, thinks I. I'll go out and give her one; for you see, I'd just had enough to make me feel like giving somebody one. So I lifted up my fist and was just going to give her one when she gives a jump. "Here, what are you doing?" she says. "What am I doing?" I says. "Do you think we're dogs' dirt?" I says, "Shut up," I says, and I give her one. "You rascal," she says, and she give me a shove that nearly sent me over, she's that big and strong. "Eh, what's that you're jawing about?" I says, and I give her a slap on the side of the face that sent her up against the stable wall and made her fall down. So I seized hold of her and as she was still jawing I shoved two or three pieces of rice-cake I'd bought for the master's kid into her mouth and while she was munching that I beat her. Then she said she wanted some more and I was feeling round for some and picked up a lump of horsedung by mistake and shoved it into her mouth and made her feel so bad that she got angry with me. So I had to promise at last that I'd give her a pair of clogs. What a bother!'

While they were amusing themselves by listening to this story they arrived on the outskirts of Kanagawa, and alighting from their horses continued their journey on foot. At Kanagawa the teahouses are all two-storied, with balustrades and flying galleries, giving a view over the sea.

The teahouse girls were standing at the gates calling, 'Come in and rest. Try our cold dishes heated up again. Cold broiled fish. Try our thick vermicelli. Our macaroni is the biggest. Come in and rest.' Thinking that they would have a little refreshment the two entered one of the teahouses.

'I say, Kita,' said Yaji, 'look how beautiful it is.'

'Aha!' said Kita. 'Quite a fine girl. What have they got to eat?'

After looking round to see what they had, Kitahachi ordered some fish and some saké. The girl wiped her hands on her apron and after warming some mackerel brought it to them with a saké bottle.

'Sorry to have kept you waiting,' she said.

'It's sure to taste nice as you've grilled it,' said Yaji.

But the girl only gave a forced laugh and went out to the front to tout for some more guests.

'Come in and rest,' she called. 'There's plenty of room at the back.'

'Of course there is,' said Kita. 'It runs all the way to Awa and Kazusa.'

Leaving the teahouse they went along joking and talking at the tops of their voices and amusing themselves with one thing and another, till they caught up, at the end of the stage, with a boy of twelve or thirteen who was going to Isé.

'Please give me a copper, masters,' called the boy.

'Of course, of course,' said Yaji. 'Where do you come from ? '

'I come from Ōshū,' said the boy.

'Whereabouts in Ōshū ? ' asked Kita.

'It's written on my hat,' said the boy.

'Chōmatsu, village of Hatayama, district of Shinobu, Ōshū,' read Yaji. 'Hatayama, eh ? I've been there. Is Master Yojirōbei in good health ? '

'I don't know anybody called Yojirōbei,' said the boy. 'But Master Yotarō lives next door to us.'

'Yes, yes,' said Yaji. 'That's him. And there should be an old gentleman named Nontarō living with him.'

'There is an old man,' said the boy.

'And Master Yotarō's wife is certainly a woman,' continued Yaji.

'Yes, Mistress Katsu's a woman,' said the boy. 'Your honour knows all about it.'

'I don't know how it is now,' said Yaji, 'but at that time the headman of the village was Denzaburō Kumano. His wife ran away after having had a love affair with a horse that her husband kept.'

'Your honour knows all about it,' said the boy. 'She went off with Master Horser as your honour says.'

'Wonderful ! Wonderful ! ' cried Kita.

'Here, boy ! ' called Yaji. 'Why do you lag behind ? Are you tired ? '

'I'm so hungry I don't know what to do,' said the boy.

'Shall I buy you some rice-cake ? ' asked Yaji. 'Come along.'

He bought the boy five or six rice-cakes in great elation.

'There you are, my boy,' he said. 'You see I know all about your village.'

Then the companion of the boy, also a lad of some fourteen or fifteen, came running after them.

'Here, Chōmatsu, Chōmatsu!' he called.

'Come along,' said Chōmatsu.

'Give me some rice-cake,' said the boy.

'Get that man in front to buy you some,' said Chōmatsu. 'All you've got to do is to say "Yes" to everything he asks you about your part of the country.'

'I'll get him to give me some too,' said the boy. He ran after Yaji and caught him up. 'Please buy me some rice-cake too,' he said.

'Where do you come from?' asked Yaji, and he looked at the writing on his hat. 'Aha!' he said, 'you are from Ōshū too. Imura, Shimosaka, eh? Look here, is there an old man named Yomosaku in your village?'

'Buy me the rice-cake first,' said the boy, 'or I shan't play up to you.'

'Get out,' said Yaji. 'Ha-ha-ha!'

'He-he-he! He had you that time,' laughed Kita.

Thus laughing and joking it was not long before they came to Hodogaya, where on both sides of the way the decoys were waiting, with their faces plastered with powder, just as if they were wearing masks, and all with blue aprons of the same pattern. It is said, indeed, that in ancient times this place was called Katabira.

Then they heard the lazy voice of a postboy singing:

> Mount Fuji has a cave wherein a horse may shelter;
> Will you not shelter me within your arms' embrace?

'Stop here, postboy,' called one of the teahouse girls.

'No, no,' said the postboy. 'Master's going to the Musashiya. But even the horse would stop for the sake of your face.'

'Hin-hin,' whinnied the horse.

After him came two or three more travellers.

'Stop here,' said the girl, seizing hold of one of them.

'Here, here!' said the traveller. 'You'll twist my arm off.'

'That won't matter,' said the girl. 'Stop here.'

'Don't be a fool,' said the traveller. 'If I lost my arm how should I be able to eat?'

'That would be all the better for us,' said the girl.

'Don't be troublesome. Let go,' said the man.

He broke loose from the girl and went on. After him came a travelling priest.

'Stop here,' said the girl.

The priest looked at her attentively.

'No,' he said. 'I think I'll go a little further.'

After him came a party of countrymen.

'Stop here,' cried the girl.

'I don't say we mightn't if it's cheap,' said one of them.

'Our charge is two hundred coppers each,' said the girl.

'Oh, oh!' said the countryman. 'We couldn't pay as much as that. We don't mind if the bath's a bit coldish, and we never have the rice-bowl refilled because we never eat more than six or seven cups of rice and soup each. And then for to-morrow's lunch we only want this basket stuffed as full as it will hold. That's all we want. We'll pay a hundred and sixty each.'

'If that's what you want you'd better go somewhere else,' said the girl.

'Well, we'll go on if you won't take us,' said the countryman, and they went on.

Laughing, Yaji and Kita went on till they reached Shina-no-zaka, when they found, to their surprise, that they had already reached the border of Musashi province.

Already the sun was nearing the western mountains, and as they intended to get as far as Totsuka that night they pushed on quickly.

'Wait a bit, Kita,' called Yaji. 'I've got something I want to talk to you about. Look here, they're sure to be always bothering us to take a girl at all the places we stop at. I've got a plan to prevent that. As I'm older than you I'll be the father, and as you're in the twenties you can be the son. Then at every place we stop at we can pretend to be father and son.'

'That's a good idea,' said Kita. 'It would be just the thing to keep them from bothering us. Must I call you father?'

'Yes, yes,' said Yaji. 'You must act like a son, you know, and do everything I tell you.'

'All right,' said Kita. 'But if there's a nice girl you mustn't try and keep her from your son.'

'Don't talk nonsense,' said Yaji. 'Halloa, here we are at Totsuka. Shall we go to the Sasaya?'

'Father,' said Kita.

30

' What is it ? '

' There are no girls here asking us to walk in.'

' No more there are,' said Yaji. ' There must be someone of importance stopping here, as all the inns have notices posted up.'

' That house over there looks all right,' suggested Kita.

' Here, my girl,' called Yaji. ' Can't you put us up for the night ? '

' There isn't an inn in Totsuka that's not engaged to-night,' replied the girl.

' Oh lor ! ' said Yaji. ' I guessed so.'

They searched the town but found that all the inns were full up and there was nowhere for them to stop. At last, at the very end of the town, they found an inn which seemed not to have been taken.

' Can you put us up for the night ? ' asked Yaji.

' Two of you, are there ? ' said the landlord. ' Yes, certainly. All the inns at this stage are taken to-night. Mine's the only one not engaged.'

' Such a clean place too,' said Yaji. ' I'm surprised they didn't engage this one also.'

' It's only just been built,' explained the landlord. ' Here, Nabé, where's the hot water ? '

Then a maid came running with hot water and their baggage was taken into a room.

' Here, Yaji,' cried Kita,—' I mean father—shall I put your sandals with mine ? '

' Yes, and just give my leggings a rub down,' replied Yaji.

' What, wash your leggings ? ' cried Kita.

He stared at Yaji, but Yaji gave him a warning look, and grumbling to himself Kita rubbed down the leggings.

' Just bring some tea,' said Kita to the maid.

The maid ushered them into a room on the ground floor and brought them two cups of tea on a tray.

' The bath is ready,' she said.

' I say, did you see that girl's face ? ' asked Yaji when she had gone out. ' It's worn away in the middle just like a mounting block.'

' So it is,' replied Kita. ' I say, Yaji.'

' Look out,' said Yaji. ' She's coming.'

' Won't you take a bath, father,' said Kita, as the maid came in with saké cups.

31

'Halloa, saké?' said Yaji. 'Whenever they see folk from Edo they always make that mistake.'

'Why do they bring out saké?' asked Kita. 'Will they charge for it in the bill?'

'Of course they will,' said Yaji.

Yaji took a towel and went off to the bath, and while he was gone the maid brought in a bottle of saké and a box of comestibles. 'Please have some,' she said.

'This is a treat,' said Kita. 'Just tell my father to make haste and come.'

The maid went off to deliver the message, and soon Yaji came in.

'Aha!' he said. 'What's this? Is this to drink? Look here, you'd better go off to the bath at once.'

'No, no, I'll go in after we've drunk it,' said Kita.

'What a suspicious chap you are,' said Yaji. 'You go on in.'

Kita accordingly went off to the bath and the landlord came in.

'Sorry I haven't got anything better to offer you,' said the landlord, 'but please drink hearty.'

'Really, landlord,' said Yaji, 'I feel ashamed to take advantage of your hospitality.'

'Not at all,' said the landlord. 'You see it's like this. I've been carrying on a different business up to now and to-day is the first day of my opening an inn. As you are my first guests I thought I would celebrate the occasion. There won't be any charge, so please make yourself at home.'

'Well, well, I must congratulate you,' said Yaji, 'though it's really too bad that you should go to this expense.'

'Oh, that's nothing,' said the landlord. 'Call for anything you want. The soup will be ready in a minute.'

'Please don't take any trouble about us,' said Yaji.

'That's all right. Take your ease,' said the landlord, and he went off hurriedly as Kita came back from the bath.

'Father, I have heard all,' cried Kita dramatically. 'Let us be thankful.'

'Instead of standing there joking,' said Yaji, 'you'd better go and get into the bath again while I drink this saké.'

'That's what struck me when I was in the bath,' said Kita. 'Halloa, my legs are still covered with mud. Never mind. Let's begin.'

'I began long ago,' said Yaji, 'but I don't mind starting again.'

'I'm going to drink out of this,' said Kita. So saying he seized a teacup, filled it and gulped it down.

'Ah, that's good saké,' he said. 'By the way, what's there to eat? Aha, white *kamaboko*,—hope it's not made of shark;— pickled ginger;—prawns. Good country fare. Here, father, these *shiso* berries will be the best for you. You'd better eat them only.'

'Nonsense,' said Yaji. 'That's the stuff that everybody leaves. By the way, I wonder when they're going to bring the soup.'

'Wait a bit,' said Kita. He turned round and peeped into the kitchen through the cracks in the door.

'It's coming, it's coming,' he cried. 'They're just serving it up. Oh lor! that's to put in front of the shrine. Ah, now it's coming.'

Kita had just sat himself down again properly when the maid brought in the soup.

'Shall I fill the saké bottle again?' she asked.

When she had gone they both eagerly took the lids off the soup bowls.

'It's red bean soup,' said Kita. 'Delicious! I hope it hasn't got any hard beans in it. By the way, where's the saké bottle?'

'Busy, aren't you?' said Yaji. 'She's just taken it away.'

'Seems as if she was just bringing it back,' said Kita.

The maid brought in the saké bottle and they both started drinking like old hands at the game, the saké cup passing so frequently from one to another that before long they were both half drunk and had forgotten which was the father and which was the son.

'Won't you have a little, miss?' said Kita to the maid.

'I never touch a drop,' said the girl.

'Don't you really?' said Kita. 'Well I never! Never mind. To-night, eh? You and I, eh? Let's plight our troth in a cup, eh, father?'

'Strikes me this son of mine is getting drunk,' said Yaji.

'Getting drunk?' said Kita. 'Well, if I am I've still got plenty of spirit. Just look at my old man's face! Ha-ha-ha!'

While they were making their drunken jokes, the maid, who was very astonished at their talk, drained the cup of saké Kita had given her and handed the cup to Yaji.

33

'What?' cried Kita. 'That old beast? Never mind, it's because of me you give it him. I'll have it next, shan't I?'

He sidled up to the girl as he spoke, but the girl, alarmed at his drunken talk, hastened out of the room.

'You're a bad man,' said Yaji, 'saying things like that in front of a woman.'

'What's the harm?' said Kita. 'There's nothing bad about it. That girl was making eyes at me. I don't want to play at being father and son any more.'

By-and-by the maid brought in the rice, and there was more joking, but I will not bore my readers by putting it all down. Although they did not behave to each other much like father and son the maid thought it was true and would not accept their suggestions. Thus they had to lie with lonely pillows, while the night deepened and the noise in the kitchen subsided, till all that could be heard was the voice of the landlady still scolding. But sleep did not come to them. The bed-clothes were dirty and the divine favour of the thousand-handed Kwannon kept them scratching. Moreover there was a draught from the crack under the door. As the effect of the saké wore off they began to think that although the girl had not come and had used them rather badly, still they had saved some money.

Then, while they were still suffering all the tortures of their wooden pillows, the dawn bell began to ring. Already in front of the inn they could hear the whinnying of the horses that were being brought for the travellers, and the songs of the carriers as they bore the baggage along.

> In the bamboo,
> Sparrows a few.
> What shall we do?
> What shall we do?

At last Yaji and Kita got up and had breakfast, making all sorts of jokes which it would be too tedious to repeat, and started off again. From the opposite direction a constant stream of carriers was passing bearing a daimyō's baggage.

> Over Hakoné,
> A twenty mile climb.
> We shall get there,—
> Get there in time.

'Look at them, Yaji,' said Kita. 'Look how easily they shoulder that heavy baggage. Look how they quiver.'

'When I see them swinging like that it makes me feel sad,' said Yaji.

'Why, why?' demanded Kita.

'It makes me think of my dead wife,' said Yaji.

'Get out,' said Kita. 'Ha-ha-ha!'

Just then, from the opposite direction there came along a ballad singer. He had a broken fan in his hand with which he beat time as he chanted.

'Aha, my prosperous gentlemen,' he chanted, 'condescend in your kindness to give me a copper.'

'Get out,' said Yaji.

But the ballad-singer only went on chanting 'Toko-toko-toko yoi toko na!'

'Look here,' said Kita, 'We haven't got any money, so clear out.'

'What?' chanted the ballad-singer. 'That can hardly be possible. Gentlemen who travel the roads must have both copper and silver, as well as stick, hat, waterproof and oil paper. The most economical cannot go on one leg. Besides you must have a change of loin-cloths, though you will save something by using the old ones as towels.'

'Here, you chatterer,' said Yaji. 'I'll give you that.' He threw a copper on the road.

'Halloa,' cried the priest, 'a four-*mon* piece? Thank you.'

'Is it a four-*mon* piece?' said Yaji. 'Oh lor! You must give me three-*mon* change.'

'Ha-ha-ha,' laughed the ballad-singer. 'What a disappointment!'

On the outskirts of Fujisawa they stopped to rest at a humble teahouse.

'Are those dumplings cold, mother?' asked Kita. 'Just warm 'em up a bit.'

'Ah, ah!' said the old woman, 'I'll warm 'em up for you.'

She raked up the fire in the brazier and fanned it till the ashes flew about, while Yaji and Kita knocked the dust off their clothes and enjoyed a whiff of tobacco. As they were doing this, an old man of about sixty, in a straw coat, carrying a bundle on his shoulder, stopped in front of the house.

'Excuse me,' he said, 'but could you tell me the way to Enoshima?'

'You want to go to Enoshima, eh?' said Yaji. 'Well, if you

go straight on you'll come to the Yugyō Temple. In front of that there's a bridge.'

'Oh yes,' broke in Kita, 'that's right. And just opposite the bridge, I remember, there's a teahouse where the mistress is a fine woman.'

'That's it,' said Yaji. 'Last year when I went to the hills I stopped there. She comes from Edo.'

'Ah, that's why she's so smart,' said Kita.

'But how do I go after I come to the bridge?' asked the traveller.

'Well, at the end of the bridge you'll see some *torii*. You must go straight past 'em.'

'If you don't go straight past 'em you'll fall into the rice-fields,' put in Kita.

'Be quiet,' said Yaji. 'And after you've got right along the road, at the edge of a village, you'll come to a place where there are two teahouses.'

'That's right,' interrupted Kita. 'They give you awfully bad food there.'

'It'll be the one on the right you mean,' said Yaji. 'The one on the left's all right. When I went there last year they gave me some perch that were still alive and a bowl of shrimps ready to jump off the dish they were that fresh, and some eggs and vegetables and mushrooms. And then I had . . .'

'Excuse me,' said the old man. 'I don't want to eat there. How do I go after that?'

'Well, if you go right along that road at the end you'll come to a stone image of Jizō.'

'That Jizō is very good to pray to if you're sick,' put in Kita. 'Our Hetanasu got cured there.'

'Talking about that,' said Yaji, 'that chap Tanekichi of the Kinbakuya in New Street went to Kusatsu, but I don't know whether he got better.'

'That's the chap that lives in Daifukuchō,' said Kita.

'Daifukuchō? Where's that?' asked Yaji.

'You must go straight along my street till you come out in Tozachō,' explained Kita. 'Then you go along Hantorichō and Tanachinchō and cross the Soroban Bridge by the Jidaiyashiki. Then you come to Daifukuchō.'

'Instead of talking about that I wish you'd show me the way to Enoshima,' said the old man.

'True, true,' said Yaji. 'Well, from the Jizō you must go straight along Daifukuchō.'

'Is there a road called that on the way to Enoshima?' asked the old man.

'No, no, that's in Edo,' said Yaji.

'I don't want to hear about Edo,' grumbled the old man. 'These folk are making a fool of me,' he muttered. 'I'll go further on and ask again.' Kita burst out laughing as the old man went off grumbling to himself.

Meanwhile the old woman had brought four or five dumplings on a tray.

'That dumpling's burnt,' said Yaji, but looking at it more closely he saw that it was a piece of hot cinder that had stuck to it.

'Here,' he said, passing it to Kita just as it was with the hot cinder on, 'try this one. You like 'em burnt, don't you?'

'Where, where?' asked Kita, and he stuck it in his mouth. 'Oh, oh!' he yelled. 'Look what you've done to me. There's a piece of hot cinder stuck to it. Oh, how it burns!'

'Ha-ha-ha!' laughed Yaji. 'I thought you liked 'em hot. That's why I gave you the one with the hot cinder on. Come, let's go.'

Kita followed grumbling and spitting after they had paid for the dumplings.

At Fujisawa they found each side of the road lined with the teahouse girls, who were calling out in chorus, 'Walk in, walk in. Our wine doesn't make you drunk. Try our hard-boiled rice.'

Then a postboy accosted them. 'Masters,' he said. 'Do you want a lively horse? I'll let you ride cheap. It's quite sound and warranted to kick.'

'Take a kago,' called a carrier. 'I'll carry you cheap as I'm on my way back.'

'How much?' asked Kita.

'Three hundred and fifty coppers,' replied the carrier.

'Too dear,' said Yaji. 'Why, I'd carry it myself for a hundred and fifty.'

'All right,' said the carrier. 'We'll make it a hundred and fifty.'

'You've come down, eh?' said Yaji. 'Very well, just hang my sandals up in front.'

'But you're not going to ride, are you?' said the carrier.
'You said you'd carry it yourself for a hundred and fifty, so I
thought I'd get a hundred and fifty too for carrying the
other end."

'That's a good one,' said Yaji laughing. 'Well, we'll make
it two hundred then.'

'It's very cheap,' said the carrier, 'but we'll take it. What do
you say, mate? Please get in.'

The price having thus been settled Yaji got into the kago
and the men started.

'I say, mate,' said the carrier in front, 'the master's rather
hard.'

'That's because he's strongly made,' said the carrier behind.

Just then the landlord of one of the teahouses called to the
carriers. 'Hi!' he said. 'When you get to Umezawa just
call at Sadoya's and tell him that the last wine had too much
water in it. Tell him to put a little saké with the next lot he
sends. Look out, you've dropped something.'

'All right,' said the carriers, and started on their way.

'Do you come from Fujisawa?' asked Yaji. 'The town's
got quite pretty. Is Master Tarozaemon, the merchant, in good
health?'

'Master knows everybody,' said the carrier in front. 'Yes,
he's quite well.'

'Is Master Magoshichi still working there?' continued Yaji.

'Yes, yes,' said the carrier in front. 'Master knows all about
everybody.'

'You fool,' said the carrier behind. 'Of course he does.
He's looking in the guidebook as he goes along. Ha-ha-ha!'

Thus going along they quickly arrived at the ferry of the
Banyū River. After crossing the ferry they went on till they
came to the village of Shirahata, where there used to be a shrine
dedicated to Yoshitsuné, whose head is said to have come flying
there.

Then they passed through Ōiso and reached Shigitatsusawa,
where they saw the statue of Saigyō made with a hatchet by
Mongaku Shōnin.

Rubbing his eyes, and yawning through the long spring day,
till he nearly wrenched his jaws out of joint, Kitahachi sought
something to amuse himself.

'Oh, how tired I am!' he said. 'I'll tell you what, Yaji,

let's amuse ourselves on the way by asking riddles. Will you guess them ? '

' All right,' said Yaji. ' Ask away.'

' Outside it's white plaster ; inside it's ton-ton. What's that ? '

' Fool,' said Yaji. ' Instead of that old stuff let me ask you something new. You and I travelling together, what are we like ? Guess that.'

' We're like people going to Isé, of course.'

' Fool. We're like two horses.'

' Why ? '

' Because we're good-goers,—geegees.'

' Ha-ha-ha ! ' laughed Kita. ' Then can you tell me where we come from ? '

' From the house of Yajirobei in Hatchōbōri, Kanda. Is that the answer ? '

' Don't make bad jokes. The answer is two pigs and ten puppies.'

' How do you make that out ? '

' Because there are two of us and we come from Kwantō.'

' Ha-ha-ha ! ' laughed Yaji. ' Here, I'll ask you a difficult one, and if you can't guess it you'll have to pay for some saké.'

' If I guess it will you pay for the saké ? ' asked Kita.

' Of course I will,' said Yaji.

' That's good.'

' It's rather long,' said Yaji. ' It's like this. The answer to where we come from is two pigs and ten puppies, which means that there are two of us and that we come from the Kwantō. What's that like ? '

' Ha-ha-ha ! ' laughed Kita. ' Whoever heard of a riddle like that ? '

' Fool ! ' said Yaji. ' Of course there's such a riddle. Try and guess it.'

' How am I to know what it's like ? ' said Kita.

' If you don't know I'll tell you,' said Yaji. ' It's like a lover who undoes his girdle and also causes his sweetheart to undo hers.'

' That's horribly difficult,' said Kita. ' What does it mean ? '

' It means that I'm making you undo (solve) again what's already been solved. Wasn't that a good one ? Come on, pay up for the saké.'

' You wait a bit,' said Kita. ' I must have my revenge.

Mine's a little long too, but the point of it is this. The answer to the riddle where we come from is two pigs and ten puppies, the meaning of which is that we are two and come from the Kwantō, which means again that if a lover takes off his girdle and gets his sweetheart to take off hers, it's not only undoing it once but causing others to do it again. What's that like?'

'Ha-ha-ha!' laughed Yaji. 'That's a tremendously long riddle.'

'Well, what's the answer?' asked Kita. 'Don't you know? It's a loin-cloth on a towel-horse.'

'How do you make that out?'

'Because you undo it when you hang it up, and undo the riddle when you answer it.'

Thus laughing and joking they soon reached Soga-no-Nagamura and passed the Koyahata Hachiman shrine. Then they came to the River Sakawa.

After they had crossed the river they met an innkeeper from Odawara who was waiting in the road.

'Are you gentlemen stopping at Odawara to-night?' he asked.

'Are you from Odawara?' said Yaji. 'We're stopping at the Koshimidzu or the Shirokoya.'

'They're both full to-night,' replied the innkeeper. 'I shall be happy to put you up at my inn.'

'Is it clean?' asked Yaji.

'Yes,' said the innkeeper. 'It's just been rebuilt.'

'How many rooms have you got?'

'There's one room of ten mats and another of eight, and the office is six mats.'

'How many baths?'

'There are two superior baths and two inferior, making four altogether.'

'How many maids?'

'There are three maids.'

'Good-looking?'

'They are very beautiful.'

'You the landlord?'

'Yes, I am the landlord.'

'Got a wife?'

'Yes, I have a wife.'

'What sect?'

'I belong to the Jōdō sect.'

'Temple near?'

'No, it is far away.'

'What time's the funeral?'

'Yaji!' cried Kita. 'What are you talking about?'

'Ha-ha-ha!' laughed Yaji. 'It slipped out.'

By this time they had come to Odawara, where, on both sides of the road the inn-maids were crying noisily, 'Walk in, walk in.'

Soon they came to the shop where *uirō*, the famous medicine of Odawara, is sold.

'Halloa!' said Kita. 'Look at the roof of this place. It's all ins and outs.'

'That's the place where they sell *uirō*,' said Yaji.

'Let's buy some,' said Kita. 'Is it nice?'

'Awfully,' said Yaji. 'It just melts in your mouth.'

'But this isn't a cake shop,—it's a medicine shop,' said Kita.

'Ha-ha-ha!' laughed Yaji.

> His face was so sweet
> When he thought it was cake,
> But now it's turned sour,
> For medicine's sake.

At last they came to the inn, where the landlord hastened in and called the maids to bring hot water. The landlord's wife brought them some tea, and in the meanwhile the maid filled a bucket with hot water and brought it for them to wash their feet. Yaji looked at the girl out of the corner of his eye.

'Look at her,' he whispered to Kita. 'She ain't so bad.'

'I'll see what she's like to-night,' said Kita.

'What are you jawing about?' said Yaji. 'I'm going to do that.'

'Look what you've done,' said Kita. 'You've put your foot in the hot water without taking off your sandal.'

'Halloa! So I have,' said Yaji. 'Ha-ha-ha!'

'The water's all dirty before I've begun,' grumbled Kita as he washed his feet.

Soon they were conducted into a room, the maid carrying their baggage and their hats and putting them on the alcove.

'I say,' said Kita to the maid. 'Just put some fire in the tobacco-box, will you?'

'What a silly thing to say,' expostulated Yaji.

'Why?' asked Kita.

'Because she'll burn the tobacco-box if she puts fire in it,' replied Yaji. 'You should have said, put some fire in the place in the tobacco-box made to hold it.'

'You've grown very particular in your language,' said Kita. 'When the days are short there wouldn't be time to smoke if one had to say all that every time.'

'By the way, I do feel hungry,' said Yaji. 'And they've only just started to cook the boiled rice apparently. How tiresome!'

'There you go. You're worse than I am,' said Kita.

'How?' asked Yaji.

'If you were to cook the boiled rice you'd turn it into gruel,' replied Kita. 'You should say, Boil the rice.'

'Don't talk nonsense,' said Yaji. 'Ha-ha-ha!'

Meanwhile the girl brought the tobacco-box.

'If the bath's hot I'm going in,' said Kita.

'There you go,' said Yaji,—'correcting other people when you don't know how to speak yourself. How can you heat a bath? You should say, If the cold water in the bath is heated I'll go in.'

Here the maid came back and told them that the bath was hot.

'Oh, the cold water's got hot, has it?' said Yaji. 'Then I'll go in.'

Taking his towel he went off to the bathroom.

Now the landlord of this inn was a man from the West Country, and the bath resembled a Goemon bath, such as is common in his part of the country. He had constructed an oven of cement and over that placed a very thin piece of iron, such as is used to bake cakes on. On this he had placed the bath, and to keep it from leaking he had put mortar all round the sides. This is a very economical form of bath because it does not require much firewood to heat the water. Such baths have no lids, but there is a piece of wood to go on the bottom of the bath and as this floats on the top of the water when it is not in use, it serves as a lid and causes the water to get hot very rapidly. When the bath is used this piece of wood is, of course, pushed down to the bottom of the bath.

Yajirobei had never seen a bath like this before, and thinking the piece of wood floating on the top was a lid he took it off quite innocently and put it on one side. Then he plunged into the bath, but as there was only the red-hot iron of the oven to stand on he burnt his feet horribly and got a terrible shock.

'Oh, oh, oh!' he shouted, jumping out. 'This is a devil of a bath.'

As he didn't like to ask how to get into the bath, he turned over all sorts of plans in his mind, till it happened that his eyes fell on a pair of clogs outside the closet. 'Aha!' he thought. 'Those are just the things.' He put them on and got into the bath, and felt so happy at his discovery that he commenced to chant to himself.

'*Her tears fell like dew,*' he chanted, when Kitahachi, who had got tired of waiting, peeped in at the door.

'Halloa!' he said. 'That's why you've been so long in the bath. Aren't you coming out yet?'

'Here, just feel me,' said Yaji.

'Why?' asked Kita.

'Don't I feel as if I had been boiled?'

'You seem to have been enjoying yourself,' said Kita.

Kitahachi went back into the room and Yaji, getting out of the bath, hid the clogs and came back to the room with an entirely innocent face.

'Won't you have a bath?' he said.

'I'm off,' said Kita.

Quickly stripping himself he plunged one foot into the bath.

'Oh, oh, oh!' he yelled. 'Yaji, Yaji, come here a moment. It's awful.'

'What a row you are making,' said Yaji. 'What's the matter?'

'Look here,' said Kita. 'How did you get into this bath?'

'Fool!' said Yaji. 'There can't be more than one way of getting into a bath. You just swill yourself down and plunge in feet foremost.'

'It's no joking matter,' said Kita. 'How can you get in when the bottom's hot?'

'Of course you can,' replied Yaji. 'You saw me in the bath yourself.'

'How did you manage it?'

'What a persistent chap you are. What is there in getting into a bath?'

'Well, it's very strange,' said Kita.

'There's no difficulty about it,' said Yaji. 'It's a little hot at first, but bear it for a time and you'll soon get used to it.'

'Don't talk like a fool,' said Kita. 'While I'm getting used to it my feet will be burnt off.'

'What an unreasonable chap you are!' said Yaji.

Yaji was so tickled over Kita's plight that he had to go back into the room to have a laugh. Kita thought of all sorts of plans for getting into the bath, and while he was looking round he came upon the pair of clogs that Yaji had hidden. 'Aha!' he thought. 'I see now,' and putting them on he got into the bath.

'Yaji, Yaji,' he called.

'What is it now?' asked Yaji.

'It's just like what you said. It's not hot when once you get in. It feels fine. *Do you not feel sorry for Ishidōmaru? Tsunren, tsunren,*' he began to chant.

Looking round Yaji saw that the clogs he had hidden had disappeared and knew that Kita had found them. He was just enjoying the joke when Kita, what with continually jumping up and down when he found a certain portion of his body was getting too hot and clattering about on the clogs inside the bath, broke the bottom out and sat down violently on the oven underneath, while the water running out of the bath turned into scalding steam.

'Help, help!' yelled Kita. 'Send the lifeboat.'

'Whatever have you done?' cried Yaji.

The landlord, startled by the noise, came running round from the back and was astonished at what he saw.

'Have you hurt yourself?' he asked.

'It's nothing serious,' said Kita. 'The bottom came out of the bath. Ah!'

'How could the bottom come out?' asked the landlord.

'Suppose I was stamping about too much on the clogs,' said Kita.

With a surprised air the landlord looked at Kita's feet and found that he was really wearing clogs.

'You are a most extraordinary person,' he said. 'Whoever heard of getting into a bath with clogs on. It's absurd.'

'Well, I got in with bare feet at first,' said Kita, 'but it was too hot.'

'Your conduct is abominable,' said the landlord.

Kita, who felt sorry for what he had done, made all sorts of excuses as he rubbed himself down, but the landlord's anger was not appeased until Yaji joined in and offered to pay for the damage.

Kita was too depressed at the thought of the money he had wasted to listen to Yaji's jokes. Supper was brought in but it was eaten quickly and silently without any jokes or laughter.

'There's nothing to be downhearted about,' said Yaji. 'We've really gained.'

'How do you make that out?' asked Kita.

'Well, knocking the bottom out of the bath has cost us two hundred coppers,' said Yaji, 'but it would have cost us more if we had gone to Yoshichō.'

'Don't make a joke of it,' said Kita. 'You don't know how I feel.'

'Well, I'm sorry you feel it so much,' said Yaji, 'because I've got something to tell you that will make you feel worse still.'

'What's that?' asked Kita.

'I've arranged for the maid to come here secretly to-night,' said Yaji. 'It's all fixed up. As you're so low spirited now I'm afraid this will make you feel worse.'

'Really, is it true?' asked Kita. 'When did you arrange it?'

'I'm pretty smart at that sort of thing,' said Yaji. 'It was while you were in the bath. I gave her something in advance and sealed the bargain with a kiss. Ain't I clever? That's how lovers are. Ha-ha-ha! Shall we go to bed now?'

While Yaji was out doing something for himself the maid came in to make the beds.

'I say,' said Kita. 'You've made some arrangement with my companion, haven't you?'

'Ho-ho-ho!' laughed the girl.

'Well, it's no laughing matter,' said Kita. 'I'll tell you secretly that that fellow's suffering terribly from disease and you'd better be careful you don't catch it. It's out of pity for you that I'm telling you. You mustn't tell anyone else.'

As he was telling her as a secret the girl thought it was true and felt shocked.

'And his legs are always covered with boils,' Kita went on seeing the impression he had made, 'and they keep breaking like beggars' hats, and he has to stick ointment over them. And then the smell of his armpits! And he's such a terribly passionate fellow that he never lets go once he has caught hold of you. And his breath smells something horrible; that's because of his

45

disease. It's really almost impossible for me to sit and eat with him. It makes me feel sick. Ugh ! '

While he was speaking Yaji came back again and the girl said good-night and quickly went out. Yaji got into bed immediately.

' I'll just warm it up a bit,' he said.

' Botheration,' said Kita. ' Everything's gone wrong to-night. First I burn myself and then I have to pay two hundred coppers, and then on top of that I've got to lie here alone while you're embracing that nice girl. I'm being knocked about by the world something awful.'

' He-he-he ! ' giggled Yaji. ' You must be patient. I know it will be rather disagreeable for you to-night, but still . . . I wonder when the little beauty is coming . . . Kitahachi, are you asleep ? Don't go to sleep yet.'

But Kita only snored by way of answer.

Yaji thought he heard the maid coming, but however long he waited there was not a sign of her, and he began to feel doubtful whether he had not wasted his money in giving her something in advance. At last he could bear the suspense no longer and clapped his hands. The landlady answered the summons.

' Did you call ? ' she asked.

' It's not about you,' said Yaji. ' I've got something I want to ask the maid. Would you mind calling her ? '

' The girl who waited on you ? ' asked the landlady. ' She comes in from outside every day. She's gone home now.'

' Oh ! ' said Yaji. ' Really ? All right, all right.'

So the landlady said good-night and went back to the kitchen.

' Ha-ha-ha ! ' laughed Kita.

' What are you laughing at, you fool ? ' asked Yaji.

But Kita went on laughing. ' I've got level with you now,' he said. ' We can go to sleep peacefully.'

' Do as you like,' said Yaji sulkily.

The unfortunate Yaji, quite unconscious of the trick that Kita had played on him, knew that he had not only wasted his treasured money but that he was also compelled to lose time by lying alone that night.

Joking they fell asleep and it was not until the sound of a distant temple bell broke into their dreams that they woke up, to find it was already dawn. Quickly getting up, they made their preparations for the day's travel and started off. That day they had to walk the twenty miles over the celebrated Hakoné range, and already they had begun the slow climb of Ishidaka road.

When they were near Kazamatsuri, Yajirobei made the following poem :—

> Oh the stony road
> O'er the mountain range !
> Well it's named the stony street,
> Beaten down by people's feet.

'We'd better buy a torch, hadn't we ? ' said Kita. 'They're famous for them here.'

'Fool ! ' said Yaji. 'What should we want with a torch when the sun's up ? '

'That doesn't matter,' said Kita. 'You get one and light it. It'll console you for last night.'

'Shut up,' said Yaji, while Kita laughed.

At Yumoto, on both sides of the road there are very fine buildings, with two or three handsome girls before each shop selling the turned woodware for which the place is noted. Kita went along peeping into every shop.

'It's like an advertisement of face-powder,' he said. 'All these girls have their faces and their hands powdered up.'

'Shall we buy something ? ' suggested Yaji.

'Please look at our wares,' said a girl. 'Please walk in.'

'Please, miss,' said Yaji, 'just show me that over there.'

But the girl was attending to another customer, and the only person to wait on Yaji was the granddame, who came hurrying out of the kitchen.

'Ay, ay,' she said. 'Is it this ye're wanting to see ? '

But as she was only the grandmother Yaji refused her help.

'It's not that at all,' he said. 'Here, miss, just show me that there.'

'Ay, ay,' said granny. 'Is it this your honour wants ? '

'No, no, I don't want that,' said Yaji. 'Here, miss, what's that you've got in your hand ? '

'Oh, this is a tobacco-box,' said the girl.

'That's what I want,' said Yaji. 'How much is it ? '

'It's three hundred coppers, your honour,' replied the girl.

'Make it a hundred,' bargained Yaji.

'Oh, that's too little,' she replied. 'We never overcharge gentlemen like you.' She gave him a glance which entirely softened his heart.

47

'Well then, two hundred,' he said.

'Won't you make it a little more?' she asked. She gave him another glance with a little laugh, though there was really nothing to laugh about.

'Well then, three hundred, three hundred,' said Yaji.

'Do make it a little more,' said the girl, and she laughed again.

'Well, botheration take it, four hundred,' said Yaji.

He flung down a string of coppers and seized his purchase.

'Come on, Kitahachi,' he said. 'Let's go.'

'Ha-ha-ha!' laughed Kita. 'That's something new, ain't it, giving four hundred coppers for something only worth three hundred.'

'I don't regret it,' said Yaji. 'That girl was awfully taken with me.'

'Get out!' said Kita. 'Ha-ha-ha!'

'She was. Didn't you notice how she was looking at me all the time?'

'She couldn't help it,' said Kita. 'Did you see her eyes? She'd got a squint.'

Here four or five shock-headed children came running up to them.

'Give us a copper,' they cried, 'and we'll go to Gongen Sama for you.'

'What's that for?' asked Kita.

'Why, to worship in your place,' they replied.

'Worship for me?' said Kita. '*Everywhere I look I see rustic faces. Who is there that I would change with? There is not one worthy of the change.* By the way, what's that bell?'

'We've got to Sai-no-Kawara,' said Yaji.

Then they came to the barrier.

> Fluttering our papers
> The spring winds blow,
> When through the open barriers
> How gratefully we go.

This stage being at the top of the pass they celebrated their arrival by exchanging numerous cups of saké.

BOOK TWO

FIRST PART

HŌMEI in his Tokaidō diary says :—' There is the music of the harp in the pinetrees and the sound of the timbrel in the waves ; the panting of the carriers is like the sound of flutes, and the stamp of the horses' feet like the boom of the big drum.'

Here begins the second book of Hizakurigé. Strike up the music.

Here we have Yajirobei and Kitahachi, two idle fellows from Hatchō-bōri in Kanda, Edo, filled with a pious desire to worship at the shrine of Isé seven times and at the shrine of Kumano three times, besides making monthly journeys to the Atago shrine, sauntering along, not at all in a hurry, till they have reached Hakoné. Ah ! the winding roads of Hakoné and ah ! the sweet saké and fish for which the mountains have been so long famous.

' Try some of our famous sweet saké,' cried a wayside dealer.

' Let's rest a bit, Yaji,' said Kita.

They sat down on a bench and Kita called to the old man to give them a drop.

' It's very black,' said Kita.

' The black kind's the sweetest,' said Yaji. ' It's like Hamamatsu in Enshū.'

' It's bad, very bad,' said Kita. ' Here, why don't you drink some ? '

' No, thank you,' said Yaji. ' Look at that cup. It's not suitable to offer to me. Now if the pattern had been convolvulus . . .'

' That's so,' said Kita. ' Look here, old man, haven't you got any pickles to eat with the rice and beans ? '

' I've only got pickled plums,' said the old man.

They took some of the pickled plums and started off after they had paid for their meal.

From the opposite direction a train of light baggage horses was coming, their bells going shan-shan-shan, and the postboys singing :—

> The smoke goes up into the sky
> From Fuji's crest. I wonder why.
> The girls at Mishima should know ;
> They light the fires of love below.

Then a postboy coming the other way called out as he passed :—' Halloa, how's the teacher from Dewa ? '

' Fool ! ' said the other, ' if I'm a teacher you're a robber.'

' Hin, hin ! ' whinnied the horses.

Just then they saw coming from the opposite direction a bevy of four or five girls riding in kago, going up to Edo as part of a daimyō's train. They were making a great chatter.

' Halloa ! ' said Yaji. ' That looks good.'

' Lively girls ! ' said Kita. ' Very fine. I say, Yaji, is it true that it makes a man's face look whiter and handsomer if he covers his head with a white towel ? '

' No mistake about it,' said Yaji.

' Then I'll do it,' said Kita.

He took out of his sleeve a piece of white cloth and wrapped his head in it. When the girls came up they all peeped at Kita's face and laughed.

' There, what do you think of that ? ' asked Kita. ' Did you see how pleased they were when they saw my face ? Ah, there's nothing like a lover.'

' They had to laugh,' said Yaji. ' They couldn't help it. Look at what you've got on your head. Look at the strings hanging down.'

' Oh, oh ! ' said Kita, looking at it. ' 'Tain't a towel after all; it's a loin-cloth.'

' Last night when you went to the bath,' said Yaji, ' you put your loin-cloth in your sleeve. It's funny you forgot about it. I suppose when you washed your face this morning you dried it with that. How dirty ! '

' Ah, that's it,' said Kita. ' I thought it had a funny smell.'

' If you weren't so stingy you wouldn't be put to shame like that,' said Yaji.

' Why ? '

' It's because you wear a cotton loin-cloth that you always mistake it for a towel. Look at me, I always wear a silk one.'

' That's all right for you,' said Kita. ' But I'm not going to repair the roof of a court lady so I don't have to wear such a thing. When you're travelling you don't have to be too particular.'

Then they came to the Helmet Stone, where Yaji made the following poem:

> By dangers of the road oppressed
>   He threw his helmet down,—
> A token of defeat confessed.

In this way they reached Yamanaka, where the girls from the teahouses on both sides of the road were calling, 'Walk in ! Walk in ! Try our best Westcountry wine and rice cakes. Please walk in and have a snack.'

'Let's rest a bit, Kita,' said Yaji.

They went into a teahouse, where they found a lot of the carriers gathered round an oven in the courtyard. Some had quilts wrapped round them, some oiled paper, some pieces of matting and others again had paper waterproofs. Then another came in smoking a bamboo pipe.

'That Red Bear of Dobuhachi,' he said, 'he's a terribly greedy chap. He asked six hundred coppers to go to Togé.'

'All right,' said another. 'We'll take forty or fifty away from him for drinks.'

'That we will,' said the other. 'That chap's too much of a swell,—going about in a cloak with a crest on it.'

'I got this yesterday at a wine-shop in Odawara,' said another carrier, who was dressed in a straw bag, 'but the tails are so long that it makes me look like a blooming doctor.'

'You chaps are all so rich' said another carrier, who had no clothes on at all ; 'you can wear what you like. The other day when I went in without anything on, old Mother Garakichi was jawing about how she'd give me an old umbrella, so as I could strip the cover off and wear that. Old fool ! "I ain't a pig," I says. "How d'ye think I'm going to wear a thing like that ? " "Well, just put this on then," she says, and she give me a straw mat. But last night, when I was going to the bath, I took it off and laid it down and one of the pack-horses come along and eat it up. Blooming shame, I call it.'

After amusing themselves by listening to the carriers' talk, Yaji and Kita started off. Soon after they had passed Nagasaka Ōshiguré they were overtaken by a traveller in a blue raincoat, who was carrying a bundle and a basket. After he had passed and repassed them several times, the traveller at last spoke to them.

'May I ask where you gentlemen hail from ? ' he said.

'We're from Edo,' replied Yaji.

'I also am from Edo,' replied the traveller, whose name was Jūkichi. 'May I ask what part of Edo you come from ? '

'From Kanda,' said Yaji.

'Why, that's where I live,' said Jūkichi. 'I thought I'd seen you somewhere. May I ask what part of Kanda ? '

'At Yajirobei Tochimenya's in Hatchō-bōri,' said Yaji. 'It's quite a big place, with a frontage of a hundred and fifty feet and a backage of two hundred and fifty. It's a corner house, built of plaster.'

'I see,' said Jūkichi. 'You live behind that house.'

'Nonsense!' said Yaji. 'Mine's not a house in a back lane. It's a detached house.'

'Oh, indeed!' said Jūkichi. 'What's the value of the property?'

'One thousand eight hundred gold pieces.'

'Do you get the first commission on the sale? If so I'll split it with you.'

'Whatever are you talking about?' asked Yaji.

'I thought you'd got a commission to sell the place.'

'No, no, that's not it at all,' said Yaji. 'Why, when I go out I usually have five or ten retainers with me, but I got tired of that, so I just take this one fellow now. I've got a whim for roughing it when I walk.'

'Yes, yes, I see,' said Jūkichi. 'By the way I met your respected mother the other day. I know her well. It was in Asakusa, just opposite the Monzeki Temple I saw her. She had a bundle in her hand and was walking with the aid of a stick. She must be very old.'

'Yes, yes,' said Yaji. 'She was probably going to worship at one of the temples. As she knows you she must certainly have spoken to you.'

'Yes,' said Jūkichi. 'When she saw me she came hobbling up, and did me the honour to say, 'Won't you give me a copper, kind master?'

At this Kita burst into a roar of laughter.

'You had me that time,' acknowledged Yaji.

'Capital, capital!' said Kita. 'I say, let's put up together to-night.'

Jūkichi agreed, and they went along joking till they got to Kunizawa, where there is a seven-sided hall erected as an offering to the gods by an Ashikaga general. Yaji paid reverence to it from a distance.

Soon the three arrived at Ichinoyama, where they saw two or three mop-headed children playing with a big turtle which they had caught.

'I say, Yaji,' cried Kita when he saw them, 'I've got a good idea. Let's buy that turtle and eat it to-night at the inn.'

'All right,' said Yaji. 'Here, boy, will you sell that turtle ? '

'We'll give it you if you want it,' said the children. 'Will you give us some coppers for it ? '

'Of course,' said Yaji. 'There's a lot of coppers for you.'

He gave the children some coppers, and wrapping the turtle in grass they carried it off, much to the delight of Kita.

'It's a good idea,' said Jūkichi. "But hadn't we better hurry on. It's nearly sunset.'

Quickening their pace the three walked on. It was now nearly dusk and far away in the distance they could hear faintly the ringing of the sunset bell. The birds were returning to their nests, and the songs of the hungry postboys, as they hurried their packhorses along, sounded spiritless. At last the three travellers arrived at Mishima, where the girls at the inns on both sides of the road began their usual chorus of 'Walk in ! Walk in ! '

'Don't catch hold of me,' said Yaji to one of the girls, who caught hold of his sleeve. 'Let go and I'll stop here.'

'Well, there then,' said the girl letting go.

'Wouldn't you like to catch me ? ' said Yaji.

But in eluding the girl he bumped into a blind shampooer.

'Oh, oh ! ' cried the blind man. 'Can't you see I'm blind, you fool ? Amma kembiki.'

'Have some spirit,' called another man. 'Here's the stuff that'll make your eyes go round in your head.'

'Now we've got away from them let's stop here,' said Kita.

'Please come in,' said the landlady. 'San, San, guests have come.'

'Welcome, gentlemen,' said the landlord. 'How many may there be in your company ? '

'Six, counting our shadows,' said Yaji.

'Dear me ! ' said the landlord. 'Where's Santarō ? Bring some hot water. Is there some tea made ? Perhaps you gentlemen would like to take a bath at once. Supper is ready, so please take a bath.'

The three travellers washed their feet and were conducted into an inner room.

'Will your honours take a bath ? ' asked the maid.

'I'll go in first,' said Yaji.

Quickly stripping himself he rushed at the first door he saw.

'Excuse me,' said the maid, 'that's the closet. This way.'

'Oh, that's the way, is it?' said Yaji, and he went off to the bath.

'By the way, what did you do with the turtle?' asked Jūkichi.

'I put it in the alcove,' replied Kita. 'We'll get them to cook it to eat with our nightcaps.'

Soon Yaji came back from the bath and Jūkichi went in his turn. Meanwhile the landlord, accompanied by the inn clerk, came in with the inn register and pen and ink. In the inn register all the addresses of travellers have to be entered.

'Excuse me,' said the landlord. 'I see one gentleman has gone to the bath. I wish to enter your names in the register. May I ask where you come from?'

'I come from Senshū,' said Kita.

'May I ask what part of Senshū?' said the landlord.

'Sakai,' said Kita, 'by name Gihei of the Amakawa.'

'Eh?' said the landlord. 'And you, sir?'

'Me?' said Yaji. 'From Yamazaki in Joshū, by name Yoichibei.'

'Dear me!' said the landlord. 'Are you Master Yoichibei? I've had the pleasure of hearing about you. How is your son-in-law, Master Kampei?'

'Kampei died before he was thirty-one,' said Yaji.

'Ah, that was very disappointing. And Karu?'

'She's very well, thank you,' said Yaji.

'And then there are Master Tanuki-no-Kakubei and Master Meppo Yahachi. They must certainly have lived in your neighbourhood.'

'Yes, yes,' said Yaji.

'And the wild boar, where is that?'

'Ah, where is that wild boar?'

'Tentsuru, tentsuru, tentsuru,' chanted the landlord. 'How's that?'

'Ha-ha-ha!' they all laughed.

'Botheration!' said Yaji. 'You've taken the joke out of my mouth.'

Meanwhile the maid had brought in the supper.

'Supper is served,' she said. 'Here, Tandon, just bring the rice-box.'

'By the way, have you got any white goods here?' asked Kita.

' Two came from Oiwaké on the Kisokaidō the other day,' said the maid. ' If you're lonely I'll call them for you."

' That would be amusing,' said Yaji. ' Are they good-looking ? '

' Not very,' said the maid. ' Just about ordinary.'

' Ha-ha-ha ! ' laughed Kita. ' Ordinary, eh ? How funny ! Just call them.'

' I'll call them then,' said the maid.

She went out to call them and just then Jūkichi came back from the bath.

' I can see from your talk that you've travelled a bit,' he said.

' How about you ? ' asked Yaji.

' Not for me,' replied Jūkichi. ' I know all about that kind of woman.' Meanwhile the maid had come back.

' I've called them,' she said. ' Please patronise them. They're here now. Come in, come in. I'll bring them in.' She jumped up and peering behind the screen caught hold of the girl standing there.

' Come in, come in,' she said.

' I'll come by myself, don't pull me,' said one of the girls, who was called Také.

' We must go in,' said the other girl, who was named Tsumé. ' Come on, Také. Let's go in quickly.'

Finally the two came in. One of them was dressed in blue cotton with a sorrel crest and a girdle with a broad striped pattern on it. The other was in a quilted scarlet dress embroidered in red, with a velvet girdle of a striped pattern. Their scarlet petticoats fluttered in and out of the folds of their dresses as they walked. They had long black pipes in their hands.

' Come along,' said Kita. ' Here, girl, take away the trays and bring some saké.'

The girl took away the trays and brought a saké bottle and some cups, together with some comestibles.

' Please have a drop,' she said.

' Well, well,' said Yaji. He took the cup and gulped it down and handed it back, and the girl, understanding what he meant, presented it to Také.

' Dear me, is this for me ? ' said Také.

She pretended to drink and then handed the cup to Kita, who took a drop and handed it to Tsumé.

' I'm much obliged to you,' said Tsumé.

'Just have one,' said Kita.

'I don't drink very much,' said Tsumé. 'But give these gentlemen plenty to drink.'

'Do all the girls at your place wear these pins, Také?' asked the maid.

She took a gold-plated pin from the head of the girl.

'They're quite fashionable in Edo,' said the girl. 'Our Kinya bought one from Hikoju of Nojiri, and she was so proud of showing it and put on such airs about it that I couldn't stand it any longer, and I made her sell it to me for twenty-four coppers.'

'Show me your comb, Tsumé,' said the maid.

'No, no, no,' said Tsumé, but as she turned her head away the maid snatched it. It was of red lacquer, gold-dusted, with a crest on it.

'Dear me,' said the maid. 'That's the crest of Master Taro-zaemon of Fuda-no-tsuji.'

'I know that,' said Tsumé, and pulling it away she pretended to strike at the maid with the comb before she stuck it in her hair.

Both of the girls spoke the dialect of Oiwaké, the place from which they had come, and the others, stifling their laughter, listened in silence. Much more was said, but I will not set it down here for fear of tiring the reader.

'Shall I spread the beds?' asked the maid at last.

'I'll sleep in the next room,' said Jūkichi.

'There's no reason for that,' said Yaji. 'You'd better sleep here.'

'No, I'll be in the way,' said Jūkichi.

'Please change your clothes,' said the maid.

She brought nightclothes, quilts and bedding, and all lay down on the quilts. Then she set small twofold screens between the beds. In the meantime Yaji's companion, Také, had come to him.

'Are you asleep?' she asked. 'It's very cold to-night, isn't it?'

'Come closer,' said Yaji. 'Don't be shy. Shall we have a little talk?'

'I feel so shy with gentlemen from Edo,' said Také. 'I don't know what to say to them.'

'Well, if you are bashful you don't show it,' said Yaji. 'How old are you?'

'I'm the same age as the moon,' said Také.

'That's thirteen and seven, making twenty,' said Yaji. 'You are a joker.'

'Ho-ho-ho!' laughed Také. 'I only came from Oiwaké the other day and I don't know how to treat guests here, especially when they come from Edo. They make me feel so shy.'

With the bed quilt drawn tightly over them, for a time they lay silent.

Meanwhile Kita's companion, Tsumé, had also come, and there was more talk, but I will not repeat it. Already the night had deepened, and the sound of the horses' bells was stilled. All that could be heard was the far-off bark of the dogs chasing the wild boar, and the sighing of the night wind as it blew coldly round the inn. Soon the oil in the night-lamp became exhausted and the light went out, leaving the room in complete darkness.

Meanwhile the turtle, which they had left lying in the alcove wrapped in straw, had bitten its way through and crept out. Softly it crawled along the floor, but not so softly that it did not waken Jūkichi, who lay and wondered what it was. Slowly the turtle crawled along, till finally it crept among Kita's bedclothes, causing Kita to wake up with a start.

'What's that?' he cried.

He lifted up his head, whereupon the turtle got alarmed and tried to run across his chest. At this Kita gave a yell, caught hold of it and flung it away. It fell on Yaji's face, and he also woke up with a start and caught hold of the turtle, which promptly bit his finger.

'Oh! Oh! Oh!' yelled Yaji.

This startled Také out of her sleep. 'What's the matter?' she cried.

'Light the lamp,' yelled Yaji. 'Oh! Oh! Oh!'

'Whatever have you done?' asked Také.

Feeling about her fingers came in contact with the turtle, whereupon, with an exclamation of surprise, she fell backwards, knocking over the screen with a bang as she did so. Then she began to clap her hands wildly.

'I can't see what's happening in the dark,' said Kita.

'Tatsudon! Tatsudon!' called Také. 'The guests have been calling you for a long time. Bring a light quickly.'

'Quick, quick!' said Yaji. 'Oh! Oh! Oh!' and he began to howl in his anguish.

Meanwhile Jūkichi had stolen the money in Yaji's loin-belt,

which Yaji had placed under his bedding, and had substituted for the money a packet of pebbles which he had prepared beforehand, afterwards carefully putting the belt back where it was before under the bedding. In truth this Jūkichi was a thief, who lived by robbing travellers on the road. He had seen that Yaji was carrying some money and had picked up an acquaintance with him in order to steal it.

At last the landlady appeared with a light and was much surprised to see the turtle.

'Dear me, how did that get in here?' she asked.

'That must be the turtle we bought last night,' said Kita. 'It's eaten its way through the grass and come out. It's caught you this time, hasn't it?'

'It's nothing to laugh about,' said Yaji. 'Look how it's made the blood come. Oh! Oh! Oh!'

'I was wondering what it was,' said Také, 'and it turns out to be a turtle. You must put your finger in water and it will soon let go.'

'Yes, that's what you must do,' said the landlady. The shutters were opened and Yaji rushed to the washbasin and stuck his finger into the water, whereupon the turtle let go.

'There,' said Yaji. 'Look what he's done to me.'

'Dear me,' said Kita. 'What an extraordinary thing! Wonderful, unheard of, most astonishing and inexplicable. Ha-ha-ha!'

After putting things straight, as it was still before dawn they went to sleep again, though not before Kita, half in fun, had composed the following poem :—

> The turtle bit his finger till it bled
> From bashfulness when getting in his bed.

Yaji also, in spite of the pain, composed this:—

> Bitten by turtle, he in pain is bound,
> And like a tortoise tramples on the ground.

But soon it was dawn and there could be heard the sound of the temple bells tolling for prayers and the cries of the hungry crows on the neighbouring roofs. Then, when everybody had got up, breakfast was brought from the kitchen.

'Where is the other gentleman?' asked the maid while they were busy with their preparations.

'Yes, where's Jū gone, I wonder,' said Kita.

'He's probably about somewhere,' said Yaji. 'We won't wait for him.'

Accordingly they began to eat their breakfast. But Jūkichi, after his usual custom, had left the inn early by the back door, and they might wait for him as long as they liked, he would never return. Yaji went out to look for him and came back with a puzzled face.

'I say, Kita,' he said, 'what's happened to Jūkichi? I don't understand it. His bundle and umbrella have gone. Looks as if he had started off while we were asleep.'

'Eh?' said Kita. 'Is there anything missing?'

They looked round but could see nothing gone.

'Nothing's wrong' said Kita.

'Yes, there is,' said Yaji, and he pulled out his belt from his sleeve and shook it. A packet fell out with a rattle, and when they opened it they found it was filled with pebbles.

'Oh! Oh! Oh!' cried Yaji.

'What's the matter?' asked Kita.

'What's the matter?' cried Yaji. 'The money's all turned to stones.'

'Oh, how awful!' said Kita.

'That rascal must have changed it,' said Yaji. 'Here, girl, call the landlord, quick, quick.'

In great excitement the maid went to call the landlord, who came in in his nightgown.

'I have just heard about it,' he said. 'What a terrible thing!'

'Look here,' said Yaji. 'You're the landlord, ain't you? We can't stand this. What do you mean by letting a thief into your inn? Do you get a share? Why did you let him start before us without telling us?'

'That's an extraordinary thing to say,' said the landlord. 'Didn't he come in with you last night? And as for his leaving this morning, I didn't know anything about it. I suppose he went out by the back door.'

'What did he leave by the back door for?' shouted Yaji. 'That's not the way to go out. You've got to bring him back, I tell you. What do you take me for? You ask up in Edo and you'll find all the friends of Yajirobei Tochimenya of Hatchōbōri, Kanda, know him quite well. You make fools of us and we'll pull your house down about your ears and turn the place into a drying-ground. Look sharp. Bring that thief back quick.'

'That's impossible,' said the landlord. 'I'm really very sorry for you . . .''

'Sorry? Sorry my eye! I'm tired of your sorry. Come, bring out that Sorry.'

'Who do you mean?' asked the landlord.

'That Sorry you let stop here,' yelled Yaji. 'You're in league with him, aren't you?'

'You are insulting,' said the landlord. 'I never let any person named Sorry stop at my inn.'

'Never let him stop?' screamed Yaji. 'Didn't he come here last night, and didn't he sleep here, and didn't he go away this morning?'

'Sorry?' said the landlord.

'Yes, Sorry . . . No, no, not Sorry, that thief.'

'Come, Yaji,' interposed Kita. 'Calm yourself a bit. It ain't the landlord's fault. We're in the wrong for bringing him here last night. I don't see what we can do but grin and bear it.'

'Yes, yes,' said the landlord. 'If he'd come alone I should have been to blame, but as he came with you, you have only yourselves to blame for your carelessness.'

'There can't be any doubt about that,' said Kita. 'Come, Yaji, it won't do any good to get excited again.'

Yaji saw that Kita was right and was silent, though his heart sank.

'Let's have breakfast, at any rate,' said Kita.

'I don't want anything more to eat,' said Yaji. 'Look here Kita, it's like this. If we can get to Fuchū I may be able to get some money there, but we've got to get along without any till we get there.'

They collected what few coppers they had about them and managed to pay the inn bill, and with the little they had left as their sole means of subsistence they set off on their travels again. Everywhere they went they inquired for the thief, but nowhere could they hear any news of him. All their jokes and idle talk were gone now and they trudged along in silence.

'Yaji,' said Kita, 'you mustn't take it so much to heart.'

'I think I shall become a priest,' said Yaji.

'Don't say such awful things,' replied Kita.

'What do you say to going back to Edo,' continued Yaji.

'We've got to get to Isé even if we have to beg our way,' said Kita, 'or our reputation will be clean gone.'

'It's all very well,' groaned Yaji, 'but I'm so hungry that I can't walk any more.'

'Well, wait a bit,' said Kita, 'there's the money that was entrusted to me in Edo,—those twelve coppers, you know. We'll buy some rice-cakes with that when we get further on.'

As they went limping along with the aid of sticks, the letter-carriers came up from the opposite direction, shouting 'Ei-sassa, ei-sassa, ei-sassa !'

'Those chaps are like Idaten,' said Kita. 'Look how fast they can go.'

'I wish I'd got their strength,' groaned Yaji. 'They must get a lot to eat.'

'You talk as if you were a beggar,' said Kita.

'Ei-sassa, ei-sassa !' cried the carriers.

'Look out,' said Kita. 'You'll get knocked down. Come more this way.'

'Ei-sassa, ei-sassa !' cried the letter carriers, and as they passed the corner of the letter box gave Yaji a knock on the head.

'Oh ! Oh ! Oh !' yelled Yaji.

But the letter-carriers passed along unconcerned, calling 'Ei-korya, ei-korya, sassa, sassa.'

'Oh !' groaned Yaji. 'How it hurts ! What a dreadful fate is mine ! How I wish I were dead !'

'Don't talk like a fool,' said Kita. 'Look out, there's a horse coming.'

'Postboy,' called Yaji. 'Is it much further to the next stage ?'

'Oh no,' said the postboy. 'It's quite near.'

'How far is it ?'

'Oh, only about nine miles,' said the postboy.

Yaji groaned.

Thus trudging along they came to Kamagafuchi. Being on the road again they could not refrain from falling into their old trick of punning on the names of the places they passed through, though their verses now savoured of their misfortune.

Here they got some rice-cake to allay the pangs of hunger a little, and by giving each other encouragement when they began to lag, at last they reached Numazu. There they entered a small teahouse at the end of the town to rest their legs.

'Ye're welcome, travellers,' said the maid. 'Would your honours like to have a meal ?'

'No, no,' said Kita. 'We ate our fill at the last stage.'

While they were resting, a samurai, travelling with an attendant and a couple of carriers, entered the teahouse. His hair was dressed in the fashion of his province and he wore a cotton cloak of a blue pattern.

'Please have some tea,' said the maid.

'What time is it?' asked the samurai.

'Two o'clock, your honour,' said the maid.

'If you've got any good saké,' said the samurai, 'let me have a little.'

'Shall I bring you some at thirty-two coppers, your honour?' asked the maid.

'Have you got any a little cheaper than that?'

'We have some at twenty-four coppers, your honour.'

'Just mix both together, half and half,' said the samurai, 'and give me a bottle.'

The maid accordingly brought the wine-heater from the kitchen, together with cups and a dish of savouries.

'How much are these?' asked the samurai, pointing to the savouries.

'Thirty-two coppers, your honour,' answered the maid.

'And these?'

'Twelve coppers, your honour.'

'Um!' said the samurai. 'Here, Densuké, you have a drink too.'

'Thankee, your honour,' said Densuké.

'That girl over there attending to the fire is very like Okuda's wife, isn't she?' said the samurai.

'Indeed she is, your honour,' said Densuké. 'That girl laughing over there ain't bad looking either.'

'Which, which?' asked the samurai. 'Yes, yes, and that one by the side of the post is a fine girl. Here, you can drink the rest, Densuké.'

'Thankee, your honour,' said Densuké.

'Now let's see what we've had,' said the samurai. 'How much is it? No, no, I didn't have any of those.'

'Yes, your honour. Then it'll be forty-two coppers,' said the maid.

'Very well,' said the samurai, and telling his attendant to pay the bill he went out. Kita and Yaji, who had been drinking tea, also started again at the same time.

'Come along,' said Kita.

64

'Much obliged,' said Yaji.

'Ye're very welcome,' said the maid.

Going along the two passed and repassed the samurai several times, while indulging in all sorts of talk, till they reached Nara-no-saka and Sembon-no-matsubara. Here Kita composed a poem, on hearing which the samurai was struck.

'Excellent, excellent!' he cried. 'I suppose you gentlemen are from Edo.'

'Yes, your honour,' said Kita. 'We had the misfortune to be stuck by a prig at the place where we stopped last night and are in great trouble.'

'I'm very sorry to hear it,' said the samurai. 'It must have been very painful to be stung by a pig.'

'No, no, your honour,' said Kita. 'Stuck by a prig,—that is a sneak.'

'A sneak?' said the samurai. 'What's that?'

'A sneak is a pickpocket, your honour,' said Kita.

'Aha, I see,' said the samurai. 'You call a person who takes other people's things a sneak?'

'Yes, your honour,' said Yaji.

'And a sneak you call a prig. I see, I see.'

'Yes, your honour,' said Kita, 'and I'd like to ask you a favour. As I said we met this thief last night and he took all our travelling money so that we are in great distress. We shall be all right when we get to Fuchū, but till we get there we shall be in great trouble. Just to get a bit of money to help us along the road I'd like your honour to buy this.'

He took off a leather purse that was hanging to his girdle and showed it to the samurai.

'I don't like buying things on the road,' said the samurai, 'but as I feel great sympathy for you in your trouble I don't mind helping you. How much do you want for it?'

'I'll let your honour have it for three hundred coppers,' said Kita.

'Oh, that's too dear,' said the samurai.

'Well, I'll let your honour have it a little cheaper.'

'I don't mind giving you sixty coppers for it,' said the samurai.

'Oh, that's too cheap, your honour,' said Kita.

'Well, I'll give you sixty-one coppers, then,' said the samurai.

'Please give a little more, your honour.'

'Well, I'll make it sixty-two coppers then.'

'Really . . .'

'It's rather like making up your mind to jump over the precipice at Kiyomidzu Temple,' said the samurai, 'but I'll even go so far as sixty-three coppers.'

'Really, your honour,' said Kita, 'if you go up like that, only one copper at a time, we shall never make a bargain. If you named a round sum now.'

'Well, what do you call a round sum ?' asked the samurai.

'A round sum is one like a hundred,' explained Kita. 'So if your honour says a hundred coppers I'll accept it.'

'Oh, a hundred is a round sum, is it ?' said the samurai. 'Well I'll give you a round sum for it then.'

'Thank you very much,' said Kita.

The purse and the money accordingly changed hands.

'It's very cheap, your honour,' said Kita. 'Including the fastener it's worth four or five hundred coppers.'

'Well, I have two sons,' said the samurai, 'and I thought it would be a good present for the elder.'

'Your honour looks too young to have two sons,' said Kita. 'They must be a great pleasure to you. If it isn't too rude may I ask your age ?'

'Give a guess,' said the samurai.

'Let me see,' said Kita. 'I should think your honour was about thirty-seven or thirty-eight.'

'I'm forty-two this year,' said the samurai.

'You don't look it, your honour.'

'It's very kind of you to say so,' replied the samurai, 'and it's quite true that among my companions Sonohara Sakunoemon, Yonekizu Jindaifu and the others, all born in the same year, I look the youngest.'

'Certainly you do, your honour,' said Kita.

'Then again the young girls say I'm as handsome as Sawamura Sōjurō.'

'Is that so ?' said Kita.

'By the way, how old are you ?' asked the samurai.

'Give a guess, your honour,' said Kita.

'Um ! Your age ? Let me see. I should think you must be twenty-seven or twenty-eight.'

'No, it's a round figure, your honour,' said Kita.

'A round figure ? What, a hundred ?'

'No, no, it's this,' said Kita, and he held up three fingers.

'Aha, three hundred. Quite a young man yet,' said the samurai.

At this they all laughed.

Thus diverting themselves they passed Ko-Suwa and Ō-Suwa and quickly arrived at Hara. There they parted company from the samurai.

'Let's have some macaroni with the money we've just got,' suggested Kita.

'Ah, that's a good idea,' said Yaji.

So they went into a macaroni shop, where Kita gave an order and the keeper of the shop brought two bowls.

'It's big macaroni, isn't it?' said Yaji. 'All the more to eat. Kitahachi, shall we have another bowl each after this?'

'No, no,' said Kita. 'It won't do to spend all the money at once. Let's go on further and then have something else. Drink plenty of the hot water.'

'Here, young fellow,' said Yaji to the shopman, 'give me some more of the hot water.'

'Ay, ay,' said the shopman.

'Ah, that's delicious,' said Yaji. 'Kita, won't you have some? Here, give me another. Oh, oh, I've burnt my mouth. It's too hot. Just put a little macaroni in it to cool it.'

'Here, young fellow,' called Kita. 'Sorry to trouble you so much, but as I'm taking medicine I'd like another cup of the hot water.'

'Ay, ay,' said the shopman.

'That's enough,' said Kita. 'But look here, my medicine won't work unless there's some sauce in it. Sorry to trouble you my man, but just put a little sauce in. Ah, that's good.'

Kita gulped it down like a fish, and then proposed that they should go on.

'Ah,' said Yaji. 'I feel very much better now.'

From there they went on to Shinden, which is famous for its eels, and their noses were tickled by the appetising smell of broiled eels coming from every house.

Passing Motoyoshihara they reached Kashiwabashi, where you get the finest view of Mount Fuji, and at Yoshihara, the next stage, the shrill voices of the teahouse girls on each side of the way greeted their ears.

'Please walk in,' they cried. 'Try our wine. Try our real rice. *Konnyaku* and onion soup served here. Walk in, walk in.'

'Kago sir. Have a kago,' called the carriers.

'How about a horse, master?' asked a postboy. 'I'll carry you cheap as I'm going back.'

'We've been riding so much,' said Yaji, 'that we thought we'd have a stroll for a change.'

'I thought you said we were having a fall for a change,' said Kita. 'Gave me quite a shock.'

At the end of the village they came upon a man wearing an old broken hat, who looked something like a rōnin. He was waving a fan and singing,

> Come, let us eat and drink our fill,
> While autumn flowers on every hill.
> Miscanthus and the bell-flower gay,
> Starwort and aster, what are they?

'I've fallen ill upon the way and am in great distress,' he said. 'Kindly contribute towards my travelling expenses, gentlemen.'

'Well, you see,' said Kita, 'we had all our money stolen by a thief last night and haven't got a penny left for ourselves. If you could spare us a bit of your savings we should be very much obliged.'

'Get out,' said the man and quickly made off.

Yaji and Kita went on laughing and just outside the next village came upon a little shed by the wayside, in front of which was hung a scroll of Kwannon. A priest dressed in a torn hempen gown was dozing outside. Directly he saw the travellers he rang his little bell and commenced to pray.

'This is the Sutra of the Lotus of the Pure Law,' he prayed. 'The children of darkness see the light, for the sound of the samisen is loud and continuous in their ears and the feasting of yesterday means the sickness of to-day and utter misery, till the neighbouring doctor is called and compounds medicines which take effect and make the stomach swell. Listen to the holy words.'

Here he rang his bell, adding, 'All contributions devoted to filling up the empty hole beneath the nose. Your kind assistance is requested.'

'Ah, that's a good prayer,' said Kita. 'Let's make a contribution.'

'Thank you very much,' said the priest. 'What name shall I put down?'

'Just put Yajirobei,' said Yaji.

'Very well,' said the priest. 'Your name on earth was Yajirobei.'

'Here, I'm not dead yet,' said Yaji.

'Eh? Not dead yet?' said the priest. 'Well then, I'll put down any heavenly name you like.'

'Oh, anything will do for the sake of Buddha,' said Kita. 'There's a copper for you.'

They passed on and by-and-by came to a place among the pinetrees where an urchin of fourteen or fifteen had made a place on the embankment for a kettle and had laid out some cakes. He was partly amusing himself and partly trying to sell the cakes.

'Come and rest, come and rest,' he was calling out.

'What do you say, Yaji?' said Kita. 'Shall we have some cakes?'

'Let's rest a bit,' said Yaji.

They sat down on some matting spread on the bank and both began to eat the cakes.

'How much are these cakes, boy?' asked Kita.

'Those are two coppers each,' said the boy.

' We've had five,' said Yaji. ' How much will that be ? '

' I don't know,' said the boy.

' Well, let's see,' said Kita. ' Two fives are three, aren't they ?
So that's three coppers. There they are.'

' That's cheap,' said Yaji. ' I'll have another. How much is
this ? '

' That's three coppers,' said the boy.

' Which, which ? ' cried Kita. ' That's fine. Here, boy, I paid
you for what I had before. We've had four since then, so three
fours make seven and a half. Knock the half off and made it
seven.'

' Halloa,' said Yaji. ' Here's some rice-cake.'

' Where, where ? ' said Kita. ' That's good. How much is
the rice-cake ? '

' They're four coppers each,' said the boy.

' If they're four coppers each,' said Kita, ' let's see, we've eaten
six of them, so five sixes are fifteen. There you are.'

' I'm not going to sell any more by arithmetic,' said the boy.
' You give me five coppers six times.'

' Eh ? ' said Kita. ' I wonder if I've got it.'

' You pay up,' said the boy.

He snatched up the coppers and counted them one at a time.

' He's done me,' said Kita. ' Come along.'

They started off but they had not gone more than a few yards
when they started to think.

' That's a smart boy,' said Kita. ' Those rice-cakes weren't
worth four coppers each really. They were only two or three
coppers. He's covered all his losses.'

' Botheration ! ' said Yaji. ' It's sticking in my throat now.
Ugh ! Ugh ! '

Half in fun they began to revile the boy, but thinking how
he had got his own back they could not help bursting into
laughter.

They walked on and soon came to Kusawa-no-Zenfukuji, where
there is a stone erected to the memory of the Soga brothers.
Then they reached the ferry across the Fuji River. As they
crossed the ferry the sun was glittering on the rim of the western
mountains, the postboys were hastening their horses while they
sang, and the sparrows were making love in the bamboo groves.
At last they reached Kambara.

SECOND PART

IT appeared that a daimyō's train had just arrived at the hostel at Kambara, and a meal was being served in the kitchen. Kitahachi peeped in cautiously from outside.

'Yaji,' he called. 'Just hold this bundle a moment.'

'What are you going to do?' asked Yaji.

'It's only for a moment,' said Kita.

He handed the bundle to Yaji and went into the hostel, where he seated himself in a corner of the kitchen, unobserved amid the general bustle. The maids of the hostel were busy bringing in the food and setting it before the many guests.

'Just bring a tray here,' called Kita.

'Ay, ay,' said one of the maids and put a tray before him. As there was so much confusion nobody took any notice of him and Kita ate to his heart's content. Then, seizing an opportunity when nobody was looking, he spread out a towel and emptied a bowl of rice into it, afterwards quietly slipping away to where the puzzled Yaji was waiting impatiently under the eaves of the house opposite.

'Is that Kitahachi?' called Yaji.

'Ay,' said Kita.

'Where have you been?'

'I've been to get something to eat,' said Kita. 'It was delicious.'

'Eh? Where did you get it?' asked Yaji.

'At the hostel. There was such confusion I got five or six helpings.'

'That was a good idea,' said Yaji. 'But you are a faithless chap. Why didn't you take me with you?'

'Well, I've brought you a present,' said Kita. He undid the towel and showed the rice.

'What's that?' said Yaji. 'Rice? Thank you. You are a smart fellow. Ah, delicious, delicious!'

Yaji gobbled up all the rice and then shook out the towel. 'What's this?' he said. 'It's a towel. How dirty!'

'What's dirty?' asked Kita.

'This is,' said Yaji. 'It's the towel you've been wiping yourself with. Ugh! I feel sick.'

'Ha-ha-ha!' laughed Kita. 'But hadn't we better go along to the end of the town and look for a cheap lodging-house.'

They went to the outskirts of the town accordingly and wandered about bewildered.

'I'd like to stop at a house where there's a fine girl,' said Yaji.

'You don't expect to find one at a lodging-house, do you?' said Kita. 'Let's see, where can it be?'

They went about peeping into all the houses, and Kita got bitten by a dog he trod on, which was sleeping under the eaves of a house.

'Oh, oh, oh!' yelled Kita.

'Bow-wow!' said the dog.

Then they heard the cry of a *sushi*-seller.

'Hi!' called Kita. 'Is there a lodging-house anywhere round here?'

'It's the house at the corner there,' said the man.

'Much obliged,' said Yaji.

They went over to the house he had pointed to, and went in. They found themselves in a room of four or five mats, the only furniture in which was a Buddhist shrine and a bamboo trunk. The master of the house, an old man of about seventy, was seated at the edge of the fire-hole in the middle of the room twisting straw-rope. A pot was hanging from a hook over the fire, and in it something was boiling furiously. Near by were a pilgrim and two palmers, one of whom was an old man of over sixty and the other a young girl of seventeen or eighteen, who had thrown herself down by the fire, with her travelling basket still on her back, and was holding her chapped feet towards the blaze. The old woman of the house, who was putting wood on the fire, accosted them.

'Come ye in,' she said.

'Can you put us up for the night?' asked Kita.

'Come in,' said the old man. 'You'll find some cold water there to wash your feet with.'

'Yaji,' said Kita, while they were washing their feet, 'did you see that nice young palmer?'

'Ay,' said Yaji. 'I'm going to have her. Everything tastes good when you're hungry.'

72

Thus laughing together they dried their feet and mounted into the room.

'Come and warm yourselves at the fire,' said the pilgrim.

'Just move up a bit, Yaji,' said Kita. He shoved Yaji along and squeezed himself down beside the girl.

Then the old woman took the pot off the hook. 'There, the gruel's ready,' she said. 'Fall to.'

'It looks nice and hot,' said Yaji.

'Nay, it's not for ye,' said the old woman. 'It's for these folk.'

'The rice they gave us to-day was all blasted,' said the old palmer, 'and half of it stones too. If ye ate this your stomach would get that heavy.'

'Master Pilgrim only brought three *go*,' said the old woman. 'Ye must divide it up.'

She gave each of them a rice-bowl and they divided up the gruel and began to eat. Yaji and Kita had to sit and look on, and as they felt awkward doing nothing, they tried to scrape up some tobacco from their tobacco pouches. The pilgrim at last finished.

'Doubtless you two gentlemen are from Edo,' he said. 'I also am from Edo, where an awful thing happened to me.'

'What happened?' asked Yaji.

'The story of the destiny which drove me to become a pilgrim,' said the old man, 'shows how impossible it is to rise in this world when fortune is against you. When I was young and lived in Edo, from early summer till late autumn, every day we had most extraordinary winds, and I was continually puzzling my brains how I could turn them to account. Finally I made a terrible mistake.'

'Dear me!' said Yaji.

'I decided to begin life as a dealer in boxes,—jewel boxes, comb-boxes, all sorts of boxes.'

'What's the wind blowing got to do with dealing in boxes?' asked Yaji.

'Well, I worked it out in this way. Every day there was an extraordinary amount of wind and as Edo is a very dusty place I thought the dust would naturally get into people's eyes and there would be a large number who would go blind. Then, according to my idea, I thought all these blind people would want to learn the samisen, so the samisen makers would get very busy, ,and a large number of cats would have to be killed, and there would be an increase in the number of rats, which would gnaw all the boxes to pieces, and thus the box trade would certainly flourish. So I laid out all my money in buying a large stock of boxes.'

'That was a good idea,' said Yaji. 'I suppose they sold well.'

'I couldn't sell one,' said the pilgrim. 'In spite of all my endeavours to hit upon a plan by which I could make a good profit, from the beginning to the end the whole thing was a failure and I was forced to seek the enlightenment of Buddha and become a pilgrim. Ah, the world is not what we think it is!'

'That's an extraordinary story,' said Kita. 'You might also tell us, Master Palmer, how you came to be a palmer.'

'Ah,' said the palmer, 'mine is a very sad tale. This girl here is my granddaughter, and we have both dedicated ourselves to the service of Buddha. I come from Nikkō, where we have many thunderstorms. One day, twenty years ago, in the summer, my Lord Thunder happened to fall at the back of my house. Unfortunately he fell on the stump of a tree, and injured himself so severely that he was unable to go back to the sky again. Accordingly I took my Lord Thunder into my house to nurse him, and while he was there he fell in love with my daughter, and I was forced to take him for my son-in-law as there was no way of separating them. Then in the summer he got a message from his parents in India to go and help with the summer thunder-showers, and he went away to the south to work for his living. My daughter and I waited for his return, and as he did not come back we began to feel anxious, fearing that he had fallen down and broken his back or that some other accident had happened to him. At last one of his friends came and told us that he had fallen into the sea and had been swallowed up by a whale. This sad news made my daughter weep very bitterly and I was at a loss what to do. Then my daughter was about to give birth to a child, and I prayed to the gods that it would not prove a demon, till at last she was delivered of this girl that you see with me. Seeing that the gods had answered my prayer and had sent a human being into the world instead of a demon, I resolved to devote myself to Buddha and become a pilgrim.'

Tears ran down the old man's face as he finished his story.

It was now growing late, and the old woman of the house

commenced to get out mats and other things for the guests to sleep on.

'It's time to sleep now,' said she. 'As the house is very small, I and the young palmer will go up into the attic.'

She brought a ladder and set it up, and she and the young girl climbed up into the attic. The pilgrim took a paper mosquito net out of his basket and put it over his head.

'Here, I've got to go out and do something,' said Kita.

'I want to do something too,' said Yaji. They both went outside the back door.

'I thought I'd have some fun with that young palmer,' said Yaji, 'but the old woman's taken her upstairs. What a nuisance!'

'I squeezed her hand and pinched her while I was talking to her,' said Kita. 'You didn't know I was making love to her, did you?'

'None of your lies,' said Yaji.

'It's not a lie,' said Kita. 'I'm going to have that girl to-night.'

'Ain't he quick!' said Yaji.

They went in and shut the door, and so to sleep. The strangeness of the place where they were spending the night, the roughness of the accommodation, the broken plaster through which the wind whistled,—all these they thought would form a subject for conversation hereafter. The night deepened and at the sound of the midnight bell Kitahachi opened his eyes. He listened and heard them all snoring; they were worn out with their travels. 'Now's the time,' he thought, and getting up softly he felt round in the darkness till he had found the ladder. Now the floor of the attic was made of interlaced bamboos, on which mats were spread, and when anyone walked on the floor it made a great creaking. This startled Kita at first, but he crawled along on all fours, feeling about, till he came to the bed in which he thought the young girl was sleeping, although in reality it was the old woman's bed. He crept in and began shaking her gently to wake her up. The old woman soon opened her eyes.

'Who's that?' she called. 'What are you doing?'

At the sound of the old woman's voice Kita discovered his mistake and endeavoured to get away. He jumped up, but unfortunately ran a splinter of the bamboo into his foot, which made him fall down, whereupon the bamboos gave way and he fell with a crash into the room below.

'What's that?' called the old man.

'Whatever can it be!' called the old woman. 'What an awful noise! Get up all of you.'

The noise had also awakened the pilgrim and the palmer.

'What a terrible noise!' said the pilgrim. 'Light the lamp. We can't see what it is in the darkness.'

Meanwhile the unfortunate Kita, having broken through the ceiling, had fallen into what seemed to him like a box, though what it was he could not well make out. His feet seemed to be caught in something and feeling about he found it was the halo of a Buddhist saint. Then he knew that he had fallen inside the Buddhist shrine, a fact which tickled his sense of humour in spite of the pain that he was suffering from his fall.

Meanwhile the old man had been getting the lamp lit.

'Seems as if it fell inside the shrine,' he said. He opened the doors of the shrine, when, to his surprise, Kitahachi walked out.

'Oh! Oh!' he said. 'It's this man.'

'Can you tell me the way to the Minobu?' asked Kita.

'Don't talk nonsense,' said the old man. 'What are you doing in there?'

'Well, I got up to go somewhere,' said Kita, 'but I lost my way.'

'Lost your way?' said the old man. 'You haven't been doing it inside the shrine, have you?' He peeped inside and saw the ceiling was broken.

'He fell through the ceiling,' he cried.

'Yes,' said Kita. 'I fell through while I was running away from the cat.'

'Are you a rat?' said the old man. 'Running away from the cat, indeed! What did you go upstairs for?'

'Well, the rats carried off my loin-cloth, and I thought it might be upstairs, so I went up to look.'

While Kita was making these excuses the old woman came down from upstairs.

'It's not that at all,' she said. 'I'm sixty years old, and I don't know what part of the country he comes from, but he came upstairs and crept into my bed.'

'What?' said the old man. 'He must be mad. Why it's twenty years since I gave up that sort of thing. Creeping into the bed of a wrinkled old woman, indeed. It's disgraceful.'

'Please excuse me,' said Kita. 'Here, Yaji, don't lie there pretending you're asleep. Get up.'

Yaji thus awakened concealed his amusement. 'He's very young,' he said, 'and never thinks of what he's doing. Do forgive him.'

The pilgrim and the palmer also endeavoured to calm the old man, and finally Kita, by the sale of a kimono, raised enough money to pay for the repair of the ceiling. The affair was thus settled.

In a short time came the dawn and Yaji and Kita quickly set out again on their travels.

'You're very unlucky, Kita,' said Yaji. 'When we stopped at Odawara you trampled the bottom out of the bath, and last night you trampled a hole in the ceiling and we had to pay three hundred coppers to get it mended. Haven't you got any sense?'

'I do feel bad about it,' said Kita.

'Ha-ha-ha!' laughed Yaji. 'Your excuse last night of losing your way was funny, and the one about the rat running away with your loin-cloth. I've been thinking out a story about that.'

'What's that?' asked Kita. 'Do tell me.'

'Well, it's like this,' said Yaji. 'There was a palmer and a pilgrim, just the same as last night, and we were stopping at a lodging-house, and you got up in the middle of the night and went wandering about. Then everybody woke up and asked you what you were doing, and you said that the rats had run away with your loin-cloth and that you were certain they had taken it upstairs. Then the pilgrim and the palmer found that their loin-cloths, which they had put by the side of their pillows, had gone too, and they thought that the rats must have taken them all. So they all went upstairs and when they got up they heard in a corner something like the sound of a samisen. 'That's strange,' they said, and peering into the rats' hole, they saw all the rats there spreading out the loin-cloths. Then one of the rats said, "I've brought the pilgrim's loin-cloth, and when you shake it it makes a noise like a samisen." Then, as the others would not believe him, he shook it out to show them and they heard the tinkle-tinkle of the samisen. "It would be funny if the pilgrim's loin-cloth only did that," said another rat. "I brought the palmer's loin-cloth. I'll shake it out and try." He took it in his mouth and shook it, and that one also went tinkle-tinkle-tinkle. "That's strange," they all thought. And then another rat said, " I brought the loin-cloth of a man named Kitahachi. It's an Etchū loin-cloth so it's short. I expect it'll only make a noise like a lute." He shook it out and it went z-z-z-z, like a *gidayu* samisen. That's funny, thought the rats. The loin-cloths of the pilgrim and the palmer make a pretty sound like an ordinary samisen. Why does this fellow's make such a strange sound ? Then a rat in the corner, after thinking a long time, said, " Oh, yes, of course. That must be the reason." " What reason ? " they asked. " Well, it's probably because that fellow Kitahachi has a *futozao*." '

' Ha-ha-ha ! ' laughed Kita. ' Splendid ! Splendid.'

While they were thus talking they arrived at Yui, where on both sides of the way the inn girls were calling to them.

' Come in ! Come in ! ' they cried. ' Try our famous sugared rice-cake. Salt ones also. Come in and rest. Come in and rest.'

' What a noisy lot they are,' said Yaji.

Crossing the Yui River they came to Kurasawa, famous for the ear and wreath shellfish which the fishermen catch and offer for sale. There they rested a little.

Then they crossed the Satta Pass and trudged on till suddenly it began to rain. This made them take out their rain-coats and pull their hats down over their brows. The scenery of the famous Tago-no-ura and Kiyomi-ga-seki they were unable to see because of the rain, and their feet began to get heavy with mud. At last they reached Okitsu, where they took a rest at a poor-looking teahouse.

' Here, granny,' called Kita to the old woman who kept the house, ' just give us some of those beanflour dumplings.'

' Dear, dear ! ' said Yaji. ' What a long time it is since I saw you last. How glad I am to see you looking so well. That reminds me, your child was quite small when I saw him last. How he's grown ! Is his sister quite well ? '

' I bain't got a child,' said the old woman.

' Well, your grandchild then,' said Yaji.

' If I bain't got any children I can't have no grandchildren,' said the old woman.

' That's true,' said Yaji. ' Well, if he isn't your grandson, whose grandson is he ? '

' It bain't a grandchild at all,' said the old woman. ' It's the son of the bearer next door.'

'Oh, that's it, is it?' said Yaji. 'Here, my boy, there are two dumplings left. You can have them.'

'Don't want 'em,' said the boy.

'Don't want them? Why?'

''Cause I don't like dumplings covered with bran,' said the boy.

'Covered with bran?' said Yaji. 'I thought it was bean flour?'

'No,' said the old woman. 'I covers 'em with bran.'

'Then that's why they tasted so gritty,' said Yaji. 'Well, I'll give them to the dog. Here, doggie, doggie.'

'Bow-wow,' said the dog.

'There you are,' said Yaji. 'Bark for them.'

'Wow!' said the dog, and Yaji gave them to him, at the same time thinking what a waste it was.

Feeling rather queer after the bran dumplings they plodded on, the rain coming down harder than ever and putting a damper on all their jokes and idle chatter, till they had passed Ejiri, when the rain stopped, and they were able to walk more easily.

By-and-by a light pack-horse came along with all its bells jingling bravely. The postboy was singing :—

> Last night I crept
> To where she slept,
> When supper was done,
> And had some fun.

Then to his horse : 'What a big-bellied brute you are ! Do you want to do it again ? Then I may as well relieve myself too.'

'Halloa, Jiro,' called a postboy in front turning round. 'Whose horse is that ?'

'It belongs to the saké shop below,' said the postboy behind. 'That chap there works it hard, but it's a good horse. It went to and from Shimizu four times yesterday, and then it had to go to Fuchū. I spent all the money I got in the fares on saké so I hadn't got anything to give it to eat, but I fastened it up to the back door of the stable and it ate all the thatched roof off the closet.'

'That woman at the saké shop's a stingy beast,' said the postboy in front. 'She used to mix chaff with my food when I was there. "Why don't you try to learn to write ?" she used to say, or "Why don't you practise figuring, and then you can be the clerk ?" That's the sort of nonsense she used to tell me, as if I should swallow such stuff.'

'Could you give me a light, postboy ?' asked Kita.

'Ay, ay,' said the postboy. 'I suppose you two gentlemen are from Edo. Edo people are so kind. Yesterday I had to take an Edo gentleman from Fuchū to Ejiri. Ah, he was a kind gentleman ! When we got to Naganuma he said, "Three hundred coppers ain't much for going to Ejiri. I'll increase it by giving you a tip of two hundred more and pay for all the saké you drink." That's what he said, and when we got as far as Yoshida he paid for all the saké, and then he said, "Here, postboy, you must be tired walking all day leading the horse. I'll get down here and you can ride." What do you think of that for kindness ? I said "No, no," but he wouldn't listen to me. "You get on," he said, "and I'll give you two hundred as travelling expenses." So I rode from Umenoki to Ejiri, and then as I had to take the horse back to Okitsu, he said, "You must be tired, so I'll give you two hundred more to take you back." You don't meet such a kind gentleman as that every day.'

Here the passenger who was riding on the horse began to snore.

'Take care, sir,' cried the postboy. 'Wake up or you'll fall off.'

'This horse is so slow,' said the passenger, 'that it makes me sleepy. Ah, that was a fine horse I had yesterday from Mishima ! And the postboy was so attentive. From Mishima to Numazu the charge is one hundred and fifty coppers, but the postboy said he was so sorry for me as the horse was so quick and I couldn't go to sleep for a minute for fear of falling off, that he wouldn't make any charge. Then when we came to Sammai-bashi, " Master," he said, " you must be tired of riding so long in the saddle. Please get down and rest here. And if master would like to take some saké or anything," he said, " I'll be glad to pay for it," and he gave me a hundred and fifty coppers. Then when we got to Numazu he said he would like to go with me to the next stage but his horse was so lively that he advised me to take another. " I'll pay for the other horse," he said, and he gave me another hundred and fifty coppers for that. Ah, there aren't many postboys like that.'

But while he was talking the postboy who was leading the horse also began to doze and commenced snoring.

While amusing themselves by listening to this talk they soon reached Fuchū. They took a room at an inn in Temma-chō, after which Yaji went off to find his friend in the town, where he succeeded in his plan for raising some money and returned to the inn greatly elated. Whatever happened they felt that they must spend the night at Abegawa-chō, of which they had heard so much. Accordingly they both made their preparations and summoned the landlord.

' We want to go sight-seeing in Nichō-machi,' said Yaji. ' Which is the way there ? '

' That's down by the River Abé,' said the landlord.

' Is it far ? ' asked Kita.

' No, only about a mile and a half,' answered the landlord. ' I'll hire horses for you, if you like.'

' Ah, that would be good,' said Kita.

' It will be fun going to buy a girl on horseback,' said Yaji. Finally they set out on horseback.

This Abekawa-chō is in front of the Abekawa Miroku. Turning off the main road you come to two big gates, where you must alight from your horse. Inside are rows of houses, from each of which comes a lively sound of music, meant to attract people to the house. In fact it is much the same as in the Yoshiwara quarter in Edo.

Visitors to the town were walking about in cotton kimono with crests and with towels laid loosely on their heads, accompanied by teahouse maids, whose clogs made a loud sound as they dragged them along. These all looked very respectable, as most of them wore wide skirts and all had cloaks. But among the townsmen, those who had only come to look on, there seemed to be a competition as to which should wear the most stylish aprons. Some of them were carrying straw bags suspended on sticks laid across their shoulders. Moving in a constant stream as they did, they looked like people who were going to worship an image of Buddha. It was impossible to know to what class they belonged or to tell the state of their fortune. One of them, looking like a gambler or other person who lives by his wits, dressed in a quilted robe of variegated pattern and wearing countrified clogs with bamboo thongs and a cotton towel round his head, was run into by another as he was going along.

'Here, keep your eyes open,' he said. 'What did you want to bump into me for?'

A friend of his, of the same type, coming up behind, joined in.

'Ya! Ichi,' he said. 'What's the matter? Knock him down.'

'It was so dark I couldn't see you coming,' said the other, and he went on with an apology.

Some of the same class were standing in front of the cages.

'That girl's face over by the wall there,' said one of them, 'is like the saintly mask of Sengen. There, she's got up and gone now. She's very short, isn't she? She's like the bamboo grass that Kajiwara's horse bit off, only half grown.'

'The dresses in this house,' said another, 'are like the lacquer-boxes in Shichiken-chō.'

'Let's go in somewhere,' said Yaji.

'Wait a minute,' said Kita. 'The girls all have different prices, —some of them are one *bu*, some ten *mommé*, and some two *shu*. I'll have that one over there by the wall. She'll be ten *mommé* I expect. What's the name of that place? Shinonoya. And there's the Chojiya, and this is the Yamamotoya. But what do you do to get in? I don't know how they manage things here.'

While they were wandering about in front of the cages, they saw a guest arrive and go in.

'Oh, oh! I see now,' said Kita. 'Let's go in here. Yaji, have you chosen one?'

'Yes, yes,' said Yaji. 'Come on.' So they went in together.

'Welcome!' said a young man at the entrance. 'Please come up.'

He conducted them upstairs and soon led them to the room of the girls they had selected. Looking round they saw there was a harp in the alcove and also some flowers. Altogether it was like a small house in the Yoshiwara at Edo. Apparently it was the custom to pay some drink-money at this stage of the proceedings.

'Will you have some saké ? ' asked the young man.

'Yes, bring some saké,' said Kita.

Meanwhile the two girls they had selected had come in. Yaji's, whose name was Kozasano, was dressed in a wadded silk robe, with a striped satin girdle and a sky-blue overmantle ; Kita's, whose name was Isagawa, was dressed in a striped crêpe-silk robe and a gold embroidered girdle, with a black silk cloak. Both of them had silk lining to their clothes. A plain wooden tobacco-box was brought in and put before them.

'Welcome ! ' said Kozasano.

'How careless,' said Isagawa. 'That girl hasn't put any tobacco in the box. Kosamé ! Kosamé ! '

'Well, girls,' said Yaji. 'Come a little closer. Here, young man, be quick with the saké.'

'It's coming, your honour,' said the youth. He went out and soon came back with a saké bottle and cups, and some comestibles. The formal cups of saké having been exchanged, Yaji offered the cup to the young man.

'Have a drop,' he said.

'Thank you,' said the youth.

At the same time Yaji gave him a silver coin, which he took and went out. In his place a little girl came running in.

'Isoji's come from the Yoshinoya,' she said, 'and wants to speak to you a minute about something.'

'I'm coming,' said Isagawa.

'Kosamé,' said Kozasano, 'is Sen of Kuno there ? '

'No,' said Kosamé.

'What a nuisance. He promised to come the other day. Making a fool of one ! '

'Come more over here,' said Kita, 'and have a cup.'

'Let me pour for you,' said Isagawa.

Then two youths and a maid came in, carrying a nest of boxes.

'Thank you for your gift,' said the maid to Kita.

'I'm Kinta,' said one of the youths, 'and this is Gonemon. We shall be glad to have your custom.' They both bowed politely.

'Aha!' said Yaji. 'Seems they don't charge beforehand here. Kinta and Gonemon are strange names.'

'What's in the box?' asked Kita. 'Aha, these are the Abekawa cakes. They're giving us something good in return for the two *shū*. Ha-ha-ha!'

Just then there was a noise in the passage, with the sound of many voices raised in dispute, and finally the persons disputing went into the next room.

'What's the row?' asked Kita.

'It's nothing,' said Isagawa. 'They've found a bad guest and brought him here.'

'Ah, that's amusing,' said Yaji. 'Let's have a look.'

He pushed open the sliding doors a little and peeped into the next room, where a large number of girls had surrounded one of the guests.

'Why do you never come here now?' they asked.

'You're always going to the Chōjiya now,' said another girl, 'and you've got no reason for it. You've made Tokonatsu quite angry.'

'Well, look here,' said the guest, who seemed to be a country fellow. 'The day before yesterday and yesterday I was coming, but I had so much to do that I couldn't get here. Then my uncle asked me to accompany him to the Chōjiya, and I went, but as I am under a vow to Tokonatsu I swear by Nitten I did not allow my heart to be turned.'

'Nonsense!' cried the girls. 'You went with Hanayama of the Chōjiya. We know all about it.'

'No, no, that's not true,' said the guest looking hurt. 'You mustn't say such things.'

Then an elder girl of the name of Tokonatsu came in. She had thrown a mantle over her shoulders and came in solemnly carrying a pipe and a tobacco pouch.

'You are welcome, Master Yatei,' she said.

'I'm sorry I haven't been able to come and see you lately,' said Yatei. 'You must excuse me.'

84

'There's no excuse for you,' said Tokonatsu. 'I'm the oldest here, and the girls call me elder sister. How do you suppose I'm going to maintain my position here if I'm put to shame like this? I'm going to punish you just as a warning to other false guests like you. Here, Natsugiku, bring that razor.'

'What are you going to do?' asked the guest.

'What am I going to do?' said Tokonatsu. 'I'm going to cut off your hair.'

The razor was brought and the girl stood up to carry out her threat.

'Spare me, spare me,' cried the guest as he tried to shield his head. 'Wait, wait.'

'There's nothing to wait for,' cried the girls.

'I can't let you cut a hair of it,' said the guest. 'Forgive me, forgive me.'

'Forgive you, indeed!' said Tokonatsu.

'Well, but look here . . .'

'We must cut it off.'

'Here, here,' cried the guest. He tried to run away, but they all got round him and caught hold of his head, whereupon all his hair came off. In truth the man had very little hair of his own and was wearing a false queue and side locks, which all fell off when they pulled it.

'There,' said the man, feeling his head, 'You've pulled off all my hair.'

At that all the girls burst into laughter. 'Ho-ho-ho!' they laughed.

'It's no laughing matter,' said the guest. 'Give me my hair and I won't go to the Chōjiya again.'

'I don't know anything about your hair,' said Tokonatsu.

'Natsugiku's hidden it,' said the guest. 'Please give me my hair quickly.'

'Will you promise not to go to the Chōjiya again?'

'Yes, yes. I won't go again.'

'Solemnly promise?'

'By Ten Shōkō Daijingu I promise not to go again.'

'Then give him his hair, Natsugiku,' said Tokonatsu.

Thus on Tokonatsu's order the hidden hair was produced and handed to the guest.

'It's not all here,' he cried.

'That's all I've got,' said Natsugiku.

'One of the side locks is missing. Isn't it there? Do look for it.'

'Is this it?' asked one of the girls.

'That's it, that's it,' said the guest.

He tried to put it on by himself but he was so excited he got it on sideways, which made all the girls laugh.

'Oh, oh!' he panted, 'a pretty game you've had with me.'

Then some saké was brought in to seal the reconciliation and there was a lot more talking and laughing.

Yaji and Kita laughed till their sides ached. 'That happens all over the place,' said Yaji, 'but it's very amusing. It was only last spring that Ikku was tied up by Katsuyama at the Nakadaya, although he doesn't like people to know about it.'

Then a maid came in. 'Shall I spread the beds?' she asked. 'Please move a little over here.'

Kita went with his companion into another room, and the maid spread the bed, and in a short time they were asleep. But their dreams were short, for the dawn soon came, with its parting.

Yaji got up, and Kita came in rubbing his eyes. Their companions accompanied them downstairs, where all were assembled, and after a hurried farewell, they hastened to Temmachō, to find their breakfast at the inn ready for them. The preparations for the road were soon made, and leaving the inn they retraced their steps to the main road and soon reached the Miroku. Here the famous Abekawa rice-cakes were on sale, and pretty teahouses made the road quite gay.

'Try some of our famous cakes,' cried the girls. 'Try our cakes.'

'I had some of them last night,' said Yaji. 'I don't want any more.'

'Nor I,' said Kita.

Just then a ferryman came to meet them. 'Are you going up to the capital, gentlemen?' he asked.

'Who are you?' asked Yaji.

'I'm the waterman,' he replied. 'I'll take you across the river cheap.'

'How much?' asked Kita.

'The rain yesterday has made the river rise,' said the waterman, 'so it will be sixty-four coppers each.'

'That's dear,' said Kita.

'Well, just go and look at the river, then,' said the waterman.

'It is running fast,' said Yaji. 'Don't let us fall in.'

'Never fear,' said the waterman. 'Just get in.'

The two got into the hand-barrow, and the watermen commenced to carry them across the river.

'Oh lor!' said Kita. 'It makes my eyes go round in my head to look at it.'

'Keep hold of my head,' said the waterman. 'Here, you're putting your hand in front of my eyes and I can't see where I'm going.'

'It is deep,' said Yaji. 'Don't let us fall.'

'There's no chance of your falling,' said the waterman.

'What would happen if you were to let us drop?' asked Yaji.

'You'd only be carried away by the current and drowned, that's all,' said the waterman.

'Don't talk of it,' said Yaji. 'Here we are, here we are. Thank you, thank you.'

He got out of the hand-barrow and paid the men. 'There's sixteen coppers each extra for you,' he said.

'Thank 'ee, your honour,' said the watermen, and went back across the river lower down where it was shallow.

'Here, Yaji, look at that,' cried Kita. 'They took us across the deep part and charged us sixty-four coppers each for it.'

From there they reached Tegoshi, where it started to rain again and soon was coming down in torrents. But they put their raincoats over their shoulders and trudged along till they got to Mariko. Here they entered a teahouse.

'Shall we have a meal?' suggested Kita. 'This place is famous for its potato stew.'

'Landlord,' called Yaji. 'Have you got any potato stew ready?'

'Yes, sir,' replied the landlord. 'Make it in a minute.'

'Then you haven't got any ready?' said Yaji. 'That's unfortunate.'

'Ready in a minute, sir,' said the landlord. 'Please wait a moment.'

He seized some potatoes and began to cut them up without taking off the skins.

'Nabé, Nabé,' he called, testily, 'what are you doing out there when I'm so busy? Come in, come in.'

A touzle-haired woman, with a baby on her back, came in at the back-door dragging her straw sandals along the ground and grumbling.

'I've only been having a bit of a chat,' she said. 'What a grumbler you are.'

'Who's a grumbler?' said the landlord. 'Here, get the things out for two guests. Look at your apron dragging on the floor.'

'What did you do with the chopsticks that were washed?' asked the woman.

'How do I know?' said the landlord. 'There we are. Now just hand me the chopsticks.'

'Do you mean these?'

'No, no. How do you think I'm going to pound potatoes with chopsticks? It's the pestle I want. Don't go to sleep. That ain't the tray. I told you to bring it here. What a fool the woman is!'

He seized the pestle and began to pound the potatoes in the mortar.

'You've got the pestle upside down,' said the woman.

'It don't matter. You look after your own business. There, the seaweed's burning.'

'What a fuss, you make,' said his wife. 'You're just like a squalling brat.'

'Here, take hold of the mortar,' said her husband. 'Don't hold it like that. I never saw such a gawk.'

'And I never saw such a fool,' replied his wife.

'What, you scold!' cried the landlord, and he brought the pestle down with a whack on her head.

'You beast,' yelled the woman, and she took the mortar and threw it at her husband, spilling all the potato stew on the ground.

This made the landlord still more angry, and giving a yell he was going to strike her again with the pestle when he slipped on the potato stew and fell to the ground.

'Do you think I'm going to give in to such a fellow as you?' cried the wife, and she was just going to grab hold of him when she too slipped on the stew and fell.

Then the good lady opposite came running over.

'Aren't you ashamed of yourselves,' she cried, 'quarrelling like this? Behave yourselves.'

But when she began scolding them both she too slipped on the stew and went over. There they were, all three, slipping about and getting their clothes all covered with the stew. It was a terrible scene.

'This isn't any use,' said Yaji. 'We'd better get out.'

'What a terrible couple!' said Kita.

Concealing their amusement they set off again, and from there reached Utsunoyama. The rain was still coming down in torrents and the road, overgrown with creepers, was very lonely. But they pressed on till they drew near to the Tōdango teahouse, where an innkeeper from Okabé met them.

'Are you stopping here, gentlemen?' he asked.

'No, no,' said Yaji. 'We must cross the river to-day.'

'The River Ōi is not passable,' said the innkeeper.

'Eh?' said Kita. 'Is the river closed?'

'Yes,' said the man. 'And there's a daimyō's train in front which has taken all the five inns at Shimada and Fujieda, so there's no place for you to stop there. You had better stop at Okabé.'

'That's what we must do,' said Yaji.

'What's the name of your inn?' asked Kita.

'It's the Sakaraya,' said the innkeeper. 'I shall be happy to conduct you there.'

Conducted by the innkeeper they descended the hill of Ōdera-ga-hara and came to Okabé.

There they put up at the inn till the river was passable, thus for a time resting their tired limbs from the weariness of travel.

YAJIROBEI

BOOK THREE

FIRST PART

THE famous Sea of Tōtōmi was calm and there was no wind to stir the pine-trees along the roads. The travellers were polite; the postboys' songs enjoyable; the carriers had no disputes, and the ferrymen did not charge more than their proper fares. The blind could walk alone, women go without protectors, and even the children who had stolen from their homes to go on pilgrimages were free from any danger of meeting robbers. Such was the Golden Age for which they had to be thankful. Wandering to all points of the compass and gathering everywhere indescribable pleasure, these two, Yajirobei and Kitahachi, unable to cross the River Ōi, had to put up at Okabé.

When they heard in the morning that the government mail-box had gone over and that the road was clear they immediately started from the inn. Already a daimyō's train, from the highest to the lowest, like the teeth of a comb for number, filled the highway with kago and baggage-horses, and was marching along in brave array. Cheerfully trudging along they crossed the River Asahina, passed the island of Yahataoni, and reached Shiroko. Here, on both sides of the road, the teahouse girls were calling, 'Walk in and rest. Good entertainment for travellers. Walk in.'

'Don't you want a horse, master,' called a postboy. 'I'll take you cheap for two hundred coppers,—just a trifle, your honours.'

'I can ride another kind of horse for two hundred coppers, you old dirt-eater,' said Kita.

'Who are you calling dirt-eater?' said the postboy. 'When did I eat dirt?'

'Hin! Hin!' neighed the horse.

'Let's have a little drink,' said Yaji. 'Here, miss, if you've got any good saké let's have a drop.' They went into a teahouse and the girl waited on them.

'Shall I heat the saké for you?' she asked.

'Yes, yes,' said Yaji. 'And what have you got to eat?'

'There's only boiled fish and onions,' said the landlord.

'What, boiled onions ? ' said Kita. 'That's good.'

'They're not boiled in water,' said the landlord. 'They're boiled in soy.' He brought the saké bottle and cups and the fish on a plate.

'Oh, I thought the onions would be cooked like we have them in Edo,' said Yaji. 'But I see they're cooked raw. All right.'

'Let's begin,' said Kita, and he took a mouthful. 'Halloa, this fish is stale. This was cooked yesterday.'

'No, no,' said the landlord, 'it's not yesterday's.'

'Well, we can't eat that,' said Yaji.

'If yesterday's is bad,' said the landlord, 'I'll give you some of the day before. I'll guarantee that'll make you drunk.'

'Drunk ? ' said Kita. 'Why, the saké's half water,' and he spat it out. 'How much is it ? '

'The fish is forty-four coppers and the drink twenty-eight,' said the landlord.

'It's nice and dear, isn't it,' remarked Kita. 'Come on, let's go.'

They paid for the food and started off and soon reached Fujieda, where, at the entrance to the town they met an old man with a bundle on his back who was riding on a very restive horse. Just as he was passing the horse came into collision with Kita, sending him sprawling into a puddle. This made Kita very angry and he jumped up and seized hold of the old man.

'Here, old chap, haven't you got any eyes ? ' he cried. 'Can't you see where you're going ? You'd better take something for it.'

'Dear me ! ' said the old man. 'I'm very sorry.'

'Very sorry ? I should say you were. But that won't do. You may think you've got hold of something easy, but I tell you I've got a glare like a gold dolphin if I'm put to it. I'm the sort of man who's bathed in cold water ever since he was born.'

'Well, if you're used to bathing in cold water it's all right,' said the old man. 'But I'm afraid that wasn't water you fell into; it was horse's stale.'

'Eh ? ' said Kita. 'Horse's stale ? What did you want to knock me down into that for ? '

'The horse began to kick when I didn't expect it,' said the old man, 'and unfortunately it ran into you. It couldn't be helped, so you must really excuse me.'

'Excuse you ? ' said Kita. 'Not I. I wouldn't care if you

were the boss of Mount Ōe come with his big rod, or Sekison with his lantern, bearing a face like that of a bear crawling in the gutter. I'm the sort of fellow that wouldn't be afraid if Hainai of Kumé were to enter my house.'

'You say such terrible things I don't understand what you are talking about,' said the old man. 'I come from Nagata, I do, and my family has always been headmen of the village. At New Year's time, too, when the village offers congratulations to the lord of the manor, I always have an upper seat. You must treat me with more respect.'

'None of your insolence,' said Kita, 'or I'll break your head.'

'Eh, eh!' said the old man. 'Haven't you got any brains? Don't you know I'm under the protection of Kwōjin? Don't chatter so much.'

'Get out, you old shyster!' said Kita. He was going to strike the old man when Yaji intervened and separated them.

'You must forgive him, Kita,' he said. 'Here, gaffer, you shouldn't be so obstinate when you know it was your own fault. Go on and don't let us have any more of it.' Yaji soothed Kita while the old man went on grumbling to himself and with his face drawn with anger.

Laughing they crossed the river to Seto, where in front of a teahouse at the end of the town they came again upon the old countryman taking a rest. Immediately he saw them he started to call to them.

'Here, here,' he cried. 'Excuse my rudeness just now. I had taken a cup too much and I'm afraid I made some foolish remarks. Kindly forgive me. Won't you take a parting cup with me? Do come in.'

'We've had a drink already,' said Yaji.

'Dear me!' said the old man. 'I did so want you to have one with me. Do just have one. Here, landlord, bring out some good saké.'

'Thanks for your kindness,' said Kita, 'but we can't stop. Come on, Yaji.'

'Dear, dear!' said the old man. 'You're such a hasty fellow. Do just come in for a moment.'

The old man caught hold of their hands and drew them in, and as their mouths were watering for the saké, they made no resistance.

'Let's have a cup, Kita,' said Yaji, 'although it's a shame to make the old gaffer pay.'

'Not at all, not at all,' said the old man. 'Here, landlord, bring out plenty to eat. But I say, it's too exposed here. Let's go into a back room.'

'This way,' said the maid, and she took the saké bottle and cups and led them round by the garden to a room at the back, where they sat on the verandah to save the trouble of taking off their sandals.

'Here, gaffer, you have the first cup,' said Yaji, offering it to the old man.

'Ah,' said the old man, 'let's try it. That's good. I'll offer the cup to the young man.'

'I'd rather have something to eat,' said Kita. 'I'm hungry.'

'What?' said the old man. 'Hungry? Then you'd better have some rice. That'll soon make you feel better.'

'I'll try a cup of saké all the same,' said Kita. 'Ah, that's good. What's the soup? Boiled sardines? I suppose we shall have pumpkin soup after this, or roasted yams.'

'What stuff you talk!' said Yaji. 'Look at these shrimps. When they jump they look like the angels painted on the ceilings of the temples.'

'Ah, that's like in Bungo-bushi,' said Kita, and he began to chant. 'Ha-ha-ha! Here, gaffer, let me give you one.'

'No, no, let me pour for you,' said the old man. 'They'll bring something to eat directly. Here, waitress, waitress, I've been clapping my hands enough to break my wrists. Why don't you bring the things I ordered?'

'Coming, your honour,' said the girl, and at last the food was brought in.

'Oh, it's come at last, has it?' said the old man. 'What's in that box? Eggs?'

'That's why they were so long in coming,' said Yaji. 'They were waiting till the eggs were laid.'

'Then they're sure to be fresh,' said Kita. 'Excellent!'

'Please drink hearty,' said the old man. 'You know you saved my life back there by forgiving me so readily. I was so excited I didn't know what I was talking about.'

'No, no, it was I who got excited,' said Kita. 'I shouldn't have said what I did. Forgive me.'

'The gaffer's so good-natured,' said Yaji. 'As for this chap he's always ready for an excuse to eat and drink.'

As the old man was paying for the feast Yaji and Kita went on flattering him up to the skies, while all sorts of good things were brought from the kitchen. When the rice came, Yaji and Kita, although they felt a little ashamed of taking advantage of the old man's kindness, made a good meal.

By-and-by the old man went out to do something.

'I say, Yaji,' said Kita, 'you owe all this to me. It's because I stood up to the old man that he's given us all this.'

'Get out,' said Yaji. 'You're not the only one. Let's have another drink while he's away.'

'I'm going to drink out of this teacup,' said Kita. Then he began to sing:

> Oh it's come! Yes, it's come!
> Oh it's come, come, come!
> Won't you have another cup with me
> When it's come, come, come.

Yaji also joined in.

> Oh, she's very like a log
> That's been cut upon the hill,
> But still she is my wife,
> So I really love her still.

'What fun we're having. By the way, where's the old fool gone?'

'He's a long time about it, isn't he?' said Kita. 'I say waitress, that old chap who was here, where's he gone?'

'He went out at the front,' said the girl.

'Eh?' said Yaji. 'What's that for? Strange!'

They waited and waited for the old man but he never came back again. They looked everywhere for him but he was nowhere to be found.

'I say, waitress,' called Kita. 'Did that old man pay the bill before he went?'

'No, it's not paid yet,' said the girl.

'Oh, oh!' groaned Yaji.

'The old fool's trying to play a game on us,' said Kita. 'I'll lay him out.'

He jumped up and rushed out, but it was like chasing a cloud. As the old man lived in the district he knew all the lanes and bypaths, and had got away quickly without anybody seeing him. Kita came back disappointed.

'I can't find him, Yaji,' he said. 'He's done us.'

'It can't be helped,' said Yaji. 'We've got to pay up. The old devil's had his revenge.'

'Yes, but why should we bear all the cost?' said Kita. 'Botheration! And we were just getting a bit jolly too! It's all off now.'

'Like that dog of Jirō and Tarō,' said Yaji.

'It's not a joking matter,' said Kita. 'Here, how much is it?'

'Ay, ay,' said the landlord. 'It's nine hundred and fifty coppers.'

'We've been cheated,' said Kita, 'but I suppose we've got to pay. The more I think about it the more annoyed I get.'

'He was a smart old chap,' said Yaji, 'and he played a clever trick on us.'

'Eh! It makes one angry to have one's eye plucked out like that,' said Kita.

But while reviling the old man Kita could not help laughing at the cleverness of his revenge.

Continuing their journey they came to the River Ōi and were met at Shimada by a ferryman.

'Do you gentlemen wish to cross the river?' he asked.

'Are you the ferryman?' said Yaji. 'How much for the two of us?'

'The river has only been passable since this morning,' said

the man, 'and it would be dangerous to carry you across. If you have a raft it will cost you eight hundred coppers for the two.'

'That's an awful price,' said Yaji. 'We're not in Echigo or Niigata. Eight hundred's too much.'

'Well, how much will you give?' asked the waterman.

'Never mind what we want to give,' replied Yaji. 'We can get over by ourselves.'

'Well, the temple will only charge two hundred coppers for burying you if you're carried away by the current and drowned,' said the waterman, 'so it's cheaper that way. Ha-ha-ha!'

'Fool!' said Yaji. 'I'll go and talk to your master. Look here, Kita,' he added as they walked on, 'it's a nuisance having to bargain with these men. Let's go and see the headman. Just lend me your dirk.'

'Why?' asked Kita. 'What are you going to do?'

'I'm going to become a samurai,' said Yaji. He took Kita's dirk and put it in his girdle with his own, pulling down the scabbard so as to make it appear that he was wearing two swords, a long one and a short one.

'There,' he said. 'Don't I look like a samurai now? You carry the bundles and follow behind.'

'Now we'll have some fun,' said Kita. He took Yaji's bundle, tied it up with his own, and put them on his shoulder. Soon they came to the headman's office.

'Ah, are you the head ferryman?' asked Yaji, pretending to speak like a samurai. 'I'm on very important business for my lord. Just call your men to put me across.'

'Certainly, your honour,' said the headman. 'How many are there in your suite?'

'Eh?' said Yaji. 'My suite?'

'Yes. Is your honour travelling in a kago or on horseback? How many packloads of baggage have you?'

'There are three horses fully laden,' said Yaji, 'and fifteen horses with lighter loads, but as they impeded my progress I left them outside Edo. Instead I am travelling in a kago with eight tall fellows to carry it. Just take a note of that.'

'Yes, your honour. And your attendants?'

'There are twelve of them,' said Yaji, 'besides spearmen,

99

sandal-bearers, and those carrying my lacquered boxes and stilts,—altogether, from the highest to the lowest, over thirty persons.'

'Ay, ay!' said the headman. 'But where are these attendants?'

'Well,' said Yaji, 'they were all with me when I set out from Edo, but they caught the measles at one time or another, so I had to leave them at different stages and there's only two of us to cross the river. How much will a raft be?'

'For the two of you a raft will be four hundred and eighty coppers,' said the man.

'That's rather high,' said Yaji. 'Can't you reduce it a bit?'

'We don't make any reduction in our charges,' said the man. 'You'd better go on instead of standing there talking like a fool.'

'Eh?' said Yaji. 'How dare you address a samurai in that way?'

'Ha-ha-ha!' laughed the man. 'A fine sort of samurai!'

'You insult a knight?' cried Yaji. 'It is unpardonable.'

'A fine knight you are,' said the man. 'Look at the tip of your sword.'

Yaji turned round to look and saw that the tip of his sword had struck against a post, and as it was only the scabbard it had bent in two. Then everybody burst into laughter and Yaji was struck dumb with shame.

'Where did you ever hear of a samurai with a broken sword?' said the man. 'You came here to deceive us, but we are not to be taken in.'

'I'm a descendant of Minoya Shirōtoshi,' said Yaji. 'That's why I wear a broken sword.'

'If we have any more of your insolence,' said the headman, 'we'll tie you up.'

'It's no use, Yaji,' said Kita. 'You can't settle it that way. Let's go.'

He took Yaji's hand and drew him away and they both sneaked off.

'Ha-ha-ha!' laughed the ferrymen. 'What idiots they are!'

'I didn't make a hit that time,' grumbled Yaji. 'Botheration!'

Laughing they hastened to the bank of the river, where they found the ferry crowded with people of all ranks. Amid the sound of many disputes they settled the price for the raft and started to cross. Soon their eyes were dizzy by the sight of the rolling waters of the river. So frightened were they that they thought at every moment they would lose their lives. There is, indeed, no more dreadful place on the Tokaidō than the River Ōi, the swift current of which sends great rocks rolling down and threatening to smash you every moment.

But in a short time they had crossed the river and had alighted from the raft. How glad they were !

Soon they reached Kanaya.

' Come in and rest,' called the girls at the wayside teahouses. ' Come in and rest.'

' Won't you have a ride, sir ? ' said a carrier. ' I'm on my way back.'

' What do you say, Yaji ? ' said Kita. ' Shall we ride ? '

' I don't feel like it,' said Yaji. ' You can ride if you like.'

' Then I'll ride as far as Nissaka,' said Kita.

After fixing the price he got in. It was raining on and off but there was an old piece of matting over the kago to keep out the rain. On Kikugawa Hill they met two or three pilgrims.

' *Ah the waves that beat the shore in far Kumano !* ' chanted the pilgrims. ' Please give us a copper, master,' they added.

' Don't bother,' said Kita.

' Oh, please, wealthy master, do please throw us a copper,' they cried.

' Didn't I tell you not to bother me, you rascals,' said Kita.

' Who are you calling rascals ? ' cried the pilgrims. ' Rascal yourself.'

' Beggars ! ' shouted Kita.

But just as he was swelling himself out with pride, somehow or other the bottom of the kago came out and he fell on the road with a bang.

' Oh, oh, oh ! ' he howled.

' Ha-ha-ha ! ' laughed the pilgrims.

' Deary me ! ' said the carriers. ' Hope you haven't hurt yourself, sir.'

' What did you rascals want to put me in a kago like that for ? ' groaned Kita.

' Very sorry, sir,' said the bearers. ' What shall we do ? '

' Go and borrow another one,—a good one,' said Kita.

' There's no place to borrow one on this hill,' said the bearers.

' I know what to do,' said one of them. ' Take off your loin-cloth, mate.'

'What are you going to do?' said his mate.

'I'll show you,' said the other.

He took off his own loin-cloth and tied it to his mate's, and tied them both round the kago, under the matting.

'Please get in,' he said.

'How absurd!' said Kita. 'You don't suppose I'm going to ride in a thing like that, do you?'

'Well, there's nothing else we can do,' said the carriers. 'It's quite safe. You could go to sleep in it without any danger of falling. Please put up with it for a little.'

As they seemed anxious to please him and the incident would serve for laughter in the future, Kita got in.

'Ha-ha-ha!' laughed Yaji. 'It looks like a funeral, you going along in a kago tied up with a white cloth.'

'Eh?' said Kita. 'Don't say such things.'

'No, it can't be a corpse,' continued Yaji. 'It can speak. It must be a criminal going to punishment.'

'That's worse,' said Kita. 'I'm going to get out.'

He got out of the kago and paid the men for as far as they had come.

Walking along they were overtaken by constant showers, which made the hills slippery, but at last they reached Sayo-no-Naka-yama. This place is famous for its white rice-cakes, which are rice-cakes with syrup inside.

While they were having some saké and eating two or three of these rice-cakes, the rain came down worse than ever.

From there they went down the hill till they reached Nissaka, the rain coming down harder and harder till it was impossible to go on, as everything was blotted out. Finally they took refuge under the eaves of an inn.

'How annoying!' said Yaji. 'Such terrible rain!'

'Well, we're not willow-trees to be planted by the road side,' said Kita. 'We can't stand under the eaves of people's houses for ever. What do you think, Yaji? We've crossed the River Ōi. Don't you think we might stop here for the night?'

'What?' said Yaji. 'Don't talk nonsense! It can't be two o'clock yet. It would be absurd to stop now.'

Then the old landlady came out of the inn.

'You can't go on in this rain,' she said. 'Please stop here.'

'I think we ought to,' said Kita. 'I say, Yaji, look! There are some women stopping in the back room there.'

' Eh ? ' said Yaji. ' Where ? That's interesting.'

' Won't your honours stop here ? ' repeated the old woman.

' Well, suppose we do,' said Yaji.

They went in and washed their feet, and were soon conducted to a room at the back next to the one where they had seen the women.

' If you have some hot water just bring a cupful,' said Yaji to the maid.

' Ay, ay, your honour,' replied the maid.

' I thought she said " Fie, fie," ' said Kita. ' Gave me quite a turn.'

The maid brought the hot water directly.

' I say, Kita,' said Yaji, ' just give me the medicine we bought yesterday.'

' Which do you mean ? ' said Kita. ' The feel-bad pills ? Wait a bit. Shall I give you a pinch of the ants' walk ? '

' Don't be a fool,' said Yaji. ' I've got an awful pain in my belly.'

' That's because you've got the bots,' said Kita. ' You ought to eat some horse beans to cure it.'

' Shut up with your silly jokes and get it out quick,' said Yaji.

' Well, seriously,' said Kita, ' you'd better have some of the Tamachi tonic pills. Hold out your hand.'

' I'll take two,' said Yaji.

He put them into his mouth and crunched them up.

' Oh, oh ! ' he cried, ' this is pepper. Whew, how hot it is ! '

' Ha-ha-ha ! ' laughed Kita. ' Wait a moment. No, there's nothing else. Yes, there is. Here's some brocade-bag pills. Will that do ? '

' It's so dark with the screens shut,' said Yaji, ' I can't see.' He let in some more light and then chewed up the pills.

' What have you given me this time ? ' he asked. ' Ugh ! '

' Let's look,' said Kita. ' Oh, that's Kwannon.'

' Then I've chawed off Kwannon's head,' said Yaji. ' Ha-ha-ha.'

' Will you have something to eat now ? ' asked the maid.

' No, we'll have supper instead,' said Kita.

' What a chatterer you are,' said Yaji. ' Do be quiet. Talk silently can't you.'

' Fancy making a row silently ! ' said Kita.

Then the supper trays were brought in and they set to work to eat, uttering all sorts of jokes.

'By the way,' said Yaji to the maid, 'the guests in the back room are women, aren't they? Who are they?'

'They're witches,' said the maid.

'What, witches?' said Kita. 'That's interesting. Let's call up somebody.'

'It's too late, isn't it?' said Yaji. 'They won't come after four o'clock.'

'It's only a little past two,' said the maid.

'Well, just ask them,' said Yaji. 'I'd like to have a talk with my dead wife.'

'Fancy wanting to do that!' said Kita.

'I'll ask them afterwards,' said the maid.

So when the meal was finished she went into the next room to ask the witches. They agreed, and Yaji and Kita were conducted into their room. There the witches produced the usual box and arranged it, while the maid, who knew what was wanted, drew some water and brought it in.

Yaji, with his mind fixed on his departed wife, poured some water over the anise leaves and the younger witch began to invoke the gods.

'First of all,' she chanted, 'I reverently call upon Bonten and Taishaku and the four gods of Heaven, and in the underworld the great Emma and the five attendants who wait on him. Of our country's gods I invoke the Seven Gods of Heaven and the Five Gods of Earth, and of the gods of Isé, Amaterasu Ōmikami, and the forty descendants of the Outer Shrine and the eight descendants of the Inner Shrine. I invoke the god of Rain, the God of Wind, the God of the Moon and the God of the Sun, the God of the North Shrine of the Benku Mirror, and the spirit of the great Sun Goddess of Ama-no-iwato, and Kokuzō, the God of Ten Thousand Good Fortunes of Asama-ga-daké, and the others in the sixty provinces of Japan, and also in the country of the gods, at the Great Shrine of Izumo. By the ninety-eight thousand gods of the country and the thirteen thousand Buddhas of the holy places, through the fearful road of the underworld I come. Ah, horror! The spirits of his ancestors crowd upon me, each couple as inseparable as the bow and the arrow. The skies may change and the waters may change, but the bow is unchangeable. One shot from it sends an echo through all the holy places of the temples. Ah! Ah! Oh, joyful sight! Well have you summoned me. I had for bedfellow a warrior famous with the bow, but alas! averse to a pure diet, in life he devoured fish even to the bones, and now, in punishment, is changed into a devil in the shape of an ox, his duty being to keep the gates of Hell, from which he has no release. Thus have I come alone.'

'Who are you?' asked Yaji. 'I don't understand what it's all about.'

'I have come for the sake of him who offered me water, the mirror of my body, my child-treasure.'

'Mirror of the body?' said Kita. 'I'll tell you what, Yaji, it's your mother.'

'My mother, eh?' said Yaji. 'I don't want to have anything to say to her.'

'Has the mirror of my body nothing to say to me?' continued the witch. 'To me, your bedfellow, whom you have thus without shame summoned from the depths? Ah, what agony I went through when I was married to you,—time and again suffering the pangs of hunger and shivering with cold in the winter. Ah, hateful! Hateful!'

'Forgive me,' said Yaji. 'At that time my fortunes were low. How pitiful your lot that you should have been brought to the grave with care and hardships.'

'Halloa, Yaji,' said Kita. 'Are you crying? Ha-ha-ha! Even devils have tears.'

'I shall never forget it,' the witch went on. 'When you were ill you gave your sickness to me. Our only child, who had to carry on our name, grew weak and thin because there was no rice to fill his empty stomach. Every day the duns were knocking at the door and the rent remained unpaid. Yet I did not complain, —not even when I slipped in the dogs' dirt in the lane.'

'Don't talk of it,' said Yaji. 'You'll break my heart.'

'And then, when through my labours I had saved enough money to buy a kimono, I had to pawn it for your sake and never saw it again. Never again did it come back to me from the pawnbroker's.'

'At the same time you must remember what a pleasant place you are in now,' said Yaji, 'while I have to worry along down here.'

'What? What is there pleasant about it? It is true that by

the help of your friends you erected a stone over my grave, but you never go near it, and you never contribute to the temple to get the priests to say prayers for my soul. I am nothing to you. The stone over my grave has been taken away and put into the wall, where all the dogs come and make water against it. Not a drop of water is ever placed on my grave. Truly in death we suffer all sorts of troubles.'

'True, true,' said Yaji.

'But while you thus treat me with neglect,' the witch went on, 'lying in my grave I think of nobody but you and long for the time when you will join me in the underworld. Shall I come to meet you?'

'No, no, don't do that,' said Yaji. 'It's really too far for you.'

'Well then, I have one request to make.'

'Yes, yes. What is it?'

'Give this witch plenty of money.'

'Of course, of course.'

'How sad the parting!' cried the witch. 'I have yet much to tell you, countless questions to ask you, but the messenger of Hell recalls me.'

Then, recovering from her trance, the witch twanged her bow.

'Thank you very much,' said Yaji. He took out some money and wrapped it in paper and gave it to her.

'Ha-ha!' laughed Kita. 'Now all your hidden shames are revealed to the world. Ha-ha-ha! But I say, Yaji, you look very downcast. What do you say to a drink?'

Yaji agreed and clapping his hands ordered the maid to bring some saké.

'How far have you come to-day?' asked the witch.

'We came from Okabé,' answered Yaji.

'How quick you are,' said the witch.

'Oh, that's nothing,' said Yaji. 'We can walk as fast as Idaten. If we're put to it we can walk thirty-five miles a day.'

'But then we shouldn't be fit for anything for ten days after,' put in Kita.

While they were talking the saké was brought in.

'Won't you have a little?' said Yaji to the young witch.

'I never touch a drop,' she answered.

'Will your companion have any?' asked Yaji.

'Mother, mother! Come here,' called the young witch.

'Oh, it's your mother, is it?' said Kita. 'I must take care what I say in front of her. But come, do have some.'

Soon they began to drink and enjoy themselves, the cup passing from hand to hand very quickly. Strangely enough, however, the witches, however much they drank, never seemed to be any the worse for it, while Yaji and Kita got so drunk they could not speak plainly. After making all sorts of jokes, which it would be too tedious to repeat, Kita at last in a drunken voice said, 'I say, mother, won't you lend me your daughter for the night?'

'No, no, she's going to lend her to me,' said Yaji.

'What an idea!' cried Kita. 'You'd better try and be good to-night. Haven't you any pity for your dead wife who spends her time in thinking of you and hoping you will join her quickly? Didn't she say she'd come and meet you after a bit?'

'Here, don't talk about that,' said Yaji. 'What should I do if she did come to meet me?'

'Then you had better be good,' said Kita. 'Now, old lady, what do you think?'

Kita here gave the young witch a loving caress, but she pushed him off and ran away, saying 'Be quiet.'

'If my daughter doesn't want to,' said the mother, 'what about me?'

'Well, if it comes to that I don't care who it is,' said Kita, who was lost in a drunken dream.

While they were talking the supper was brought in and there was a good deal of joking too tedious to repeat, and finally Yaji and Kita, the effects of the saké having already passed off, went back into their own room, where, as soon as it was dark, they went to bed. In the next room also the witches were apparently going to bed, worn out by their travels.

'That young witch is sleeping on this side, I know,' said Kita in a low voice. 'I'll creep in to her after a bit. Yaji, you'd better go to sleep.'

'Get out,' said Yaji. 'I'm going to be the one to get her.'

'Isn't he bold?' said Yaji. 'It would make a cat laugh.'

Thus talking they crept into bed and fell asleep. It was already about nine o'clock, and the night watchman's rattle, as he went round the inn, echoed through the pillows of the travellers. In the kitchen the sound of the preparations for the next morning's meal had died away, and all that could be heard was the barking of the dogs. It was just when night was at its darkest and eeriest hour that Kitahachi judged it the right time to creep out of bed and peep into the next room. The night-light had gone out, and he felt his way in very softly and crept into the bed where he thought the young witch was sleeping. To his surprise the witch, without saying anything, caught hold of his hand and pulled him in. Delighted with his reception, Kitahachi sank down under the coverlet with her arm for a pillow and soon realised his desire, after which they both fell asleep quite unconscious of their surroundings.

Yajirobei, who was thus left sleeping alone, soon opened his eyes. 'I wonder what time it is,' he muttered. 'I must go to the closet. It's so dark I can't see the way.'

Thus pretending that he was going to the closet he crept into the next room, quite unconscious of the fact that Kitahachi was already in there. Feeling about he came to the side of the bed where Kita was lying, and thinking in the darkness that it was the young witch's lips from which moans were coming, he put his lips to those of Kitahachi and took a bite.

'Oh! Oh!' yelled Kitahachi.

'Halloa! Is that you, Kitahachi?' said Yaji.

'Oh, it's Yaji, is it?' said Kita. 'Ugh! Ugh! How beastly!' and he began spitting.

At the sound of their voices the witch into whose bed Kita had crept woke up.

'What are you doing?' she said. 'Don't make such a noise. You'll wake my daughter up.'

This was another surprise for Kita, for it was the old witch's voice. Cursing himself for his stupidity he got out of the bed and crept away softly into the next room. Yaji was going to do the same when the old witch caught hold of him.

'You mustn't make a fool of an old woman by running away,' she said.

'No, no,' stuttered Yaji. 'You've made a mistake. It wasn't me.'

'You musn't try to deceive me,' said the old woman. 'I don't make a regular business of this, but when I meet a traveller on the road and sleep with him I like to get a little just to help me along. It's a shame to make a fool of me by running away. There, just go to sleep in my bosom till dawn.'

'What a nuisance you are,' said Yaji. 'Here, Kitahachi, Kitahachi.'

'Take care,' said the old woman. 'You mustn't call so loud.'

'But I don't know anything about it,' said Yaji. 'It's that chap Kitahachi that's got me into all this mess.'

Thus saying Yaji struggled out of her grasp, only to be caught again and thrown down. But at last, after a good deal of kicking, he managed to get away into the next room, where he repeated to himself

By stealth I entered, witch's love to earn,
But which was witch I could not well discern.

SECOND PART

DAWN seemed to come in no time, and awakened by the bustle of the travellers preparing for the road and the neighing of the horses, Yaji and Kita rubbed their travel-wearied eyes, got their breakfast, and forthwith set out, amused by the old witch's angry looks. Passing through Furumiya and Honda-no-Hachiman, they came to Shūto-no-Hata, which means mother-in-law's field, and to Yome-ga-Ta, which means bride's rice-field. Then said Yaji,

> The dried-up mother-in-law is cast aside
> And turns again into the juicy bride.

From there they reached the River Shōi, where the rain of the previous day having been heavy and the bridge presumably having been swept away, travellers were taking off their pants and pulling up their clothes to ford the river. Yaji and Kita were just about to follow their example when two blind men, going up to the capital and in doubt whether they could walk across the stream, accosted them.

' Can you tell me,' said one of them whose name was Inuichi, ' whether the water is only knee-deep.'

' Yes, yes,' said Kita, ' but the current's rather fast, so it's a little dangerous. Mind how you go.'

' Yes,' said the blind man, ' I can tell by the sound that it's running fast.'

He took a stone and threw it in. ' It seems shallow here,' he said. ' Here, Saruichi,' he called to the other blind man. ' We needn't both of us take off our leggings. You're younger than I. Take me across on your back.'

' Ha-ha-ha ! ' laughed Saruichi. ' None of your tricks. We'll play for it, and the one who loses will have to carry the other across. What do you say ? '

' All right,' said Inuichi. ' Come along. Three times, you know.'

' Ryangosai ! Ryangosai ! ' cried Saruichi, as they waved their right hands, while with their left hands they felt what each other was doing.

'I've won, I've won,' said Inuichi.

'What a shame!' said Saruichi. 'Well, tie my bundle up with yours and put them on your back. Are you all right? Come along then.'

He turned round for the other to get on his back, when Yaji, seeing his chance, stepped forward and got on instead. Saruichi, who thought he had Inuichi on his back, stepped into the water and was soon across. Inuichi, who had in the meantime been waiting on the other side, here began to call out.

'Saru, Saru,' he cried. 'What are you doing? Why don't you carry me across the river quick?'

Hearing Inuichi calling to him from the other side of the river, Saruichi began to get angry.

'None of your jokes,' he cried. 'Didn't I carry you across the river just now, and there you are on the other side again? Who are you fooling?'

'Don't talk nonsense,' said Inuichi. 'You went across alone. No cheating.'

'It's you that are cheating,' retorted Saruichi.

'You shouldn't talk like that to your elder,' replied Inuichi. 'Come and carry me across at once.'

Inuichi was beginning to show the whites of his eyes, so Saruichi, seeing that there was nothing to be done but to go back again, crossed the river once more.

'There, there,' he said. 'Get on my back.'

He turned round, and Kita, rejoicing at his luck, jumped on and Saruichi set out once more to cross the river. Inuichi now began to get very angry.

'Saruichi,' he cried. 'Where are you?'

Hearing this Saruichi stopped in the middle of the river. 'Halloa!' he said. 'Who's this I've got on my back?'

Thereupon he promptly dropped Kita into the river.

'Help! Help!' cried Kita, and as he was being carried away by the current he began waving his arms and legs about till Yaji jumped in and pulled him out, wet to the skin.

'Look what that blind beggar's done to me,' moaned Kita.

'Well, take off your kimono and wring it out,' said Yaji.

'It was your fault,' continued Kita. 'If you hadn't got him to carry you across I shouldn't have tried it myself.'

'Ha-ha-ha!' laughed Yaji. 'What a shame to drop you in the river like that!'

Thus enjoying the joke Yaji made a little poem on it :

> Fooling the blind he had a little spill,
> The current was swift, the punishment swifter still.

'I don't want to listen to your jokes,' said Kita. 'Shut up ! Oh-h, it's cold.'

He shivered as he tried to wring the water out of his kimono.

Just then the blind men, who had at last got across the river, passed them.

'You can't wear that wet kimono,' said Yaji. 'You'd better get another out. We'll get it dried when we get to a fire.'

'I shall catch cold,' said Kita. 'What a shame !'

Grumbling and sneezing he got out another kimono, and having hung the wet one over his arm they went on.

Soon they got to Kakegawa, where at the last teahouse the girls were calling out, 'Stop here and eat. Try our fish-soup. Try our boiled cuttle-fish. Walk in, walk in.'

Then there were the baggage-carriers singing their songs:—

> Blow ! Blow ! Blow ! Blow ! Blow !
> Heave her up ! Heave her up ! On you go.
> Light as a feather,—its feathers you know.
> Light as feathers. Do you think they know ?
> No ! No !
> Do you think they know ?

'Hin, hin,' whinnied the horses.

'Look, Kita,' said Yaji. 'There are those two blind men in that teahouse.'

'That's good,' said Kita. 'I'm going to have my revenge on them for throwing me into the river.'

They went into the teahouse and Kita sat down by the side of the blind men.

'Shall I bring you a meal ?' asked the maid.

'No, no, we're bursting already,' replied Yaji.

The two blind men went on drinking their saké, quite unconscious of their presence.

'We've drunk all the saké,' said Inuichi. 'Let's have some more.'

'So we have,' said Saruichi. 'Here, landlord, landlord, bring a little more drink.'

'Coming, sir,' cried the maid.

'By the way,' said Inuichi, 'I wonder what became of that rascal you threw in the river.'

'Oh, him,' said Saruichi, laughing contemptuously. 'Let's wet the other eye.'

He filled the cup and after taking a sip put it down by his side, when Kitahachi, softly stretching out his hand, took up the cup, drank off the contents and put it back where it was before.

'He was a rogue,' continued Saruichi. 'Got on my back as bold as brass, he did, but it was quite a different thing when he got into the water. Did you hear him calling "Help! Help!"? He was in a terrible fright. He's one of those chaps who go about bamboozling people. Probably he's a pickpocket.'

'That's about it,' said Inuichi. 'You can depend upon it he can't be up to any good. He's the sort of chap that would come to a place like this and go off without paying. Let's have another drink.'

'Oh, ah!' said Saruichi, 'I'd forgotten about the drink.'

He felt for the cup and was going to drink when he found that there was nothing in it.

'That's funny,' he said. 'I must have spilled it.' He felt about again. 'It's strange,' he said. 'However, let's fill it again.'

He filled it up again, took a sip and put it down. Immediately Kitahachi again reached for the cup, drank the contents and put it back.

'It would be funny if those chaps were to come in here,' said Inuichi.

'Not they,' said Saruichi. 'They're probably wandering about down there wringing out their clothes and trying to dry them. They're both stupid rascals.'

Feeling for the cup he took it up, only to find that again there was nothing in it.

'Now, how's that?' he said.

'What's the matter?' asked Inuichi. 'Spilled it again? How careless you are.'

'No, I didn't spill it,' said Saruichi. 'There's something very strange about this.'

'That's what you always say,' said Inuichi. 'I believe you drank it yourself.'

While they were disputing Kita got hold of the saké bottle and filled his teacup twice, afterwards softly putting the bottle back where it was before.

'Here,' said Inuichi, 'you give me the cup.'

He snatched it from Saruichi and picked up the bottle to fill it.

'Hullo!' he cried. 'Why, you've drunk it all.'

'Nonsense!' said Saruichi. 'What are you talking about?'

'Well, the bottle's empty.'

'Then it was never full,' said Saruichi. 'Here, landlord,' he called, 'do you think we are fools because we are blind? We've only had two sips out of this bottle of saké and it's empty. What do you mean by it?'

'It was full when I gave it you,' said the landlord. 'Perhaps you've spilled it.'

'Spilled it, indeed!' said Saruichi. 'You dealers are all the same. At any rate we won't pay for it.'

Thus he began to get very angry. Now there happened to be a little girl loitering at the door of the teahouse and she had seen all that had happened.

'That man there,' she said, pointing to Kita, 'took the blind man's saké and poured it into his teacup.'

'What's the child talking about?' said Kita. 'I'm drinking tea.' He quickly drank up all the saké left in his teacup.

'You smell of saké,' said the landlord, 'and your face is red. Perhaps you've drunk the gentlemen's saké.'

'What?' cried Kita. 'You say the same? It's outrageous. My face is red because I'm drunk with tea. Persons who get drunk on saké get tongue-tied, and in the same way persons who get drunk on tea, say "tea, tea, tea" all the time. That's why tea's so. Ha-ha-ha!'

'No, no,' said Saruichi. 'You don't fob us off in that way. What the child says is true. This man has drunk my saké on the sly and he's got to pay for it.'

'You're tea-tea-totally wrong,' said Kita. 'What I tea-tea-took was tea, as I tea-tea-told you, only you will tea-tea-talk so much.'

'What's the good of playing the fool that way?' said Inuichi. 'You thought nobody would see you, but the child is a witness.'

'There's a certain proof, landlord,' said Saruichi. 'Smell his teacup and see whether it smells of saké.'

Kitahachi, feeling that he was caught, tried to hide his tea-cup, but the landlord seized it and smelled it.

'It does, it does,' he cried, 'and it's sticky with it too. There can be no mistake, you drank it and you must pay for it.'

'I won't pay for the saké because I didn't drink it,' said Kita, who saw that he was in a corner, ' but I'll pay anything you like for the tea. How much is it ? '

' Very well, then, pay for the tea,' said the landlord. ' You've had two bottles of tea. That will be sixty-four coppers.'

' What ? ' cried Kita. ' For two bottles of tea ? It's outrageous.'

' Here, we've had enough of this,' intervened Yaji. ' Pay up. You're always getting into trouble. Better pay up before anything happens.' He gave Kita a warning look, and there being nothing else to do Kita paid the money.

' Really,' said Saruichi, ' these people are outrageous. Probably they are the same people who played the trick on us at the river. To drink another person's saké on the sly. It's robbery.'

' What, you call us robbers, you blind beggar ? ' cried Kita flying into a passion.

' We're in the wrong,' interposed Yaji. ' You must forgive him. When he gets drunk with tea there's no holding him. I'll tea-tea-take him away.'

He dragged Kita away and made him walk fast till they had left the stage far behind.

' Ha-ha-ha ! ' laughed Yaji. ' You're the biggest fool I've ever met.'

Passing through Sawada and Hosoda the two travellers came to Sunegawa Hill, where the trees on each side of the road were so thick that they made it quite dark and they were unable to distinguish people who passed them. Suddenly they heard a voice calling, ' Halloa there ! Halloa there, master travellers ! ' Turning round they saw a man running towards them in the shadow of the trees. He had his hand in his bosom and he wore an old wadded garment like a dressing gown, with a queer shaped hat on his head. His face was bushy with hair and he looked very dirty. Yaji and Kita, who had never seen such a strange-looking man before, felt very frightened as he came up to them.

' What do you want running after us like this in broad daylight ? ' stammered Yaji.

' He-he-he ! ' tittered the man. ' I only wanted to ask your honours to give me a copper.'

' What a thing to ask ? ' said Kita. ' Is that all you were running after us for ? There's a copper.'

'Frightening people out of their wits,' grumbled Yaji. 'I never saw such a fool of a beggar.'

From there they quickly arrived at Fukuroi, where on each side of the way the teahouses were busy serving the travellers with saké and food.

After passing this stage they overtook a Kyōto citizen. He was wearing a wadded kimono, had a gold-mounted dirk, a flower-coloured woollen overcloak, and a waterproof. He was travelling with one attendant. After they had passed and repassed several times he spoke to them.

'You gentlemen are from Edo, I suppose,' he said.

'Yes,' said Yaji.

'Edo is a very prosperous sort of place,' the traveller went on. 'I go there every year and I have been invited occasionally to the Yoshiwara to take my pleasure. People are always asking me about it, but I really don't know how much it costs to go there. You gentlemen must certainly have been there. About how much does it cost?'

'I have to sell from five to ten pieces of land every time I go there,' said Yaji, 'but for such courtesans as you speak of it's only a trifle,—say one *bu* and two *shu*. Then there's a *bu* for the teahouse and another *bu* for the geisha. If they make it one *kin* one *kin* that would come to about four hundred each.'

'Dear me!' said the traveller. 'I've been to several of the big houses, but I never heard tell of that one *kin* one *kin* business. What is it?'

'Well,' replied Yaji, 'there's saké one *kin* and food one *kin*. That's when you can't drink the saké in the house and they have to fetch it from outside.'

'Aha!' said the traveller. 'There was nothing like that at the house I went to. They didn't bring in any saké we couldn't drink. It was very good saké.'

'Oh, but it's the way of Edo people not to drink saké that's drinkable,' said Yaji.

'Then the Edo girls all want ready money,' the traveller went on.

'What are you talking about?' said Yaji. 'They'll give you any amount of credit if only they can send someone home with you to collect the money.'

'Ha-ha-ha!' laughed the traveller. 'You gentlemen have evidently never been to a large establishment. I have heard my shopmen talking about it and I have heard that they never give any credit if you go to buy a superior courtesan.'

'What do you mean by saying we've never been there?' asked Yaji. 'Why I've got corns on my backside through sitting in a kago and being carried there.'

'Well then,' said the traveller, 'what house do you go to?'

'We go to the Ōkiya,' said Yaji.

'Whose is the Ōkiya?' asked the traveller.

'Tomenosuké,' said Yaji.

'Ha-ha-ha!' laughed the traveller. 'I was talking about the Matsuwaya. They haven't got the superior courtesans at the Ōkiya. You're very low-class.'

'Of course they have them there,' cried Yaji. 'Haven't they, Kita?'

'I've been listening to you all this time without saying anything,' replied Kita, 'but I must say, Yaji, you're giving yourself airs. You've never been there yourself. You've only been listening to what other people told you. You ought to be ashamed of yourself, spoiling the reputation of your native place by talking at random like that.'

'You fool!' cried Yaji. 'What's the good of talking like that? Didn't I take you with me as one of my company?'

'Do you mean at the time of the landlord's funeral?' asked Kita. 'One of your company, indeed! I remember now you only paid two *shu* as a tip. I paid for the drinks and the fish salad, and everything.'

'It's a lie,' said Yaji.

'A lie, indeed!' said Kita. 'And moreover I remember that a fish bone stuck in your throat and you had to gulp down five or six helpings of rice to get rid of it.'

'Don't talk nonsense,' said Yaji. 'It was you who did that when you burnt your mouth by drinking sweet saké at Tamachi.'

'And then,' continued Kita, 'you let your purse drop in the ditch and picked up a piece of dog's dirt instead. Shame!'

'Ha-ha-ha!' laughed the traveller. 'You gentlemen are really very low-class.'

'Whether we're low-class or high-class, you get out,' said Yaji. 'I've never met such an infernal old chatterer.'

This angered the traveller, who went on in front with a stiff apology and a hurried bow, and soon disappeared.

'Botheration!' said Yaji. 'That chap was too much for me. Ha-ha-ha!'

While they were thus talking they passed Mikano Bridge, climbed Okubo Hill and soon reached Mitsuké.

'Oh, I am tired,' said Kita. 'Let's ride for a bit.'

'Won't you have a ride?' asked a postboy. 'I've got a fine horse here that wants to get home. I'll take you cheap. Have a ride.'

'What do you think, Kita?' asked Yaji.

'If it's cheap I'll ride,' said Kita.

After bargaining over the price Kita got on. As the postboy was a country farmer he was very polite.

'Isn't there a short cut to Tenryū, postboy?' asked Yaji.

'Yes, if you go up there you'll cut off over two miles,' said the postboy.

'Can a horse get through?' asked Yaji.

'No, there's no horse road.'

Yaji therefore decided to take the short cut by himself, leaving Kita to keep to the main road. Soon Kita crossed the bridge over the River Kamo and came to Nishizaka Sakaimatsu.

'Come in and rest, come in and rest,' called the teahouse girls.

'Try some of our famous cakes,' called an old woman.

'Eh, mother,' said the postboy, 'what strange weather we're having.'

'Good morning to ye,' said the old woman. 'That eldest girl of Shinta's is waiting to go with you. And look here, I've got a message for the old lady at Yokosuka. I've got a sermon for her dissipated uncle, so tell her to come and see me.'

'All right,' said the postboy. 'I'll be back directly.'

'This horse is very quiet,' said Kita.

'That's because she's a mare,' said the postboy.

'Ah, that's why it feels nice riding her,' said Kita.

'Master,' said the postboy. 'Where's Edo?'

'Edo?' said Kita. 'Why, it's the principal city.'

'Ah, it's a wonderful place,' said the postboy. 'When I was young I went there once as one of the lord's retainers. It was full of traders.'

'It's got to be,' said Kita. 'Why, I keep seventy or eighty attendants in my house.'

'Think of that now!' said the postboy. 'It must be terrible hard work for your wife to boil all the rice for them. What does rice fetch in Edo, master?'

'Why, one *sho* two *go*,' said Kita. 'If it's good, about one *go*.

'And how much would that be, master?' asked the postboy.

'A hundred coppers, of course,' said Kita.

'Does master buy a hundred coppers' worth at a time?' asked the postboy.

'Don't talk nonsense,' replied Kita. 'We buy it by the cartload.'

'Then how much can one get for a *ryo*?' asked the postboy.

'What, one *ryo*?' said Kita. 'Let's see. Twice one is eight and twice five are ten and twice eight are sixteen, when she can be pressed, and four fives are twenty, when you can undo her girdle, which makes three *to* eight *sho* seven *go* five *shaku*.'

'Eh?' said the postboy. 'The rice business in Edo must be very difficult. I don't understand it a bit.'

'Of course you don't,' said Kita. 'No more do I. Ha-ha-ha!'

While they were talking they arrived at Tenryū. The river here flows out of Lake Suwa and the town on the left bank is called Great Tenryū and that on the other bank Little Tenryū. A ferry connects the two towns. Here Kita found Yaji waiting for him and together they crossed the ferry.

Leaving the boat on the other side they went through the town. This place is exactly half way between Edo and Kyōto and is therefore called Middle Town.

From there they passed through Kyamba, Yakushi and Shinden. When they were near Toriimatsu they were met by an inn tout from Hamamatsu.

'If you're stopping at the next stage, gentlemen,' he said, 'I can recommend my inn.'

'We'll stop if you've got any nice girls,' said Kita.

'We have many,' said the inn tout.

'Will you give us something to eat if we stop?' asked Yaji.

'To be sure I will,' answered the inn tout.

'What kind of vegetables have you got?'

'We are noted for our yams.'

'They're common. Haven't you got anything else?'

'Yes, we have mushrooms and water-leek.'

'Have you got any beancurd soup with vegetables in it?' asked Kita.

'No, no,' said Yaji. 'We want something lighter. We'll keep that to the hundredth day after.'

'What strange things you say,' said the inn tout. 'Ha-ha-ha! But here we are.'

'What, are we at Hamamatsu already?' said Yaji. 'I didn't think it.'

The inn tout ran forward to announce that the guests had come and the landlord came out to welcome them.

'Welcome, gentlemen,' he said. 'Welcome. Here, San, bring some tea and some hot water.'

'Our feet are not so dirty as all that,' said Yaji.

'Well then, please have a bath at once,' said the landlord.

'Where's the mortuary?' asked Kita. 'Yaji, you'd better die first.'

'What a chap he is for saying improper things,' said Yaji. 'You go first.'

A maid conducted Kita to the bathroom, while Yaji was shown into a room and the baggage taken in.

'Would you like to have a shampoo, sir?' asked a shampooer.

'I think I will,' said Yaji. 'Halloa, I see you're not blind.'

'No, sir, fortunately I can see quite well with one eye,' said the man. 'For ten years I was afflicted with total blindness and had to go round shampooing, till at last I got back the use of the left eye.'

'When you got your sight back everybody must have looked strange to you,' said Yaji.

'Yes,' replied the shampooer, 'they did.'

'You'd better get the other eye treated,' said Yaji, 'and if it gets better you'll be able to see with two. Kita's a long time in the bath.'

Just then Kita came back. 'I've had a fine bath,' he declared. 'It was so hot that it's made my body stretch.'

After that the maid brought in the supper and there was more talk which I will not put down. At last supper was finished and Yaji, having had a bath, called the shampooer again.

'Just give me another rub down,' he said. 'By the way, as I was coming from the bath I saw a woman,—I suppose the mistress of the house. She looked rather ill and very untidy, but she was very beautiful.'

'She's mad,' said the shampooer.

'Don't they take care of her?' asked Kita.

'Listen,' said the shampooer. 'She's saying her prayers.'

They listened and could hear a prayer bell sounding endlessly from the direction of the kitchen.

'She was a servant in this house,' the shampooer went on in a low voice. 'The landlord fell in love with her, which made his wife so jealous that she beat her and slapped her and finally turned her out of the house. But the landlord took pity on her and took her under his protection, which made his wife all the more angry, till finally she went mad and hanged herself. Then the landlord brought the girl back into the house again, and that night the ghost of the landlord's dead wife appeared and the girl went mad. That's why she prays endlessly every night.'

Yaji and Kita pretended to be very brave on hearing this story, but at heart they were filled with fears.

'What did you say?' asked Kita. 'The ghost appears in this very house?'

'In this very house,' said the shampooer.

'It's not true,' said Yaji.

'It's quite true, I assure you,' said the shampooer. 'The ghost appears every night, all in white.'

'Lor!' groaned Kita. 'What a place we've come to!'

'Its face is just the colour of the woman who hanged herself,' the shampooer went on, 'and it has green eyes and it grinds its teeth just as if it was alive.'

'Where does it appear?' asked Kita.

'At the end of the verandah just behind you.'

'Terrible, terrible!' groaned Kita. 'It gives you a shudder down your backbone.'

'Isn't the sound of the rain mournful?' said Yaji.

'It's just the sort of night for the ghost to appear,' said the shampooer.

'Don't talk of such dreadful things,' said Kita.

'The sound of that bell seems to go right through you,' said Yaji.

'What a dreadful inn we've come to!' moaned Kita.

'What timid chaps you are!' said the shampooer laughing.

'Have you finished?' asked Yaji. 'Will you have a turn, Kita?'

'I'm going to bed,' said Kita.

The shampooer said good-night and went off and the maid spread their beds. All their jokes and idle talk forgotten, the two lay down, but could not get to sleep.

'Listen to that bell,' said Yaji. 'Kita, don't you think we might start again now?'

'What?' said Kita. 'Walk along that lonely road in the dark after hearing that story? Not me.'

'But this house seems so eerie that it gives me the creeps,' said Yaji.

They lay with their eyes wide open listening and were startled by the squeaking of the rats in the roof.

'Even the rats want to frighten us,' said Kita. 'I've got to get up and relieve myself.'

'I want to too,' said Yaji. 'Just listen to the rats. Yah! What's that soft thing touching my legs?'

'Where? What?' asked Kita.

'Miaou!' went the cat.

'Shoo! Shoo! Get out, you beast,' cried Yaji.

The interminable sound of the bell, chang-chang-chang, mingled with the pitter-pitter-patter of the rain on the eaves. Now and again they could hear the sound of the crier going round ringing his bell and calling for a lost child, but they covered their heads with the bedclothes and tried not to listen. At last Kita peeped out.

'Yaji,' he whispered, 'are you still alive?'

'Lord preserve us! Lord preserve us!' prayed Yaji. 'But I say I must get up or I shall do it in the bed.'

'We're both in the same trouble,' said Kita.

'Let's get up together without thinking about it,' suggested Yaji.

'We can open the shutters and do it there,' said Kita.

So they both got up trembling and opened the shutters.

'There you are, Yaji,' said Kita.

'No, no, you go first,' said Yaji.

'There's something there,' said Kita, falling back. He had seen something white fluttering in a corner of the garden.

'Where? What is it?' asked Yaji.

'I don't know what it is,' said Kita, 'but it's there. Look for yourself.'

'What is it?' asked Yaji.

'It's something white standing there. You can't see the bottom part.'

Trembling with fear Yaji peeped out and was so startled by what he saw that he fell into the garden.

'Here, Yaji, Yaji! Where are you?' called Kita.

The noise they made brought the landlord running in from the kitchen, and he dragged Yaji in and helped to restore him to consciousness.

'Whatever happened?' he asked.

'We were just going outside to relieve ourselves when we saw something white in the corner,' explained Kita. 'It gave us quite a fright.'

The landlord went out to have a look.

'That's a white petticoat,' he said. 'Here, San, San! Why didn't you take the washing in when it grew dark. And it's been raining for a long time, too. How careless you are! I'm sorry you were frightened,' he added.

'We really don't know what fear is,' said Yaji, 'but somehow to-night we got a bit nervous.'

'Well, good-night,' said the landlord.

'Oh dear!' said Yaji, as the landlord went off to the kitchen. 'I did have a fright.' Plucking up his courage he went to the end of the verandah and saw that it was really a woman's petticoat that was hanging there. Then the two, having done their business, went back to bed, and with their hearts relieved of fear fell into a sweet doze. They were just in the middle of a pleasant dream when they were awakened by the stout crowing of the cocks. Already the bells of the horses could be heard jingling and the songs of the postboys as they prepared for an early start:

> If you come to-night
> For you I'll wait;
> Steal round to the back,
> Don't try the front gate.

Then came the whinnying of the horses and the caw-caw of the crows.

'It's dawn already,' said Yaji.

Forthwith he and Kita got up and having breakfasted started off again. Passing through the village of Wakabayashi they reached Shinohara, where Kita spied some rice-cakes covered with bean-flour.

'How tasty they look,' he cried. 'Here, granny, give me some.'

He took up one of the cakes and tried to bite it. 'Oh! it's hard,' he said.

'That's the one kept for show, master,' said the old woman.

'So it is,' said Kita looking at it. 'It's made of wood; no wonder it's hard.'

'How many shall I give you?' asked the old woman.

'Three will do,' said Kita.

After paying for them he ran after Yaji, who had gone on ahead.

'Yaji, Yaji,' he called.

'What is it?' asked Yaji. 'Give us one if they're good.'

'They're awfully good,' said Kita.

'Well, let's have one then.'

'Take one,' said Kita.

But as he was holding them out on the palm of his hand a kite suddenly swooped down and snatched them away.

'Ha-ha-ha!' laughed Yaji.

'Botheration!' said Kita, 'the kites here must be teetotallers.'

They passed Hasanuma and Tsuboi and reached Maisaka, where they embarked on the public ferryboat for Arai.

Journeying by boat being a change after the labours of the road, all the passengers were at first very lively, talking and laughing and cracking jokes. But at last, weary of talking, some of them began to doze, while others fell silent looking at the scenery.

Among the passengers was a countryman of about fifty, dressed in an old wadded garment, who seemed to have lost something, as he was continually looking under the passengers' knees or lifting up the matting on which they were sitting. At last he began feeling Yaji's sleeve.

'What are you doing?' said Yaji, catching hold of his hand. 'What do you mean by feeling my sleeve?'

'Beg your pardon,' said the man. 'It's nothing, it's nothing. I've only lost something.'

'Then you should ask people first before you claw them,' said Kita. 'If you brought it on to the boat it must be somewhere. What is it? Tobacco box or pipe?'

'No, no,' said the man. 'It's nothing like that.'

'Perhaps it's some money you've lost,' said Kita.

'No, no,' said the man. 'It's nothing like that. We'd better not say anything more about it. It doesn't matter.'

'If it doesn't matter,' said Yaji, 'why do you go about disturbing people when they're dozing?'

Then all the people on the boat began asking, 'What is it? Tell us what you've lost. It must be here somewhere.'

'No, no,' said the old man. 'It don't matter. It's all right.'

'It isn't all right,' said Yaji. 'What have you lost?'

'Well, I'll tell you then,' said the old man. 'But you'll be a bit startled.'

'Ha-ha-ha!' laughed Kita. 'Why should we be startled because you've lost something?'

'What is it you've lost?' asked Yaji.

'Well, it's a snake,' said the old man.

'Yah!' yelled Kita. 'A snake? What kind of a snake?'

'Well, it's alive,' said the old man.

Then all the people on the boat began to scream.

'What a thing to bring on a boat!' said Yaji. 'What were you doing with a snake?'

'It makes me feel quite creepy,' said Kita. 'Wonder if it's on me,' and he jumped up.

Then all the people on the boat began to jump about and shout: 'There it is, under that plank.—It's coiled itself up there.—No, it's gone over there.—It makes me shudder to think of it.—It's got under the luggage.—I never thought I'd come to travel with a thing like that.'

While they were going on throwing the things about, the old man spied the snake beneath a bundle and quickly picked it up and put it in his sleeve.

'Fancy handling a snake like that!' said Kita. 'It will get away again if you put it in there. Throw it into the sea.'

'No, no,' said the old man. 'I'm on a pilgrimage and I was fortunate enough to find this snake on the way. So I kept it and exhibit it to people for a small sum so as to help me on my way. I couldn't think of parting with it.'

'I don't care about that,' said Yaji. 'You've no right to bring it here. Here, boatman, what did you want to let this thing come on board for?'

'I didn't know anybody was carrying a snake,' said the boatman.

'I don't care what you say,' said another passenger. 'We can't allow you to keep the snake on the boat. Throw it overboard.'

'No, no,' said the old man. 'I can't do that.'

'If you don't get rid of it I shall have to throw you into the sea too,' said Kita. 'What do you say to that?'

'Let's see you do it,' said the old man. 'Two can play at that game.'

'What an obstinate old chap it is,' cried Kita. He jumped up and caught hold of the old man's coat. But just then the snake put its head out, and Kita gave a yell and jumped back. Yaji then tried to hit the old man with his long pipe. This made the old man angry, and he caught hold of Yaji and commenced to struggle with him, while all the other people in the boat tried

to separate them. Then the snake put its head out of the old man's bosom and began twisting it round and round.

'There it is,' they all cried. 'Kill it, kill it.'

Kita pulled out his dirk and gave the snake a blow on the head. Upon this the snake twined round the dirk, and when Kita tried to throw it into the sea the dirk slipped from his hand and both the snake and the dirk went overboard and disappeared in the water. The loss of his dirk disconcerted Kita, but all the people cried, 'We've got rid of the snake, at any rate, though it's a pity about the dirk.'

'It's the first time I've ever seen a man fling away his weapon,' said the old man.

This made Kita angry, and he seized hold of the old man and tried to beat him, when Yaji intervened.

'There, there, Kita,' he said. 'This is a public ferryboat. You can't make a row here.'

While he was trying to soothe Kita the boat arrived at Arai. 'Here we are at the barrier,' cried the boatmen. 'Don't forget your hats. Take care, we're going to touch.'

Then all the passengers got off the boat with cries of thankfulness that they had arrived in safety and went through the barrier. Yaji and Kita also landed, consoling themselves with the idea that throwing away your weapon is such an uncommon thing that it would make a good subject for talk on future occasions, and then, to celebrate their safe arrival, they went into a teahouse and had some saké.

KITAHACHI

BOOK FOUR

UENSAI TEIRYU in a poem says that he does not know what was the result of blowing a conch-shell in ancient times, but now, at any rate, it brings a favourable wind. But how was it with Imagiri, for there, from beyond the hills, there came the sound of too many conch-shells, and from that time the passage by sea became dangerous, till in the era of Genroku an official order was issued that breakwaters should be constructed to make it safe for the ferry, for which act of benevolence all were duly grateful.

But the sea was calm and the wind gentle and there was no danger when Yaji and Kita crossed over and stuffed themselves with the famous eels of Arai. While they were resting after the crossing a continual stream of people of all classes kept passing and repassing. Some were hastening down to the landing stage, calling to the ferry-boats to wait for them, while the head factor scolded and shouted his orders about the horses. Then there were the inn attendants running about and the teahouse girls bounding along with their aprons all awry, to say nothing of the baggage carriers with their chants and the postboys with their eyes in all directions.

> My heart is as black as Hamana's bridge;
> It has ceased to beat, it has ceased to live

they sang.

'Come in and rest! Come in and rest!' screamed the teahouse girls.

'Here, postboy, put me down here,' said a voice.

'Yes, sir,' said the postboy. 'Look out for your head, sir.' The postboy led the horse beneath the eaves of the teahouse.

The person who had asked to be put down was a samurai, who was dressed in a grey cotton robe with a black cloak. The samurai alighted from his horse, and Yaji and Kita sat down on a bench opposite.

'Can I give your honour some tea?' inquired the maid.

The samurai took the tea, and after drinking it stared hard at the maid. 'What time is it?' he asked.

'It's two o'clock, your honour,' she answered.

'It's the same time as it was yesterday at this time,' put in the postboy.

'I'll have something to eat,' said the samurai. 'What have you got?'

'We have some broiled eels, your honour,' said the girl.

'Beg pardon, your honour,' said the postboy. 'Shall I put your honour's baggage here,—five pieces?'

'Just give me my money,' said the samurai.

'Yes, your honour,' said the postboy. 'With your honour's leave I'd like to take a drink.'

'Oho!' said the samurai. 'Are you fond of liquor?'

'Yes, your honour,' said the postboy. 'I'm fonder of drinking than I am of eating.'

'Get what you like,' said the samurai. 'If I were drinking I would give you some, but I don't drink myself.'

'Even if your honour doesn't take any,' said the postboy, 'I should like some.'

'Oh, I see,' said the samurai. 'You want some drink money, do you? I can't allow that. We fixed the price for the journey and I shall certainly not pay anything extra for drink.'

'Yes, but your honour . . .'

'If you demand any more you must give me a receipt so that I may send it to your employer's office when I return.'

'The luggage is very heavy, your honour, for this light horse,' said the postboy. 'I should like to stop here.'

'Very well,' said the samurai, 'then I'll give you eight coppers more.' He took out his purse and counted out eight coppers.

'Won't you make it sixteen coppers, your honour?' asked the postboy.

'Well, I'll give you four coppers more,' said the samurai. He counted out four coppers and threw them down, whereupon the postboy reluctantly picked up the money and led his horse away.

'Wait, wait,' cried the samurai. 'Where on earth are you going? There, he's gone and he hasn't given me the sandals that were fastened to the horse. I valued those sandals very much. I was going all the way to Edo in them.'

He went on grumbling to himself till Kita, who had been watching the scene with amusement, addressed him.

'Is your honour going to Edo?' he asked.

'Yes,' said the samurai.

'I overheard your honour say that you wore only one pair of sandals all the way to Edo. Your honour must be a very careful walker.'

'No, no,' said the samurai. 'But those sandals were made by myself very carefully, and that is why they last the journey there and back.'

'Truly your honour must be a very clever walker,' chimed in Yaji. 'Do you see these sandals of mine, your honour? I used them the year before last to go to Matsumae, and as they were as good as new when I got back I put them by for another time. Last year I wore them to Nagasaki, and as they are still quite good I am using them again.'

'Dear me!' said the samurai. 'You must be more careful than I am. How do you manage to make them last such a long time?'

'Oh, that's easy,' said Yaji. 'I can make them last longer than my leggings.'

'How do you do that?' asked the samurai.

'Oh, that's because I always ride,' said Yaji.

'Get out!' laughed the samurai. 'Ha-ha-ha!'

'Come, let's go,' said Yaji.

So with apologies to the samurai they started off again. They took kago as far as Futagawa, but after they had passed Mount Takashi they met two kago coming from the opposite direction.

'Shall we change?' called out one of the carriers. 'What do you say?'

'How much will you give?' asked the other party.

'I'll give a fist,' responded the first. 'Will that do?'

'What do you say, partner? Shall we take it?'

The bargain was thus struck and the carriers requested Yaji and Kita to alight and take the other kago, while the people in the other kago took theirs.

'Master's in luck,' said one of Kita's carriers. 'This is an inn kago, so it has a cushion. You've gained by making the exchange, master.'

'So it has,' said Kita. Putting his hand down to feel the cushion he found under it a string of coppers, which he concluded had been left there by the person riding in the kago before him and had been forgotten when he alighted. Saying nothing about it he secretly slipped the money into his sleeve.

After they had passed Shirasuka one of the carriers pointed

to a hill. 'Do you see that hill, your honour?' he asked.
'There are deer on that hill.'

'Which?' said Kita. 'That's interesting.'

'Gentlemen from Edo are generally very interested in that,'
said the carrier, 'as they don't see such strange animals up there.
One made a poem about it yesterday.'

'I've made one up already about it,' said Kita, 'but I suppose
it would be wasted on your ears. It's like this:—

> Deep in the hills I hear the stag's cry,
> And thick in my path the maple leaves lie.
> 'Tis autumn goes by with a sigh.

Isn't that good?'

'Your honour is certainly very clever,' said the carrier. 'As
for me I don't know anything about such things. You seem to
make them up as you go on, which is certainly remarkable.'

'I can turn them out at any time,' said Kita, 'and in return for
your praise I'll treat you to a drink. Is this a stage?'

'This is Saru-ga-bamba, your honour,' said the carrier, and he
called to his mate to stop in front of the teahouse.

'You can all have a drink,' said Kita. He called to the
maid to bring out some saké and something to eat.

'Kita, Kita,' cried Yaji from his kago, 'what's the matter
with you? You've got very generous.'

'What are you talking about?' said Kita. 'Isn't it the usual
thing to give the men a drink?' He pulled out the string of
coppers that he had found in the kago and showed them to Yaji.

'You're not going to spend all that, are you?' asked Yaji.

'Of course I am,' replied Kita.

'Then I'll have some too,' said Yaji. He got out of his kago
and went and sat in front of the teahouse. The maid now brought
out the saké.

'Thank'ee very kindly,' said Kita's carrier. Then he called to
his mates to come and join him. 'Come along,' he said,
'Sarumaru Taifu is treating us to drinks.'

Yaji also began to enjoy himself at Kita's expense. 'Landlord,' he called, 'the gentleman in the kago will pay for all this.
How much is it?'

'Yes, sir,' said the landlord. 'It will come altogether to three
hundred and eighty coppers.'

'Oh, indeed,' said Kita. 'Well, you've had quite a feast.'
Reluctantly he paid the money.

'Oh, by the way,' called Kita's carrier to his mate, 'what did you do with that string of coppers I gave you?'

'Oh, that,' answered his mate. 'Please, master,' he said to Kita, 'if you don't mind getting up for a minute, there's some money down by the side of the cushion.'

'What?' said Kita, startled. 'I never saw it.'

'It must be there,' said the carrier. 'I put it there myself.'

'I saw it myself,' said Yaji. 'Kita, wasn't that the money you took from under the cushion and twirled about?'

'That's it, that's it,' said the carrier.

Kita felt very angry at having been discovered, and he cast an angry look at Yaji, who turned away and pretended not to notice. There being no help for it Kita took the coins out of his sleeve and secretly slipped them under the cushion again. 'Oh, yes,' he cried, 'here it is.'

'That's all right,' said the carrier. 'Now we can go on again.'

They started off again and by-and-by came to the town of Futagawa, where all the teahouse girls were in the street calling to the travellers to come in. 'Come in and try our hot soup,' they called. 'Try our raw fish and saké.'

Then a carrier who was standing by the corner of the teahouse called to the men who were carrying Yaji and Kita:—'Hi, Hachibei, you'd better go home and look after your wife. There's bad goings on in your house.'

'Fool,' replied one of Yaji's carriers. 'Don't you know your father's hung himself, you old dirt-eater? Ha-ha-ha!'

Yaji and Kita alighted in front of the kago house and walked on. A daimyō's train was taking a short rest at this stage, his palanquin being set down in front of the hostel and a number of samurai and retainers gathered round the entrance, while the contractors for carrying the baggage were hurrying about.

'Halloa, the master of the house wears two swords also,' said Kita.

'You think everybody's the owner as long as they are wearing a *hakama*,' said Yaji.

'Look at that kago,' went on Kita. 'Look how the cushions are piled up on it.'

'Of course,' replied Yaji. 'Look at the persons who ride in them. They're all *fukusuké*. Ha-ha-ha! Look out, there's a horse.'

'Hin-hin-hin!' whinnied the horse, and 'Oh, oh, oh!' yelled Yaji. 'What an awkward place to put a kago.'

Hearing Yaji grumbling, a man who looked like some sort of upper retainer began to revile him. 'What do you mean by treading on the kago with your muddy foot?' he demanded. 'I'll knock your head off.'

'Ha-ha-ha!' laughed Yaji. 'You've got to do it first.'

'What's that?' said the man. 'Do you want me to cut you down?'

'Do you think your rusty sword would cut anything?' jeered Yaji.

'If you speak like that I must cut you down,' said the man. 'Here, Kakusuké, lend me your sword.'

He began pulling at his companion's sword, but the man resisted. 'If you want to cut anybody down,' he said, 'why don't you use your own sword?'

'Don't make such a fuss,' replied the other. 'What does it matter whose sword it is?'

'No, no,' said Kakusuké. 'You can't have mine.'

'What a stingy chap you are,' said the other. 'Just let's have it for a moment.'

'No, no,' said Kakusuké. 'What an obstinate fellow you are. You know the spearman Tsuchiemon took my real sword for the two hundred coppers I owed him.'

'Oh ah!' said the other. 'I'd forgotten. Well,' he added, turning to Yaji, 'I'll forgive you this time. You can go.'

'Go?' said Yaji, pushing up against him. 'I shan't go. Why don't you cut me down?'

At this the retainers who stood round began to laugh and seemed too amused at the scene to think of interfering.

'Well, then, there's no help for it,' said the retainer. He drew his sword, but as it proved to be only a piece of lath, Yaji caught hold of him and threw him down, whereupon the fellow began to bawl loudly, 'Murder! Murder! Help! Help!'

But the daimyō was now leaving his lodgings and the signal for the train to form was given. The quarrel thus ended, and fortunately Yaji was able to get away with Kita.

'Ha-ha-ha!' laughed Yaji. 'That was a funny quarrel.'

As they went along Kita began to yawn. 'Heigho!' he said, 'I am tired. What a trouble it is to have to carry even this small amount of baggage. I'll tell you what, Yaji. Suppose one of us carries the lot and we'll play the priest game.'

'That's a good idea,' said Yaji, 'and luckily here's a bamboo that someone's thrown away which will come in very handy for carrying our things on.'

They slung the baggage on to each end of the bamboo so that one of them could carry it on his shoulder. 'There, you carry first,' said Yaji.

'You're older than I am so you'd better carry it first,' said Kita.

'We'll play for it,' decided Yaji. So they played for it and Kita lost. He shouldered the baggage grumbling and they went on, but they had not gone far before they met a man who looked like a priest of the Hokké sect. He was chanting 'Dabu, dabu, dabu! Fumiya, fumiya, fumiya! Dabu, dabu, dabu!'

'There you are, Yaji,' said Kita. 'Take hold of the baggage.'

'Oh, oh!' groaned Yaji. 'I hope we meet another priest soon.'

Then came a postboy and a horse, the bells of the horse going shan-shan-shan, while the postboy sang to himself:

> She in the valley,
> I on hilltop withdrawn:—
> Oh, she looked pretty
> Bleaching the lawn.

'Kita,' called Yaji. 'Look at that priest on the horse.'

'It's too soon,' grumbled Kita as he took the baggage. Then they came upon a cripple by the side of the road.

'Take pity on a poor cripple, travellers,' he cried.

'He's a priest, too,' said Kita. 'Give him a copper.'

'He may look like a priest in front,' said Yaji, 'but he's got hair on the nape of his neck.'

'Get out,' said Kita.

Then there came up behind three nuns who were singing and keeping time with clackers in their hands.

> However humble I may be,
> Oh, let me share my dreams with thee,
> However humble I may be.

'What fine voices they've got,' said Kita. 'Who are they?' He turned round to look and found that they were nuns. 'Here, Yaji,' he cried, 'take the baggage.'

'What a nuisance!' grumbled Yaji.

'It looks awfully well to have somebody carrying your baggage for you,' said Kita. 'It's as though you were travelling with a servant. I say, Yaji, that nun looked at me with such a charming smile, the little dear.'

'There's no charm about her,' said Yaji. 'Her face is all out of shape.'

The nuns passed and re-passed them. One of them was about twenty-two or three and the other was considerably older. They had with them a little girl of about eleven or twelve. At last the younger nun stopped Kita. 'Could you give me a light?' she asked.

'Certainly, certainly,' said Kita. 'I'll strike a light for you in a minute.' He pulled out his flint and commenced striking.

'There you are,' he said. 'By the way, where are you going?'

'We're going as far as Nagoya,' said the girl.

'I should like to stop with you to-night,' said Kita. 'Come as far as Akasaka. Let's go together.'

'Thank you,' said the woman. 'Could you give me some tobacco? I've forgotten to buy any.'

'Pull out your tobacco pouch,' said Kita. 'I'll give you all I've got.'

'I'm afraid you'll want some yourself,' said the girl.

'No, no, that's all right,' replied Kita. 'By the way, I'm astonished at a beautiful girl like you shaving her head. It seems such a shame.'

'Why, nobody cares if I cut my hair off,' said the girl.

'I do,' said Kita. 'I care very much. Won't you care for me?'

'Ho-ho-ho!' laughed the girl.

'I wish we could stop together,' added Kita. 'I say, Yaji,' he called, 'shall we stop at the next stage?'

'What a fool you are,' scolded Yaji. 'I wish we had never met these nuns.'

They passed Hiuchizaka and reached Nikenchaya, when the nuns turned off into a side road.

'Here,' called Kita. 'Where are you going? That's not the way.'

'Goodbye,' said the nun. 'We've got to leave you here.' They went along a field path while Kita looked after them very disappointed.

'Ha-ha-ha!' laughed Yaji. 'You're in bad luck to-day.'

'It's a shame,' groaned Kita. He continued to look behind him at the nuns as he went along till at last he ran into a man who was going the other way.

'Oh, oh!' yelled Kita. 'Can't you use your eyes? Who are you?' He turned round to look, and it was a priest.

'There you are,' said Yaji. 'You take the baggage now.'

'It's not fair,' said Kita, as he reluctantly took the baggage.

Thus going along they passed Yoshida, and soon caught up with a party of five or six pilgrims, rather more smartly dressed than usual, who were talking loudly. One man, dressed in a wadded garment of a bright pattern and carrying a bundle on his shoulder, turned round and called to the man behind him.

'Hi, Genkuro Yoshitsuné,' he called. 'Come along, come along.'

Yaji and Kita, struck by the name Yoshitsuné, took a closer look at the man thus called. He was wearing a lined kimono with wide sleeves, and was also carrying a bundle on his back. His face was deeply pitted with pock marks, and he was a little bald on one side.

'Brother Kamei and Brother Kataoka are that quick on their feet,' he said. 'Mine are all chapped, so I can't walk quick on the rough stones.'

'What's happened to Lady Shizuka?' asked Kamei.

'I'll tell you,' said Yoshitsuné. 'At the last stage Lady Shizuka got an attack of his old complaint lumbago. He was in terrible pain and we had great trouble with him. And Lady Rokudai also, he made himself sick by eating thirty dumplings, and he was writhing in agony. Besides that Benkei got a skewer from one of the dumplings stuck in his throat, and he was crying and crying, so that I and Niiya-no-Tomomori had to nurse him. They're all coming on behind. You were lucky in starting early and getting out of all the fuss.'

Yaji and Kita were greatly amused at this talk, and after passing and repassing the pilgrims several times, Yaji at last spoke to them.

'Where are you gentlemen bound for?' he asked.

'Oh, we're going to Isé,' said Yoshitsuné.

'I heard you just now calling each other Yoshitsuné and Benkei and so on,' said Yaji. 'What's the reason of that?'

'It must have sounded strange to you,' said Yoshitsuné. 'I'll tell you. Just before we left our village there was a festival and we acted in the piece called "The Thousand Cherry-trees," and as we all took part, and one was Yoshitsuné and another Benkei and so on, we got into the habit of calling each other by those names and even now continue it.'

'I see,' said Yaji. 'Then I suppose you took the part of Yoshitsuné?'

'Yes,' said Yoshitsuné. 'Before that we had some players down from Edo who acted "Tenjinsama" and what do you think happened? I'll tell you. There's a bad man in the play named "Shihei" or "Gohei" or something like that, who caused Tenjinsama to be banished because he said he had spoken disrespectfully of the Emperor, and there he was in his palanquin, going into banishment, and all the people coming out to see him, and all the old women and the young women weeping and wailing. It was like the passing of an Imperial Abbot. And all the people in the theatre were throwing rice and money on to the stage because they felt so sorry for him. Then a horsebroker in the audience named Yogoza, a man of no account, ran up on the stage and shouted, "This play is no good. Why should Tenjinsama be banished to an island? That noble who appeared before, who looked like Emma at the Chōraku temple, he is the bad man. Tenjinsama isn't guilty. No matter if it is only a play, they shouldn't make fools of the people. I, Yogozaemon, will take Tenjinsama's punishment on myself; I will battle for him with Shihei,—I, who am strong enough to lift up two bales of rice." Then all the people in the theatre were astonished, but there were none to say him nay, and they all cried out, " You are right, Master Yogoza, you are right. Let us take this man Shihei and beat him." Then some of the young men of the village bounded into the greenroom with the idea of beating Shihei, and the actor who was doing the part, seeing them coming, cried out in fear and tucked up his skirts and ran. Then the chiefs of the village called a meeting and it was decided that henceforth actors from Edo should not be allowed to enter the village. So we had our own theatre after that, and I can tell you we attracted more people than the actors from Edo. The theatre was crammed to bursting, so popular we were.'

The pilgrim got very excited over the tale he poured forth and was evidently very proud of their success. Very soon they reached Taiunji, where the pilgrims stopped, while Yaji and Kita hastened on.

The sun was now reaching the horizon and it would soon be twilight. They quickened their pace, but their feet were getting tired.

' How slow you are, Yaji,' said Kita.

' I'm awfully tired,' replied Yaji.

' I'll tell you what,' said Kita. ' We stopped at a dreadful place last night, so I'll go on ahead to Akasaka and look for a good inn. As you're tired you can come on slowly behind and I'll send someone from the inn to meet you.'

' That's a good idea,' said Yaji, ' but mind you pick out a good inn,—one where there's a nice girl.'

' Trust me,' said Kita. Leaving Yaji he went on ahead.

Yaji trudged on, but by the time he got to Goyu night had already fallen. The inn girls, with their faces painted up as though they were wearing masks, caught hold of his sleeves and tried to stop him, but he pulled himself away. At the end of the town he went into a small teahouse to take a short rest. The old woman who kept the teahouse welcomed him.

' It's only a little way to Akasaka, isn't it ? ' he asked.

' It's about a mile,' said the old woman. ' But if you're travelling alone you'd better stop here, as there's a wicked old fox lives in the pinewood you have to pass, and he's bewitched a lot of travellers.'

'That's bad,' said Yaji, 'but I can't stop here. My mate's gone on ahead and he'll be waiting for me. I shall be all right.'

He paid the old woman and started off again. When he left the teahouse it was already dark, and soon it got darker and darker and he began to feel nervous. Still he went on, though taking the precaution to rub some spittle on his eyebrows. Just then he heard the bark of a fox a long way off. 'There it's barking,' he thought. 'Come over here and show yourself, you beast. I'll soon beat you to death.' Keeping up his courage by these boasts he went on.

Meanwhile Kitahachi had gone on ahead as fast as he could till he came to that very place. He also had been told that a wicked fox lived there, and becoming afraid that the fox would bewitch him, he determined to wait there for Yaji, so that they could go on together. He was sitting down by the side of the road enjoying a whiff of tobacco when Yaji came along.

'Halloa, is that you Yaji ? ' he called.

'Halloa ! ' replied Yaji. 'What are you doing here ? '

'I was going on ahead to arrange rooms at an inn,' said Kita, 'but I heard that a wicked old fox lived here, so I thought I would wait for you so that we could go on together.'

Now Yaji had conceived the idea that the fox had changed itself into Kita for the purpose of deceiving him. 'Don't talk nonsense,' he said boldly. 'That's not the reason at all.'

'What are you talking about ? ' asked Kita. 'I brought some rice cake as I thought we might get hungry. Have some ? '

'Hold your tongue,' said Yaji. 'Do you think I'm going to eat that filth ? '

'Ha-ha-ha ! ' laughed Kita. 'Don't you know me ? '

'Know you, indeed ! ' replied Yaji. 'You're just like Kita, —just his shape, you devil.' He struck Kita with his stick and made him howl.

'Eh ! Eh ! That hurts,' yelled Kita. 'What are you doing ? '

'What am I doing ? I'm going to beat you to death.' Catching Kita off his guard, Yaji then knocked him down and began to jump on him.

'Oh, oh, oh ! ' roared Kita.

'Well, if it hurts,' said Yaji, 'why don't you change into your proper form.'

'What are you feeling my behind for?' roared Kita.

'Put out your tail,' replied Yaji. 'If you don't, this is what I'll do.' He seized Kita's hands and twisting them behind his back tied them with a towel. Kita was so surprised that he let himself be tied up.

'Now,' said Yaji, 'get up and walk.' Holding Kita behind he pushed him along till they came to Akasaka. As it was late there were no innkeepers in the road to greet the travellers and no girls waiting at the doors of the inns. Yaji wandered about in the hope that he would meet the inn servant that was to be sent to meet him.

'Yaji,' pleaded Kita, 'do let me loose. Think how bad it would look if anyone was to see me.'

'Shut up, you beast,' said Yaji. 'I wonder where the inn is?'

'How could anybody take a room for us at an inn if I'm here?' asked Kita.

'Will you still be talking, you beast?' said Yaji.

Just then they met an inn servant. 'Are you gentlemen stopping at this stage?' he inquired.

'Have you come to meet us?' asked Yaji.

'Yes,' said the man.

'There,' said Yaji. 'What do you think of that, you cheat?'
Here he gave Kita a whack with his stick.

'Ai!' yelled Kita. 'What are you doing?'

'Have you any others with you?' inquired the man, looking surprised.

'No, no,' said Yaji. 'I'm alone.'

'Oh, then it's a mistake,' said the servant. 'I understand that the party I am to meet numbers ten.'

He went off hurriedly. Then an innkeeper called to them from the front of his inn. 'Won't you stop at my house to-night, gentlemen?' he asked, as he came running out and caught hold of them.

'No, no,' said Yaji. 'My companion came on ahead and he must be here somewhere.'

'That's me,' said Kita.

'What an obstinate brute you are,' scolded Yaji. 'Put out your tail. Wait a bit. There's a dog. Here, doggie, doggie, go for him, go for him. Aha, the dog doesn't seem to mind. Perhaps he isn't a fox after all. Are you really Kita?'

'Of course I am,' said Kita. 'I call it a cruel joke you have had with me.'

'Ha-ha-ha!' laughed Yaji. 'Then we'll stop at your place after all,' he added, turning to the innkeeper. Feeling sorry for Kita he then untied him.

'Please come in,' said the landlord. 'Here, bring some hot water. Is the room ready?'

'What a time I've had,' groaned Kita as he washed his feet. The maid took their baggage and ushered them into a room.

'I'm very sorry, Kita,' said Yaji. 'I really took you for a fox.'

'You made a fool of me all right,' growled Kita. 'I feel quite sore.'

'Ha-ha-ha!' laughed Yaji. 'But yet I don't know; he may be a fox after all. Somehow I've got a strange sort of feeling. Here, landlord, landlord.' He commenced bawling for the landlord and clapping his hands.

'Did you call, sir?' asked the landlord.

'Look here, there's something strange about this,' said Yaji. 'Where am I?'

'At Akasaka, sir,' replied the landlord.

'Ha-ha-ha!' laughed Kita. 'What's the matter with you, Yaji?'

'Are you still trying to bewitch me?' said Yaji, beginning to wet his eyebrows again. 'Landlord, isn't this a graveyard?'

'Eh?' said the landlord. 'What did you say, sir?'

'Ho-ho-ho!' laughed Kita. 'How funny you are.'

Just then the maid came in from the kitchen. 'Will it please your honours to take a bath?' she inquired.

'There, Yaji,' said Kita. 'You go and take a bath. It'll calm you down.'

'I suppose you think you'll lead me into some dirty water, you beast,' replied Yaji. 'You don't catch me that way.'

'No, no,' said the landlord. 'The bath is filled with pure spring water and is quite clean, your honour. Please try it.'

The landlord went off to the kitchen and the maid brought in some tea. 'If you feel lonely,' she said, 'I'll call some courtesans.'

'Fool!' said Yaji. 'Do you think you're going to catch me embracing a stone image?'

'Ha-ha-ha!' laughed the girl. 'What strange things you say!'

'Well, I'll go first then,' said Kita. He went off to the bathroom and while he was gone the landlord came in again.

'I've something to tell your honour,' he said. 'I'm having a little celebration in my house to-night and I should be glad if you would join us in a bottle of wine.' As he spoke a dish of savouries and a bottle of saké were brought in from the kitchen.

'Oh, please don't take any trouble about us,' said Yaji. 'What's the occasion?'

'Well,' said the landlord. 'The truth is that my young nephew is going to get married to-night. We're just going to hold the marriage ceremony, so I'm afraid it'll be a bit noisy.'

He went off busily to the kitchen just as Kita came back from the bath. 'What's that he said?' asked Kita.

'There's a marriage ceremony here to-night,' said Yaji. 'I'm getting more bewitched every minute. I shan't go in any of your spring-water baths.'

'Try and control yourself and don't be so nervous,' said Kita.

'No, no,' said Yaji. 'You don't catch me off my guard. For all I know this food they've brought in may be dirt, although it looks so nice.'

'Yes,' said Kita. 'I wouldn't touch it if I were you. Just

look on while I eat. I won't be angry. Excuse me not standing on ceremony.' He helped himself to the saké and gulped it down.

'It makes me feel quite bad to see you,' said Yaji, with a look of disgust on his face.

'Don't be so nervous,' said Kita. 'Try a cup.'

'No, no,' said Yaji. 'I know it's some filth,—horse's stale or something. Let's smell it. It smells all right. I can't stand this ; I must have some.' He poured himself out a cup and drank it off.

'Yes, it's saké all right,' he said, smacking his lips. 'What have they got to eat ? I don't like the look of those eggs. I'll try a prawn. Yes, it's a prawn all right,' he added after he had munched it. Thus he began to eat and drink.

Meanwhile there were sounds of preparation from the kitchen, where there was great bustle and confusion. It appeared that the wedding feast was already beginning. Now they could hear the sound of chanting :—

> On the four seas
> Still are the waves ;
> The world is at peace.
> Soft blow the time winds,
> Rustling not the branches.
> In such an age
> Blessed are the very firs
> In that they meet
> To grow old together.

'Yan-ya !' cried Kita joining in the chant.

'What a noise !' said Yaji.

'They can be as noisy as they like for me,' said Kita. 'Aren't you going to let go of that wine-cup ? Just pass it over, will you ? If you think it's horse's dung or stale I'll take the risk and drink it all myself. Ha-ha-ha !'

'I really thought I was bewitched,' said Yaji, 'but now I know I wasn't. What a time I've had !'

'It doesn't compare with me being tied up and beaten,' said Kita.

Just then the supper was brought in, and as the door opened they could hear the sound of another chant :—

> Through ages unchanging,
> From generation to generation,
> Like pine tree and plum,
> May they flourish together ;
> Like two tender seedlings

May they grow both together,
Till old age shall find them
Still happily joined.
Rejoice ! Rejoice !
He has taken a bride from the best in the land.

Then followed the clapping of hands and the sound of talking and laughing. Soon the maid came in and asked whether she should spread the beds.

'You might as well,' said Yaji.

'Is the marriage ceremony over ? ' asked Kita. ' I suppose the bride is very beautiful.'

'Yes,' said the maid. 'The bridegroom's a handsome fellow and the bride's very beautiful too. Unfortunately they have to sleep in the next room, where everybody will be able to hear their love-talk.'

' What a nuisance ! ' said Yaji.

' Awful ! ' said Kita.

' Good rest,' said the maid.

She went off, leaving them to get into bed, and soon they heard the sound of the door being opened in the next room. Apparently the bride and bridegroom were going to bed. Then they heard whispers and other movements, from which they judged it was not the first time that the couple had tasted the delights of love. The sounds kept Yaji and Kita from going to sleep.

' This is awful,' said Yaji.

' We've come to the wrong inn again,' said Kita. ' They don't mind us. How loving she is, the little beast.'

' They've stopped talking,' said Yaji. ' Now's the time.' He crawled softly out of bed and listened to what they were doing. Then he stood up and peeped through the cracks in the sliding door. Kita also crawled out of bed.

' I say, Yaji,' he whispered. ' Is the bride beautiful ? Just let me have a peep.'

' Don't make a noise,' said Yaji. ' It's the critical moment.'

' Eh ? ' said Kita. ' Just let me look. Move away a little.'

But Yaji was peeping through the crack like a man in a dream, and what with Kita shoving him and his own obstinacy, they managed between them to push the sliding door out of its grooves, and it fell suddenly forward into the next room with

Yaji and Kita on top of it. This startled the newly married couple.

'Oh, oh!' shouted the bridegroom. 'What's that? The door's fallen out of its grooves.' Jumping up he overturned the lamp and plunged the room into darkness. Yaji had already fled back into his own room and jumped into bed, but Kita was not quite so quick and got caught by the bridegroom.

'Excuse me,' said Kita. 'I was going out to do something and mistook the door of my room. Really the maid is very careless putting the lamp in the middle of the floor. I'm sorry you tripped over it. But I really must go if you'd just leave loose of me.'

'Such outrageous conduct!' said the bridegroom. 'Everything's covered with oil. Here, San, San, get up.'

The maid came out of the kitchen with a lamp and put things to rights, and Kita, looking very foolish, put the door in its grooves again and went very dejectedly to bed. Then as the night deepened all was still in the inn save only for the snores of the travellers.

Part of old Tokaidō road.

SECOND PART

EN thousand cocks were crowing and horses neighing bravely when Yaji and Kita woke up next morning. They ate their breakfast and quickly left Akasaka behind them, but just outside the town they caught up with three travellers who were going in the same direction. Apparently they were from Edo and, by their manner of speaking, three braves.

'I say,' said one, 'wasn't it funny last night?'

'What, about those fellows in the back room?' asked another. 'They were a couple of fools. Because there was a wedding at the inn they got envious, and in peeping through the cracks of the door they got so excited that they knocked the door over. They were the laughing stock of the place.'

'And the way they apologised to the bridegroom,' said the third man. 'I wasn't able to sleep for all the row they made.'

'And one of the rascals called the landlord earlier in the evening and asked him if the inn was a graveyard. He must have been cracked.'

It appeared from their talk that these men must have stopped at the same inn as Yaji and Kita. Yaji grew hot as he heard their talk, and quickening his step he caught them up.

'Look here, you three,' he said. 'I've been silent up to now, but I'd like to know why you call me a rascal.'

'It hasn't anything to do with you,' said the first man. 'We were talking about our own affairs.'

'Your own affairs, indeed,' said Yaji. 'Weren't you jawing about what happened at the inn? The person who made the door fall down, you said, was a rascal. That's me.'

'Oh, you're the rascal, are you?' replied the brave.

'Yes, I'm the rascal,' said Yaji.

'Ha-ha-ha!' laughed the brave. 'Well, if you're the rascal that's why we called you a rascal. Ain't that all right?'

'Look here, I won't stand any of your jokes,' said Yaji.

'Oh, go and eat dung,' said the brave.

'Eat dung?' said Yaji. 'That's easy. I'll eat it if you get it,' for he was so angry that he didn't know what he was saying.

The traveller picked up a piece of dung on his stick and held it out to Yaji. 'There it is,' he cried. 'Eat it, eat it.'

'No, no,' said Yaji. 'I don't like it.'

'Don't like it?' said the brave. 'But you must like it.'

Then the three men surrounded Yaji to make him eat it by force. Kita, who had been looking on amused, now intervened.

'Let him go,' he pleaded. 'It's much the same as if he'd eaten it, isn't it?'

'Ha-ha-ha!' laughed the three braves. 'Well, we'll let him off at that.' With that they went off.

Yaji tried to bottle up his anger, but he went on reviling them under his breath for a long time.

After they had passed Fujigawa they came to a poor little teahouse by the side of the road.

'I feel rather queer,' said Kita. 'Here, old lady,' he called to the teahouse keeper, 'have you got any hot water?'

'I ain't got any hot water for drinking,' said the old woman, 'but I can give you some cold.'

'I want to drink some medicine,' said Kita. 'Cold water's no use. Where's the convenience?'

'What's the good of your asking where it is and wandering about the house like that?' asked Yaji. 'It's not on the mats. You'd better go round at the back.'

'I see, I see,' said Kita. 'It's at the end there.'

He went round to the back and did his business, and looking about him afterwards, saw that a store-room had been turned into a house and that there was a girl of eighteen or nineteen alone there. Her hair was rather disordered, but she was a very pretty girl and she was alone.

Kitahachi, with his usual impudence, walked in smiling. 'Sorry to trouble you,' he said, 'but could you let me have some water to rinse my hands.'

While he was rinsing his hands the girl kept on giggling. 'What are you laughing at?' asked Kita. 'Do you live here alone? Isn't it dangerous?'

He looked round and saw nobody but the girl. Thereupon he seated himself and pulled out his pipe and tobacco. 'What are you laughing at?' he asked again. 'Is there anything to laugh at? Well, then, come and laugh here.'

He caught hold of her and pulled her down beside him, the girl making no objection, and Kita was just congratulating himself on his good fortune when a little boy came running by and saw them.

'Eh!' he shouted. 'Here's a man making love to the mad girl.'

Bursting into laughter the boy ran off. The startled Kita also wanted to run away, but the girl held him and would not let him go.

'Eh, young fellow,' she said. 'You're not going yet.'

But Kita was by this time rather frightened and he struggled so hard that he was able to break loose just as the girl's old father came on the scene.

'What are you doing with that young girl?' asked the old man.

'I'm not doing anything,' replied Kita.

'Then why did you come here?' asked the old man.

'I went to relieve myself and then I asked her for some water to rinse my hands,' said Kita.

'No, no, no,' said the old man. 'This girl is mad, and it is quite plain you came here with a bad intention.'

'How absurd!' said Kita.

'You can't deceive me,' went on the old man. 'You knew this girl was mad and so you came here to make a fool of her.

I can't accept your excuses. It is unpardonable.' The old man spoke in a loud voice and was evidently intent on making a scene.

In the meanwhile Yaji, after waiting some time in the teahouse in front for Kita to return, had come round to the back and had, indeed, been secretly watching the scene for some time, much to his own amusement. Now he thought it was time that he showed himself, so he came slowly forward.

'Excuse me,' he said. 'I'm in charge of this man and I happened to hear what had taken place. I may tell you that this chap's a bit off his head, as you can see by his looks. Please pardon him. Eh, you rascal! You give me a lot of trouble, don't you? Just look at his face. See for yourself the restless look in his eye. Isn't that enough to show his condition? Your lunatic is a woman, so you can manage her, but this looney gives me all sorts of trouble.'

'No, no, it can't be,' said the old man. 'Is he really mad?'

'Look at his expression,' replied Yaji. 'You can see his condition at once.'

'What?' said Kita. 'I mad? How absurd.—That is . . . Well . . . It's falling, falling, falling! There, there! The flowers are blooming and falling, blooming and falling. Oh, the poor things cannot sleep. Ah, ah, there's my wife. No, she's not a good wife. Halloa! Halloa! Oh, oh, oh!'

'That's the way he goes on,' said Yaji. 'Look at his eyes. You can see he's a love-maniac. That's why he gets so excited when he sees a woman. He's quite lost to shame and reason. He's my younger brother. I never thought such a fate would overtake him.'

'You can talk of your affliction,' said the old man, 'but I have mine also. This girl that you see so afflicted is my only daughter. She's given me great trouble.'

'I expect so,' replied Yaji. 'Now then, you rascal, what are you giggling at? Well, gaffer, we must be going now. Sorry to have disturbed you.'

'Won't you have a drop of tea before you go?' asked the old man.

'No thank you,' said Yaji. 'We must really be going. Now then, looney, come along.'

Thus keeping up a ceaseless chatter Yaji settled the matter and led Kita away. It was not until they had quite escaped from observation that they burst into laughter.

'You're too bad, Kita,' said Yaji. 'Fancy getting hold of a mad girl! You're really too shameless.'

'I do feel a bit ashamed myself,' said Kita. 'But I say, Yaji, your idea of making out that I was mad was a master-stroke.'

'Yes, you ought to treat me to saké for that,' said Yaji. 'I'll tell you a story about that. There was once a crooked sort of fellow just like you, who got hold of a mad girl, but when he began to make love to her, her father came in and got very angry. "What do you mean, you rascal," he said, "coming into a person's house without permission and trying to make a fool of his daughter? It's inexcusable." But you wouldn't give in and you cried out angrily, "You're like a Yotsuya kite sharpening its beak on me." "If I'm like a Yotsuya kite," replied the old man, "you're like a pigeon of the Hachiman shrine." This struck me as curious. Why should Kita be like a pigeon? Then the old man explained: "Because he eats the beans of the mad woman."'

Laughing over their joke they passed on till they came to Okazaki, which is a famous place on the Tokaidō. Here, on both sides of the road are many teahouses and the place is filled with life.

'Take a rest, sirs,' cried an old teahouse keeper. 'Meals served at once. Try our best saké. Come in! Come in!'

'I feel rather hungry,' said Yaji. 'How would it do to take a short rest here?'

They went into a teahouse, accordingly, and were welcomed by the maid.

'We'll have a meal, miss,' said Yaji. 'Got anything nice?'

'We have some nice trout,' said the girl.

'What?' said Kita. 'Did you say high-priced trout?'

'Ho-ho-ho!' laughed the girl. She brought them two trays of boiled trout.

'Let's see,' said Yaji. 'Ah, that tastes good. How white the rice is!'

'What a thing to say!' exclaimed Kita. 'Look how you've made the girl laugh. She's got a dimple in her face.'

'It would be all right if it was a dimple,' said Yaji, 'but her face is all worn away like a stepping stone. Ha-ha-ha!'

Thus were they joking away in their usual fashion. Meanwhile in the next room three guests were talking loudly. Apparently they lived somewhere in the neighbourhood and had lingered

on amusing themselves but were now on the point of departure.
They had for companions some courtesans, who had come thus
far with them on the road and with whom they were now having
a final feast. They were all very merry and were singing a
popular song :

> She has twisted the flowers to fence her round
> And I cannot enter that sacred ground.

As they were making a great noise Yaji and Kita took a peep
at them.

'Now then, Taihyō,' said one of the men. 'What have you
done with that saké cup ? '

'Nihyō's got it,' said Taihyō.

'Here it is,' said Nihyō.

'Drink up and pass it round,' said Taihyō.

Nihyō emptied the cup. 'I mustn't drink any more,' he said.
'Shall I give it to you ? '

'I'll have just a little,' said Taihyō. 'Shall we go round by
Monmokkō and go to the Masuya or the Chojiya ? '

'Listen to Master Taihyō,' said one of the girls. 'He must be
drunk talking about going somewhere else. You mustn't go.'

'It's not that,' said Taihyō. 'I've got a bill from the
Tachibanaya about some goods, and I must go.'

'Oh, that's it, is it ? ' said the girl.

'Of course, of course,' said Nihyō, and he began to chant—

> The plum in the hothouse may think it is spring,
> But I'm not deceived by any such thing.

Meanwhile three riding horses had been brought and tied under
the eaves of the inn, and the postboys now came through the
garden to tell the guests that they had arrived.

'Much obliged, much obliged,' said the guests. 'Well, we
must part now.'

'Goodbye ! ' cried the girls. 'Please come again. You are
going to see Tsuru at Narumi, we know.'

At this Taihyō and Nihyō laughed. Amid the farewell
greetings of the people of the inn, the three guests got on their
horses and rode off, while the girls made all sorts of jokes. Yaji
and Kita were very much amused at the idea of going to buy a
courtesan on horseback.

Passing on they came to Imamura, where an old woman in a
teahouse pressed them to come and try the sugar rice-cakes for
which the place is famous.

'How much each are those rice-cakes?' asked Kita.

'They're three coppers each,' said the old woman's husband.

'That's cheap,' said Kita. 'And how much are these with beans on?'

'They're three coppers also,' said the old man.

'They're dear for three coppers,' said Kita. 'I'll tell you what. Make these two coppers each and in return I'll give you four coppers for those round ones.'

'This is a strange sort of fellow,' thought the shopkeeper, 'but at any rate I shan't lose by it. Very well, your honour,' he said aloud, 'take what you like.'

Kita took two coppers out of his purse. 'I meant to have bought one of the round ones,' he said, 'but I've only got two coppers so I'll have to have one with beans on.'

He caught up the cake and walked off munching it.

'Ha-ha-ha!' laughed Yaji. 'Bravo, Kita! You did astonish that shopkeeper.'

'Ah, he'll know better next time,' said Kita.

'You are a rascal really,' exclaimed Yaji. 'I couldn't do a thing like that. Ha-ha-ha!'

Soon they arrived at Chirifu, where they heard a postboy singing,—

> Shall I stop at Miya
>   To see the girl who loves me well ?
> Or shall I go to Okazaki,
>   Where the light-o'-loves all dwell ?

'What a bother,' said Yaji. 'My feet are beginning to get sore in these straw-sandals. I'll have to walk in a pair of the other kind for a time. Here, shopman, how much are these sandals ? '

'Sixteen coppers, your honour,' said the man.

'That's cheap,' said Yaji.

Now the shopman was from Isé and was a clever trader. 'Yes, they're cheap enough,' he said. 'My sandals are all very well made and don't come to pieces.'

'Perhaps they will when we get along the road a bit further,' said Kita.

'That's because you wear them,' replied the shopkeeper. 'If you put 'em by they'd never wear out.'

'Yes,' said Yaji. 'Your sandals are just right because they've all got thongs.'

'Where can you get sandals without thongs ? ' asked Kita.

'Well, they're very cheap at any rate,' said Yaji. Then he took a pair that were hanging down in front of the shop. 'Why, they're not a pair,' he cried ; ' one's bigger than the other. That big one's cheap for eight coppers, but the small one's dear at the price. I'll tell you what I'll do. I'll give you nine coppers for the big one and seven coppers for the small one.'

'Very well,' said the shopkeeper.

'Halloa ! ' said Yaji. 'I haven't got enough change. I thought of buying a pair, but I've only got seven coppers, so I'll only buy one.'

'Ha-ha-ha ! ' laughed Kita. 'You've trying to imitate me. It's all right for cakes, but it won't do for sandals.'

'You must buy the pair,' said the shopkeeper. 'I can't sell one sandal separately.'

'What ? ' said Yaji. 'You won't let me buy one sandal. Really, it's very inconvenient buying things in the country.'

'I've never heard of them selling one sandal even in Edo,' said Kita.

'If you don't like those, take this pair,' said the shopkeeper. 'I can let you have them for seven coppers.'

'I don't want horses' sandals,' said Yaji. 'Don't make a fool of me.'

'You'd better buy a pair, Yaji,' said Kita. 'What are you going to do with one sandal?'

'Go a little further and buy another,' replied Yaji.

'I see,' said the shopkeeper, laughing. 'Well, I'll let you have the pair for fourteen coppers.'

'Then why didn't you say so before,' said Yaji. He took off his old straw-sandals and threw them away and put on the new ones.

When they arrived at Arimatsu they found all the shops filled with a kind of cloth made in the district, of different patterns. It was hanging in front of the shops, and all the shopmen were out in the street shouting their wares.

'Come in,' they cried. 'Come in and buy some of our famous Arimatsu cloth. Buy, buy, buy!'

'Eh!' said Yaji. 'What a noisy lot they are!'

'What do you say, Yaji,' said Kita. 'Shall we buy a piece?'

'We'll make 'em sell it to us cheap,' said Yaji.

'All right,' agreed Kita. 'We'll look as if we were going to buy the lot.'

They walked up and down the street looking at the things till they came to a small shop at the end of the town, which had a lot of the cloth displayed outside. There they went in.

'How much is this cloth?' asked Yaji.

But the shopkeeper was absorbed in a game of chess. 'Dear me!' he murmured. 'I've made a mistake. By the way, what have you taken?'

'Halloa! Halloa!' said Yaji. 'How much is this cloth?'

As he spoke in a loud voice the shopkeeper was startled. 'Eh?' he said. 'What's that?'

'How much? How much?' asked Yaji.

'Let's see,' muttered the shopkeeper. 'What did you say? Well, I'll move this, then.'

'Here, here, I can't stand this,' cried Yaji. 'Isn't this cloth for sale? What's the price?'

'Dear me!' said the shopkeeper. 'What a hasty temper you've got. Just turn it over and you'll see the mark on it. You can't tell without that?'

'This is a funny sort of a shopkeeper,' said Yaji. 'It's marked with an *a* and an *e*.'

'Oh, indeed,' said the shopkeeper. 'That'll be three *bun* five *rin*.'

'That's too dear,' said Yaji. 'You won't lose if you come down a bit.'

'Lose?' said the shopkeeper. 'What, to such a bungling chess-player as he is?'

'Come, come, Master Jihyō,' said his friend. 'Attend to business, why don't you? Please wait a minute, gentlemen,' he added to Yaji and Kita.

'Never mind them,' said the shopkeeper, still lost in his game. 'They won't buy anything that's certain. They haven't got the gold and silver. I've got them in my hand.'

'What are you talking about, you rascal?' said Yaji angrily. 'Haven't got any money, indeed. Is that the way to treat people? We'll buy something now just to show we have. How much is this loin-cloth?'

'What? You want to buy a loin-cloth?' said the shopkeeper. 'What impertinence!'

'How dare you talk to me like that?' yelled Yaji. 'What impertinence is there in wanting to buy something that's for sale, old snotty-face?'

This woke the shopkeeper up and he at last rose from the chessboard. 'Excuse my inattention,' he said, as one coming out of a dream. 'I'll let you have anything cheap. Please pick out what you want.'

'Come now,' said Kita. 'We're going to buy quite a lot. Yaji, you'd better buy a present for your mother or your wife. How much is that?'

'That's four *mommé* eight *bu*,' said the shopkeeper.

'How much is that over there?' asked Yaji.

'That's fifteen *mommé*,' said the shopkeeper.

'Haven't you got any better ones?' asked Yaji.

'Certainly,' said the shopkeeper. 'This one is twenty-one *mommé* and this is twenty-two *mommé*. That below is nineteen *mommé*.'

'I want something better than these,' said Yaji.

'I'm sorry to say they're all I have,' replied the shopkeeper.

'Then you'd better take care of them,' said Yaji. 'Somebody will buy them perhaps some day. I'll take some of that stuff I looked at first. Just cut me a towel out of that piece.'

'Oh, indeed!' said the shopkeeper. Lost in astonishment he

cut a towel out of the cloth and handed it to Yaji, who paid and walked off.

'What a fool!' he said, when they were outside. 'He took us for a couple of country bumpkins. He did get a shock. Ha-ha-ha! But we've wasted a lot of time. We must get on.'

Quickening their pace, they went on and it was just getting dusk when they got to Miya, where the girls were crying shrilly outside each inn. 'Stop here, gentlemen,' they cried. 'The bath is quite ready. There's a vacant room for you. Stop here, stop here.'

'Where shall we stop?' asked Yaji. 'At the Zeniya or the Hyotanya.'

'What's that inn over there?' said Kita. 'The Kagiya.'

'Please stop here,' said a girl.

'All right,' said Kita. 'How much do you charge?'

'Don't trouble about that,' said the girl, laughing. 'Please walk in.'

'Don't they make any charge here?' asked Kita.

'So much the better,' said Yaji. He took off his hat and went in.

'I'll bring some hot water,' said the landlord, 'but never mind washing your feet if they're not dirty. You can go straight to the bath.'

Their baggage was taken in and Yaji and Kita, after they had removed their sandals, were shown into a back room. Soon the maid brought some tea.

'Would you like a rub down?' asked a shampooer.

'I would,' said Kita, 'but I'm feeling very hungry just now.'

'We'll have some macaroni,' said Yaji. 'It's very good here.'

'I'll call again afterwards,' said the shampooer.

Then came two or three persons carrying lanterns. 'Are you gentlemen stopping here?' they asked. 'Onbako is the patron god of this place and we're erecting a fountain in his honour. Won't you make a small contribution towards the cost?'

'All right,' said Yaji. 'Give them something, Kita.' Kita gave them eight coppers and they entered it in a book.

Then came a priest. 'We're erecting a monument to the sixty disciples,' he said, 'and should be very glad if you could spare us something.'

'What's that?' said Yaji. 'Donation for a stone monument?

What a nuisance you people are ! Here, take that,' and he gave him eight coppers also.

Just then the landlord suddenly thrust his head in at the door.

'What are you helping to erect ? ' called out Yaji. 'Do you want eight coppers also ? '

'No, no,' said the landlord, coming in. 'I only came to ask if you were going by boat in the morning or going round by Saya ? '

'Let's go direct from here by boat,' suggested Kita.

'The boat's all right,' said Yaji, 'but the trouble is that I always want to make water when I am on the sea, and as we have to go seventeen miles I can't retain it all that time. I think we'd better go round by Saya. What do you say, Kita ? '

'I can give you something that will make it all right,' said the landlord. 'I always provide my guests with a bamboo tube for use on such occasions.'

'Well then, I'll have one of those,' said Yaji.

'Very well,' said the landlord. 'I'll send your supper in now.'

The maid accordingly brought the supper-trays and there was more talk which I will not relate, till at last the trays were taken away and the shampooer came in.

'Shall I rub you gentlemen down now ? ' he asked.

'All right,' said Yaji.

While Yaji was being shampooed two blind girls in the next room began to sing an Isé chorus to the music of the samisen for their own amusement :—

> As fine as a flower,
>> Formed to make all hearts ache,
> Who would not loose her girdle
>> For such a lover's sake ?

'Ain't they got good voices ? ' said Kita. 'I say, shampooer, you don't know what a dancer I am. If you could see I'd show you how I can dance to that music.'

'I'm very fond of dancing,' replied the shampooer. 'I like to hear the sound of it. Won't you give us a dance ? '

'All right,' said Kita. 'But I hope you'll applaud me. I must have a little encouragement. I'll tell you what. When I've finished a dance I'll just touch your head so that you can know when to applaud. Is that all right ? Now I'm going to begin.'

Then the girls in the next room began singing again :—

No parting thought the twain, but three,
Four, five days pass, and out to sea
The waiting barque must sail again.
Such partings in this world of pain!

Kita, clapping his hands to the music, pretended that he was
dancing. Then at the end he touched the shampooer's head
with his foot.

'Bravo! Bravo!' said the shampooer. 'Capital! Capital!'

'Wasn't it good?' said Kita. 'Shall I dance again?'

Then the girls began singing again and he went through the
same performance :—

With you I'll pull together
Across the waves of life,
A pillow for our rudder,
Your true and loving wife.

'Ha-ha-ha!' laughed Kita when they had finished. 'Wasn't
it good?'

Then the maid came in to ask if they would take a bath.

'Have you finished, Yaji?' asked Kita. 'If so you'd better
go to the bath, and as the shampooer has been so kind as to
praise my dancing I'll let him rub me down for a bit.'

Yaji accordingly went off to the bath and the shampooer began
to rub Kita.

'By the way, sir,' he asked, 'are you going to call a girl?'

'No,' said Kita. 'I'd rather know something about those girls
in the next room.'

'They're blind singers who came to stop at the inn two or
three days ago,' said the shampooer. 'They've got good voices,
but I'd like you to hear mine.'

'All right. Go on,' said Kita.

'But I'd like you to applaud me so as to give me some
encouragement,' said the shampooer, 'so please praise me when
I've finished.'

'All right, all right,' said Kita.

'Then I'll begin,' said the shampooer.

Thereupon he began to sing in a loud voice which made Kita's
head ring :—

Oh he's drunk, drunk, drunk,
'Cause he's drunk such a lot.
If he hadn't drunk so much
He would not, not, not . . . .

Then he thrust his fingers into Kita's ears. 'This is the chap,' he
chanted 'who was kicking me on the head. May the fool be

eaten up with disease and never come to any good ! May he be hung by the neck as he deserves ! '

Then he pulled his fingers out of Kita's ears and pretended that he was still singing the chorus,—' Yatosanosé ! Yatosanosé ! '

As he had stopped up Kita's ears, Kita was quite unconscious of all the bad things that the shampooer had said about him, and joined in the chorus,—' Yanya ! Yanya ! '

' Jaja janjan ! ' sang the shampooer, so loudly that Kita's head rang and he had to squeeze up his face. Nevertheless he cried ' Bravo ! Bravo ! ' when the shampooer had finished.

' Shall I sing you another ? ' asked the shampooer.

' No thank you,' replied Kita. ' My head won't stand it.'

' Ha-ha-ha ! ' laughed the shampooer. ' Wasn't that amusing ? '

Yaji, who had come back from the bath while the song was going on, had enjoyed Kita's torments. ' Sing us another,' he said to the shampooer.

' I'm going to the bath,' said Kita. ' I've had enough shampooing.'

He went off to the bath accordingly and the shampooer retired. Then the maid came in to spread the beds, and before Kita came back from the bath Yaji was in bed.

' Are you asleep already ? ' asked Kita. ' By the way, did you see those girls sleeping in the next room. They're awfully pretty.'

' But they're blind,' said Yaji.

' Well, they're none the worse for that,' said Kita. ' Just when I came from the bath I found one of them wandering about trying to find the wash-bowl and I had a little talk with her. She's quite a nice girl.'

' Which one's that ? ' asked Yaji. He crawled out of bed and went to peep through the crack in the door into the next room.

' I see her,' he said. ' She looks quite nice from behind. I must see what I can do.'

' No, no, that won't do,' said Kita. He drew the bedclothes over him, thinking in his heart all the time that he would himself crawl out afterwards. But as he lay there pretending to sleep, sleep overcame him and soon his snores echoed to the roof.

All was now quiet in the next room; apparently the two blind girls had gone to sleep. Night deepened and soon the midnight bell sounded, whereupon Yaji got up, and after assuring himself that Kita was sound asleep, crawled to the door into the next room and opened it softly. Creeping in he saw that the two girls were sound asleep. Yaji had intended to slip into the arms of one girl as she lay asleep, but he found that, being blind, she had taken the precaution of keeping her bundle in bed with her and was clasping it tightly with both her hands. As the bundle was in the way, Yaji began carefully to remove it, but immediately she felt it being taken away the girl woke up, and seizing the bundle with one hand with the other caught hold of Yaji.

' Thief ! Thief ! ' she screamed. ' Landlord ! Landlord ! '

At her screams, finding that he had missed his aim and thinking that it would be annoying to be found out, Yaji snatched himself from her grasp, darted back into his own room and jumping into his bed pretended to be sound asleep. Kita had also woke up and was laughing to himself over the affair.

Meanwhile the landlord came rushing from the kitchen. ' What's the matter ? ' he cried. ' What's the matter ? '

' Somebody tried to take away my bundle that I was holding,' said the blind girl. ' Are the shutters open ? Just look and see.'

' No, no, everything's shut,' said the landlord.

' Then where can the thief have come from ? ' said the girl.

' Aha ! ' said the landlord. ' The door into the next room is open. Are you asleep, gentlemen ? '

' Ga ! Ga ! ' snored Yaji.

' Aha, there's something dropped here,' said the landlord. ' Why, it's a loin-cloth. Gentlemen, is this yours ? '

When he heard this Yaji realised that it must be his own loin-cloth. Softly raising his head he saw to his amusement that the loin-cloth was stretched out between the two rooms, from the pillow of the blind girl to his own pillow. While he was hesitating what to say, Kita, seeing a chance of teasing Yaji, jumped up.

' What a noise you're making,' he said. ' Where's the loin-cloth that was dropped. Oh, that's it, is it ? Why, Yaji, isn't that your loin-cloth ? '

' What a silly thing to say,' replied Yaji, giving Kita's bedgown a secret tug. The landlord, though outwardly he appeared satisfied, thought there was something strange in the affair.

' It's as well to take care when you're travelling,' he said. ' Please be careful. I bid you good-night.'

' I feel so nervous that I know I shan't be able to sleep,' said the blind girl. ' Please see that everything is shut.'

'Good-night,' said the landlord.

When the landlord had gone Yaji softly put out his hand and drew the loin-cloth into his bed, while Kitahachi murmured,

> A blind girl's love he sought to prove,
> For who is blind if 'tis not love.

Now, as night deepened, they all sank to rest, but they had hardly had time to enjoy one pleasant dream before the dawn wind began to blow through the trees and the sound of the waves echoed through their pillows. Aroused by the ringing of the dawn bell they opened their eyes to find that it was daylight and that the crows were already cawing to each other and the horses whinnying. Then they heard the songs of the carriers :—

> Climbing the hill,
> Through shine and shower,
> Look how the clouds
> Over Suzuka lour.

'Who's for the boat? Who's for the boat?' called a voice. Then the maid came to wake them and to tell them that the first boat was just about to start.

'Shall I bring in your breakfast?' she asked.

'Wake up, Kita,' said Yaji. Jumping up they washed and breakfasted and were just making preparations to start when the landlord came in.

'Are you ready, gentlemen?' he asked. 'I'll show you the way to the landing stage.'

'That's very kind of you,' said Yaji. 'Come, Kita, let's go.'

Having finished their preparations they started off to a chorus of farewells from the maids of the inn and the hope that they would stop there again on their return journey.

'Thanks for your trouble,' said Yaji.

At the landing stage the landlord called to the boatmen. 'Here are two passengers,' he cried. 'Please look after them.'

'By-the-by, landlord,' said Yaji, 'you've forgotten to give me what you promised yesterday,—the bamboo tube, you know.'

'That's so,' said the landlord, 'and I had it out all ready. I'll go and get it now.'

He hastened off to get the tube and meanwhile the two travellers paid their fare of forty-five coppers each and went on board with their bundles. Then the landlord came back with the piece of bamboo.

'I'll throw it to you,' he called.

'Why, it's only a fire-blower,' said Kita.

'It's for when I want to make water,' said Yaji. 'Thank you very much, landlord. I shall be all right with this. Ha-ha-ha !'

Then the boat started with all the travellers feeling very adventurous, and the wind being favourable they sped over the waves like an arrow. The sea was calm and all the passengers were in great spirits, talking enough to dislocate their jaws and laughing so shrilly that it almost seemed as if they were quarrelling with each other. Yaji went to sleep, and was only awakened by a number of trading boats which came up to them.

'Buy some saké,' cried the men in the boats. 'Try our broiled eels. How about some dumplings ? Try our pickles.'

'I've had a good sleep,' said Yaji. 'What a distance we've come. But I must relieve myself.'

He took the bamboo tube which the landlord had given him for the purpose, but as the tube was exactly like a fire-blower and had a hole at each end, as fast as he made water into it at one end it came out at the other into the boat. Soon the passengers began to be astonished at the water in the boat.

'What's this ?' they cried. 'Everything's covered with water. Where's it coming from ? Somebody must have upset a teapot.

Dear, dear ! My tobacco and paper have got all wet. What a nuisance ! Why, surely somebody's been making water.'

Their cries threw Yaji into confusion and he hurriedly hid the piece of bamboo.

'What have you been doing, Yaji ? ' said Kita. 'If you want to make water you should go to the side of the boat so that it will fall into the water. You've made the boat all wet inside. How dirty ! '

'I was going to empty it into the water afterwards,' explained Yaji.

'How disgusting ! ' said the passengers. 'Everything smells horribly. Here, boatman, haven't you got any more mats ? '

'What's that ? ' said the boatman. 'Somebody been making water ? He's defiled the patron god of the boat. Be quick and dry it up.'

'You haven't got any commonsense,' said Kita.

'Look out, it's running out of the bamboo still,' cried the boatman. 'Throw it away.'

'No, no, no,' said Yaji. 'I'll put it up here. We can use it as a fire-blower afterwards.'

'What, when you've made it all dirty ? ' said Kita. 'Who would use it as a fire-blower now ? Be quick and dry up the mess. How slow you are ? '

Yaji took no notice of Kita's teasing, but undid his loin-cloth and mopped up the mess, while Kita turned the mats over and put things straight.

'There,' he said, 'that's all right now. You can all come and sit down.'

'I hope you'll excuse me,' said Yaji dejectedly. 'I'm afraid I've disturbed you all.'

The passengers laughed sarcastically but said nothing, and soon the boat arrived at the shore at Kuwana.

'Here we are, here we are,' they all cried. 'The boat's got here safely in spite of its being defiled. Thank goodness for that.'

So they all went on shore and indulged in saké in honour of their safe arrival.

BOOK FIVE

THUS Yajirobei and Kitahachi, having passed over the calm waves for seventeen miles, by the grace of heaven arrived safely at Kuwana amid great rejoicing. There they partook of the baked clams for which the place is famous, and having poured out sundry cups of saké, started on the road again. As they started they heard the travellers singing a popular song :—

> Send her a present of clams, lover mine,
> But oh ! for the tortoise that lives at the shrine !

' I'm on my way back, masters,' called a postboy. ' Won't your honours ride ? '

' No, no,' said Yaji.

' I'll only charge you a hundred and fifty,' said the postboy.

' No, no,' said Yaji.

' What do you say to four coppers cash down ? ' asked Kita.

' No, no,' said the postboy.

' Hin-hin,' whinnied the horses.

Then came the songs of the carriers,—

> Spread the sail and speed away,
> At Atsuta we wish to stay.
> What have you done with Hachibei ?
> The horses ate him on the way.
> Dokkoi ! Dokkoi !

' I say, Yaji,' said Kita. ' Let's do something to amuse ourselves. Let's tie our baggage together so that one of us can carry it, and we'll pretend for half a day that one of us is the master and the other the servant.'

' That would be amusing,' said Yaji. ' Let's do it. I'll be master first.'

' All right,' said Kita. ' It's two o'clock now, so we'll go on till four. Of course we must treat each other as master and servant and not change over till the time's up.'

' Of course,' said Yaji.

They found a bamboo and tied their baggage on at either end so that Kita could carry it on his shoulder.

'As you are older, you must be the master,' said Kita, 'and I'll play the part of the servant. You'll see what a good servant I make.'

He shouldered the baggage and came on behind Yaji. 'Master,' he cried.

'What is it?' said Yaji.

'Fine weather to-day, master,' said Kita.

'Yes,' said Yaji. 'The wind's gone down and it's warm.'

'Yes, your honour,' said Kita.

Thus as master and servant for the time being they went on talking. Soon they came to Ofukemura, which is noted for its baked clams. Here they saw all the travellers gathered round the braziers in the teahouses, baking the clams in the hot ashes.

'Come in, come in,' cried the teahouse girls. 'Try our fine wine. Have a snack. Have a snack.'

'Take a kago, master,' cried a carrier. 'I'll take you cheap for this stage.'

'I don't want a kago,' said Yaji.

'Get your master to ride,' said the carrier to Kita. 'I'm on my way back, so I'll take him cheap.'

'My master likes to walk,' said Kita.

'All the same I suppose he'll ride if it's cheap,' said the carrier.

'I don't care about your making it cheap,' said Yaji. 'I'll ride if you make it dear.'

'Well, then,' said the carrier. 'I'll make it dear and charge you three hundred coppers.'

'No, no,' said Yaji. 'Can't you make it a little dearer than that?'

'Well,' said the carrier, 'I'll charge you three hundred and fifty then.'

'If you charge one thousand five hundred coppers I'll ride,' said Yaji.

'Eh?' said the carrier. 'What extravagance! It'll spoil my business. I couldn't take such a price from you. I won't take more than four hundred coppers.'

'That's too cheap,' said Yaji.

'What are you talking about?' cried the carrier. 'That's not cheap. Look here, as a last offer I'll go as far as seven hundred coppers.'

'Don't bother me,' said Yaji. 'I won't go below one thousand five hundred coppers.'

'Oh, dear!' said the carrier. 'Whatever shall I do? Won't you go a little below that?'

'Never,' said Yaji.

'What a strange thing for the kago-carrier to have to beat the customer down,' said the carrier. He turned to his mate. 'Shall we carry him for one thousand five hundred coppers, mate? Get in, sir.'

'You accept, then, do you?' said Yaji. 'Well, in return for my paying you dear you must give me a tip.'

'Oh, yes,' said the carrier. 'We'll give you a tip.'

'Then I'll draw one thousand four hundred and fifty coppers,' said Yaji, 'and you can have the remaining fifty. Do you agree to that?'

'Oh, no,' said the carrier. 'That won't do.'

'Then the bargain's off,' said Yaji. 'Ha-ha-ha!'

'Master got the better of them there,' said Kita.

Thus joking they reached Toda, which is also celebrated for its clams. Both sides of the road were filled with teahouses, their eaves nearly meeting, and the girls were all in the road calling to the travellers to come in.

Going into a teahouse to take a rest, Yaji, as master, mounted on to the boards of the verandah, while Kita, as the servant, waited down below.

'Kitahachi,' said Yaji. 'We'll have something to eat.'

'Yes, your honour,' said Kita, and turning to the maid he ordered two meals.

'Will you eat your rice with clams?' inquired the maid.

'No, we'll eat it with chopsticks,' said Yaji cheerfully.

'Ho-ho-ho!' laughed the maid. Then she put a handful of pine cones into a box-shaped oven and began to fan it.

'Have you got any good saké?' asked Yaji. 'I don't like the bad stuff we usually get. And look here, we come from Edo, where we are used to all kinds of delicacies, and we can't eat the common stuff they give you on the road. Really, it's very painful travelling. Riding on a horse is dangerous and the kago gives you a crick in the back. They recommended me to try the inn kago and I found them so much better that now I can't ride in the ordinary ones. Kitahachi, I think we'll walk for a bit now, and if we find any good sandals we'll buy a pair. I can't walk in straw sandals any more. Look, my feet are all covered with chaps.'

'So they are, your honour,' said Kita. 'That's because this is the first time your honour's worn straw sandals and your old chaps are coming out again.'

'Don't talk nonsense,' said Yaji. 'It's because my feet are too soft and the strings of the sandals have eaten into them. But where are the clams?'

'They're ready now,' said the maid. She brought them each a plateful.

'Ah,' said Kita, 'that girl likes me. She's only brought you a little and look how she's piled them up for me. I feel like a starved devil going from rice bowl to rice bowl.'

'Fool!' said Yaji. 'She didn't give you a lot because she's in love with you. It's because she despises you.'

'Why?' asked Kita.

'All the servants travelling with their masters are served that way,' explained Yaji, 'so that people can tell which is the master and which is the servant.'

'Oh, that's it, is it?' said Kita. 'How stupid!'

'Ha-ha-ha!' laughed Yaji. 'Let's have some more clams.'

The maid brought another large plate of clams.

' I expect your clam is nicer still,' said Yaji, giving her a pinch behind.

' Ho-ho-ho ! ' she laughed. ' Master's full of jokes.'

' I'm full of jokes too,' said Kita, giving her another pinch.

' You be quiet,' said the girl. ' I don't care for you.'

' Whatever I do she despises me,' said Kita, and he was going on grumbling to himself when the temple bell began to ring.

' What time's that ? ' asked Kita.

' It's four o'clock,' answered the maid.

' Oh then, my time's up,' said Kita. ' You've got to be the servant now. Here, Yajirobei, I'm tired of riding on horses and in kago. After this we'll walk at our leisure. Buy me some good sandals. These are no good. See how dirty my feet are.'

' Don't be a fool,' said Yaji. ' Your feet are so split up that they look like claws.'

' You mustn't talk to your master like that,' said Kita. ' Here, take the baggage.'

' What a strict master you are,' groaned Yaji. ' Just put it down there.'

' No, no,' said Kita. ' That won't do.' He gave the baggage a push which caused Yaji to roll over and upset all the plate of hot clams into his sleeve.

' Oh, oh ! ' yelled Yaji. ' They're hot. You've upset all the gravy.'

' Where ? ' asked Kita. He thrust his hand into Yaji's sleeve to seize the clams, but they were so hot that he had to let go and they all slipped down inside Yaji's kimono. Kita endeavoured to get hold of them but only succeeded in burning Yaji more, till at last Yaji undid his loin-cloth and they all slipped out.

' Ha-ha-ha ! ' laughed Kita. ' That's what I call an easy delivery.'

' It's no joking matter,' said Yaji. ' It gave me quite a shock.'

' Hope you haven't hurt yourself.'

' No, I haven't hurt myself,' said Yaji, ' but it made me smart.'

Starting off again they had almost reached Yokkaichi when they met an inn tout. ' Welcome, gentlemen,' he said. ' May I recommend my inn ? '

' We're going to the Obiya,' said Yaji.

' There's a daimyō's train stopping in the town,' said the man, ' and both houses of the Obiya are full up. You'd better stop at my inn.'

This was not true, as it was only a petty official who was travelling through and he had put up at one of the smaller inns. They were too simple-minded to see through the trick, however.

'How much will you put us up for?' asked Yaji.

'Whatever you think proper to pay,' replied the man.

'They treated us very well at the Yokiya at Miya,' continued Yaji. 'The charge was one hundred and fifty coppers for board and lodging and they said nothing about the saké and cakes they gave us. I did think of giving them two hundred extra, but I didn't do so in the end, so it was very cheap altogether. Will you treat us as well as that?'

'Certainly,' said the man.

Thus talking they came to the outskirts of Yokkaichi, where the inn tout ran forward.

'This is the place,' he said. Then he called to the inn people to announce that guests had come, and a maid came out and welcomed them. While they were taking off their sandals they looked about and saw that it was a very dirty place; a broken cupboard and a cracked kitchen stove stood in the entrance, and the walls were covered with soot.

'We're very crowded this evening,' said the landlord. 'I hope you gentlemen won't mind sharing a room with other travellers.'

'Not at all,' said Yaji.

'Then please come this way,' said the maid. She led them along the passage to a room at the back, where there were two countrymen, who greeted them as they entered.

'Eh! I am tired,' said Kita. Then, at the invitation of the maid he quickly went off to the bath.

Soon a boy of fourteen or fifteen came in with a box in a wrapper. 'Do you want any tobacco?' he asked. 'Or toothbrushes, or powder, or some nose paper?'

'I got some Morning Willow tobacco from a girl at the Otaké when I dropped in there some time ago,' said one of the countrymen, 'but I've smoked it all.'

'Haven't you got any of the fine tobacco at four coppers?' asked the other countryman.

'Sorry I haven't got any of that,' said the boy. 'Try some of this.'

'What's that?' asked the countryman. He took some of it and put it in his pipe and puffed. 'Why, this hasn't got any taste,' he said. 'Let's try the other.' Then he puffed away at the other.

'How do you find that?' asked the boy.

'I can't keep it alight,' said the countryman. 'Look, it goes out when I puff at it.'

'That's because it's burning your knee,' said the boy.

'Oh, oh, oh! I've burnt a hole in my best kimono,' cried the countryman as he blew the tobacco off his knee. 'No, no, I don't want any tobacco that burns holes in your clothes. Take it away.'

'All right,' said the boy, and he went off grumbling.

Then Kita came back from the bath. 'Aren't you going in, Yaji?' he asked.

'Please take a bath,' said the maid.

'Eh! She's a fine girl,' said Yaji. 'Quite dazzling.'

'I've just made an agreement with her in the bath-room for to-night,' said Kita in a low voice. 'Quick, ain't I?'

'Is it true?' asked Yaji. 'How did you do it?'

'She came into the bathroom while I was there and asked if the bath was hot enough,' explained Kita, 'so I made an agreement with her. There's another nice woman, somewhat older. If you go and wait in the bath probably she'll come and you can fix it up with her.'

'All right, I'll try,' said Yaji, and he went off to the bath.

Then a liquor seller came in. 'Have some spirits?' he said. 'Try some white saké.'

'Just give me a little of the spirit,' said Kita. 'That's enough.'

The man poured some spirit into a cup, and Kita, after he had paid the man, filled his mouth with it and blew it on his feet.

'That feels better,' he said. 'I'm so tired I think I'll lie down. Please excuse me all of you. Ah, that feels good,' he added as he stretched himself out on the mats.

Meanwhile Yaji had gone to the bathroom and was waiting and waiting for the woman to come, without ever a sign of her. He washed himself over and over, each finger and each toe, and, in fact, spent such a long time in the bath that he began to feel faint. Finally he could no longer stand and he fell over the side of the bath.

Just then Kita, feeling anxious because Yaji had been so long in the bath, came along and peeped in at the door.

'Yaji, Yaji,' he called when he saw the state Yaji was in,

'what's the matter?' He threw some cold water over Yaji's face and Yaji responded with a groan.

'Do you feel better?' asked Kita. 'What's the matter?'

'Oh!' groaned Yaji. 'You have played an awful trick on me.'

'How?' asked Kita.

'I was waiting and waiting in the bath for that woman to come,' said Yaji, 'and the result was that I stayed in too long.'

'And then you felt faint, I suppose,' said Kita. 'Ha-ha-ha! That shows you haven't got any sense.'

'My legs are all trembling,' said Yaji. 'It's all your fault.'

'Ha-ha-ha!' laughed Kita. 'What a joke. There, stand up.' He put Yaji's kimono on him and managed to support him to the room, where Yaji fell flat on the floor as if he had no strength left.

'Ah, I feel a little better,' he said.

'What a dreadful thing,' said Kita. 'You ought to have come out before.'

'I thought the woman would come as you said,' moaned Yaji, 'and I waited and waited. There was a woman there washing something, and I thought she might be the woman you meant, so I asked her to scrub my back. But she turned out to be an old woman of sixty. She came with a scrubbing brush and asked if she should scrub my back with that.'

'That was a good one,' said Kita. He was lying on his stomach listening to Yaji's story in a half dream and amusing himself by tweaking the ear of the countryman, who lay stretched out at his feet, with his toes. Apparently the countryman was a good-natured sort of fellow, for he only moved his head aside gently when Kita did this.

'What did you do then?' asked Kita.

'Just listen,' said Yaji. 'I was feeling awfully vexed, and then that dreadful old woman comes along with a scrubbing brush. "What are you going to do with that?" I asks her. "Ay, ay," she says and she goes off and brings back a broken old kitchen knife. "Shall I scrape the dirt off your back with this?" she asks. "Do you think I'm a pot or a pan?" I says. "Idiot!"'

'Ha-ha-ha!' laughed Kita. 'Bravo! Bravo!' Once again he lapsed into a sort of dream. His foot stole out unconsciously and he began feeling round the head of the countryman till he

176

found his ear. He was just beginning to play with it again when the countryman caught hold of his foot.

'I've borne it in silence up to now,' he said, 'but this time I want to know what you mean by playing with my ear.'

'Eh?' said Kita, startled. 'Excuse me, excuse me.'

'I shan't excuse you,' said the countryman. 'I don't mind your doing it once unconsciously while you're talking, and so I moved my head aside without saying anything; but then you deliberately go and do it again. What do you mean by touching my head with your muddy foot. It's unpardonable.'

'He's very sorry,' said Yaji. 'You must excuse him. In a public inn you never know what destiny has in store for you. You really must excuse him.'

'Since you're so ready to apologise I won't be hard on you,' said the countryman, 'but you shouldn't make a fool of a person.'

'I'm a little bit drunk,' said Kita, 'so you must excuse me.'

'You're still trying to make a fool of me,' said the countryman. 'I've been lying here watching you and I haven't seen you drink a drop of saké. I can't believe you're drunk.'

'No, I haven't been drinking any saké,' said Kita. 'It's my feet that are drunk.'

'As if your feet could drink saké!' said the countryman. 'Don't be a fool.'

'Don't get so excited about it,' said Kita. 'I tell you my feet are drunk, because I blew some spirit on to them. They're mad with drink. Look at them. Look how they're trembling and how they want to play with your head. There, there!'

'Really, your feet are very ill-mannered when they're drunk,' said the countryman.

'Yes,' said Kita. 'It's much better to have feet that don't drink. My feet give me a good deal of trouble.'

'Well, I won't say any more about it then,' said the countryman. 'Don't you think it's time we went to sleep?'

He called to the maid to spread the beds and the two countrymen tumbled into them, and in a second were sound asleep and snoring. Yaji and Kita dropped numerous hints to the girl who came to spread their beds and there were many jokes made, but finally the girl went off into the kitchen.

'Kita,' said Yaji, in a low voice, 'did you really arrange something with that girl?'

'Of course,' said Kita. 'But she's not coming here. You've

to go along by the wall in the next room and open the door at the end. She's sleeping there.'

'I'll go first,' said Yaji.

'You'd better go to sleep instead of getting so jealous about it,' replied Kita.

Kita turned his back and pretended to go to sleep, and Yaji also pretended to go to sleep while planning how he could spoil Kita's game. In the end, however, worn out with their travels, they both fell fast asleep, and some time elapsed before Yaji woke up with a start to find the night lamp out and the room plunged in darkness. As it was now quite quiet Yaji thought it would be a good time to steal a march on Kita. Softly he got up and crept very quietly into the next room. Feeling his way along by the wall, unhappily he raised his hands too high, and by some mishap unhooked a hanging shelf, which slipped down into his hands to his astonishment. 'This is strange,' he thought. 'I must have put my hands up too high and unfastened it. If I take my hands away it will fall to the floor with all the things on it and wake everybody up, which would be very annoying.'

He tried to hook the shelf on again, but all in vain, and he had to stand there in his undershirt holding the shelf up with both hands and feeling very cold and miserable.

While Yaji was standing there wondering what to do, Kita, quite unconscious of what had happened, also woke up. Crawling into the next room he also felt his way along by the side of the wall till he got to where Yaji was standing.

'Kitahachi! Kitahachi!' whispered Yaji, who could just distinguish him in the dim light.

'Who's that?' said Kitahachi. 'Is it Yaji?'

'Don't make a noise,' said Yaji. 'Come here quick.'

'What's the matter?' asked Kita.

'Just hold this,' said Yaji. 'Come a little more this way.'

'Where, where?' asked Kita, stretching up his hands, whereupon Yaji carefully put into his hands the shelf he had been holding up.

'What's this?' asked Kita. 'Yaji, Yaji, what's this?' He tried to take away his hands, but as soon as he did so the shelf began to fall and he had to clutch on to it again. 'I'm in a fix now,' he thought.

'Yaji, Yaji,' he whispered. 'Where are you? My arms are getting tired. Whatever shall I do!'

Confused by the darkness Yaji crept along by the side of the wall till he came to the door into the kitchen. There, by the dim light of a lantern shining from a room across the garden, he saw a recumbent figure by the side of the door, which he took to be that of the girl whom Kita had spoken of. He put out his hand to wake her up, when to his surprise his hand encountered something cold as stone, exactly like a dead person. This is strange, he thought, and feeling round further he found that it was wrapped in a piece of rough straw matting. This gave Yaji a shock and he commenced to shiver and shake as he turned round and made his way back to Kita.

'Are you there?' he whispered, his teeth chattering.

'Is that you, Yaji?' said Kita. 'Just come here a moment.'

'No, no,' said Yaji. 'There's something wrong about this house. There's a dead body covered with a mat over there.'

'What's that?' said Kita. 'You don't mean it?'

'It's true,' said Yaji. 'It's just there. What a horrible place we've come to! Dreadful! Dreadful!'

With that he crept quickly back to his own room.

'Here, here,' whispered Kita. 'Don't leave me here like this. What shall I do? I feel so bad, I can't stand it any more.'

Here he began trembling so violently that he was unable to hold the shelf up and it fell with a crash to the ground with all the things on it. Heedless of what he had done, Kita tried to find his way to his own room, but he was so bewildered that he could only wander round and round.

At the sound of the crash the landlord's voice could be heard from the kitchen. Apparently he was lighting a lamp to come out and see what was the matter. The two countrymen in the inner room were also getting up and they would be coming in and find him there. More and more bewildered finally Kita lay down and covered himself over with a piece of matting which he fortunately found there. Thus covered he stifled his breath and listened to what was happening.

At last the landlord came in carrying a light. 'Whatever's all this?' he said. 'Why, the shelf's fallen down and all the trays and boxes are broken.' While he was picking up the pieces the two countrymen came in.

'What a terrible noise it made,' cried one of them. 'Why, one of the boxes has fallen on our statue of Jizō and broken its nose. Oh dear! Oh dear!'

'Where, where?' asked the other. 'So it has. The nose is broken right off. Is it there? Halloa, who's this sleeping here?'

At the cries of the two countrymen Kita lifted up his head, and peeping out from under the mat saw that what Yaji had taken for a dead body was a stone statue of Jizō, which was wrapped in a coarse piece of matting.

'Who are you?' cried the landlord when he saw Kita. 'Aren't you one of the guests stopping at this inn? What are you doing here? There's something strange about this. Your conduct seems to me suspicious,—very suspicious. Perhaps you are a thief. Did you come here to steal something? You'd better confess.'

'Perhaps this is the man who threw down the shelf and broke off the nose of Jizō,' said one of the countrymen. 'It's a statue of Jizō that we're going to set up in our village. We received it from the stonemason yesterday, and we were going to set it up to-morrow at the Chōtaku temple. Now the nose is broken off it's useless. You'll have to make it good.'

It appears the two countrymen had been sent by the people of the village to bring back the statue of Jizō which was to be erected in the village temple, and as it had become late they had decided to spend the night at the inn.

This made the landlord all the more suspicious. 'The nose of the Jizō can't be helped,' he said, 'but are you sure your baggage is all right? There's no doubt he's a suspicious character, though I don't suppose he'll confess anything.'

'No, no,' said Kita. 'I'm not that sort of man at all. Don't make such assertions. We're quite respectable travellers.'

'He's probably telling a lie,' said one of the countrymen. 'What's he sleeping here for then if he's respectable?'

'I was just going to the closet,' said Kita.

'Don't talk nonsense,' said the landlord. 'Whoever heard of a closet being in a room. Besides you went early in the evening. I can't accept such an excuse as that.'

'Well, I'm really ashamed to say the real reason,' said Kita, 'but I suppose you won't understand unless I do, so I'll tell you quite frankly.'

'You must tell us,' said the landlord. 'What was it?'

'Well, I really feel ashamed to tell you,' said Kita, 'but the reason why I was wandering about here like this was because I was on a love adventure. It was the shelf falling down that upset me.'

'Love adventure, indeed!' said one of the countrymen. 'Don't be absurd. A love adventure with a stone Jizō!'

'The more you talk the more foolish you appear,' said the landlord.

'This is getting serious,' said Kita. 'Here, Yaji, Yaji.'

Yaji, who had been listening for some time convulsed with laughter, at this appeal came into the room.

'Sorry he's given you so much trouble,' he said. 'I'll guarantee his respectability. Please excuse him. As for the broken nose of the Jizō, I'll hold myself responsible for that and see that it's made good.'

Thus Yaji went on uttering all sorts of excuses and apologies until the landlord was fain to accept them, especially as he himself was of the opinion that they were respectable characters. Thus the dispute was settled and they all went to bed again, though it was not long before the cocks were crowing in the dawn and the horses were whinnying in front of the inn.

Aroused by these noises, Yaji and Kita got up, had their breakfasts and started off again.

After they had passed Hamada and were approaching Akaori, they came upon a crowd of men and women gathered in groups on the road. They stopped to see what it was, and Yaji accosted an old man.

'Excuse me,' he said. 'Can you tell me what's the matter?'

'Wait and see,' said the old man.

''Taint a fight, is it?' asked Kita.

'No, no,' said the old man. 'Takoyaku of the Tengai Temple is making a public progress to Kuwana and will pass this way.'

'Aha! I see,' said Yaji. 'He's coming now.'

Along the road came a procession of villagers, with a banner carried in front of them on which the name of the village was inscribed. They were all chanting, 'Namada! Namada! Namada!'

'They don't boil their octupuses here evidently,' said Kita. 'They eat them raw.'

'Look at the face of that chap carrying the banner,' said Yaji. 'He doesn't look as if he had much sense.'

'Make your offerings. Make your offerings,' called the leader of the procession. 'This is the holy Takoyaku of the Tengai

Temple, who came up from the sea and appeared in the middle of a potato field. Believers are required to make offerings of any amount they think fit. Come, who'll make an offering ? '

' I had three platefuls of him this morning,' said Kita.

' Look, he's come,' said Yaji.

The sacred box containing the god here appeared. It was carried on the shoulders of a number of men, and after it came the priests of the Tengai Temple riding in palanquins, at the sight of whom all the old women and wives in the crowd began to cry out for a prayer.

' A prayer, a prayer,' called an acolyte, whereupon the bearers set down the palanquins and opened the doors for the priests to come out. These proved to be fat men, with faces as red as boiled octopuses, all heavily pock-marked.

Immediately the priests got out they all began very earnestly to recite the prayer, ' Namuami ! Namuami ! Namuami ! ' whereupon the crowd repeated ' Namuami ! Namuami ! Namuami ! ' Then the priests repeated it again still more loudly, ' Namuami ! Namuami ! Namuami ! ' and the crowd imitated them, ' Namuami ! Namuami ! Namuami ! ' Then at the end of the prayer something tickled the noses of the priests and they all sneezed simultaneously, ' Akishu ! ' Then all the people, thinking this was a part of the prayer, also sneezed in chorus, ' Akishu ! ' Then the priests in a low voice said, ' Botheration ! ' and all the people said ' Botheration ! ' after them.

' That's a funny prayer,' said Yaji. ' Seems as if the priests wanted to go to Heaven by sneezing.'

After this the procession formed again and the leaders took up their chant of ' Namada ! Namada ! '

Continuing their journey the two travellers soon arrived at Oiwaké, which is famous for its cakes.

' Try our hot cakes,' called the girls at the teahouses. ' Come in and rest. Try our rice-cake stew.'

' That girl to the right is not bad-looking,' said Kita.

' Quite attractive,' said Yaji.

They went in and sat down. ' Will you have some tea ? ' asked the maid.

' Yes, and we'll try some of your cakes,' said Yaji.

The maid went away and soon came back with a tray. There was another traveller sitting in the teahouse, a man who was apparently a pilgrim to the Kompira shrines. He was wearing a short white coat over a heavy, wadded garment.

'Let's have some more cakes,' said Yaji. 'I feel as if I could eat them for ever.'

'That's only your talk,' said Kita.

'You gentlemen are from Edo, I suppose,' said the pilgrim, who was eating rice-cake broth.

'Yes,' said Kita.

'Ah!' said the pilgrim, 'When I was in Edo I ate twenty-eight cakes at the Torikai of Izumi. Very extraordinary!'

'The Torikai?' said Yaji. 'Why, that's quite close to my place. We used to eat fifty or sixty every day for tea.'

'You must have been remarkably fond of them,' said the pilgrim. 'I myself am fond of rice-cakes. As you see I have eaten five platefuls of this rice-cake broth without choking myself.'

'I've eaten fourteen or fifteen of these cakes,' said Yaji, 'and you see I'm still alive. Indeed, I feel as if I hadn't had enough.'

'They're so sickly,' said the pilgrim, 'I don't suppose you could eat any more. Fourteen or fifteen must be about all you can eat.'

'Oh no,' said Yaji. 'I could easily eat some more.'

'You only say that,' said the pilgrim. 'You know you couldn't eat any more.'

'Couldn't eat any more,' cried Yaji. 'If it wasn't that I didn't want to waste my money I'd eat a lot more. If anybody likes to feed me I'll go on eating with pleasure.'

'How interesting!' said the pilgrim. 'I hope you won't mind my offering to pay for those if you eat them.'

'Of course I can,' said Yaji.

'It will be your loss if you fail,' said the pilgrim.

'Of course, of course,' said Yaji. He began to eat with great confidence and got through ten of them. Then he began to feel uneasy, but nevertheless he was not going to let himself be beaten by the pilgrim, and he forced himself to eat the remainder.

'Wonderful! Wonderful!' said the pilgrim. 'I could never do that.'

'Have a try,' said Yaji. 'I could eat any amount of these small ones.'

'I don't think I could really,' said the pilgrim. 'But still I don't like to give in. I'll eat ten of them just to see.'

'What, only ten?' said Yaji. 'Eat twenty. Look here, if

you eat them all up and don't leave one, in return I'll pay for
the cakes and contribute a hundred coppers towards your
expenses.'

'Thank you,' said the pilgrim. 'I'll trust in heaven and have
a try.'

He seemed rather afraid to begin, but at last he started and
munched steadily through ten of them. He made a wry face
over the remaining ten, but finally managed to eat them all up.

Yaji was astonished. 'Wonderful, wonderful!' he said.

'As we agreed,' said the pilgrim, 'may I ask you to pay for the
cakes and to make an offering of a hundred coppers?'

'All right,' said Yaji, 'but it's so wonderful that if you eat
twenty more I'll contribute three hundred coppers, but if you
fail you must give me two hundred coppers. How's that?'

'Fine, fine!' said the pilgrim. 'I'll try even if I burst myself.'

'We'll put up the cash,' said Yaji. 'Just put up two hundred
coppers.'

He himself put out three hundred coppers, thinking that he
would get back the hundred coppers that he had lost and interest
on it into the bargain. He'll never be able to eat twenty more,
he thought as he ordered the cakes. But this time the pilgrim,

without any demur, gulped down the twenty cakes very quickly, and pocketed the three hundred coppers.

'Thank you very much,' said the pilgrim. 'Just pay for the cakes as well, will you? I didn't think I should have such a feast. Ha-ha-ha! Don't disturb yourselves for me,' and he slung his bag on his back and went off without even troubling to look behind him. Yaji was dumbfounded.

'That's a good 'un,' laughed Kita. 'I thought it would turn out like that.'

'It's just my luck,' groaned Yaji. 'I thought I should get that hundred coppers back, but instead of that I've lost some more. What a nuisance!'

Just then a kago came along. 'Won't your honour take a ride?' asked the carriers.

'I'm not worrying about a kago,' said Yaji. 'I'm worrying about the three hundred coppers I lost seeing who could eat most cakes.'

'Aha, that would be the pilgrim we passed just now,' said one of the carriers. 'That fellow's always up to those tricks. He's Kamashichi of Ōtsu, a well known juggler. The other day he had a try who could eat most rice-cakes and made out he'd eaten seventy-eight. He gets people to bet that he can't eat so many cakes and then pretends to eat a lot, but all the time he's putting them up his sleeve. You honour's been tricked. Ha-ha-ha!'

While they were talking two boys on their way to Isé came to the door with three or four cakes in their hands.

'Master,' they cried, 'we've run away to go on pilgrimage. Won't you give us something to help us along the road?'

'Where did you get those cakes, boys?' asked Kita.

'A pilgrim gave them to us out of his sleeve,' said one of the boys.

'Then he only pretended to eat them and cheated me,' cried Yaji. 'I'll run after him and give him a beating.'

'Let him be,' said Kita. 'We're on a pilgrimage ourselves so we must be careful what we do. It was all our own stupidity. Ha-ha-ha.'

'That's all right,' said Yaji, 'but ain't it enough to make your blood boil.'

'It's because you treated me so badly last night,' said Kita. 'It's a punishment on you.'

'It's nothing to laugh about,' said Yaji. 'Here, miss, how much are the cakes?'

'It will be two hundred and thirty-three coppers altogether, your honour,' said the girl.

Yaji paid the money grumbling.

'Just to change your luck, your honour,' said the kago carrier, 'we'll carry you cheap.'

'No, no,' said Yaji.

'Just for drink money,' persisted the carrier.

'Do you drink saké?' asked Yaji.

'Yes, your honour,' said the carrier. 'We're very fond of saké. Won't your honour treat us?'

'No, no,' said Yaji. 'Do you think I'm going to waste more money on saké? Not I. Come on Kita. Let's get on.'

Site of former barrier at Hakoné.

SECOND PART

THEY turned off along the road to Isé, where it separates from the road to Kyōto, and leaving the town on the left they plodded along the moorland road. Soon they came in sight of a man sitting sideways on a farm horse and singing in a shrill voice :—

> She is so hot,
> He who aspires
> To sleep with her
> No clothes requires.

'See how I'll get that man off his horse,' said Yaji. He pulled his dirk out until it stuck a long way out of the scabbard, and then drew his waterproof over his arm so that it appeared as if he was carrying a long sword. When the man came up to him he got off his horse.

'How's that?' asked Yaji triumphantly.

Then came a postboy, also riding sideways and singing :—

> I'll stop the night, I thought, and then,
> Once more I changed my mind again ;
> I cannot call on her without
> My clothes, which are all up the spout.

'I'll get him off his horse too,' said Yaji. He gave a yell, and the postboy got off his horse in alarm immediately.

'What do you think of that, Kita?' asked Yaji.

'Everybody knows that it is the proper thing to alight from your horse when you pass a samurai,' said Kita.

'That's just it,' said Yaji. 'They take me for a samurai.'

'Nonsense,' said Kita. 'Look behind. There are two samurai coming.'

'Are there really?' said Yaji, and turning round he ran into a samurai.

'Can your honours tell me how far it is to Kambé?' he asked, for they looked like two country samurai, acquainted with the neighbourhood.

'At that point between the river bank and the sky,' said one of the samurai, 'it is half way.'

'Thank you, your honour,' said Yaji.

'At that point between the river bank and the sky?' said Kita. 'Boa-constrictors don't crawl on the ceiling. Ha-ha-ha! By the way I wonder what's the name of this river.'

'It's two coppers each,' said the bridge-keeper, 'and this is the River Utsubé.'

Later they crossed the River Takaoka and quickly arrived at Kambé, where they went into a small teahouse on the outskirts of the place to have a rest. By-and-by along came a postboy.

'Won't your honours take a ride?' he asked.

'Well, if you are on your return journey we might ride,' said Yaji.

'I'm going back to Ueno,' said the postboy. 'I'll take you and your baggage for two hundred and fifty coppers.'

'We'll give you a hundred and fifty coppers to carry both of us,' said Kita.

'I haven't got the gear for carrying two people,' said the postboy. 'It's nine miles to Ueno and Shiroko's half way. You might one of you ride and one of you walk and change over there.'

'We don't want to go if we can't both ride,' said Yaji.

'Then how will it do if I tie you both in the saddle?' asked the postboy. 'I've got a rope and it will be quite safe.'

'What an idea,' said Kita. 'We shouldn't be able to smoke.'

'Suppose we take turns in riding and give you a hundred and fifty coppers,' suggested Yaji.

To this the postboy agreed, and their baggage having been fastened on, Kita took the first turn.

'I'll walk on slowly in front,' said Yaji. 'Look out, Kita, the baggage is all on one side.'

'He-he-he!' whinnied the horse and started off with all its bells jingling.

Soon from the opposite direction they saw a man coming towards them. He was dressed in a blue-striped cloak that had been washed and was carrying some strings of coppers in a wrapper over his shoulder.

'Halloa!' he cried on seeing the postboy. 'Aren't you Chota of Ueno? I was just going there. Lucky I met you.'

'Oh, it's Master Gombei, isn't it?' said the postboy. 'Dear me! I feel quite ashamed to meet you.'

'I should think so, I should think so,' said Gombei. 'You know you were to pay me back every month, but you haven't brought me a penny of it. What are you going to do about it? That's what I want to know.'

'Please come over here,' said the postboy. He led the way to a shady place by the side of the road and sat down on the bank. Apparently he was going to explain why he had not been able to pay a debt.

'Don't be angry,' he said. 'Sit down a bit. Take care, there's some dirt there. If I'd known you were coming to-day I'd have had it cleaned. I'm sorry I can't give you some tea or order any saké, Master Gombei, because we're on the road.'

'Look here,' interrupted Kita. 'Can't we be getting on?'

'Don't be in a hurry,' said the postboy. 'Wait a bit. I've got some important business to attend to. You see, Master Gombei, it's like this. My old woman, she's been very sick since last winter and I've got a lot of hungry little devils crying for food, and I can't get even the roughest kind of work. However, I promise I'll bring you the money in four or five days.'

'No, no,' said Gombei, 'that won't do. You always say that but you never bring it. It's three years since I lent you the money. With interest it amounts to over twenty thousand coppers. You must pay up. If you can't I'll take the horse. I got the papers all ready in case they were wanted. No excuses now. Here, master, I'm very sorry, but that horse is wanted to pay off a debt. Please get down.'

'It's enough to drive a fellow silly,' said Kita. 'I've just got on the horse and now you want me to get off. Well, I haven't paid for it yet, so I suppose I may as well.' He got down from the horse.

'Master, master,' said the postboy. 'Don't get off the horse or he'll take it. Please get on again.'

'No, no,' said Gombei.

'It's a shame to take the gentleman's horse,' said the postboy. 'Please get on, sir.'

'Get on again?' said Kita. 'Well, here goes,' and he got on again.

'What are you doing, Chota?' said Gombei, who was getting furious. 'Please get off, sir.'

'What, get off again?' said Kita. 'You're playing with me. I'm getting tired of this getting on and off.'

'Yes, but it's my horse,' said Gombei. 'Please get down.'

'What a trouble you are,' said Kita, peevishly, and he jumped off again.

'Don't get off, don't get off,' said the postboy. 'Look here, Master Gombei, I'll tell you what. I can't do anything here. Wait till I get to my house. Or if that won't do I'll give you these clothes.'

'I know you,' said Gombei. 'You want to get away.'

'No, no,' said the postboy. 'Please, master, get on.'

'What, get on again?' said Kita. 'You'll have to excuse me this time. I'm going to walk, I am, I don't care how cheap it is, I don't want to ride.'

'Don't say that, sir,' said the postboy. 'It's all right this time. There!'

He caught hold of the horse's bridle and held it, so there was nothing for Kita to do but to get on again.

'Just hand over those clothes, as you promised,' said Gombei.

'No, no,' said the postboy. 'You must wait till I get home.'

'None of your tricks,' said Gombei. 'Master, please get off that horse again.'

'The country bumpkins!' said Kita. 'Now they say I've got to get off again! No, no, I've had enough of that. Let's get on.'

'That's right, master,' said the postboy. 'Don't get off.'

'He must get off,' said Gombei angrily, but as he went to catch hold of the horse the postboy struck it hard, and the horse started off at full gallop with Kita on its back.

'Stop, stop,' shouted Kita, pallid with fear. 'Help, help!'

'What did you want to make the horse run away for?' said Gombei, and he ran after it.

Kita clung on to the saddle with both hands, for dear life, while the horse went on helter-skelter, till at last, able to hold on no longer, he fell off, catching his feet in the bridle as he did so and turning head over heels.

'Oh, oh, oh!' he groaned. 'Where's everybody? Oh, oh!' and he lay there groaning till the postboy came running up.

'Hope you haven't hurt yourself,' he said, as he ran up to Kita. But just then he caught sight of Gombei trying to catch the horse and he rushed off to stop him, leaving Kita to look after himself.

'Here, wait for me,' called Kita. 'Look what you've done to me.'

Grumbling he got up. He felt very angry, but he had hurt himself too badly to run after them, and all he could do was to limp along till he reached the village of Yabasé.

In the meantime Yaji had gone along quite unconscious of the trouble about the horse, but as he thought it strange that Kita did not overtake him he decided at last to wait till he came up.

'Halloa!' he cried when Kita came in sight. 'What's the matter?'

'I can't tell you what I've suffered,' said Kita, and he told Yaji all that had happened to him, much to Yaji's amusement.

At Isoyama they came upon a stall where an old man was inviting passers-by to test their skill with a blowpipe.

'Try your luck,' he called. 'Here's the Forty-seven Rōnin in eleven scenes. Try that. Blow up. Blow up. Everything you hit turns into something else. Here you are! Here you are!'

'Eh, what's this?' said Kita. '*The dream-pillow of Kampei and Okaru?* Let's have a try at that.'

He put an arrow in the blowpipe and blew, striking the tablet, which fell with a click.

'What's that come out?' said Yaji. 'Why, it's a big mushroom. Ha-ha-ha! This is amusing. What's that over there? The dark night of Koyue Yoichibei? Wonder what will come out there.'

He blew a dart and struck the tablet. 'Halloa!' he cried. 'It's the priest Mikoshi. Ha-ha-ha! What's that over there, Kita. Try that one.'

Just as he was going to blow, however, he trod on a dog that was sleeping in front of the stall, making it howl.

'Get out, you cur,' said Yaji, and he struck at the dog with the blowpipe, whereupon the dog bit him. It was now Yaji's turn to howl, and he was running after the dog when he slipped and fell. Just where he fell was a tobacco pouch lying on the ground.

'I shan't lose by falling,' he said. 'Here's a tobacco pouch.'

He was just about to pick it up when a little boy on the other side of the road drew it away with a string he had fastened to it.

'Well, I'm blowed!' said Yaji. 'What a sell!'

'Fool, fool!' screamed the small boy and went off laughing.

'That's a good trick,' said Kita. 'Come on.'

They paid the blowpipe man and were going along again when they saw a tobacco-pipe lying by the side of the road.

'Ain't you going to pick that up, Yaji?' asked Kita.

'No, no,' said Yaji. 'I'm not to be caught twice. Let that old chap following us pick it up.' They went past it and then turned round just in time to see the old man pick it up, shove it in his bosom, and walk off quickly.

'Well I never!' said Yaji. 'It wasn't a sell after all.'

'That makes you feel bad, doesn't it?' laughed Kita.

Thus joking and laughing they went on till they reached Ueno, where they were accosted by a man in a cloak, who was accompanied by an apprentice.

'Excuse me, gentlemen,' he said. 'Are you from Edo?'

'Yes,' said Yaji.

'I have been walking after you from Shiroko,' said the man, 'listening to your poems, and although I am only an amateur in such matters, I must say I was considerably impressed.'

'Oh, that's nothing,' said Yaji. 'I made all those up on the spur of the moment.'

'Really,' said the stranger. 'I am surprised. The other day I had a visit from Shunman Shōsadō and others from Edo.'

'Did you really?' said Yaji. 'Aha!'

'May I ask under what name you write?' continued the stranger.

'Oh, I'm Jippensha Ikku,' said Yaji.

'Indeed,' said the man. 'That's a very celebrated name. Are you really Jippensha Ikku? I'm very glad to meet you. My name is Kabocha Gomajiru. Are you going to Isé on this journey?'

'Yes,' said Yaji. 'I came on this journey especially to write Hizakurigé.'

'Dear me,' said Gomajiru. 'That's a strange way of writing a book. I suppose your friends at Nagoya, Yoshida and Okazaki, will come and meet you.'

'Well, you see,' said Yaji, 'as I have to call at every place on the Tokaidō and as the entertainments offered me naturally delay my journey, I thought it would be a bother to them to have to wait for me, so they've all gone straight there. That's the reason why I'm travelling in common clothes just like an ordinary person, —so that I can take my ease and do just as I please.'

'That must be very enjoyable,' said Gomajiru. 'My house is at Kumotsu. I should be very glad if you would pay me a visit.'

'Thank you very much,' said Yaji.

'Truly you would be a most welcome guest,' continued Gomajiru. 'I should like to introduce you to some people in the neighbourhood. In any case I should like to accompany you for the next stage. How extremely fortunate it was that I met you just when I did. But here is Ogawa, which is famous for its cakes. Shall we take a rest?'

'No, no,' said Yaji. 'I've had enough cakes. Let's go straight on.'

Proceeding on their way, therefore, they soon reached Tsu. This is the place where the road from Kyōto meets the road to Yamada, and in consequence the streets are very lively with people from the capital, all dressed in the same kind of clothes, riding on led horses, and singing :—

Oh come, and I will show to you
The famous sights, the temples high,
The hill of Otowa and there
Where Kiyomizu and Gion fair
Tell of days gone by.

193

Within a pearly haze they lie
Of cherry blossoms in full flower;
So dark it is that one would think
It was the evening hour.

'Look, Kita,' said Yaji. 'How beautiful the girls all look.'

'They're Kyōto people,' said Gomajiru. 'But although they all look so grand they don't waste their money.'

Just then one of them stopped Gomajiru and asked him for a light.

'Take one from here,' said Gomajiru, and he held out the pipe which he was smoking. The Kyōto man put his pipe to it and sucked.

'Can't you get it?' asked Gomajiru. Still the stranger went on sucking without saying a word.

'What's this?' said Gomajiru. 'Why, you haven't got any tobacco in your pipe. I've heard of this before. You pretend you want a light, and all the time you go on smoking other people's tobacco. That's enough, that's enough. There,' he added, turning to Yaji. 'That's how stingy the Kyōto people are. Ha-ha-ha! Would you oblige me with another pinch of your tobacco.'

'Well, I don't know about Kyōto people being stingy,' said Yaji, 'but I notice you're very fond of smoking my tobacco.'

'I didn't bring my tobacco pouch with me,' said Gomajiru.

'Did you forget it when you came out?' asked Yaji.

'No, no, I didn't forget it,' said Gomajiru. 'The fact is I haven't got a pouch, the reason being that I'm such an inveterate smoker that I found I was spending too much money on tobacco. So I gave up carrying a pouch and only carry a pipe.'

'Is that so that you can smoke other people's tobacco?' asked Yaji.

'Yes, certainly,' said Gomajiru.

'So while you call Kyōto people stingy, you're stingy yourself.'

'Ha-ha-ha!' laughed Gomajiru. 'That's so, that's so. But hadn't we better walk a little faster, as it's getting late.'

Quickening their pace they soon arrived at Tsukimoto, from which place, they learnt, there is a road to Karasu-no-miya. Then they came to Kumotsu, where Gomajiru led them to his house. This appeared to be an inn, although there were no other guests there just then. They were shown into a back room and treated with great respect, evidently because Yaji had told a lie about his name. Both he and Kitahachi thought it all very amusing, and after taking a bath they put themselves at their ease. Then Gomajiru came in.

'You must be very tired,' he said. 'Please make yourselves comfortable. Unfortunately there is no fish to-day, so I shall not be able to give you much of a feast, but as the *konnyaku* here is very good I thought you would like to try that.'

'Please don't take any trouble about us,' said Yaji. 'But, landlord, I'd like to introduce my friend.'

'Oh really,' said the landlord. 'To whom have I the pleasure of speaking ? '

'I'm Jippensha's best pupil,' said Kita, 'by name Ippensha Nanryo. This is my only excuse for troubling you.'

'Not at all, not at all,' said Gomajiru. 'Please make yourself at home.'

The maid here announced that the meal was ready.

'Then you'd better have it at once,' said Gomajiru. 'Please take your time.' He hurried off to the kitchen and the maid brought in a tray and put it before Yaji.

'Not bad, is it ? ' said Yaji looking at the tray.

'Fine girl,' said Kita. 'But as you're a poet now you've got to be good.'

Then a small girl of eleven or twelve brought in another tray and put it before Kita, and they both took up their chopsticks to eat. On both their trays there was a black thing, about the size of a bean-cake, put on a flat saucer beside the *konnyaku*, which was heaped up in a bowl, and some bean-paste on a small plate.

'Whatever's this ? ' said Yaji in a low voice to Kita,—'this round thing on the saucer ? '

'I don't know I'm sure,' said Kita. He felt it with his chopsticks, but it was so hard that he couldn't make an impression on it. Examining it more closely he found it was a stone.

'It's a stone,' he said.

'What, a stone ? ' said Yaji. 'Here, waitress, what's this ? '

'It's a stone, your honour,' said the maid.

'Dear me,' said Kita. 'Just give me a little more soup.'

He gave his soup bowl to the girl and waited till she had gone out.

'What a swindle ! ' said Yaji. 'How can we eat stones ? '

'Wait a bit,' said Kita. 'There must be some way of eating it as they've served it. He said he'd give us some of the things this place is noted for and I suppose this must be one of them.'

'I never heard of such a thing,' said Yaji.

'Wait a bit,' said Kita. 'You know they call dumplings stones in Edo. Perhaps it's a dumpling.'

'Aha!' said Yaji. 'That's it, that's it. It can't be a real stone.'

He poked it with his chopsticks, but still it appeared to be a real stone. Then he struck it with the bowl of his pipe, and it sounded like a stone.

'It's a stone all right,' he said. 'I suppose it would make him angry if we asked him how we were to eat it, but it's very strange.'

Then Gomajiru came in.

'Really I'm ashamed of the poor fare I have to offer you,' he said, 'but please eat heartily. I'm afraid the stones have got cold. Let me change them for some hot ones.'

At this the two travellers became more and more puzzled as to how the stones were to be eaten, but still they didn't like to ask for fear of offending the landlord.

'Don't trouble, don't trouble,' said Yaji, trying to look as if he had been eating the stone. 'One stone will be enough, though they're very nice. In Edo, you know, they serve gravel pickled in hot pepper sauce or with boiled beans, and we also give stones to troublesome mothers-in-law as a kind of medicine. They're my favourite food. Why, when I was living in Fuchū, we used to have stones stewed like turtles. Really, when I had eaten four or five my stomach used to get so heavy that I couldn't stand up. I had to be tied to a stick and be carried along like a kago when I wanted to go anywhere. Your stones are especially delicious but I'm afraid of eating too many for fear I should incommode you.'

'What's that?' said Gomajiru. 'Have you been eating the stones?'

'What of it?' said Yaji.

'It's incredible,' said Gomajiru. 'Why, to eat stones you would have to have terribly strong teeth. Besides, you'd burn yourself.'

'Why?' asked Yaji.

'Those stones are red hot,' replied Gomajiru. 'They're meant to lay the *konnyaku* on so as to take out the water and improve the flavour. That is why they're hot. They aren't to eat.'

'Aha! I see, I see,' said Yaji. 'Now I understand.'

'You shall see for yourselves,' said Gomajiru. He ordered the maid to change the stones for hot ones. Then Yaji and Kita put the *konnyaku* on the stones as he had told them, which made the *konnyaku* hiss, and then they ate it with the bean sauce and found it exceptionally light and well-flavoured. They were greatly impressed.

'I never saw such a strange way of cooking before,' said Yaji. 'The stones are all so much alike.'

'I have a store of them,' said Gomajiru. 'Shall I show you?' He went into the kitchen and brought in a box such as soup bowls are kept in.

'Look,' he said. 'I have enough here for twenty guests.' Sure enough there were the stones inside, while written on the box was '*Konnyaku* stones for twenty people.'

By this time all the poets in the neighbourhood had begun to assemble at the door. 'Excuse us,' they cried.

'Dear me!' said Gomajiru. 'Is that you, Master Baldpate? Please all come this way.'

'Are you Jippensha Ikku?' said the first to enter. 'This is

the first time I have had the honour of meeting you. I am Awfully Funnyman. The gentleman next to me is Master Gaptooth, then comes Master Snottyface, and the one farthest away is Master Scratchy. Please give us all the honour of your acquaintance.'

'By the way, master,' said Gomajiru, 'if it is not troubling you too much, would you be so kind as to write one of your poems on a fan or a scroll?' He brought out a fan and a scroll as he said this.

Yaji was greatly perplexed as to what he should do. Should he carry out his joke boldly? But then he had no poems of his own and he couldn't think of one on the spur of the moment. He decided that he would write a poem by somebody else, and he wrote one.

'Thank you, thank you,' said Gomajiru. 'The poem reads:

> Where can I hear the cuckoo sing?
> Far from the wine-shop's roistering;
> Far from the cook-shop's guzzling throng,
> There can you hear the cuckoo's song.

'Dear me!' said Gomajiru. 'I seem to have heard that poem before.' Then he read another:

> Would you know of lovers' sorrow?
> Ring the dawn bell once again;
> For it brings the fatal morrow
> Tells them they must part in pain.

'But isn't this poem by Senshuan?' asked Gomajiru.

'What are you talking about?' said Yaji. 'That's one of my best poems. It's a very well known poem in Edo. Everyone knows it.'

'Yes, but when I was up in Edo last year,' said Gomajiru, 'I saw Sandara and Shakuyakutei Ushi and others, and I brought back that very poem and pasted it on the screen behind you. It is in the poet's own handwriting.'

Yaji turned round and saw on the screen the very poem that he had written.

'My master's very careless,' put in Kita, 'and can't tell the difference between his own poems and those of others. Look here, Yaji—I mean master—write one of the poems you made up on the road.'

Yaji, though he was rather out of countenance, put his usual bold face on it and commenced to write another poem, one of those he had made up on the road.

Meanwhile Kita, who had nothing to do, fixed his eyes upon a screen.

'Aha!' he said. 'That's a picture of Koikawa Harumachi. What's that phrase (*san*) written above it.'

'That's a poem (*shi*),' said Gomajiru.

'And that poem (*shi*) above the god of good luck,' asked Kita, 'who did that?'

'No, that's a religious maxim (*go*) written by the priest Takuan,' said Gomajiru.

'What a chap this is,' thought Kita. 'When I say it's *san* (three) he says it's *shi* (four), and when I say it's *shi* (four) he says it's *go* (five). Whatever I say he always goes one more. I'll catch him yet.'

'I say,' he said aloud, after he had looked round, 'that written on top of that hanging scroll,—I suppose that's *roku* (six).'

'I don't know whether it's six or what it is,' said Gomajiru. 'It was taken as a pledge (*shichi*=seven).'

Just then the maidservant came in. 'A letter has come from Master Higetsuru,' she said.

'Dear me!' said Gomajiru. 'I wonder what it is about.' He opened it and read it aloud:—'This is to inform you that Jippensha Ikku has just arrived at my house from Edo and has brought letters of introduction from his friends at Nagoya. I hasten to inform you at once of the news and shall later take the liberty of accompanying him to your house. This in the meantime.'

'What can be the meaning of this?' said Gomajiru. 'I can't understand it at all. You hear what my friend says, master. It seems that this man is taking your name. Luckily he will soon be here and you will be able to confront him. Don't you think we should have some fun with him?'

'I never heard of such impudence,' said Yaji. 'But still I don't think I'd care to meet him.'

'Why, why?' asked Gomajiru.

'Well, just a minute ago,' said Yaji, 'I felt a touch of my old complaint, the colic. If it hadn't been for that I should have shown him up. It's a great nuisance.'

This unexpected coincidence made Yaji feel very miserable, and his behaviour increased the suspicions of the landlord and his guests that he was trying to deceive them. They now began to press him with questions.

'Look here, master,' said Master Funnyman, 'this is a very strange thing that's happened. Even if you don't feel well I think you certainly ought to meet the false Jippensha.'

'Don't ask me, don't ask me,' said Yaji.

'By the way, master,' said Master Snottyface, 'where is your house in Edo?'

'Let's see,' said Yaji. 'Where is it? Is it in Toba, or Fushimi, or Yodotaké?'

'Oh yes,' said Master Scratchy, 'you cross the ferry at Yamazaki and ask for Master Yoichibei. Get out. Ha-ha-ha!'

'But I see you have written on your hat Yajirobei, Hachō-bōri, Kanda, Edo,' said Gomajiru. 'Who is this Yajirobei?'

'Aha!' said Yaji. 'Where have I heard that name before? Oh yes, of course. My real name is Yajirobei.'

'Oh, you're one of the Yajirobeis that go round begging with the dolls I suppose,' said Gomajiru.

'That's it, that's it,' said Yaji.

'Well, Master Yajirobei,' said Funnyman, 'shall I bring the false Ikku?

'No, no,' said Yaji. 'No, no. I'm just going.'

'Why, what do you think the time is?' said Gomajiru. 'It's ten o'clock.'

'Maybe, maybe,' said Yaji. 'It's my colic. If I sit like this it gets worse and worse. When I get out in the cool night air and walk a bit it soon gets better.'

'So you're going to start now,' said Gomajiru. 'Well, I'm agreeable. At any rate you can't stop here,—taking other persons' names like that and deceiving everybody. Get out.'

'How have I been deceiving you?' asked Yaji.

'How have you deceived us? Didn't the real Jippensha bring letters from his friends at Nagoya?' said Gomajiru. 'There's no getting over that.'

'I thought they were cheats from the first?' said another. 'Get out before we throw you out.'

'Throw us out?' said Yaji. 'Don't be ridiculous.'

'Look here, Yaji,' said Kita. 'Don't let's have a row. We're in the wrong. Let's go somewhere else and stop, even at a cheap lodging house. We're very sorry if we've done anything wrong.'

Kita thus went on repeating apologies to the landlord, who was half angry and half amused.

While they were getting ready to start, all the people in the house came to see them off and jeered and laughed and clapped their hands. Yaji, with a very angry face and a dignified air, walked out followed by Kita.

It was now past ten and everybody had gone to bed. Yaji and Kita walked on, but they could not see any inn, nor anybody in the street to ask, the only things astir being the dogs under the eaves of the houses, and they only barked at them.

'These curs!' said Yaji. 'I'll serve them out,' and he picked up a stone and threw it at the dogs. This only made them more angry, and they ran after the travellers, barking furiously.

'Don't take any notice of them,' said Kita. 'Even the dogs despise us. What are you making those strange signs for?'

'When you're attacked by dogs,' said Yaji, 'if you make the character for tiger in the air and show it to them they'll run away. They don't seem to run away here, though. Perhaps the dogs in this town can't read. Here, shoo, shoo!'

In one way and another they managed to get rid of the dogs, and then went on. Very soon they unexpectedly came to the end of the town.

'We're in a fix now,' said Yaji. 'I'll tell you what. Let's walk all night. That would show our mettle. Come on.'

'Don't be a fool,' said Kita. 'It isn't midnight yet. There must be some place to stop at.'

'There isn't a house where they haven't gone to bed,' said Yaji. 'Yes, there is. You can see a faint light over there. Let's go and ask there where there's an inn.'

'That's a good idea,' said Kita. 'But isn't it a lantern?'

'What nonsense,' said Yaji. 'The light's coming through the cracks of a door.'

'Yes, it's a light in a house,' said Kita. 'At any rate we'll ask'

They walked along faster, but as they drew nearer they were startled to see that the light was moving along in front of them.

'Halloa!' said Yaji. 'That house seems to be walking along too.'

'So it does,' said Kita. 'That's funny.'

'I don't see anything funny about it,' said Yaji. 'It seems to me rather queer. Did you ever hear of a country where the houses walked?'

'It's like what happened when we stopped at Akasaka,' said Kita, 'when the foxes bewitched us. If we don't put a brave face on it they'll bewitch us again. Let's walk faster and not take any notice.'

So they plucked up their courage and walked faster and faster until they caught up to the light, which proved to be only a brazier on a cripple's barrow, where he had lit a fire to make himself some tea. He was pushing the barrow along while the water was getting hot. They laughed over their mistake and passed him, but the loneliness of the road soon made them fearful. Sometimes the moon came out of the clouds for a little, but generally it was dark, and to walk in the dead of night, with no one out on the road and everything silent, made them tremble, however bold they pretended to be.

At last they heard someone coming up behind them, and Yaji turning round to look saw that he was a tall man wearing a long sword.

'There's a suspicious-looking man behind us,' whispered Yaji to Kita. 'Let's get on a bit faster.'

But the faster they walked the faster the man behind came on.

'Wait, wait,' cried Kita. 'I shall burst unless I relieve myself.' But when he stopped to do this the man behind also stopped.

'I say,' called out Yaji in a trembling voice, 'where are you going?'

'I'm going back to Matsuzaka,' said the man in an unexpectedly mild voice, 'but I was so afraid of the dark that I was thinking what I should do when I heard you coming along. Then I thought I should have good company, so I was trusting in you.'

'Well, you don't seem very brave by your voice,' said Kita. 'But why are you wearing that long thing stuck in your sash?'

'Oh this?' said the man. 'This is a bamboo stick I picked up,' and he pulled it out of his girdle and showed them that it was a cane.

'Oh, it isn't a sword then,' said Yaji. 'You seemed so frightened that we've been wondering for a long time what sort of man you were. Really, you are a coward,—quite different to me.'

'There's three of us now,' said Kita, 'so it's perfectly safe.'

'But there's something dreadful ahead,' said the man.

'What sort of thing?' asked Yaji.

'I'll tell you,' said the man. 'I had to go as far as Edo Bridge to-day, and going back I got such a fright. A little further on there's a pinewood, and when I got up to that I saw a great white thing standing there. It was swaying backwards and forwards and shivering and shaking. I tell you it gave me a real fright. I thought I should have died. I was too frightened to go on so I turned round and came back to see if I could meet anyone to go with me, and then I saw you.'

' Eh ! ' said Yaji. ' Where did you see this great white thing ? '

' It's just a little further along,' said the man.

' What can it be ? ' said Yaji. ' I'll go along and see. You come with me.'

They went along all together till they came to the pinewood.

' There,' cried the man suddenly. ' Don't you see it ? ' and he began trembling violently.

By the pale light of the moon they could see a strange white thing right in the middle of the path. What it could be they could not guess. Sometimes it looked big and sometimes it looked small, and sometimes it disappeared altogether.

' Whatever can it be ? ' said Yaji.

' It's not got any feet, so it must be a ghost,' said Kita.

' Yes,' said the man. ' However can we pass it ? '

' We can't go this way,' said Yaji. ' We'll have to turn back. It gives me the creeps to see it.'

' I had to turn back before,' said the man, ' because I was too frightened to pass it by myself. Now I've got you with me you're frightened too, so if we turn back to find others we may spend the whole night going backwards and forwards.'

' It's all in white, so it must be a ghost,' said Yaji.

' Do you see that blue light ? ' said Kita.

' It looks as if it was coming this way,' said the man.

' What shall we do ? ' said Yaji. ' We can't go on.'

As the three stood there trembling, with pale faces, occasionally looking behind them to see if anybody was coming, they heard a sound of singing.

> The load of love !
> Ah, who can say
> What weight it does
> Upon them lay ?

Soon they distinguished three workmen coming along the road.

' Where have you come from ? ' asked Yaji in a trembling voice.

'Oh, we live in the neighbourhood,' replied one of them, 'and we're just going to Tsu on business.'

'However did you come this way?' asked Yaji.

'What's the matter with the man?' they replied. 'Didn't we say we were going to Tsu?'

'You're not ghosts, are you?' asked Yaji. 'I don't see how living beings could come through it.'

'What are you talking about?' they cried. 'We can't understand you.'

'Look here,' said Kita. 'There's a ghost along the road you came. How did you pass it?'

'You've been bewitched by the fox of Miwatari,' they cried.

'Well, see for yourself,' said Kita.

'See what?' they asked.

'That white thing there,' said Kita.

'White thing?' they said. 'Oh, that. That's a fire smouldering in the middle of the road. The smoke looks white by the light of the moon.'

'Ha-ha-ha!' laughed Yaji. 'That's it, is it? Thank you, thank you,' and breathing a sigh of relief they went on. When they got to the place they found that somebody had swept up a quantity of rubbish and had set it alight, and it was the smoke rising from the fire that they had seen.

Continuing on their way the two travellers arrived at Matsuzaka, where, as it was very late and they did not want the expense of going to an inn, they got their companion to show them to a cheap lodging-house, where they spent the night.

Starting off early next morning, the two travellers went on till they came to Myōjō, where they took a rest at a teahouse. Here they found a Westcountryman who was bargaining with a postboy for a ride. He was dressed in a broadstriped cloak of a gay pattern, and carried an account book and a bundle on his back.

'Masters' said the postboy, 'wouldn't you like to let this horse carry your baggage and one of you ride with this gentleman?'

'You gentlemen are bound for the Grand Shrine, I suppose,' said the countryman. 'I myself am going as far as Furuichi to collect a bill. If one of you would ride with me no doubt we could have some pleasant talk.'

'I do feel a bit tired after last night,' said Yaji. 'I think I'll ride, Kita.'

'Then carry the baggage too,' said Kita.

After they had fixed a price with the postboy, Yaji and the countryman, with all the baggage, got on the horse.

'Hin-hin-hin!' whinnied the horse, and off they started.

'You are from Edo, I suppose,' said the countryman.

'Yes,' said Yaji.

'Edo's supposed to be a fine place,' said the countryman, 'but I had a bad time of it when I went there last year. It didn't suit me at all because wherever I went I found the closets so dirty. I must have gone a hundred days without doing anything, and then when I was leaving Edo I got to a place called Suzu-ga-mori, I think. I was glad. I'll do it here, I thought, and I poured into the sea all that I had saved up. I must have done seven gallons at one go. It was a relief. It was the prettiest and largest jakes ever seen. Ha-ha-ha!'

'Nowadays it's in such demand that they exchange vegetables for it,' said Yaji. 'Pity you wasted it in the sea. You could have exchanged it for five or six horseloads of vegetables. Also, when you want to break wind you ought to run out into the garden and break it over the vegetables to make them grow.'

'Yes,' said the countryman. 'Vegetables treated like that are sliced up and mixed with plaster, when they call it wind-vegetable-plaster.'

'Kyōto people are generally frightfully stingy,' said Yaji. 'Last time I went there was in March, when all the flowers were in full bloom. The people were all sitting outside surrounded by curtains and admiring the flowers, and eating out of magnificent embossed lacquer boxes. But what do you think they were eating? Pickles and bean-powder. I was astonished.'

'Well, when I was up in Edo,' said the countryman, 'they were boasting about the beautiful cherry-blossoms at Yoshiwara. So I went to Yoshiwara on purpose to see them, but I couldn't find any cherry-blossoms there at all.'

'At what time of the year did you go?' asked Yaji.

'It was in October,' said the countryman.

'Whoever heard of cherry trees being in flower in October?' cried Yaji.

'Yes, but at Omuro and Arashiyama in Kyōto,' said the countryman, 'we have cherries all the year round.'

'That would be only the trees,' said Yaji. 'The flowers don't bloom all the year round.'

'Well, I don't know about that,' said the countryman. 'And

then at Edo they're very fond of those long songs, but they don't compare with the Kyōto Miyazono and Kunidaiyu.'

'What sort of a song do you call a Kunidaiyu?' asked Yaji.

'It's like this,' said the countryman, and he began to sing very solemnly :—

> When I am free,
> If you'll marry me,
> We'll live together
> In close company.

'That's good,' said Yaji, when he had finished. 'I must get you to teach me.'

'Oh, that's easy,' said the countryman. 'You've only got to imitate me.'

Kita, who was following behind, here stopped and picked up a bamboo wand that was lying by the side of the road. He thought that the countryman was boasting too much and he had an idea of paying him back. The countryman, however, was quite lost to the world, and, unconscious of what Kita was intending to do, sang another song :—

> That women are spiteful is quite true,
> For after death they'll torment you;
> As demons there among the dead,
> They'll raise their wands to strike your head.

Then, just at the end of the song, Kita brought down his stick on the countryman's head with a tremendous whack.

'Hi! Hi!' shouted the countryman. 'What's that? You'll break my head.'

'Ha-ha-ha!' laughed Yaji. 'Just sing it again.'

The countryman was persuaded to sing it again, but again, just at the end, Kita brought his stick down on his head.

'Oh! Oh!' yelled the countryman. 'Stop it. Stop it.'

He turned round to see who it was, but Kita had hidden himself on the other side of the horse and he could see no one.

'That's a good song,' said Yaji, 'but the tune's awfully difficult. Just sing it once more.'

'I don't mind singing it as many times as you like,' said the countryman, 'if you don't hit me on the head.'

'Of course,' said Yaji. 'I'll take care of that.'

'Then I'll sing it again,' said the countryman.

> That women are spiteful is quite true,
> For after death they'll follow you,
> Tormenting demons in hell they'll be
> To use their whips on you and me.

Kita was going to hit him again on the head at the end of the song, but somehow he missed his aim and instead hit Yaji.

'Oh! Oh!' yelled Yaji. 'That's my head, Kita. What are you doing?'

'It was you that hit my head, was it?' said the countryman. 'What did you want to do that for?'

'I don't remember doing it,' said Kita.

'You can't deny it,' said the countryman.

'I don't know anything about it, I tell you,' said Kita. 'What an obstinate chap you are.'

'Who are you calling chap?' asked the countryman. 'You're very free with your tongue.'

'Get out, you old fool,' said Kita. 'It's you that have been talking big. I'll throw you off the horse if you say much.'

'Oh, indeed,' said the countryman. 'Let's see you do it.'

'All right, I'll make you turn head over heels,' said Kita, and he gave the horse a whack on the loins which made it rear up.

'Oh, oh!' yelled the countryman. 'What are you doing?'

'Oh, oh, oh!' yelled Yaji in turn.

'Woa! Woa!' cried the postboy.

By this time they had got to Kobata, where Yaji and the country-man got off the horse and they all went into a teahouse.

'What do you mean by hitting me on the head?' said the countryman to Kita.

'There, there,' said Yaji soothingly. 'All sorts of things happen to you when you're travelling. Just make it up and I'll buy you some saké.' He called to the maid to bring out some saké.

This started a drinking bout, in the course of which the country-man got very mellow.

'I'm awfully drunk,' he said. 'But, Master Yaji, I like you, though I don't like your friend,—don't like him at all. But as you're travelling together that can't be helped. I'll tell you what we'll do. We'll stop in Myōkenchō at Yamada and then go on to Furuichi together and enjoy ourselves. They know me well there. I'll show you the Tambourine Chamber at the Chizukaya and the Pine Chamber at the Kashiwaya. Won't you come? What do you think?'

This is a boastful old chap, thought Yaji. I'll encourage him in his boasting and go with him. 'That's splendid,' he said aloud. 'Come on, let's go together.'

'We'll have a meal at the Matsuzakaya at Sako,' said the countryman, 'and then go on to the Fujiya at Myōkenchō. Come along, come along.'

'Yes, let's go,' said Yaji.

Paying for the saké they started off and soon arrived at Yamada.

THIRD PART

THE town of Yamada, a name which is stated in the Kawasaki *Ondo,* the song which they sing at Yamada in Isé, to be derived from the name Yōda, has twelve streets and nine thousand houses, all neatly arranged and showing great simplicity of structure and dignity of style. Naturally, as residents in the capital of the gods, the people have a suavity and calmness which distinguish them from those of other parts, and as the town is visited by a constant stream of travellers, it is, of course, exceedingly prosperous. As Yajirobei, Kitahachi and the countryman went through the streets they saw that each house had a tablet at the door bearing the name of a Shintō priest, this giving the houses the air of being places of business. A number of samurai, assistants of the priests, in full ceremonial dress, were riding rapidly backwards and forwards to meet the travellers as they came through the streets. One of them drew near to Yaji.

'May I ask where you are going?' he said.

'We're going to the Grand Shrine, of course,' replied Yaji.

'No, I mean to what priest,' said the man.

'Lord Gidayu Takemoto,' said Yaji.

'Gidayu?' said the samurai. 'Where is he?'

'Oh, he's in Dotombōri, in Ōsaka,' said Yaji.

'He's well known also at Shijō in Kyōto and at Fukiyachō in Edo,' put in Kita.

'Are you beggars then?' asked the samurai.

'If we have any of your insolence you'll get a beating,' said Kita.

'Listen to the boaster,' said the samurai. 'Ha-ha-ha!'

'Let's go and have a rest somewhere,' said the countryman.

'This place seems awfully dirty,' said Kita. 'It looks as if all the priests were engaged in doing some business for themselves.'

'Get out,' said Yaji. 'Ha-ha-ha!'

The three then went into a teahouse for a short rest. While they were sitting there a party of Westcountry people, both men and women, all dressed in the same style, came along singing, and following them was a band of twenty pilgrims, riding in kago sent from a temple, with one of the priests' assistants as a guide.

'Here it is,' he called. 'Here it is. Everybody will alight here and take a rest.'

At this all the pilgrims got out of the kago and came into the teahouse. Apparently they were from Edo. Each of them wore a tight-sleeved kimono and carried a short sword. Among them was a man who immediately accosted Yaji when he saw him.

'Halloa, Master Yaji,' he said. 'Have you come to Isé?'

Yaji was astonished for a moment, but looking at the man attentively he recognised him as the rice-dealer Tarobei, who lived in the same street in Edo. It fact, he was the very rice-dealer whose bill he had left unpaid when he set out from the city.

'Halloa, Master Tarobei,' he said shamefacedly. 'Glad to meet you, though it's rather embarrassing.'

'Not a bit,' said Tarobei. 'I'm one of a party here,—in fact they look upon me as the leader, so I had to come. But I'm glad to see you. It does one's eyes good to see an old friend when you're travelling. Let's go in and have a cup.'

'Thank you,' said Yaji.

'Who's your companion?' asked Tarobei. 'I think I've seen him before. Glad to meet you both. Won't you join our party? It won't cost you much, or if you join as my servant it won't cost you anything, and you can have a good feed. What do you say?'

'I should like nothing better if I may,' replied Yaji.

'That's all right,' said Tarobei. 'I'm the leader of the party so that will be all right. Come in, come in.'

Yaji took off his sandals and having told the countryman to wait for him, went in.

'Come along, come along, the two of you,' said Tarobei, and Kita also went in.

The countryman continued to sit in front of the teahouse and drink his saké, while inside all were feasting and talking and laughing. Soon another party of travellers arrived in kago, the leader this time being a Westcountryman.

'Ho-yoi-yoi! Ekkorasassa! Ekkorasassa!' cried the kago carriers and the kago were set down and all the party entered the teahouse. They were ushered into an inner room by a maid, and they also began to feast and make merry. It so happened that both parties finished their repast at the same time and came out of the teahouse together.

'Please get into your kago,' called out the leader of the Edo

party, and after a great deal of running about and confusion everybody got into a kago.

'Come along, Yajirobei,' said Tarobei, who was a little flushed with saké. 'You must ride in my kago.'

'No, no,' said Yaji. 'I couldn't think of it.'

'I want to walk for a change,' said Tarobei. 'Get in, get in.'

'You're very kind,—exceedingly kind,' said Yaji, and he got in.

Both parties starting at the same time, and there being much confusion, Yaji's carriers made a mistake and got among the carriers of the Westcountry party without knowing it. Nobody took any notice and they went quickly through the streets of Yamada. Now the priest attached to the Edo party belonged to a different shrine to the priest attached to the Westcountry party, so that the Edo party branched off at a turning to the left and the Westcountry party went straight on. Yaji's carriers being mixed up with the Westcountry party kept straight on, and turned with the others into a building, out of which came a gentleman in ceremonial attire to meet them. All the party got out and went inside and Yaji went with them, but he was astonished when he got inside to find that they were all strangers.

'That's strange,' he said. 'Please can you tell me where Master Tarobei, the rice-dealer, has gone?' he asked one of the party.

'What's that?' answered the man. 'Master Tarobei? I haven't seen you before. Who are you?'

'I'm Master Tarobei's neighbour,' answered Yaji. 'There must be some mistake. I wonder what's become of Kitahachi.'

Yaji wandered about looking at each of them like one bewildered, and the members of the party all looked at him and whispered and nudged each other, and kept their eyes on their baggage because they thought he might be a thief. At last two or three of them went to the leader of the party.

'Who is this strange man?' they asked.

'Who can he be?' said another. 'Why's he looking all about him?'

'If I could only see Master Tarobei, the rice-dealer, it would be all right,' said Yaji.

'There's no such man in the party,' said the leader. 'You must be here for some bad purpose.'

'Doesn't this gentleman belong to your party?' asked the priest.

'No,' said the leader.

'Dear me!' said the priest. 'What are you doing here? I must ask you to leave at once. You are taking great liberties.'

'He must be a thief,' said the leader. 'Let's throw him out. There's something strange about him.'

'What are you talking about?' said Yaji. 'Throw me out, indeed! What insolence!'

'Aha!' said the priest. 'You seem to be an Edo man from your talk. I think I see what's happened. There was a party from Edo at the place where we stopped and your kago carriers must have got confused with our party.'

'Oh, that's it, is it?' said Yaji. 'Then where's the place I ought to have gone to?'

'How am I to know?' said the priest.

'Whoever heard of a person not knowing where he was going?' said the leader. 'It seems to me that you got mixed up with our party on purpose in order to get yourself treated at our expense.'

Then all the other members of the party began to get very

angry and to threaten him. 'Such insolence!' they cried. 'Let's give him a thrashing.'

'What are you talking about?' said Yaji. 'Do you think I can't pay my own way? That's easy enough for an Edo man. I'll pay for the lot of you.'

Here Yaji sat down proudly on the floor.

'What?' said the priest, astonished. 'You'll pay for all? That's splendid.'

'Of course I can,' said Yaji. 'I don't care how much it is. Here you are.' He pulled out two hundred coppers wrapped in a piece of paper. This gave the priest another surprise.

'Ha-ha-ha!' he laughed. 'That's no good. At the least it will cost you fifteen gold pieces.'

'What?' said Yaji. 'Isn't this enough?'

'Of course not,' replied the priest.

'Well, if it won't pay for everything,' said Yaji, 'it will pay at least for the oranges.'

'Ha-ha-ha!' laughed the leader. 'That's a good one.'

'He's making a fool of us,' said the priest. 'We've had enough of this. The place you ought to go to must be the Naigu. That's where the priest who was with your party belongs. You must go to the old market in Myōkenchō and then ask again.'

'Oh, that's the place, is it?' said Yaji. 'Well, thank you very much. Sorry to have disturbed you.'

'What a fool the man is!' said the leader and they all began laughing and jeering at him and clapping their hands.

Yaji felt very angry, but as there was nothing to be done he went off and retraced his steps to the place where he had branched off from the other party. As he walked he wondered what had become of Kita,—whether he had been taken away by the rice-dealer, and whether the Westcountryman had gone to Myōkenchō alone. Thus thinking he walked along till he came to Hirokōji. There he was accosted by an innkeeper in front of an inn.

'Are you looking for an inn?' he asked. 'You'd better stop here.'

'Is it far to Myōkenchō?' asked Yaji.

'No, no,' said the innkeeper's wife. 'It's only a little further.'

Yaji went on trying to remember the name of the inn in Myōkenchō where the Westcountryman said he was going to stop. He thought and thought, but the name of Fujiya had slipped his memory. It seemed to be on the tip of his tongue, but he couldn't get it off, though he had a vague idea that it was connected with something hanging down.

'Is there a hanging inn in Myōkenchō?' he inquired of a passer-by.

'A hanging inn?' said the man. 'I never heard of such a place.'

'They don't seem to know it here,' thought Yaji as he went on. 'I'll go a bit further and ask again.'

He went on quickly till he saw a sign marked 'Mankintan, Shichiemon Yamahara, Myōkenchō.'

'It must be somewhere here,' he thought. 'I'll ask again.'

'Do you know of a place about here somewhere that's hanging down?' he asked a passer-by.

The man looked at him puzzled. 'Hanging down?' he said. 'What sort of a place can it be hanging down?'

'It's an inn,' said Yaji.

'There's no inn like that,' said the man.

'I've forgotten the name,' said Yaji.

'I don't know any place like that,' said the man. 'Hanging down? Aha, perhaps if you go over to that house at the corner where that man's standing and ask there they'll know. Last year there was a man hanged himself there, so perhaps it's the hanging inn.'

'No, no,' said Yaji. 'It isn't that sort of hanging.'

'Well, you might go and ask,' said the man. 'It's an inn.'

Yaji started off again on his search, getting more and more bewildered and flustered, till at last he spoke to a man standing at the door of an inn.

'Excuse me,' he said. 'I've just got a question I want to ask you. Was it you who hanged himself last year?'

The man, who happened to be the landlord, was thunderstruck at such a question. 'Never,' he said. 'I never hanged myself.'

'Then where can it be?' said Yaji.

'I don't know any place where a man hanged himself,' said the landlord, 'but there's a place a little further along where a man died from a rice ball which fell from a shelf and stuck in his throat. Perhaps that's the place.'

'That would be it,' said Yaji. 'I know it was something about something hanging down.'

He went on till he came to the house and then he asked at the gate. 'Is this the house that fell from a shelf?' he inquired.

'Never,' said the mistress. 'My house has always been here. It's never been put on a shelf.'

'Dear me!' said Yaji. 'Isn't there any other.'

'You've made a mistake,' said the woman. 'Isn't it the house that fell from a hill? That would be Yojiro's hut. It was blown by the wind into the valley the other day. That must be what you want.'

'No, no, that's not it,' said Yaji. 'I don't know what to do. I'm all at sea. I've been asking all over the place and I'm quite worn out. I'll just take a rest and a smoke.'

He sat down in front of the inn, and the landlord, who quite sympathised with him in his distress, brought out a tobacco-box from the inn.

'Please take a whiff,' he said. 'Where do you really want to go to? Haven't you any companions?'

'Yes, I had two,' said Yaji, 'but I've lost them and that's why I'm in such trouble.'

'Isn't one of your companions a man from Edo and the other a Kyōto man with a wen beside his eye about this big?'

'That's them,' said Yaji.

'Then they're stopping in this house,' said the landlord. 'They've sent out to look for you.'

'Is that so?' said Yaji. 'Well, I am glad. By the way, what's the name of your inn?'

'Look for yourself,' said the landlord. 'It's written on that board hanging up there,—Fujiya.'

'That's it, that's it,' said Yaji. 'I knew it was something hanging down from a ledge. Where are my companions?'

'They're inside waiting for you,' said the landlord, and as he spoke the Westcountryman, who had heard Yaji's voice, came running out.

'Here you are at last,' he said. 'I knew you'd be asking for us. We've been asking all over the place for you. Come in, come in.'

Kita and the Westcountryman had followed the Edo party, but not being able to find Yaji, and being surrounded by strangers, they had felt rather embarrassed. After making inquiries in vain, they had gone on to the Fujiya in Myōkenchō in the hope that

Yaji would ask his way there. Yaji told them of his adventures, at which they laughed heartily.

Kita had sent for a barber and was having himself shaved when Yaji arrived.

'It's lucky we've all got together again without any accident,' he said.

'I'm the only one that's suffered,' said Yaji. 'By the way, barber, I'll have a shave too after you've done.'

'Then you'd better have a bath while you're waiting,' suggested Kita.

Yaji accordingly went off to the bath and Kita began talking to the barber. 'Mind you do my hair up tight, barber,' he said. 'Somehow my side hair always gets loose and makes me look so untidy. You know when a woman's hair is dressed to make it look very big they say she's got the Chikuma pot on her head.'

'Yes,' said the barber, 'but at the same time they look very pretty.'

'They may look pretty,' said Kita, 'but they shouldn't relieve themselves in public.'

'Well,' said the barber, 'those Edo girls have such large mouths that when they yawn it takes all your love away.'

'But then, Edo's famous for its courtesans,' said Kita. 'They're so full of spirit. Here they treat everyone the same and never refuse anyone. That's because they don't have enough faith.'

'Yes,' said the barber, 'they wouldn't even refuse a gentleman like you, so that's all right.'

'I'm telling the truth,' said Kita, 'so it's no use trying to make light of what I'm telling you.'

'If you talk so foolishly,' said the barber, 'I shall cut you.'

'It's painful enough as it is,' said Kita.

'It's bound to be painful,' said the barber. 'I haven't sharpened the razor for a long time.'

'What an extraordinary thing,' said Kita. 'Why don't you sharpen it?'

'If I sharpened it too much,' said the barber, 'it would wear it out. Let me see. It must be three years since people began to complain how sore their heads felt when I shaved them with this razor.'

'I can quite understand that,' said Kita. 'It's so painful that it feels as if you were pulling each hair out by the roots.'

216

' Well, it doesn't matter how much it hurts as long as your life's not in danger,' said the barber.

' Of course, of course,' said Kita. ' But don't shave my pate too much.'

' You don't seem fond of being shaved,' said the barber.

' How do you expect me to like being shaved with that razor ? ' said Kita. ' I expect you've taken all the skin off my head. Don't shave it any more. Just do my queue up nice and tight.'

' All right, all right,' said the barber. ' What a lot of scurf you've got. There's a way of getting rid of that.'

' How do you get rid of it ? ' asked Kita.

' By shaving your head and becoming a priest,' said the barber.

' Eh ? ' said Kita. ' What stupid things you say ! '

' Does your queue feel all right now ? ' asked the barber.

' No, no, do it tighter,' said Kita. ' Look how clumsily you've done it on this side. Don't you know how to tie up a queue tightly ? Such clumsiness ! '

' How will this do then ? ' asked the barber, and he twisted up Kita's queue so tightly that he drew the skin on his head into wrinkles and made him turn up his eyes. Kita felt as if his hair was being pulled out of his head, but he wouldn't give in and tried to keep a straight face.

' That's all right,' he said. ' It feels very comfortable.'

' I think it will be all right,' said the barber.

' You've done it so tight that he looks as if he couldn't bend his neck,' said Yaji, who had come back from the bath.

' Shall I do your hair too ? ' asked the barber.

' No, I feel chilly after my bath,' said Yaji. ' I must have caught cold. I'll put it off till to-morrow.'

The barber took his leave and the maid brought in supper and served it to each person, upon which the countryman, who had been lying down, woke up.

' Let's have supper,' he said.

' I'm sorry we have no fish to-day,' said the maid.

' It's quite a feast,' said Yaji. ' Come along, Kita.'

' Where are my chopsticks ? ' asked Kita.

' They're lying on the tray before you,' said Yaji. ' What a chap you are ! '

' Please give 'em to me,' said Kita. ' I can't bend my head to look down.'

217

'What's the matter?' asked Yaji. 'Halloa, your face is funny. Your eyes are pulled up so that you look just like a fox.'

'It's that barber,' groaned Kita. 'He did my queue up so tight. It's so painful that when I bend my neck it feels as if all my hair was being pulled out by the roots.'

'You're spilling all your soup,' said the Kyōto man. 'Look, you've put your soup on top of your rice. There, you've spilled it. Haven't you any manners?'

'Wipe it up, Yaji, will you?' said Kita.

'What a bother you are,' said Yaji. 'What did you want to have your queue tied up so tightly for? You should have had it done loose. I expect you annoyed the barber.'

'That's it,' said the countryman. 'That's why he did it up so tight.'

'I can't even talk,' groaned Kita. 'Ain't there anything to be done, Yaji?'

'I'll make it looser for you,' said Yaji, and he gave Kita's queue a good hard pull.

'Ow! Ow!' yelled Kita. 'What are you doing?'

'That feels better, doesn't it?' said Yaji.

'Ah, I can bend my neck a little,' said Kita. 'What an unfortunate chap I am.'

Supper being over, the dishes were removed and they began talking about how they should amuse themselves.

'Let's go to Furuichi to-night,' suggested the Kyōto man.

'Well, it seems rather bad to go there before we've been round the temples,' said Yaji, 'but we might as well enjoy ourselves as not.'

'Come on,' said the Kyōto man. 'I've spent thousands there year after year so they'll be quite willing to let me be responsible. Come on, let's go at once.'

'I wish I'd had my hair dressed too,' said Yaji.

'Landlord, landlord,' called the Kyōto man. 'Just come here a minute.'

'Ay, ay,' answered the landlord. 'Did you call me?'

'The gentlemen from Edo wish to go mountain climbing.'

In the vulgar language of the place, going to see the courtesans is called climbing the mountain.

'Very well,' said the landlord. 'I'll go with them.'

'Let's go to the Gyūsharō or the Chizukatei,' said the Kyōto man.

'To the Drum Chamber, or whatever they call it,' said Kita.

'It's not the Drum Chamber,' said the landlord. 'It's the Tambourine Chamber. That's at the Chizukaya.'

'Well, let's go to the Chizukaya then,' said the Kyōto man.

It was already dusk before they were ready, and this being the proper time the three sallied out with the landlord for their guide.

Furuichi is just along Myōkenchō. There the houses are set so closely that their eaves meet and from every house come the lively notes of the samisen playing the Isé song. Soon they reached the Chizukaya, where all the girls came running out to meet them.

'Welcome, welcome,' they cried. 'Please come upstairs.'

'Well, I may as well go upstairs too, I suppose,' said the landlord of the Fujiya. 'I'll show you the way.'

With the landlord leading the way they went upstairs and sat down.

'By the way, Master Yaji,' said the Kyōto man, 'suppose we pretend that you're the head-clerk of a big shop?'

'Ah, that's a good idea,' said the landlord of the Fujiya.

'But you must take care about your language,' said the Kyōto man, 'as you're supposed to be at the head office. It would be better if you spoke like the Kyōto people.'

'That's easy,' said Yaji. 'You just hear me talk like a Westcountryman. Here, girls, just come here a moment. For some reason I cannot explain my throat is uncommonly dry. Please bring me a cup of tea.'

'Ay, ay,' said the girls.

'Ain't I good at the Kyōto language?' said Yaji. 'What do you think, my dear?'

'Bravo! Bravo!' said the Kyōto man.

Meanwhile the maids had brought saké and some comestibles, and the landlord of the Fujiya had passed the cup round.

'Here, waitress,' called the Kyōto man, 'where are the girls? This is a very wealthy gentleman from Edo, so bring out the best girls you have. If he takes a fancy to them he won't mind staying three or four months with you. He doesn't care what he spends.'

'Yes, yes,' said the landlord of the Fujiya. 'When I was in Edo last year I passed his shop. It is a big place. That exchange shop of yours is quite a big place too,' he added turning to Kita.

'My place is not very big,' said Yaji. 'The frontage is scarcely more than thirty-three houses, but as there are ,thirty-

three thousand three hundred and thirty persons inside they make a fearful row.'

'His Kyōto establishment is in Juzuya-machi, Rokujō,' said the landlord of the Fujiya.

'That's so," said Yaji. 'My father and mother are very anxious about me because I'm always climbing the mountain. I'm afraid I'm a bad lot.'

Then the maid called for the girls to come in and four or five of them came and bowed politely to the guests. 'Welcome all,' they said.

'Aha !' said Yaji. 'Very pretty.'

'Just pass them the saké cup,' said the Kyōto man.

'Ay, ay,' said Yaji. 'I'll give them one.'

He took a saké cup and handed it to the most beautiful of the girls with a smile.

'I say,' said Kita. 'I want to see the Drum Chamber.'

'You're always talking of the Drum Chamber,' said the Kyōto man. 'It's the Tambourine Chamber.'

'There's a guest from Edo in the Tambourine Chamber,' said the waitress.. 'He's got all the girls in there dancing and singing. Listen.'

From the Tambourine Chamber came the sound of samisen and of girls singing.

> The mist is wafted by the breeze,
> And far and near the shadows break,
> While deep within the encircling trees
> The moon's face floats upon the lake.

'They're having a dance in the other room,' said the Kyōto man. 'Let's do something too,—something out of the common.'

'All right,' said Yaji. 'I feel just ready to enjoy myself. I can't be bothered with the Kyōto talk any more. Yoi, yoi, yoi!'

'Tochin, tochin!' chimed in the Kyōto man.

Then from the back room there came another song :

> All my love affair is known.
> What care I ?
> Play upon the samisen
> A softer melody.
> Stay my tottering feet. To-night
> I must haste to love's delight.

'Bravo! Bravo!' cried the Kyōto man. 'But where is my darling companion? What is your name? Ben? Oh, how thankful I am. I, Yotakurō Henguriya, living north of Nakadachiuri, Sembon-dōri, Kyōto, respectfully and thankfully announce that I have for companion Ben of the Chizukaya of Furuichi in Seishū, as lovely and as charming as St. Benten. Come a little closer.'

He took her hand as he spoke and pulled her closer to him. He was a little drunk and had a habit when in that condition of repeating himself at length. The girl was the one to whom Yaji had presented the saké cup and who, he thought, would be his companion. Now that she was claimed by the Kyōto man he began to feel very jealous.

'Here, Master Kyōto,' he said, 'that girl's my companion.'

'What are you talking about?' said the Kyōto man. 'Here, waitress, what's your name?'

'My name is Kin,' said the girl.

'Then I, Yotakurō Henguriya, living north of Nakadachiuri in Sembon-dōri, Kyōto, call upon you, Kin, waitress at the Chizukaya at Furuichi, in Seishū, to say whether I did not a little while ago secretly engage Ben, as beautiful and charming as St. Benten, namely I, Yotakurō Henguriya, living north of Nakadachiuri . . .'

'That's enough, that's enough,' said Yaji. 'I don't care where you live. Tell me this. Didn't I first hand my saké cup to that girl?'

It is the custom in Edo, when one goes to such places, for the man to hand his saké cup to the girl he wishes to select. In the West country it is different, however. There these matters are arranged secretly with the goodwife of the house or some other woman. Thus the Kyōto guest had already arranged with the waitress that he should have the best looking of the girls and that others he had selected should be given to Yaji and Kita. Of this Yaji was quite ignorant, and following Edo custom he thought that the girl he had presented his saké cup to was to be his companion. This was how the dispute arose.

'There, there,' said the waitress, trying to soothe Yaji. 'This girl is this gentleman's companion. Yours is the one with the chignon.'

'Don't talk nonsense,' said Yaji. 'I saw that girl first and there's no mistake I was the first to hand her a saké cup, so she's mine.'

'You don't understand how these matters are arranged,' said the Kyōto man. 'Whereabouts in Edo do you come from?'

'I'm Yajirobei Tochimenya of Hatchōbōri in Kanda, Edo,' said Yaji, 'and I'm a ticklish chap to handle.'

'Aha!' said the Kyōto man. 'So this terrible man to handle, Yajirobei Tochimenya, of Hatchōbōri, Kanda, Edo, meeting Yotakurō Henguriya who lives north of Nakadachiuri, in Sembon-dōri, Kyōto, claims as his companion Ben of the Chizukaya in . . .'

'What are you jawing about?' said Yaji. 'Bother your Yotakurō Henguriya!'

'So Yajirobei Tochimenya of Hatchōbōri, Kanda, Edo, miscalls Yotakurō Henguriya, who lives north of Nakadachiuri, in Sembon-dōri, in Kyōto, and the said Yotakurō Henguriya, who lives north of Nakadachiuri, in Sembon-dōri, Kyōto, hearing the said Yajirobei . . .'

'Oh do shut up,' said Yaji. 'What an infernal chatterbox you are!'

'I want to see the Drum Chamber instead of listening to this,' said Kita. 'What about the Drum Chamber?'

'There's no such place as the Drum Chamber,' said the waitress. 'Do you mean the Tambourine Chamber?'

'Yes, yes,' said Kita. 'Tambourine, of course.'

'That's a different question altogether,' said the Kyōto man.

'What we have to decide now is who is the companion of Yotakurō Henguriya.'

'I don't like this sort of joking,' said Yaji. 'There can be no doubt that the Tambourine Chamber is mine and I'm going to have her.'

'Ha-ha-ha!' laughed the landlord of the Fujiya. 'Do you mean you're going to embrace that large room?'

'Never mind whether she's big or small,' said Yaji, 'she's mine.'

'No, no, no,' said the Kyōto man. 'I can't allow that.'

'What is it you can't allow?' said Yaji. 'I don't care what you say, she's the companion of Yajirobei Tochimenya of Naka-dachiuri, Sembon-dōri, Kyōto.'

'No, no,' said the Kyōto man. 'She belongs to Yotakurō Henguriya just above Hatchō-bōri, Kanda, Edo.'

'Ha-ha-ha!' laughed Kita. 'You've got yourselves so mixed up you can't tell which is which.'

'I thought this gentleman was from Kyōto,' said the waitress, 'but now he's talking like an Edo man.'

'Don't be a fool,' said Yaji. 'Do you think this is a time for me to talk like a Kyōto man?'

'But while you gentlemen are disputing,' said the waitress, 'all the girls have run away.'

'Botheration!' said Yaji. 'I'm going home.'

'No, don't do that,' said the waitress.

'Let's arrange it this way,' said the landlord of the Fujiya. 'Suppose we go and see the Pine Chamber at the Kashiwaya, or else all go to the Asayoshi.'

'I'm not going,' said Yaji. 'I'm going back to the inn.'

'No, don't do that,' said the landlord of the Fujiya.

Yaji got up to go in spite of all the apologies of the waitress, and broke away from her when she tried to detain him by force. Just then the courtesan named Hatsué, who had been selected for him, came running in.

'What's the matter?' she asked.

'I'm not going to be stopped,' said Yaji. 'Let go, let go.'

'Is it because you don't like me that you want to go?' asked the girl.

'No, no, it's not that,' said Yaji. 'Let go, let go.'

'No, no, no,' said Hatsué, and while he was trying to get away from her she caught hold of his cloak and pulled it off.

223

'Here, what are you doing with my cloak?' cried Yaji. 'Let go, let go.'

Then she took away his purse and his tobacco pouch, all the time scolding him for being so obstinate. As he still persisted in saying that he would go, she then caught hold of his girdle and undid it and began to take off his kimono. As Yaji had only got a dirty loincloth on underneath he did not like to have himself exposed and felt greatly embarrassed.

'Here, here,' he cried, catching hold of his kimono with both hands, 'forgive me, forgive me.'

'You'll stop here then?' asked Hatsué.

'Yes, yes,' said Yaji.

'Take pity on him, Hatsué,' said the waitress.

'There, there,' said the landlord of the Fujiya, 'everything's all right now. Come along.'

He took hold of Yaji's hand and made him sit down again. The dispute being thus over, the waitress cleared up the room, and having pulled the drunken Kyōto man to his feet she led him and Kita away to other rooms, leaving Yaji to follow.

Yaji, who was very vain of his personal appearance, was anxious lest anybody should see his dirty loin-cloth, so while he was going along he took it off and flung it through the lattice of a window out into the garden. He looked round as he did so to see if anybody had observed him, and nobody being in sight, he followed the waitress with his peace of mind restored.

As it was now late the singing in the back room was hushed and the only sound to be heard was the snoring of the travellers. But soon the four o'clock bell rang, and then followed the crowing of ten thousand cocks, while through the window of the dawn came the dim light of day. Rubbing their eyes the travellers arose.

'Come along' said the Kyōto man. 'Let's get up. It's time to start.'

'Come on, Yaji,' called Kita. 'The sun's risen. Let's go.'

Going into the room where Yaji was sleeping they woke him up from a deep sleep.

'I did sleep well,' he said.

'Won't you stay another night?' asked the girl.

'Never, never,' said Yaji. 'Let's go.'

After they had made their preparations to start all the girls came out to bid them farewell, and one of them happened to peep out through the lattice window.

' Halloa ! ' she said. ' Look there. There's a napkin hanging to the pine tree.'

' Let me look,' said Hatsué. ' So there is. Whose is it ? '

' That's funny,' said Yaji. ' It reminds one of the feather-robe pine tree, eh ? The tree with a loin-cloth is funnier still.'

' Isn't that yours, Yaji ? ' asked Kita.

' So it is,' said Hatsué. ' Isn't it your loin-cloth ? '

She looked at Yaji and laughed, but Yaji, although he was secretly amused that the loin-cloth he had flung out of the window should have caught on to the pine tree, put on an innocent face.

' Nonsense ! ' he said. ' What should I be doing with a dirty loin-cloth like that ? '

' Yes, but when I pulled off your kimono last night,' said Hatsué, ' you had a loin-cloth on just like that.'

' That he had,' said the Kyōto man.

' It's all nonsense,' said Yaji. ' I don't like cotton loin-cloths. I always wear silk.'

' Ho-ho-ho ! ' laughed Hatsué. ' It's not true. It's his.'

' I know it quite well,' said Kita. ' That's it. If it's a lie show us the one you have on. I believe you're like the spearmen of a daimyo's procession, with nothing on.'

' Ha-ha-ha ! ' laughed Hatsué. ' Here, gardener,' she called through the lattice. ' That loin-cloth belongs to a guest. Just get it for him will you ? '

The gardener picked it off the tree with a bamboo and thrust it through the lattice. ' There it is,' he said.

' Oh, how it smells ! ' said Hatsué.

' There you are, Yaji,' said Kita, laughing. ' Take it.'

' What spiteful things you say,' replied Yaji. ' I tell you it's not mine.'

' Well, show us the one you've got on, then,' said Kita. He seized hold of Yaji's girdle to undo it, but Yaji broke away and fled down the passage to the amusement of them all.

It was thus that they left the house.

' Botheration ! ' said Yaji. ' You put me to shame, Kita.'

' Well, a loin-cloth in a pine tree is rather a curious thing,' was Kita's reply.

Returning to the inn in Myōkenchō they determined, as the day was a fine one, that they would immediately start to go round all

the temples. Their hurried preparations finished, they returned
to Furuichi, where the keepers of the stalls and sideshows were
calling to the people to come in, and there they saw Sugi and
Tama, who allow people to throw coppers at their faces while
they play on the samisen and sing a song which nobody under-
stands.

'I'll see if I can't hit that girl on her dimple,' said Yaji.

He took two or three coppers and threw them, but each time
the girl bobbed her head to one side so that he missed.

'Let me have a try,' said Kita. He threw, but he also missed.

'You'll never be able to hit her,' said the Kyōto man.

'You see this time,' said Yaji. Then he threw, but missed
again.

'I've thrown a whole string of coppers and not hit her once,'
said Kita. 'There must be a way of doing it. I'm going to hit
her ugly mug somehow.'

He picked up a pebble and threw it, but the girl caught it in
her mouth and spat it out, so that it hit Yaji on the face and made
him yell.

'Ha-ha-ha!' laughed Kita. 'That was a good one.'

Passing on they reached Naka-no-Jizō, on the lefthand side of which stands the Honsei Temple, where a fine view is to be obtained. There also is the famous Samukazé, the Gochi-no-Nyōrai, the Nakagawara, and many other places too numerous to mention. From there they came to Ushiyazaka, where a number of young beggar-girls were asking the passers-by for money. Some of the girls were dressed in coloured paper hats.

'Please give us some money, Master Edo,' they cried. 'Throw us some money.'

'Shut up,' said Yaji. 'Be off with you.'

'Oh, don't say that, Master Edo,' they cried. 'Do please give us a little.'

'Well, you mustn't pull me about,' said Yaji. 'There, I'll give you some.'

He took out some coppers and scattered them on the road and the beggar-girls all picked them up with many thanks.

A little further on they came upon a boy of seven or eight, who had a white towel tied round his head and was wearing a cloak without any sleeves. He was dancing and waving a fan at the same time, while behind him a man in a woven hat was rubbing two pieces of bamboo together and singing.

'Give us some money,' they cried.

'There, there's a four-copper piece for you,' said Yaji.

'If it's a four copper piece,' they said, 'you must give us three coppers change.'

'They're a sharp lot,' said Yaji. 'This is Ujibashi, I suppose.'

'Yes,' said the Kyōto man. 'And look. There are the men with nets to catch your money.'

'Where?' cried Yaji.

Looking over the bridge he saw some men standing in the river bed with nets fastened to the end of long poles, with which they were catching the coppers flung by the travellers.

'I say, Master Yaji,' said the Kyōto man, 'just lend me some small change.'

He took Yaji's money and flung it down, whereupon the men under the bridge caught it in their nets.

'Isn't it wonderful how they do it,' said the Kyōto man. 'Let's try again. Here, Master Kita, just let me have a few coppers. Look out, I'm going to throw some more. Ha-ha-ha! Wonderful!'

'You're very fond of throwing other people's money,' said Yaji. 'Suppose you throw some of your own.'

'It wouldn't make any difference; they'd catch it just the same,' said the Kyōto man.

'I know,' said Yaji, 'but you're a little bit too stingy.'

'When I was here last time,' said the Kyōto man, 'there was a terrible fool here. He must have thrown from forty to eighty pounds of coppers over the bridge, and then because they caught it all so well he got spiteful and thought he would like to break their nets. So he took a large silver coin that he had in his pocket and threw it just to see, and they caught it in their net just like any other coin. So he asked them how they managed to catch it, and one of them said, 'That's easy. It's because the net has eyes (holes) to see it with.' Ha-ha-ha ! That beat him. Come on, let's go.'

They passed through the first *torii* and then through to the Yotsuashi Gate and the Sarukashira Gate, and finally prostrated themselves before the Honsha. This is the place where the Holy Mirror and the Holy Sword have keen kept since the days of the great god Amaterasu.

> Bright shines the sun on sacred ground,
> Divine the breeze that's wafted round.

Here they saw the Asai Shrine, Toyo Shrine, Kawaguya-furu-dono Shrine, Taka Shrine, Tsuchi Shrine and many others too numerous to mention, all of which filled them with such awe that their jokes were forgotten and their idle talk silent. Thus for a time they went round looking at the shrines with serious faces, and then, having finished the round, they returned to Myōkenchō. There they parted from the Kyōto man and started at midday for the Gekū Temple, which is dedicated to the Toyouke Daijin, who is the god called Kunitokodachi, one of the seven divine generations. Afterwards they went round the Shinji Shrine, the Hōken Shrine and many others, till, when they were climbing up to the Ama-no-Iwato, Yaji, for some reason, began to suffer from a stomachache. Quickly reaching the top they rested for a time, while Yaji took some pills they had with them. The pain did not abate, however, so they returned quickly to Hirokōji to look for an inn. While they were wandering about there the landlord of an inn addressed them.

'Won't you stop here for the night, gentlemen?' he asked.

'Well,' said Kita, 'my companion's taken rather sick so I think we had better.'

'Please come in,' said the landlord, and he called to the maid to show them in.

'You look very bad, Yaji,' said Kita. 'This must be a punishment on you for something you've done.'

'I don't remember doing anything bad,' said Yaji. 'It must have been the rice this morning.'

'You must have been eating something you're not accustomed to,' said the landlord.

'You haven't got any pluck,' said Kita.

He assisted Yaji into a room and the landlord brought in their baggage.

'It seems rather serious,' he said. 'Have you tried any medicine? As it happens my wife has just sent for the doctor, as she is expecting a baby. She's been feeling unwell from yesterday, so I've just called him. Would you like to see him too?'

'Yes,' said Yaji, 'if you don't mind calling him.'

'Certainly, certainly,' said the landlord, and he went off to the kitchen.

Meanwhile Yaji got worse.

'How would it do to take something?' said Kita,—'some hot water, or tea, or saké?'

'Don't talk nonsense,' said Yaji. 'How my stomach's rumbling! Where's the closet, Kita. Just ask.'

'Where have you put it?' said Kita. 'Perhaps it's up your sleeve.'

'Don't talk like a fool,' said Yaji. 'Fancy having the closet up your sleeve! I want you to look where it is.'

'I see,' replied Kita. 'Well, I'll have a look. Oh, there it is, fallen down in front of the verandah.'

'What are you jawing about!' groaned Yaji. 'Ugh, how it hurts!' He got up slowly and went off to do his business. Then a girl came from the kitchen and announced that the doctor had arrived.

'Show him in,' said Kita.

The doctor was evidently only the doctor's assistant, not the doctor himself. He was dressed in a dark brown cotton kimono with a crest and a black silk cloak.

'What unseasonable weather we're having,' he said. 'Let me feel your pulse.'

He seated himself beside Kita and began to feel his pulse.

'It isn't me that's sick,' said Kita.

'We can tell whether a person is ill or not,' said the doctor, 'by comparing their pulse with that of a healthy person. Just let me see.'

He felt Kita's pulse for some time very gravely.

'No, no,' he said at last. 'There's nothing the matter with you.'

'No,' said Kita.

'How is your appetite?' asked the doctor.

'Well, this morning I had three goes of rice and three bowls of soup.'

'Yes, yes,' said the doctor. 'I thought so. And you couldn't eat any more?'

'No,' said Kita.

'I thought I was right,' said the doctor. 'I thought from your pulse there was nothing wrong with you.'

'Yes,' said Kita.

'I'm right, ain't I?' said the doctor. 'The first thing in medicine is to feel the pulse. You needn't be anxious. Well, I must be going now.'

'Please look at the patient before you go,' said Kita.

'Oh yes,' said the doctor. 'That's right. I always forget to feel the patient's pulse when I am called in. It's a bad habit of mine. It's really not necessary but I may as well see him. Where is the patient ? '

' He's just gone to the closet,' said Kita. ' Here, Yaji, Yaji. The doctor's come. Come out quick.'

' I can't come out,' said Yaji from inside the closet. ' Please tell the doctor to come here.'

' Nonsense ! ' said Kita. ' Who ever heard of such a thing ? What a rude thing to say ! '

' Well, I'll come out then,' said Yaji. He came out slowly and the doctor felt his pulse as if it was a matter of life and death.

' Aha ! ' he said. ' You're suffering from dizziness. Your confinement must be close at hand.'

' I don't remember becoming pregnant,' said Yaji.

' Isn't it pregnancy ? ' asked the doctor. ' How strange ! That's the fault of my master. He sent a man to call me from the Igagoya in Hirokōji and told me that a patient was going to be confined and that probably she was suffering from dizziness and I must give her some medicine. Aren't you the patient ? '

' I see, I see,' said Kita. ' There is a case of that here. But this gentleman is not suffering from it.'

' Dear me ! ' said the doctor. ' That's my mistake. But if you would suffer from the same complaint then I could administer the same medicine. That would save a lot of trouble.'

' That's so,' said Kita. ' Yaji, you'd better do as the doctor tells you and feel dizzy.'

' What are you talking about ? ' said Yaji. ' Men don't get dizzy.'

' Well, well,' said the doctor, ' perhaps it would be better for you to have another kind of illness. That will give me more practice. What do you say you're suffering from ? '

' I've been suffering from grinding pains in the stomach for some time,' said Yaji.

' Probably only inside the stomach,' said the doctor.

' Yes, only in my stomach as you say,' replied Yaji. ' Not outside.'

' Ah, I thought so, I thought so,' said the doctor. ' Here,'— he called to the maid—' tell my man to bring my medicine-box in, will you ? '

The maid went out but soon returned to say that she could not see the doctor's man.

'No wonder you couldn't see him,' said the doctor. 'I didn't bring him. I brought the chest in myself.' He opened a cloth he had brought and took out his medicine-chest.

'What a duck of a spoon you've got,' said the maid as she looked in the chest.

'That's because he's a quack doctor,' said Kita. 'Ducks always quack. But why have you got pictures on the medicines instead of names? What's the reason of that?'

'Ahem!' said the doctor. 'That's rather an embarrassing question, but I may tell you that from the time I was born I have never received any instruction in letters.'

'Then you can't read?' asked Kita.

'No,' said the doctor, 'I can't read at all. So I have the names of the medicines done in pictures.'

'That's interesting,' said Kita. 'What does that picture of the Dōjō temple stand for?'

'That stands for cinnamon,' said the doctor.

'And this picture of Emma stands for rhubarb, I suppose. What's the meaning of the dog on fire?'

'That's dried orange peel.'

'And that picture of the woman in childbirth and somebody making water by her?'

'That's jasmine root, of course.'

'And that seal with the hair on it?'

'That's lizard tail.'

'And the devil breaking wind?'

'That's aegle.'

'Ha-ha-ha!' laughed Kita. 'How funny! But what about the medicine?'

'You must boil the medicine as usual,' said the doctor, 'and add a slice of ginger to it.'

'Wouldn't horseradish do?' suggested Kita.

'Don't be a fool,' said Yaji.

Just then they heard sounds from the kitchen as of people rushing about and the voice of the landlord calling, 'Here, Nabé, Nabé, send someone for the midwife. Here, heat some water, quick, quick. Have you got some *hayamé*?'

In the midst of all these noises Yaji went on groaning.

'How is it, Yaji?' asked Kita.

'This won't do,' said the doctor. 'You mustn't come near the patient.'

As he drove Kita away there came from the kitchen the old midwife that had been summoned for the landlord's wife. The maid, all in a fluster, dragged her to where Yaji lay groaning under the bedding.

'Eh ?' said the old woman. 'You mustn't give way. Sit up, sit up.' She dragged Yaji up and in doing so accidentally scratched his face and made him yell. 'You must be patient,' she went on. 'Here, where's the mat. Somebody bring the mat.'

'Oh, oh, oh !' groaned Yaji.

'There, there,' said the old woman. This midwife was in fact a little blind and moreover so agitated that she had mistaken Yaji for a woman in labour. She now began to hold him up.

'Here,' she called. 'Somebody come and help me. Quick, quick.'

Kita, who was enjoying the old woman's mistake, kept a straight face and began to help her to hold Yaji up.

'What are you doing, Kita ?' said Yaji. 'Oh, how it hurts.'

'You mustn't be so timid,' said the old woman. 'You must try and bear it.'

'How do you think I'm going to bear it ?' said Yaji. 'I'm off to the closet. Let go.'

'No, no,' said the old woman. 'You mustn't move.'

'But if I don't it will all come out here,' said Yaji.

'Well, let it,' said the midwife. 'There, there, it's head's coming out.'

'Oh, oh !' yelled Yaji. 'That's not a child. Let go. Oh, oh, oh !'

He began to struggle, and as the old woman held him tight, he finally lost his temper and give her a box on the ear. This astonished the old woman, but she still kept her arms locked round him, as she thought the patient was delirious.

Meanwhile from the kitchen came the cry of a newly born infant. Apparently the goodwife of the house had given birth to the child.

'There,' said the midwife. 'It's born. Why, it isn't here. Where can it be ?'

The midwife letting go of him to look for the baby, Yaji

233

immediately rushed away to the closet, while the landlord came out of the kitchen.

'Here, granny, granny,' he cried. 'I sent for you a long time ago. The baby's born now. Quick, quick.'

He dragged the old woman off into the kitchen, where could be heard cries of, 'What a fine boy! The finest boy ever born in the three countries. Congratulations! Congratulations!'

At receiving these congratulations the landlord was all over smiles. 'I'm sorry you've been disturbed,' he apologised to the guests. 'Happily my wife's had an easy birth.'

Just then Yaji came out of the closet. 'Congratulations,' he said. 'I also have had an easy delivery. I feel as if I had never had anything the matter with me at all.'

'You are also to be congratulated,' said the landlord.

Then saké was served in honour of the event and there was great talking and laughing over the midwife's mistake.

BOOK SIX

FIRST PART

THE proverb says that shame is thrown aside when one travels, and names and addresses are left scrawled on every railing. Yet it is a consolation when one is travelling to meet people from one's own province, even although they have the word ' deaf ' written on their hats. Naturally one is curious about the people who are travelling the same roads, and those whose fates are linked together at the public inns do not always have their marriages written in the book of Izumo. They are not tied by convention as when they live in the same row of houses, but can open their hearts to each other and talk till they are tired. On the road, also, one has no trouble from bill-collectors at the end of the month, nor is there any rice-box on the shoulder for the rats to get at. The Edo man can make acquaintance with the Satsuma sweet-potato, and the flower-like Kyōto woman can scratch her head with the skewer from the dumpling. If you are running away for the sake of the fire of love in your heart, you can go as if you were taking part in a picnic, enjoying all the delights of the road. You can sit down in the shadow of the trees and open your little tub of saké, and you can watch the pilgrims going by ringing their bells. Truly travelling means cleaning the life of care. With your straw sandals and your leggings you can wander wherever you like and enjoy the indescribable pleasures of sea and sky.

Here we have Yajirobei and Kitahachi, from Hatchō-bōri, Kanda, in the eastern capital, two lazy vagabonds, who have been wandering round the shrines of Isé and are now going along the shady Nara highway, hastening to the capital. Now they have reached Kyō Bridge at Fushimi. The sun is sinking in the west and the travellers are pressing onward, while the boatmen call noisily to those who are going down the river to Ōsaka.

' Come along,' they cry, ' The boat's starting now. All aboard for the Hakkenya in Ōsaka.'

' Aha ! ' said Yaji. ' This will be the night-boat down the River Yodo. I'll tell you what, Kita. We were going to see Kyōto first, but what do you think of going to Ōsaka first after all ? '

'All right,' said Kita. He called to the boatman to know whether it was a public boat.

'Yes, yes,' said the boatman. 'Come on board quick, please. We're just going to start. Hi, you mustn't come on board with your sandals on. Don't you know that?'

'Who are you talking to?' said Kita. 'Impudent fellow!'

'I'll tie our two bundles together, Kita,' said Yaji.

'Here, boatman,' called Kita, 'where do we sit?'

'Squeeze in by the side of that priest,' answered the boatman.

'Excuse me,' said Kita, and they squeezed in with the rest of the passengers.

'It's very crowded to-night,' said one of the passengers. 'Here, boatman, haven't you got any cushions?'

'Take them from over there,' replied the boatman. 'Are you all ready? Please sit down while I put the cover on.'

'Change, change,' called a hawker. 'Do you want any change?'

'Sugar-cakes, sugar-cakes,' called another.

'Hot saké, hot saké,' called another. 'Finest flavour.'

Meanwhile the boatmen had spread a rush mat over the top of the boat and had got out the sweeps.

> The wind has changed. Let's hoist the sail
> And it will waft us o'er.
> My tired body longs for rest,
> So I will toil no more.

'Halloa!' they cried. 'Look how the sky has changed. We're going to have rain.'

'Ah, boatmen,' cried a passenger. 'You must have been to Chujō Island and not purified yourselves properly. That's why it looks like rain. Ha-ha-ha!'

'I hope you're all sitting comfortable,' said one of the passengers. 'You'll be stiff later on if you don't.'

'Move up a bit,' said a Kyōto man. 'You're sitting on my supper.'

'Dear me,' said an Ōsaka man. 'How very awkward of me. By the way, as we're all travelling together, I hope we shall become better acquainted.'

'Yes, yes,' said the Kyōto man. 'What part of Ōsaka do you come from?'

'I come from Dotombōri.'

'All the people who live in Dotombōri can sing,' said the Kyōto man. 'Won't you oblige us with a song?'

'Ah, that's a good idea,' said a Nagasaki man. 'I think we each ought to do something to keep us from going to sleep in the boat. I'm a Nagasaki man, I am, so I'll give you a piece from the play called "How the Hair-pins were broken by the Pumpkin Pillow of Nomokawa Island."'

'That's a good piece,' said another man. 'I come from Echigo myself, so if the gentleman from Nagasaki does that, I'll give you something from Okesa and Matsuzaka.'

'That would be interesting,' said Kita. 'Please begin, Master Nagasaki.'

'All right,' said the Nagasaki man, 'this is what I'll give you.' Earnestly clapping his hands the while, he sang :—

> Oh leave not one
> Who loves you true,
> Nor shake off her
> Who dotes on you.
> To catch a frog,
> In his hop-hop-hop,
> Over his head
> A tub you pop.
> Or if a tub
> Is of no avail,
> You still can secure him
> Under a pail.

'Bravo! Bravo!' cried all the passengers.

'Now I'll sing one,' said the Echigo man. 'But you must all say "Tokoton, Tokoton" as the chorus.'

'All right,' said the Nagasaki man. 'We understand.'

Then all the passengers began to clap their hands and to chant 'Tokoton, tokoton' in chorus.

> And how d'you do this morning,
> Mrs. Chō, Mrs. Chō?
> How d'you do this morning,
> Mrs. Chō?
> (Chorus) Tokoton! Tokoton!
> Here's a comb that's made of horn,
> Mrs. Chō, Mrs. Chō,
> That I brought from Niigata,
> Mrs. Chō.
> (Chorus) Tokoton! Tokoton!
> I bought it for my true love,
> Mrs. Chō, Mrs. Chō.

And six hundred cash it cost me,
Mrs. Chō.
(Chorus)   Tokoton ! Tokoton !

'Ha-ha-ha ! ' laughed Yaji. 'That's good.'

'Now it's the turn of the Edo gentleman to do something,' said the Kyōto man.

'I can't sing anything without an accompaniment,' said Yaji, 'and we haven't got any musical instruments here.'

'Well, you can give us an imitation of someone,' said the Kyōto man. 'Imitate some Edo actor.'

'I can imitate twenty or thirty of them,' said Yaji. 'Which one shall I do ? Gennosuké or Mitsugoro ? No, I'll do Kōraiya. But I'm afraid you won't be able to understand Edo talk and it won't be interesting.'

'No, no,' said the Ōsaka man. 'That will be all right. Just try.'

'Without boasting,' said Yaji, 'I may say that I'm the best imitator in Edo. I'll do anyone you like to mention.'

'Anyone we like to introduce, eh ? ' said the Kyōto man. 'Very well, I'll play the accompaniment on my mouth.' He began to imitate the sound of a samisen.

'You must suppose this is a well-known theatre in Edo,' said Yaji, 'and that I am Kōjirō Matsumoto.'

'Bravo, Matsumoto,' cried all the passengers.

'*The roll is mine,*' chanted Yaji. '*I have succeeded in obtaining it. Now I shall be able to make progress. For this success I am truly thankful.*'

'That's no good,' said the Kyōto man. 'I only came back from Edo the other day after living there five or six years. Matsumoto doesn't speak like that.'

'Let me try to imitate him,' said the Ōsaka man.

'No good at all,' went on the Kyōto man. 'Who are you going to imitate ? '

'The same actor,' said the Ōsaka man. This Ōsaka man had been in Edo and he gave a very successful imitation of the actor.

'Bravo Matsumoto ! ' cried all the passengers.

'That was good,' said the Kyōto man. 'Master Ōsaka has done it very well. Yours was no good at all,' he added turning to Yaji.

'Of course not,' said Yaji. 'I was imitating his understudy, Dōshirō, who comes from Shinshū.'

'What a lie!' said the Kyōto man. 'Ha-ha-ha!'

Then all the people in the boat began to laugh at Yaji, who was so disconcerted that he did not know what to say.

By this time the boat had passed Yodo.

'By the way, Kita,' said Yaji, 'I forgot to relieve myself before I got on the boat. You know I get so nervous in a boat that it always make me feel that way. What a nuisance it is! Here, boatman. Just put in to the shore for a minute.'

'Do you want to land?' asked the boatman.

'I want to relieve myself,' said Yaji.

'Lean over the side of the boat and do it,' said the boatman.

'That would be all right if I could, but I can't,' said Yaji.

Seated next to them was a party of two, consisting of an old man and a young boy. The old man had been talking to Yaji and Kita earlier in the evening, but was now lying down covered with a quilt.

'Excuse me,' he said, 'but if you want to relieve yourself there's a pot over there. Here, Chōmatsu. Wake up. He's too sleepy. You'll find it just over there. Please take it.'

'Thank you very much' said Yaji. He searched about in the dark and behind a brazier he found a teapot of a kind hardly ever seen in Edo. Yaji thought it must be the pot the old man meant and pulled it out.

'Here it is,' he cried. 'It's the usual kind, I see.'

In reality it seemed to him a strange-looking pot. He thought at first the handle must be the mouth, but he found there was no hole. Then he thought it must have a stopper in, and stuck his finger in to see. He was in such a hurry to relieve himself that he kept twisting the teapot about in all directions till at last the lid fell off. 'Oh, there's a hole here,' he thought, and he did it in the top.

'Thank you very much,' he said to the old man, and put the teapot back where he had found it.

'It's very cold,' said the old man. 'Chōmatsu, get up and make a little fire. We'll warm some saké. Can't you open your eyes? Wake up, wake up.'

The old man got up himself at last and raked together the fire in the brazier. Then he lit a small lantern, hung it on the gunwale and took up the teapot.

'What's this in the teapot?' he said. 'Oh, yes, we were going to make some tea and filled it with water.' With that he threw the contents of the teapot into the river and having put some saké in it put it on the brazier to warm.

'Won't you Edo gentlemen have some saké ? ' he asked.

'I shall be delighted,' said Kita.

'It's warm now,' said the old man. He brought out some comestibles and poured out some saké into a cup.

'It's nice and hot,' he said, ' but it has a funny smell. Seems as if the saké had gone bad. But it can't be that. Just try a cup.'

He handed the cup to Kita who drank it off at a gulp. It seemed to him to have a very strange salty taste and made him feel sick, but he said ' Thank you.'

'Won't your friend have some ? ' said the old man.

'Here, Yaji,' said Kita, and he handed him the cup.

Yaji, who had been looking on, felt sure that the pot in which they had warmed the saké was the one into which he had relieved himself, and he noted their grimaces after they had drunk. The situation seemed to him very funny, but he concealed his amuse-ment, and when Kita handed him the saké cup declined to have any.

'I don't know how it is,' he said, ' but I don't feel like drinking saké to-night. But let me pass the cup to you.'

'Won't you have some ? ' said the old man.

'Why he bathes in it usually,' said Kita. 'Won't you really have some, Yaji ? Generally the very mention of saké makes your mouth water. It's very strange.'

'Aha ! ' said the old man. 'I understand. Your friend mis-took the pot in the dark and did it in here. I thought it tasted like that. We can't drink it now.'

'I never dreamt of it,' said Kita. 'When we were crossing the Kuwana ferry he made a mess in the boat and caused no end of a row, but I didn't think he would be as careless as this. Ugh ! How dirty ! '

'That's why the teapot was full when I took it up,' said the old man. 'I thought this lad had filled it with water and I emptied it into the river, but I must have left some in.'

'What a horrible thing,' said Kita. 'I feel sick.'

'So do I,' said the old man. 'Ugh ! Ugh ! '

'I'm really very sorry,' said Yaji. 'Shall I give you some medicine ? Though I don't know what sort of medicine would be good for it. Has any body got any pills for this complaint ? ' he asked the other passengers.

'No, no,' said the passengers. 'We haven't got any medicine that would be good for that.'

'What a nuisance!' said Yaji.

'Just lift up the cover a little, Yaji,' said Kita.

'What for?'

'I want to do something.'

'Do something?'

'Yes, with my mouth.'

'Then you'd better go to the side of the boat and stick your head over. I'll hold on to you. How do you feel now? Is there some more? It's a pity there's no dog in the river.'

'What do you want a dog for?'

'Why if there was a dog I could call "Shirokoi! Shirokoi!"'

'Don't be a fool! Ugh!'

'Chōmatsu,' said the old man. 'Just rub my back. Ugh! Ugh!'

Soon the old man ceased to feel sick and washed his mouth with the river water.

'How's the other gentleman?' he asked.

'Well, I feel a little better now,' said Kita. He washed out his mouth also and sat with a very sad face. Yaji continued to conceal his mirth at the incident and the old man took him for a very good-natured person and did not get angry with him.

'I'm very sorry you've been so unfortunate,' he said. 'We might drink the remainder of the saké to take away the taste, but unfortunately I haven't got anything to warm it in. What shall we do?'

'There's a new pot here,' said Chōmatsu. 'We might use that to warm the saké in.'

'That's true,' said the old man. 'A clean pot's all right. I bought it at Fuji-no-mori to-day and it hasn't been used once yet. Let's heat it in that.'

'You'd better take care,' said Kita. 'You might make a mistake.'

'Nonsense!' said Yaji. 'You drink tea out of a teapot, so why shouldn't you drink saké out of another kind of pot?'

'What, drink saké out of a pot?' cried Kita.

'Well, after all,' said Yaji to the old man, 'perhaps you'd better use the small teapot.'

'I threw it into the river,' said the old man. 'The pot's quite new and clean.'

243

He put some saké from the tub into the pot and put it on the brazier.

'Just pass me that teacup, Chōmatsu,' he cried. 'There, now we'll have some good saké.'

When the saké was warm he invited Yaji to have some, and at the same time passed him some comestibles.

'What's this?' asked Yaji.

'That's whale meat with the fat taken off,' said the old man.

'It's very nice,' said Yaji. 'Here, Kita, have a drink.'

Kita seized the cup and poured himself out a drink from the pot. As it was a new pot he had no hesitation in drinking the saké and swilled it off with gusto. 'It gives it a new flavour drinking it out of a pot,' he said. 'Shall I give you some?'

'Please all have a drink,' said the old man.

Kita accordingly passed the cup on to the person next to him, who happened to be the man from Echigo, and he expressed himself as very pleased. When Kita began to pour from the pot, however, his expression changed. 'Isn't that a pot to make water in?' he asked.

'You needn't be frightened,' said Kita. 'This is a new pot so it's quite clean.'

He poured out some saké and the Echigo man drank it off. 'Ah, that's good,' he said. 'Here, my Nagasaki friend, come and enjoy yourself.'

He passed the pot to the Nagasaki man, who also expressed himself as very pleased.

'Let everybody have a drink,' said the old man.

The Nagasaki man accordingly passed it to the man next him. This was a man who appeared to be sick, since he was very pale and dirty and had something round his neck. He was lying down and had an old man with him as attendant.

'I don't drink saké,' said the sick man, 'but my companion does.'

He handed the cup to his companion, who showed no reluctance in taking it, as he had heard them saying that the pot was quite new and clean.

'Would you please hand me the pot,' said the attendant. 'I'll pour for myself.'

The old man was apparently fond of saké, for he drunk two cups of it in quick succession before he returned the cup to Yaji.

'Now, Master Gaffer, you have a cup,' said Yaji to the owner of the saké.

'No, no, you have one,' said the old man.

'Very well,' said Yaji. 'Just pass that pot over will you, please?'

'Yes, yes,' said the attendant on the sick person.

He passed the pot along and Kita having filled Yaji's cup to the brim Yaji gulped it down at a breath. Immediately he flung the cup away.

'Oh, oh, oh!' he yelled. 'What a dreadful thing I've done. Ugh! Ugh!'

'What's the matter, Yaji?' asked Kita.

'The matter is that it's not saké,' said Yaji. 'It's somebody's stale.'

'Deary, deary me,' said the old man with the sick person. 'I've been very careless. I changed the pot with that of the invalid here. Here's the one with the saké in. Please give the other back.'

'Ha-ha-ha!' laughed Kita. 'That's a good one.'

'What shall I do?' said Yaji. 'What shall I do? I've never drunk anybody's stale before, and that sick man's stinks horribly. Ugh! Ugh!'

'Ha-ha-ha!' laughed Kita. 'Look at that sick man's face. He's got the pox. Look how his face is covered with boils.'

'Don't talk of it,' moaned Yaji. 'My throat's fit to split. Oh, oh! I do feel sick.'

'It's a punishment on you,' said Kita. 'It ought to be prohibited on boats.'

The commotion caused by the incident had wakened all the passengers, who laughed heartily at it. Just then, when they were drawing near to Hirakata, a trading boat came alongside.

'Halloa!' cried the man in the boat. 'Do you want to buy something to eat and drink? Wake up everybody. What a sleepy lot you are.'

He brought his boat alongside and without any ceremony pulled back the matting that covered the boat. The ways of these trading boats are well known, and give rise to many disputes.

'What have you got to eat?' asked one of the passengers. 'Have you got any good saké?'

'I'm hungry,' said Kita. 'I'd like something to eat.'

'Want something to eat, do you?' said the boatman. 'There

you are, eat that. What about the chap over there? He's got a hungry look. Haven't you got any money?'

'Get out you rascal,' said Yaji. 'What do you suppose we are?'

'This soup's half cold and has no taste at that,' said one of the passengers.

'Mix some water with it then,' said the man.

'Shut your jaw,' said the passenger. 'These vegetables are all bad.'

'What else did you expect,' replied the man. 'I kept all the best ones for myself.'

'What an insolent knave he is,' said the Nagasaki man. 'I never heard of such a thing.'

'Shall I knock him off the boat,' said the man from Echigo.

'Don't talk nonsense, but just pay up,' said the man. 'That old man over there hasn't paid me.'

'You thief, I paid you just this minute,' said the old man. 'I suppose your wife's a beggar and eats raw rice, which makes her swell up and froth at the mouth.'

'And you've got a hovel in the river bed at Shijō, I suppose,' replied the man. 'It's going to rain, so you'd better go home before it's washed away.'

'What a rascally knave he is!' said Yaji.

'Don't get angry,' said one of the passengers. 'All the men are like that. The place is noted for it.'

'Yes, but it's too much of a good thing,' said Yaji.

'Fools, fools,' shouted the man as he shoved off.

'Who are you calling fools?' shouted Yaji angrily. 'You just wait a minute.' He jumped up, treading on the knee of one of the passengers as he did so.

'Oh, oh, oh!' yelled the passenger. 'That's my knee.'

'Now you're stepping on me,' yelled the Nagasaki man.

'I'm very sorry,' said Yaji, and he sat down again.

As the boat was thus proceeding down the river, suddenly the sky got dark and rain fell and as the cover of the boat leaked the passengers began to complain. At last the boat put in to the bank at a place half way between Fushimi and Osaka, where the boats going up and down the river pass each other, and waited there for the weather to clear up. This was not for some time, but at last the rain ceased, the clouds parted and the moon came out. Then all the passengers began to feel more cheerful.

Yaji and Kita drew back the cover of the boat to look at the scenery.

'What will be the time, I wonder,' said Yaji. 'By the way, Kita, I'm in trouble again. I want to do another little job for myself.'

'You only think of dirty things,' said Kita.

'Well, you can't do it in the boat,' said Yaji. 'Look here, as we're lying by the bank I think I'll jump up on the embankment and do it.'

'Yes, I see people are getting off the other boats to relieve themselves,' said Kita. 'But be quick. I'll come with you as I want to do something too. Here, boatman, is it all right to get up on the bank?'

'If you want to do something you must be quick,' said the boatman. 'As soon as I've had my supper I'm going to start again.'

'Where are my sandals?' said Yaji.

'Never mind your sandals,' said Kita. 'We can wash our feet when we come on board again.'

The two then climbed up on to the bank.

'What a lovely view it is!' said Yaji. 'Where shall I do it?'

'Look out, there's a pool there,' said Kita. 'Go a bit further along. It is a fine night, isn't it?'

While they were gazing at the scenery one of the boats at the bank began to prepare to start, and it seemed to Yaji and Kita that it was their boat which was going on again. The boatmen were getting out their sweeps, and all the people who had got off the boat were rushing down the bank and jumping on again in great confusion. Yaji and Kita pushed through the crowd and jumped on board the boat, which had come from the Hakkenya at Ōsaka and was going up the river, although, confused by the boatmen's cries, the two thought it was the boat by which they had come from Fushimi. They thus got on to the wrong boat. As all was dark under the cover of the boat they did not dream that they had made a mistake, especially as they had seen some of the persons from their boat walking on the bank, and these, they thought, had also got aboard. But they could not see their faces in the darkness and there was nobody to warn them of their mistake. As everybody was tired of talking they had all squeezed into their places and were all lying down. Yaji and Kita felt about in the dark, and finding somebody's bundles mistook them for their own, and using them for pillows were soon lost in the world of dreams.

Meanwhile the boat was being towed and punted back to Fushimi, and it was near dawn when they passed Yodo and quite light when they got to Fushimi. The daylight streaming through the openings in the cover and the cries of the crows awakened the passengers, and when the boat reached its destination they all began to get ready to go on shore. Kita and Yaji drew back the cover and taking their hats and their bundles went on shore to the inn at the landing stage. They were surprised to find that they did not recognise any of the passengers, and they kept looking round to find those they had talked to the night before.

'Where's the old man who gave me the saké?' asked Yaji.

'And where's the man from Nagasaki and the man from Echigo? Perhaps they didn't come ashore here. Let's take our time and have something to eat.'

'Will any gentleman stop for a meal?' asked the maid of the inn.

'Yes,' said Yaji. 'We two will.'

The maid brought them some boiled rice in a beancurd bowl, which was the custom at that inn, but the two travellers, not having had a meal there before, still thought they were at Ōsaka and were quite unconcerned.

'I'll tell you what we'll do,' said Yaji. 'We'll go first to the Fundokawachiya in Nagamachi, the place recommended by the teahouse at Hasé, and put up there. What do you say to going to a theatre then?'

'I want to see Shinmachi first,' said Kita.

'Of course, of course,' said Yaji. 'How hot this soup is! Phew!'

Just then some other passengers came off the boat and ordered a meal.

'What did you do with the cakes you bought at the Toraya, Master Tahei?' asked one of the passengers.

'Would you believe it, Master Rokubei?' was the reply. 'I went to the Toraya yesterday on purpose to buy them and then I went and left them at the Kawaroku.'

'Well, you'd better go and get some more,' said his companion. 'It's only twenty-five miles.'

'Ha-ha-ha!' laughed Tahei. 'That's a good one.'

This struck Yaji as very strange.

'Excuse me,' he said, 'but that Toraya you mentioned just now, it must be in Ōsaka.'

'Of course,' said Rokubei.

'And that Kawaroku where you left the cakes, where is that?'

'That's near the Nippon Bridge.'

'And how far is that?'

'It's twenty-five miles.'

'Dear me!' said Yaji. 'I didn't think Ōsaka was such a big place, did you, Kita?'

'What are you talking about?' said Kita. 'They're making fools of us. Whoever heard of its being twenty-five miles from here? Nonsense!'

'Why, where do you think you are?' asked Tahei. 'This is Fushimi.'

'What?' cried Yaji. 'Fushimi? You're making fun of us, as Kitahachi said. We came from Fushimi last night.'

'Then you must have been bewitched by the Momoyama fox,' said Tahei. 'We'd better keep away from you.'

'Yes, you'd better,' said Kita. 'Bewitched by a fox, indeed! Why, we come from Edo. Absurd!'

249

At this point in the dispute two or three more of the party came in.

'What's that?' said one of them. 'What were you talking about? But instead of that just listen here. What do you think has happened to us? We've lost our bundles on the boat. Just think of it. We've hunted for them everywhere but can't find a trace of them.'

Just then one of them caught side of the bundles that Yaji had by his side.

'Here they are, Master Gonsuké,' he cried. 'I told you it would be better to come ashore and make inquiries about them.'

'Yes, that's it,' said Gonsuké, and he caught them up and was going to carry them off when Yaji stopped him.

'What are you doing?' he said. 'Those are our bundles.'

'What are you talking about?' said the other. 'Taking other people's things! Here's my name on it, see?'

Yaji looked at the bundles again and was startled to see that they were not their own.

'Well, I never,' he said. 'It's my mistake. They're yours right enough. I wonder where ours are.'

'What are you talking about? How should I know anything about your bundles?' said the man.

250

'This is awful,' said Yaji. 'What shall we do, Kita?'

'You tied mine up with yours,' said Kita, 'and it was by your side all the time. I don't know anything about it.'

'It's very strange,' said Yaji. 'Here,'—turning to the other travellers—'is this really Fushimi?'

'Ha-ha-ha!' they laughed. 'What's he saying? Just look at him. What a silly face he's got.'

'You're an impudent lot,' said Kita.

'Never mind whether we're impudent or not,' they replied. 'You're a couple of thieves. But we've got the bundles back so we won't be hard on you. You can go.'

'This is dreadful,' said Yaji. 'I don't understand what's happened. Do you, Kita?'

'Not me,' said Kita. 'What day was it yesterday?'

'Yesterday? Let's see,' said Yaji. 'There was a moon last night, wasn't there? It must be the twenty-fourth or twenty-fifth day.'

'Is it a long month or a short month. What day was it yesterday?'

'Where was it that we stopped the other day when they said it was the day of the rat?' asked Yaji.

'Oh yes,' said Kita. 'That was the place where we had such good food.'

'I never saw burdock leaves so big before,' said Yaji.

'Ha-ha-ha' laughed the other travellers. 'They certainly can't be in their right senses. Ha-ha-ha!' and they laughed till their sides ached.

'I see what they've done,' said an older man named Tarobei, after thinking awhile. 'They're neither of them clever enough to try and steal other people's baggage. What they've done is this. They went down the river from Fushimi last night, and when they got to the place where the boats stop they went on shore, leaving their bundles in the boat.'

'That's it, that's it,' said Yaji.

'I told you so,' said the old man. 'And then there were a lot of people getting in and out of the boats and when the boatman called out that the boat was starting everybody rushed to get in and they got into this boat instead of their own. So while they thought they were really in the boat they had travelled in, they were in another which brought them back again.'

'That's right,' said Kita. 'It was so dark when we got into the boat that we didn't notice any difference, and we were so tired that we went straight off to sleep. And when we got here this morning and looked round all the faces were strange and we were thunder-struck.'

'I thought it looked like a place I had seen before,' said Yaji. 'And now I look again I know it is! Ha-ha-ha! That's how we came to take your bundles, you see. Very sorry.'

'Ah, now I see it all,' said Kita.

'Yes, but where are our bundles gone to?' said Yaji.

'Your bundles were left on the boat,' said the old man, 'and they would be taken to the Hakkenya at Ōsaka. You'd better ask there.'

'Ha-ha-ha!' they all laughed.

'What a shame!' said Kita.

'Never mind,' said Yaji. 'There's nothing in the baggage but a change of clothes. I've got all my money in my belt. Let's just let it go. We're Edo people, we are.'

So although they wanted the baggage, they agreed that it would be rather foolish to go all the way to Ōsaka to get it, and they therefore decided to go straight on to Kyōto. Parting with the other travellers they set out with dejected faces to the capital.

After leaving Fushimi they soon came to Sumizomé, where there is a small pleasure-quarter. Suddenly a girl parted the sunblinds hanging from the eaves of one of the houses and ran out. She was dressed in a blue cotton dress with a velvet collar and her face looked quite white with the powder that was plastered on it.

'I say,' she said, seizing hold of Yaji's sleeve. 'Come inside for a little and amuse yourself.'

'No, no,' said Yaji. 'Let go.'

He shook her off and then she caught hold of Kita.

'How about you?' she said.

'How about me,' said Kita, and he put his finger to his lower eyelid and pulled it down.

'Won't you come?' she asked.

'Not even if I was Yoshihidé,' said Kita. 'Let go.'

'Oh, that's it, is it?' said the girl and she disappeared in the house.

Going on they came to Fuji-no-mori, where they worshipped at an Inari shrine.

'What do you say to having a drop here?' suggested Kita.

'All right,' said Yaji.

They parted the sunblinds and went into a small teahouse.

'I see they've got some sweet saké,' said Yaji. 'Here, granny, give us a cupful.'

'Ay, ay,' said the old woman. 'I'll draw you some in a minute.'

'Seems as if the old woman had fallen in love with you, Yaji,' said Kita. 'She keeps looking at you all the time in such a queer way.'

'Don't be a fool,' said Yaji. 'Here, old woman, hurry up.'

'Ay, ay' said the old woman. 'In a minute.'

Every time the old woman looked at Yaji her tears began to fall.

'What's the matter with your eyes, old lady?' asked Yaji. 'Are they bad?'

'It makes me feel sad every time I look at you,' said the old woman.

'Why's that?' asked Yaji.

'Wai-wai,' sobbed the old woman.

'That's strange,' said Kita. 'What makes you feel so sad?'

'I lost my only son the other day,' said the old woman, 'and he was just like that gentleman,—just like him.'

'Was he like me?' said Yaji. 'Then he must have been very good looking. What a pity he died!'

'He'd got a hoarse voice just like you,' said the old woman, 'and his face was pock-marked and black like yours, and he had a turn-up nose just like yours, and his eyes were crooked like yours.'

'Well, he seems to have had all my bad points,' said Yaji.

'He couldn't have had any of the good ones,' said Kita, 'because there ain't any.'

'Not only that but he was bald just like you,' went on the old woman, 'with such a little queue. Oh, he was just like you.'

'When you've finished taking stock of my face, perhaps you'll let us have that saké,' said Yaji.

'Oh dear, I forgot all about it,' said the old woman, and she brought out two cups and filled them with the saké.

'It's very weak,' said Kita when he'd tasted it.

'That's because it made me so sad to look at the gentleman that my tears fell into it,' said the old woman.

'What?' said Yaji. 'It ain't only tears. Seems to me as if your nose ran into it too.'

'Well, to tell you the truth,' said the old woman, 'it ran from my nose and my mouth too.'

' Oh, how nasty ! ' said Kita. ' I can't drink any more.'

' I've drunk all mine,' said Yaji. ' How horrid ! Come on, let's go.'

' How much is it ? ' asked Kita.

' That'll be six coppers,' said the old woman.

' You don't charge for the snot I suppose,' said Kita, and he went out spitting.

They walked on and on and gradually grew nearer and nearer to the capital. The road become busier and busier, and they noted the courteous manners of the people and the gay dresses of the women. Soon they came in front of the Great Buddha.

' What a fine big temple,' said Kita, ' and there's a Buddha at the top there.'

' Ah, this will be the Great Buddha,' said Yaji. ' I've heard about it, but it's bigger than I thought. Look at the enormous stones. Wonderful ! Wonderful ! '

Thus talking they went in at the gate and climbed the steps up to the central hall in which stood the figure of Buddha.

SECOND PART

IN the Great Hall of the Hokwō Temple the principal image is a carving of Rushana in a sitting position. It is six *jō* and three *shaku* high. The Hall, which faces the west, is twenty-seven ken from east to west and from south to north forty-five ken.

'It's much finer than I thought,' said Yaji. 'Look at his great palms, the size of a room.'

'And he's got whatyoumaycallems as big as a badger,' said Kita.

'What improper things you say,' said Yaji. 'A man could walk up his nostrils with his hat on.'

'If he sneezed he'd get blown out pretty quick,' said Kita.

'Don't talk foolishness,' said Yaji. 'Let's go round to the back and see what's there. Halloa, there's a window at the back.'

'That's where he breathes,' said Kita.

'He's not a whale,' said Yaji.

'I say,' said Kita. 'Look at those holes in the beams.'

'So there are,' said Yaji. 'That's strange.'

At the bottom of the beams supporting the roof were cut holes just large enough to allow a person to wriggle through, and the country visitors were amusing themselves by getting through the holes. Kita also got through.

'That's interesting,' said Kita. 'I can get through, but I don't think you could, Yaji. You're too fat.'

'What are you talking about?' said Yaji, and pushing Kita out of the way, he went down on all fours and wriggled halfway into the hole. Then he found that he couldn't get any further and tried to get back, but the hilt of his dirk caught sideways in the hole and hurt him unbearably.

'Oh, oh!' he groaned, red in the face. 'What an awful thing I've done.'

'What's the matter?' said Kita. 'Can't you get out?'

'Here, just pull my hands,' said Yaji.

'Ha-ha-ha!' laughed Kita. 'What fun!' and he caught hold of Yaji's hands and gave them a good pull.

'Oh! Oh!' said Yaji. 'That hurts.'

255

'What a weakling you are,' said Kita. 'Have a little patience.'

'Try pulling me by the legs,' suggested Yaji.

'All right,' said Kita, and he went round to the other side and caught hold of Yaji's legs.

'Ya-en-sa! Ya-en-sa!' he cried as he pulled.

'Oh! Oh! That hurts more,' groaned Yaji.

'Have a little patience and bear it,' cried Kita. 'You've come out quite a lot. Ya-en-sa! Ya-en-sa!'

'Wait a bit, wait a bit,' said Yaji. 'You'll pull my legs off. It's better from the other end.'

Accordingly Kita went round to the other side and began to pull his arms.

'Ya-en-sa! Ya-en-sa!' he cried. 'You've come out quite a lot.'

'Oh! Oh!' yelled Yaji. 'I can't stand it, Kita. Just go round to the other end and pull like you did before.'

'How you change your mind!' said Kita, and he went round to the other side and caught hold of his legs again.

'Ya-en-sa! Ya-en-sa!' he cried.

'Wait, wait,' said Yaji. 'It's better when you pull my arms after all.'

'If I go on pulling you first at one end and then at the other,' said Kita, 'we'll go on all day. Wait a bit, I've got an idea.' He called to some pilgrims who were standing by.

'Just come here a minute, will you?' he said. 'If you pull in front I'll go and pull behind.'

'Don't be a fool,' said Yaji. 'How are you going to get me out by pulling at both ends?'

'Well, we can't get you out pulling first at one end and then at the other,' said Kita.

'If we pulled at both ends,' said one of the pilgrims, 'we'd stretch you a bit and you'd come out easily.'

'I know what to do,' said Kita. 'We'll go and buy a bottle of vinegar for you to drink, Yaji.'

'What's the good of that?' asked Yaji.

'Why, you know vinegar makes you thin,' said Kita.

'Ha-ha-ha!' laughed the pilgrims. 'But we haven't time for that. What we'd better do is to get a hammer and hit him on the head, so as to drive him out.'

'I never thought of that,' said Kita. 'That's a good idea. But don't you think we might hurt him?'

'Then I don't see how we're going to get him out,' said the pilgrim.

Here a countryman joined in.

'I'm from a far province,' he said, 'but I don't like to see the gentleman in such a fix.'

'Well, if you can suggest anything,' said Kita, 'let's hear it.'

'Well, I think if we were to cut his leg and rub some hot pepper in he'd get such a shock that he'd get out by hisself.'

'That's like the girl and the snake,' said Kita. 'It's a good idea.'

'What I think,' said another pilgrim, 'is that you want to make

his bones soft. Then we could pull him out. What we ought to do is to get some quicklime and sprinkle it on him.'

'Ah,' said the countryman, 'and you might get him a coffin at the same time. If we break his arms and legs we could probably get him in.'

'What foolishness you're talking!' groaned Yaji. 'What's the use of saying such silly things? Can't you help me, Kita?'

'Wait a minute,' said Kita. 'Ah, I see. The scabbard of your dirk has got caught crossways,' and he put in his hand and felt about till at last he managed to take off the dirk.

' Ah, that feels easier,' said Yaji.

' There,' said Kita. ' Now if you'll all push in front I'll pull his legs from behind. Ya-en-sa ! Ya-en-sa ! '

' He's coming. He's coming,' said the pilgrim. ' Just a little more. Shove up.'

' Oh, oh ! ' groaned Yaji.

' Ha-ha-ha ! ' laughed Kita. ' What a joke ! '

' Oh, oh ! It hurts,' groaned Yaji.

' Can't be helped,' said Kita. ' En-ya-en-ya ! There you are,' and he pulled Yaji out on to the floor.

' Thank you, thank you,' panted Yaji, wiping his face. ' Thank you all. Now I know that it hurts the person being born more than it hurts the person bearing. My bones did crack when I was coming out. And look at my kimono how torn it is.'

Going out of the temple grounds into the bustling streets of the city they fell into admiration of the manners of the citizens, the gentleness of the men and women, even down to the postboys and the baggage-carriers, and the precise way in which they were dressed. As they were thus walking along looking at the strange sights, suddenly there was an agitation in the crowd, and they saw all the people, young and old, start running violently, uttering wild cries, ' Ho-u-ho, yoi-yoi. Ekkorasassa. Ho-u-ho, yoi-yoi. Ekkorasassa.'

' What are they all running for ? ' asked Yaji. ' There's something happened over there. What a fearful crowd ! I say,' he called to a passer-by. ' Can you tell me what the trouble is about ? '

' There's a terrible quarrel going on over there,' replied the man.

' A fight in the capital ? ' said Kita. ' That should be worth seeing,' and they hurried on till they came up to the crowd, which completely filled the street. Pushing their way to the front to get a look they saw the two men who had quarrelled. One of them appeared to be a fishmonger from the fish-tray that was on the ground beside him. His opponent seemed like a workman,—a very stalwart young man. In the capital people are not easily moved to anger, and although it was a quarrel, the two did not try to hit each other, but stood together in the sunshine quite quietly.

' I beg your pardon,' said the fishmonger. ' It was not I that collided with you. I am sure you do not wish me to knock your head off.'

'You talk big,' replied the workman, 'but if you move a finger I shall be compelled to retaliate.'

While he was speaking he folded his towel neatly and bound it round his head.

'You wag your jaw too much,' said the fishmonger. 'Where do you come from at all ? '

'I ? ' said the workman. 'I come from Ame-no-kōji in Horikawa.'

'What's your name ? ' asked the fishmonger.

'I am called Kihei,' replied the workman.

'How old are you ? '

'I am twenty-four.'

'Don't talk nonsense,' said the fishmonger. 'You can't be as young as that. You must be lying.'

'What are you talking about ? ' said the workman. 'It's perfectly true. My wife unfortunately died this year.'

'That was a great misfortune,' said the fishmonger. 'You must have been sadly grieved.'

'That is not all,' continued the workman. 'I am burdened with the care of a baby, which gives me great trouble.'

'I can imagine so,' said the fishmonger. 'I am two years older than you.'

'Then I am the younger of the two,' said the workman. 'Where is your house ? '

'It's the first street to the east in Inokuma-dōri,' replied the fishmonger.

'Really ? ' said the workman. 'A blind doctor named Sumpaku lives there.'

'Well,' said the fishmonger, 'and what about him ? '

'Oh, nothing, save that he is a relative of mine,' replied the workman. 'If you go that way you might remember me to him.'

'Excuse me,' said the fishmonger. 'I see no reason why I should carry your messages. You must be a big fool.'

Here the people looking on began to yawn.

'Come on, Jūbei,' called one. 'Let's go.'

'Wait a bit,' said Jūbei. 'They're just going to begin to fight.'

'But I left a visitor at home,' expostulated the other.

'Then go and bring him here,' said Jūbei. 'And you might bring a mat along at the same time.'

Many of the spectators were sitting down on mats under the eaves of the houses, pulling the hairs from their chins to pass the time.

'The fellow over on the other side is the best,' said another man in the crowd.

'No, no,' said his friend. 'The one on this side is a good talker too.'

'Yes, he talks all right,' said the first man. 'By the way, that reminds me, how's your missus ? Is she better ? '

'Thank you,' replied his friend. 'She got very much better, but yesterday she got very bad again and last night she died.'

'Ah, that must have given you great distress,' said the other. 'When is the funeral to take place ? '

'It had just started,' said his friend, 'when I saw all the people running and heard there was a terrible quarrel going on here. So I told them to wait while I went to see.'

While the people in the crowd were thus talking the quarrel was going on.

'Come a little more this way,' said the workman. 'We are in the shade and it feels a little cold.'

'Well, and what if I do ? ' asked the fishmonger.

'I think you were pleased to call me a fool just now,' continued the workman. 'May I ask why I am a fool ? '

'You are a fool because you are a fool, I suppose,' said the fishmonger.

'What are you talking about ? ' said the workman. 'From your observation I should judge you were the fool.'

'Oh, no, not at all,' replied the fishmonger. 'I am a very intelligent person.'

'If you are intelligent,' said the workman, 'then I must be also.'

'Is that so, indeed,' said the fishmonger. 'Then I think that this quarrel had better cease.'

'Yes, indeed,' replied the workman. 'It would be a pity to spoil our clothes, so I think we had better give it up.'

'It's getting late, too,' said the fishmonger. 'I must really go.'

'Well, I'm going your way,' said the workman. 'Let's go together. What pleasant weather it is to-day.'

'Yes,' said the fishmonger, 'it's getting quite warm.'

They went off together quite amiably and the crowd dispersed, while Yaji and Kita held their sides and laughed.

'Ha-ha-ha!' laughed Yaji. 'These Westcountry people have got long tempers. Did you ever see such a gentle quarrel as that?'

'They were thinking what they would get out of it,' said Kita.

Passing along they came to Kiyomizu, where the teahouses are thick on each side of the road and outside all the girls stand screaming, 'Come in. Come in. Come in. Try our famous macaroni. Come in. Come in.'

'We'll go a bit further before we have something to eat,' said Yaji.

Soon they came to the Kiyomizu Temple, in the main hall of which stands the Eleven-faced Thousand-handed Kwannon. Yaji and Kita rested here a while and then wandered round the precincts till they came to where an old priest, standing by a table on an elevated piece of ground, was calling to the crowd of pilgrims.

'A picture of the holy Kwannon of this temple may be obtained here,' he cried. 'Try its wonderful virtues. It makes the blind to talk and the dumb to hear. The cripples who have walked all the way here are able to walk all the way home again. Those who worship it just once, even though they are strong and healthy, enter Paradise immediately. The devout who desire salvation should not leave without receiving one of these pictures. Offerings may be made to any amount. Are there no believers here?'

'What a chattering old priest,' said Kita. 'By the way, Yaji, I've heard a story about people jumping off from this place.'

'From ancient times,' said the priest, 'those who have made a vow to Buddha have jumped from here in perfect safety.'

'They'd be smashed to pieces if they did,' said Yaji.

'Do they ever do it now?' asked Kita.

'Yes,' said the priest. 'Even naturally timid people have been known to come and jump off here. There was a young girl jumped off here the other day.'

'What happened to her?' asked Kita.

'She jumped and fell,' said the priest.

'Yes, but what happened after she fell?' asked Kita.

'What an inquisitive person you are,' said the priest. 'Well, as she was full of sin, the Buddha, for punishment, made her turn up her eyes.'

'Didn't her nose turn up too?' asked Kita.

'Well, she hadn't got any nose when she started,' replied the priest.

'Did she lose her senses?' asked Kita.

'Yes, she became unconscious,' answered the priest.

'And what happened then?' asked Kita.

'What a persistent fellow you are,' said the priest. 'What do you want to know all this for?'

'It's a bad habit of mine,' said Kita. 'I'm never satisfied till I hear everything to the end.'

'Well, I'll tell you?' said the priest. 'When the girl got to the ground she went mad.'

'Dear me,' said Kita. 'And what did she do then?'

'She began reciting the million prayers,' said the priest.

'And what then?' asked Kita.

'She struck the bell.'

'And what then?'

'Namu Amida Butsu.'

'And after that?'

'Namu Amida Butsu.'

'And what came next?'

'Namu Amida Butsu.'

'Yes, but what came after that?'

'Namu Amida Butsu.'

'Yes, yes, yes, but what came after the prayers?'

'Well, you must wait till she's finished. She's got to say it a million times.'

'What?' cried Kita. 'Have I got to wait till she's done reciting the prayer a million times? How awful!'

'Well, you said you liked to hear about everything to the end,' said the priest, 'so if you have patience you'll know. If you get tired of waiting you might help her say the prayers.'

'Ah, that would be interesting,' said Kita. 'You help too, Yaji. Namu Amida Butsu. Namu Amida Butsu.'

'You must strike the bell too,' said the priest. He struck the bell loudly while he recited the prayer. 'Namu Amida Butsu. (Chan-chan.) Namu Amida Butsu. (Chan-chan.)'

'This is quite amusing,' said Kita.

'Here, just hold the bell a minute. I've got to go somewhere,' said the priest.

He thrust the bell into Kita's hand and went off. Kita took the bell and went on praying, 'Namu Amida Butsu. Namu Amida Butsu. (Chan-chan. Chiki-chan-chan. Chiki-chan-chan.)'

'You don't strike the bell properly,' said Yaji. 'Give it here.'

'What?' said Kita. 'Don't I do it properly?'

He began striking the bell so loudly and making such a row that a priest came out of the temple and fell into a terrible passion when he saw what was going on.

'Here,' he cried. 'What are you doing at that holy shrine. Don't you know any better than to behave in that uncouth manner in a sacred place?'

'The priest in charge went away,' said Kita, 'so we thought we'd just keep things going.'

'Don't make any of your silly jokes here,' said the priest. 'Where do you think you are?'

'This is Kiyomizu, Atsumori's burial place, ain't it?' said Kita.

'You must be mad,' said the priest.

'Yes, that's why we're saying the million prayers,' replied Kita.

'Nonsense,' said the priest. 'Go away at once. This is a holy place of prayer.'

The priest got so angry and spoke in such a loud voice that many more priests came running out of the temple, and as they looked very threatening Yaji and Kita slunk down the hill.

'That comes of being too clever with the bell,' said Kita.

It was now four o'clock and the two thought they had better set off for Sanjō to look for an inn for the night. As they were going along they saw a man coming from the opposite direction carrying a tub and some radishes.

'Radish stale,' he kept calling out. 'Radish stale.'

'Well, I've heard of pumpkins playing the flute, but never of radishes relieving themselves,' said Kita.

'I suppose he wants to exchange the radishes for the stale,' said Yaji.

'Here you are,' cried the man. 'Big radish stale.'

As he was going along calling, two men, apparently lower retainers of some sort, came up and began to bargain with the man.

'Here,' cried one of them. 'We'll give you our stale for three radishes.'

'Well, just come down here and show me how much you've got,' said the man.

He led them down a side road, and Yaji and Kita, anxious to see what they were going to do, followed after.

'There, do it here,' said the man, putting the tub down.

After they had done it the man tilted the tub on one side to see how much there was. 'Is that all ?' he asked.

'I broke wind at the end,' said one of the retainers, 'so there can't be any more.'

'That's no good,' said the man. 'Just shake yourselves and try again.'

'We're not keeping any back,' said the retainer. 'There's nothing left.'

'Then I can't give you three radishes,' said the man. 'Take two.'

'Yes,' said the other retainer, 'I know it's only a little, but it's very good. Other people only live on rice and tea, but we live on nothing but meat.'

'Yes, but there's nothing of it,' said the man.

'Well, don't make such a fuss,' said the retainer. 'Take it home and mix some water with it and it will make quite a lot. Give us the three radishes.'

'You say nothing but "give, give,"' said the man, 'but I want something in return. Go and drink some tea, and see if you can't do some more.'

They were going on disputing, when Kitahachi, who had been enjoying the joke, spoke to the retainers.

'Excuse me,' he said, 'but fortunately I want to relieve myself, and if it's not being too rude I'll let you have it. If you add mine to yours he'll let you have three radishes.'

'Thank you very much for your kind offer,' said one of the retainers, 'but I'm afraid we trespassing on your goodness too much.'

'Not at all,' said Kita. 'I haven't very much to offer, but if the little I have is of any service to you . . .'

'Well, we'll accept your offer then,' said the retainer.

The tub was brought and put before Kita.

'No, no,' he said. 'Put it further away. My distance is a couple of yards.'

'That's wonderful,' said the man with the radishes. 'You can't be a native of this place. Theirs is so thin it's no use.'

'I've always been a great man at that sort of thing ever since I was born,' said Kita. 'I'm the sort of man that has to carry a tub around with him.'

'How lucky you are !' said one of the retainers.

'Well then, just put the tub on your shoulder and I'll go with you,' said the scavenger.

'Well, I'm not quite so frequent as that,' said Kita.

'You've got a friend with you, I see,' said the man. 'Doesn't he want to do something ?'

'No, thank you,' said Yaji. 'I'm the sort of man that does four to eight gallons at a time without any difficulty, but lately I haven't been able to do any at all, which gives me much trouble.'

'There's a way to cure that,' said the man.

'How's that ?' asked Yaji.

'Well, you know, if saké won't run well from the bung of a saké tub they bore a hole in the top of the tub and then it comes out very fast. If yours won't come out all you have to do is to bore a hole in your forehead and it'll come out all right then.'

'Ha-ha-ha !' laughed Kita. 'That's a good one. But it's getting late. Let's go.'

As they were going along they saw coming from the opposite direction two or three girls wearing veils, as is the custom in the capital. They looked very fair and graceful, and Kita was quickly on the alert.

'Halloa !' he said. 'Look at these girls. Ain't they pretty ?'

'They look a frolicsome lot,' said Yaji. 'What have they got their clothes over their heads for ?'

'Those are veils,' said Kita. 'I'm going to speak to that pretty little one.'

'Excuse me,' he said, going up to one of the girls, 'but could you tell me the way to Sanjō ?'

Now this girl was an attendant at the Palace and very haughty.

'If you wish to go to Sanjō,' she replied, 'you must go straight along here till you get to Ishigaki and there you must turn to the left and you'll come to Sanjō bridge.'

As she was a Palace attendant and Kita appeared to her a little impudent and forward, she had directed him to Gojō Bridge instead of Sanjō, as a punishment.

'Thank you very much,' said Kita, quite unconscious of the trick that had been played on him, and they continued on their way.

'That girl had a very haughty way with her,' said Kita.

'Yes,' said Yaji, 'she treated us very disdainfully. What a shame! Ha-ha-ha!'

They went on till they got to Ishigaki and then turned to the left as they had been told till they came to Gojō Bridge. By this time it was getting quite dark. Then a man stopped them

'Can you tell me the way to Shirudani?' he asked.

'Yes,' said Kita. 'Go straight along and you'll get to Shirudani. If you fall you must get up again and go on, and don't mind if you tread on some cow's dung.'

'What do you mean by answering in that way, you cur?' said the man.

'What do you mean by calling me a cur?' said Kita. 'Haven't I told you the road?'

'You talk big,' said the man. 'Do you want me to cut you down?'

Then they saw that the man had two or three companions with him, all strongly built, with long swords at their thighs. They looked like wrestlers.

Kita immediately altered his tone.

'Excuse me,' he faltered.

'He's half drunk, your honours,' said Yaji. 'Just overlook it this time.'

'That I cannot,' said the wrestler. 'What are you?'

'We're only two travellers, your honour,' said Yaji.

'If you're travellers,' said the wrestler, 'you must have an inn. Where is it?'

'We were just going to our inn at Sanjō, your honour,' said Yaji.

'What are you talking about now?' said the wrestler. 'Sanjō,

266

indeed ! We've just come from the Amigasaya at Sanjō. This is Gojō Bridge.'

'Isn't this Sanjō ? ' said Yaji. 'There, Kita, that girl who showed us the way played a trick on us.'

'Where do you come from ? ' asked the wrestler.

'We came from Kiyomizu.'

'Ha-ha-ha ! ' laughed the wrestler. 'They've been bewitched by a fox. Don't let's waste any more time on them. Get out, get out. You're a couple of fools.'

The wrestlers went on their way laughing, and Yaji and Kita crossed the bridge, sore at heart and grumbling at having been misdirected, and wandered on through the busy streets, till, past the bridge, they found a street on the left where lanterns were hanging from all the eaves and the air was filled with the sound of the samisen, coupled with lively songs.

Men with their heads tied up were prowling round and peeping into the houses. This street is called Gojō Shinchi and is a small pleasure-quarter. The wicket of each house was open and at each door stood a girl. One of them caught hold of Yaji as he passed and whispered something to him. Turning round to look, he saw that inside the house there were a number of courtesans.

'I say, Kita,' he said, 'this is a courtesans' quarter. Suppose we spend the night here.'

'So it is,' said Kita. 'Well, we haven't got any baggage, so it will look all right.'

'Please come in,' said the girl.

'We'll go in,' said Yaji, 'but how much do you charge ? '

'Do you want to stop all night ? ' she asked.

'Of course,' said Yaji.

'It's early yet,' said the girl, 'so it will be seven *mommé*.'

'They say you can beat down these Westcountry courtesans,' said Kita. 'Make it half.'

'Say four hundred coppers each,' said Yaji, 'and we'll stop. If you can't do it for that we'll give it up.'

'Very well,' said the girl. 'Please come in.'

'Is that all right ? ' said Kita. 'I suppose you've got two courtesans not engaged.'

The girl conducted them upstairs, where, as the roof was low, Yaji bumped his head and groaned.

'What's the matter?' asked Kita.

'Please take care,' said the girl.

She brought a tobacco-box and with her came two courtesans named Kichiya and Kingo, each wearing a thick silk robe with a black velvet collar. As the room upstairs was so low that their hairpins scraped against the ceiling, they walked with a stoop, holding their skirts up at one side. When they had entered the room they sat down, crying out that they were tired.

'The lantern's very dark,' said Kita. 'Come more this way.'

'Where do you gentlemen come from?' asked Kichiya.

'Let's see, where did I meet you before?' said Yaji.

'Ho-ho-ho!' laughed Kingo. 'You're just like someone I met at the Rokkaku morning market. You talk with an accent so I suppose you are travellers.'

'You must be pilgrims,' said Kichiya.

'Something like that,' answered Yaji.

'Won't you have some saké?' asked Kichiya.

'Yes, yes,' said Yaji. 'Let's have some saké quickly.'

'And what would you like to eat with it?' asked Kichiya.

'I think riceballs would be nice,' said Kingo.

'I think *kachin* would be nicer,' said Kichiya.

'Well, I don't care whether it's *kachin* or *yachin*,' said Yaji, 'only let's have it quickly.'

'I'll bring it at once,' said Kichiya.

She went downstairs to get it and while she was away the other courtesan took a looking-glass out of her sash and re-powdered her face. At last the saké bottle and cups arrived, together with two big bowls on trays. This astonished Yaji.

'It's strange giving us a bowl each,' he said. 'I've always heard that Kyōto is a stingy place, but they don't seem to be so here.'

'It's cheap at four hundred,' said Kita.

They thought that the saké and the comestibles were included in the four hundred coppers.

'Well, let's have a drink,' said Yaji.

'All right, said Kita, and he gulped down a cupful. 'What's in the bowl? It looks like onions, but it's all burnt black.'

'That's *kachin*,' said Kichiya. This is a Westcountry dish of rice-cake and onions. As the girl was not fond of drinking and

268

liked this dish, she had ordered it for the guests. Kita did not know what it was.

'I've never heard of *kachin*,' he said. 'What is it?'

'It's nice,' said Kichiya.

Kita took a taste. 'Why, it's rice-cake,' he said.

'Get out!' said Yaji. 'These Westcountry people are strange. Fancy eating rice-cake with saké! Whoever heard of such a thing?'

'I'll bring you something else,' said Kingo.

She went downstairs and soon came back with a dish of rice-balls done in the Westcountry style. As she was very fond of them she had ordered them.

'What's this?' asked Kita. 'Why, it's rice and fish.'

'It's cockles and rice,' said Kingo.

'Everything they bring is stranger and stranger,' said Yaji. 'I'm not going to drink any more saké.'

There was some more talk, but to cut it short the bedding was brought in and screens were put up between the beds. Just then a woman of about forty, apparently the mistress of the house, came upstairs with the bill and pulled aside the screen. 'Excuse me,' she said.

'Who is it?' asked Yaji.

'I've come for the money,' said the woman. She presented a paper to Yaji, who opened and looked at it.

'What's this?' said Yaji. 'I thought we had to pay four hundred each, that is eight hundred, but here's four hundred for the rice-cake, two hundred for the rice balls, one hundred and eighty for the saké, fifty for the candles, altogether one thousand six hundred and thirty coppers. This is terrible. Are these all extra? I thought they were included in the charge. Here, Kita, what do you think of it?'

'What's that?' said Kita. 'You people must think we come from the country. It's very dear if you charge for the saké extra. Is this four hundred for the rice-cake we had in the bowls? Why there were only three or four pieces of rice-cake and a scrap of onion. Everybody knows that Kyōto people are stingy, but I didn't think they were as stingy as all that. Even down to the candle! You must cut it down.'

'Ho-ho-ho!' laughed the woman. 'So you think Kyōto

people are bad, do you ? And you won't pay even fifty coppers for a bit of candle ? Do you think it's right of you to complain of things being dear after you've eaten everything up ? '

' Oh, don't let's have any argument,' said Yaji. ' There's a gold piece for you. You must make that do.'

He threw her a gold piece as he spoke, and the woman took it and went down the stairs grumbling.

' Ain't it awful, Kita,' said Yaji.

' I don't like giving in to them,' said Kita. ' Can't we get our own back ? '

Just then Kichiya came in.

' What did you want to go and leave me alone for ? ' she asked. ' What are you doing ? Aren't you going to bed ? '

She seized hold of Kita's hand and dragged him away.

' Here, here,' said Kita. ' What are you doing, taking off my girdle ? '

He spoke loud so that Yaji should hear him.

' It's warm to-night,' she said. ' I'll make you comfortable.'

It is a rule among the courtesans in the West Country that when they have a guest for the first time they let it appear as if their sash-band had come undone by itself. This Kichiya, however, was a middle-aged woman and not very knowing, so she unfastened her sash, and took off Kita's kimono as if she were on terms of the closest intimacy with him. Thus they lay down.

Soon the night began to deepen, and only the lonely sound of the dogs barking far off could be heard and the sound of drums. It was two o'clock before Kichiya opened her eyes and spoke to Kitahachi.

' How sound you sleep,' she said.

' What is it ? ' asked Kita.

' I want to go somewhere,' said the girl.

She got up and put on Kita's kimono, which had been thrown down beside the pillow, and fastened her sash.

' Lend me your kimono for a bit,' she said. ' I want to look like a man and deceive the people downstairs.'

' It suits you fine,' said Kita. ' What a joke ! '

' I must tie something round my head,' she said. Then she took a towel and tied it round her head and went downstairs.

Kita did not go to sleep again, but lay and waited for the girl to return. 'Perhaps she's gone to another guest,' he thought, and continued to wait. Then the bell sounded for four o'clock and soon day began to dawn. Deciding that he could wait no longer, Kita clapped his hands loudly and the mistress of the house came upstairs in answer to his call.

'Who's that calling?' she asked.

'I did,' said Kita. 'That girl I had went downstairs some time ago and I've seen nothing of her since. Just call her, will you?'

'There's a row going on downstairs about her,' said the woman.

'What's the row?' asked Kita.

'The girl's run off in a man's kimono.'

'What?' said Kita. 'Do you mean to say she's run away? How awful! That man's kimono was mine.'

'What was she doing with your kimono?' asked the woman.

'She said she wanted to give them a surprise downstairs,' said Kita, 'and asked me to lend it to her.'

'And did you lend it to her?' asked the woman.

'Yes,' said Kita. 'I didn't know she was going to run away. How was I to tell? Haven't you got a kimono you could lend me? Just go downstairs and ask at once.'

'I'll tell 'em that downstairs,' said the woman, and she went down.

Soon a big man in a dressing gown, apparently the master of the house, came upstairs, accompanied by the cook and two or three other men. They came stamping up the stairs and stood round Kita's pillow.

'Are you the fellow that lent the girl a kimono?' asked the landlord.

'Yes, that's me,' said Kita.

'You, is it?' said the landlord. 'You villain! Get up and let's look at your face.'

'What are you making such a fuss about it for?' asked Kita.

'Making a fuss?' said the landlord. 'If you lent her your kimono you must know where she's gone. Tell me the truth.'

'Don't talk nonsense!' said Kita. 'I don't know anything about it.'

'It's no use telling me that,' said the landlord. 'I know you had something to do with it.'

'Nonsense.!' said Kita.

'He talks big, don't he?' said the landlord. 'Drag him out.'

The men immediately dragged Kita out of the bed, awakening Yaji, who jumped up when he saw what they were doing.

'Here, that's my mate,' he said. 'What are you going to do with him?'

He tried to push the landlord aside but was held by the other men.

'They're working together,' cried the cook. 'Let's take 'em both.'

Yaji and Kita were then dragged downstairs. Yaji was completely mystified as to what the trouble was about till, to his surprise, he heard the story from Kita, who was now quite repentant of having lent the girl the kimono. But the master of the house would not listen to their excuses and tied them to a post in the kitchen, where, as the day advanced, all the people in the neighbourhood came to stare at them, much to their mortification.

Among the visitors who came to see them was a man named Jūkichi, who was apparently the owner of the house.

'I've heard about Kichiya running away,' he said. 'Where are the fellows who helped her?'

'There they are, tied up there,' said the landlord.

'They look like thieves,' said Jūkichi.

'They pretend they're travellers,' said the landlord, 'but I don't suppose they have any home of their own.'

'I feel sorry for them though,' said the owner.

He and the landlord both came nearer to have a look at them.

'You've got yourselves into a nice fix by your wickedness,' said Jūkichi. 'Aren't there some more of you? You'd better confess all you know.'

'I don't know anything about it at all,' said Yaji. 'We only came here to spend the night. Can't you help us? My hands are tied so I can't hold them up in prayer to you, but I'll do it with my feet. Here, Kita, help me.'

'All right,' said Kita, and he began praying to Kompira. 'Praise be to the Great Gongen Sama Kompira and may he remove from me this misfortune. Namu Kimyō Chōrai. Namu Kimyō Chōrai.'

'What's the good of praying to Kompira,' said the landlord. 'That won't help you. Fortunately you haven't got any clothes on, so you're just right for trying the cold water penance.'

'No, no,' said Kita. 'I'm really a believer in Kompira, but you see I'm not like other believers. I've taken a vow against the cold water penance. I only get the protection of the god when I wear plenty of clothes, and drink warm drinks and get near the fire. Won't you let me have a kimono so that I can get warm ?'

'You're a cunning rogue,' said the landlord.

'No, it's really quite true,' said Yaji. 'It's a great misfortune for me to have to associate with this fellow. I suffer from chronic spasms. Oh !'

'If you've got spasms,' said the landlord, 'I'll tie the rope a bit tighter round your waist. That will cure you.'

'No, no,' said Yaji. 'If you'll just untie the rope so that I can jump about I'll soon be better.'

'Ha-ha-ha !' laughed Jūkichi. 'This is a clever fellow. You'd better let him go. They're both of them fools. I expect he only lent the girl the kimono.'

'Yes,' said the landlord. 'They neither of them seem very bright. Perhaps I'd better let them go after all.'

'Oh, thank you, thank you,' said Kita. 'But I can't go out without any clothes.'

'Get out,' said the landlord. 'I don't want to listen to any of your excuses.'

'I'll go then,' said Kita. 'I'll go.'

'Go along with you,' said Jūkichi. 'A couple of fools !'

They untied the ropes and released them.

'See what you got us into, Kita,' said Yaji.

'What about me ?' said Kita. 'I got my kimono stolen. Oh, how cold it is ?'

'Ha-ha-ha !' laughed the landlord. 'Well, I'll take pity on you and lend you something to cover you.'

'Thank you, thank you,' said Kita. 'Anything will do. I shall be so grateful.'

273

'Oh, you've turned beggar, have you?' said the landlord. 'Bring a piece of matting from the shed. That'll suit you.'

'There's that straw bag that the things came in yesterday,' said the servant. 'Wear that.'

'What, put that on?' said Kita. 'How cruel you are!'

'Do you despise my kindness?' said the landlord. 'Won't you wear it?'

'Thank you, thank you,' said Kita. 'I think I'd like best to go as I am.'

'What a chap you are,' said Yaji. 'Here, I'll lend you my raincoat.'

He took off his raincoat and put it on Kita, and they started off.

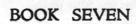
BOOK SEVEN

BOOK SEVEN

E read in the poem that the capital is famous for its flowers and its temples, which, there is no denying, are very large and impressive. Then there are the flowers in spring and the maples in the autumn. In all directions beautiful scenery is to be found, and if you take with you a tub of the famous saké of Kamogawa your spirits will be lifted up to the skies. The merchants there are dressed in clothes different from those of other parts, for in Kyōto, they say, people will spend their money on clothes at the expense of their stomachs till they faint with hunger in the streets. This is because the cloths from the Nishijin looms have the colour of delicate flowers and are as pure as the waters of the River Hōri. Then there is the face powder of Kamamoto, and the toilet powder of Kawabata, as white as snow. The folding fans of Mieidō, the open fans of Fushimi, the rice-cakes of sweet-smelling Kōdōmae, the Daibutsu rice-cakes of Maruyama, the spikenard shoots of Daigo, the leaf buds of Kurama, which are noted in the Teikinōrai, the turnips of Tōji, the vegetables of Mibu—these are some of the things of which the Kyōto people are proud.

Thus it was that, for the first time, those rowdy travellers, Yajirobei and Kitahachi, came to the city of so many famous products. They had completed their stolen journey to Isé and were now taking an opportunity to see the capital, after they had boarded the wrong boat on the River Yodo, lost their baggage, drunk a cup in the pleasure-quarters of Gojō in the best of spirits, and had paid heavily for it.

Kitahachi had lost his good name and was only kept from being naked by Yajirobei having lent him a cotton coat which he fortunately had. Penniless amid all the amusements of the capital, Kita wandered on shivering in the keen morning air, till he got to Gojō Bridge, where of old Ushiwakamaru fought with Benkei. Turning to the west there, they passed by the historic remains of Kawara-no-in and of Kadodé Hachiman, along by the bank of the River Takasé, where all day the boats are being hauled along.

' It makes me madder every time I think of it,' said Kita. ' If we could only find an old kimono somewhere. I'd like a wadded one,—just one would do. Haven't you any advice to give me, Yaji ? '

'You don't want to buy a kimono,' said Yaji. 'When Edo people go on stolen pilgrimages it's the custom for them to come back naked.'

'But it's so cold,' said Kita.

'Well, luckily, there's a bath-house there,' said Yaji. 'Go in and warm yourself.'

'That's an excellent idea,' said Kita, and he darted off to the bath-house.

There was a wicket door in front of the house and a curtain. Kita dived through the curtain and rushed into the shop.

'What can I do for you ? ' asked the keeper of the shop, who was astonished at this abrupt entrance of a naked man. 'What is it you require ? '

Kita looked round and saw that it was not a bath-house. 'What a shame ! ' he said. 'I thought it was a bath-house.'

'Ha-ha-ha ! ' laughed the shopkeeper. 'That's because you saw the character for bath on the door, I expect. You thought it read *Public Bath,* but it's the name of a medicine to put in the bath.'

'So it is,' said Yaji. 'What a joke ! '

'Oh-h ! ' shuddered Kita. 'I'm colder than ever now.'

Thus Kita went on grumbling till they came to a shop where a number of second-hand kimonos were hung out for sale. At the entreaty of Kita, Yaji picked out a blue wadded garment and asked the price.

'Good day, good day,' said the shopkeeper. 'Please sit down and have a smoke. I'll get you some tea. Oh, the fire's gone out. Bring some fire, boy.''

'Never mind the tea,' said Kita, shivering. 'How much is this kimono ? '

'Yes, yes,' said the shopkeeper. 'That's a good one. I'll let you have it cheap.'

Here the apprentice brought the tea. 'This tea's cold,' said the shopkeeper. 'Why don't you bring some hot tea ? '

'The missus said I needn't make any tea as she was going to have rice gruel this morning,' said the boy, 'so I didn't make any. I've brought what was made yesterday.'

'Yesterday's tea ! ' said Yaji. 'It's like the wind let by a *kappa.*

278

By the way that reminds me.   Excuse my rudeness, but could you show me the convenience ? '

' Do you want to go there ? ' asked the shopkeeper.

' It's not lukewarm,' put in the boy.   ' It's boiling.'

' Who boiled it ? ' asked his master.

' I've just been there,' said the boy.   ' Go and look.   It's steaming like anything.'

' You dirty young rascal,' said the landlord.

' Never mind about that,' said Kita, ' but just tell me how much this kimono is.   Let's settle it quick.   I'm so cold I can't stand it.'

' Get more over there in the sunshine if you're cold,' said the shopkeeper.   ' There was a gentleman here yesterday who said this was a very warm house, and after he'd basked in the sun all day he said he didn't want a kimono if he could come here every day and warm himself in the sun.'

' Oh, bother the sun ! ' said Kita.   ' Do you want to sell this kimono or don't you ? '

' Yes, yes,' said the shopkeeper.   ' Is this the one you want ? '

' You must make it cheap,' said Kita.

' It's the blue one, isn't it ? ' said the shopkeeper.   Here he brought out his abacus.   ' I can't let you have that under three thousand five hundred coppers.'

' That's too dear,' said Kita.   ' I come from Edo and I know all about the price of old clothes.   Don't try to fool me.   Tell me the right price.'

' Ah, perhaps you're in the business too,' said the shopkeeper.

' No, no,' said Kita.   ' I'm in the pawning business.'

' Do you receive goods or do you pawn them ? ' asked the shopkeeper.

' His business is to pawn them,' said Yaji.

' That's how I know what things are worth,' said Kita.   ' You wouldn't get more than a thousand coppers on a kimono like that.   The pawnbroker would lose if he gave more on it.'

' What are you talking about ? ' said the shopkeeper.   ' Any widow pawnbroker would certainly lend you a gold piece on a kimono like that.'

' Nonsense ! ' said Kita.   ' Do you think I'd lend a gold piece on a thing like that ? '

' Anybody would lend a gold piece on it,' said the shopkeeper.

' Do you think I'd get it back ? ' asked Kita.

' Of course you would,' said the shopkeeper.

'That's what you say,' said Kita, 'but you're not to be depended upon. Where's the money that I lent you the other day for those pants? Then there's the lined kimono that I lent you money on, when you said your children were all sick and that your wife had died of the plague and you hadn't got enough money to pay for the funeral. I lent you the money then because you pleaded so earnestly, and now you can't repay it. Do you call that being honest? I think I ought to take this cotton garment as security for that lined kimono.'

'What nonsense are you talking?' said the shopkeeper angrily. 'How dare you say that my wife died of the plague?'

'Don't mind him,' said Yaji. 'He says all sorts of bad things. Just let us have that kimono for a thousand coppers.'

'Well, it's my first sale this morning,' said the shopkeeper, 'so I'll let you have it for that.'

Thereupon he clapped his hands to show that the bargain was concluded.

'Then the kimono's mine,' said Kita, and he put it on while Yaji was paying for it and returned Yaji his coat.

Kitahachi's spirits immediately rose when they got out of the shop. 'I say, Yaji,' he cried. 'Don't I look smart? We talked that old clothes man over, didn't we? It's cheap at a thousand coppers. Look, the collar's not dirty a bit.'

'It looks like a servant's blue coat,' said Yaji. 'It's just right, because now I look like the master.'

'What do they call this place, I wonder,' said Kita. 'There are a lot of fine girls going about.'

'Some of them have got purple hoods on their heads, I notice,' said Yaji, 'so I suppose it's Miyagawa-chō.'

'Look at that beauty just coming along,' said Kita. 'Lucky I bought a kimono. That coat of yours was better than being naked, but I couldn't have passed her in it without feeling ashamed.'

He hastily arranged the collar of the kimono and folded it straight in front as two singing girls passed him. After they had passed one of them turned round to look at Kita's kimono.

'Look at that man's kimono, Hatsuné,' she said. 'What big crests it's got on it. How funny! Ho-ho-ho!'

'What a fool he looks!' said Hatsuné. 'Who'd care for a fellow like that? Ho-ho-ho!'

They went on their way laughing, while Yaji examined Kita's new kimono.

'I say, Kita,' he said, 'look at your kimono. There's a big crest on your back, all on one side.'

'Where, where?' asked Kita. He twisted round to look and saw that the kimono was made of pieces of flag sewn together and dyed, and covered all over with big crests.

'Oh, how dreadful!' said Kita.

'Ha-ha-ha!' laughed Yaji. 'There's a big carp going up a waterfall on your sleeve. This kimono's made of pieces of flags.'

'That old dealer's got the better of us,' said Kita. 'That's why it was so cheap. I'll go back and give him something.'

'Leave him alone,' said Yaji. 'You shouldn't be such a fool. It's his business to sell his goods, so it can't be helped.'

Kita went on grumbling till they came to Shijō-dōri, where is situated the fashionable and prosperous Gion-machi. From the theatres on both sides of the road came the inspiriting sound of the drums and the hoarse cries of the two ticket-sellers, who were both dressed in bright costumes of the same pattern.

'Here you are, here you are!' they cried. 'Come in and see the famous Sangoro commit suicide. Come and see Arakichi and Tomokichi in their famous performance.'

At Kyōto and Ōsaka the theatre attendants are all girls. One of these caught hold of Kita and Yaji by the sleeve. 'Come in and see one act,' she said.

'What do you say, Yaji,' said Kita. 'Shall we just take a peep at the Kyōto theatre?'

'That's a good idea,' said Yaji. 'How much is it?'

'That's all right,' said the girl. 'I'll arrange it all for you. Come in.'

She caught hold of their hands and dragged them in and took them upstairs, where the box-opener showed them to their seats. The curtain was down and the vendors were crying their wares.

'Uji tea, Uji tea,' cried one.

'Have some cakes,' called another.

'Tea, tea,' called another. 'Who wants some tea?'

'There's quite a crowd, isn't there?' said Yaji. 'But it's only half of what would be in the theatre in Edo.'

'What a bore it is waiting,' said Kita. 'I could do with a cup.'

'I feel hungry,' said Yaji. 'Let's buy some cakes or something.'

' Have some cakes,' said a vendor.

' Just give us three or four of those cakes,' said Kita.

' They're three coppers each,' said the man.

' Here,' said one of the audience. ' What are you doing, cake-man. You're treading on my lunch.'

' Ay, ay,' said the vendor. ' Excuse me.'

' Oh, oh ! ' cried Yaji. ' Now you're treading on my foot.'

' Ay, ay ! ' said the man. ' Just excuse me, will you ? '

' Don't step over me,' said Kita. ' I don't want your stomach on my head.'

' I say, Gombei,' called one of the audience. ' What did you buy ? '

' Wait a bit, Master Tarobei,' said Gombei. ' I've got some-thing nice in my box. Come over and look. Won't you come ? ' He brought out a package wrapped in a bamboo leaf.

' Oh, it's rice and fish balls, is it ? ' said Tarobei. ' Splendid, splendid. Let's have it instead of lunch and eat it with our saké. What do you think ? '

Very well,' said Gombei. ' Let's have a cup.'

He took out a small cup and a bottle.

' Look there, Yaji,' said Kita in a low voice. ' Ain't they lucky. They've got a drink.'

' What a greedy chap you are,' said Yaji.

' Here, my boy,' said Kita, ' there's a cake for you,' and he gave one of the cakes he had bought to a little boy who was with the two men in the next box. He did this because he wanted the men to offer him a drink.

' Thank you, thank you,' said Tarobei.

' I see you're enjoying yourselves,' said Kita.

' Are you fond of saké ? ' asked Tarobei.

' Yes, yes,' said Kita. ' It's better than food.'

' Yes, it's very pleasant,' said Tarobei. ' Master Gombei, let's have another drink. Ah, this is very good saké.'

' Yes,' said Gombei. ' I'm afraid you're not enjoying your-self,' he added, turning to Kita. ' Won't you have a cup of tea ? '

He held out a tea cup and Kita took it hurriedly, with many thanks.

' I'm afraid it's cold,' said Tarobei. ' Have some from the kettle.'

Kita, with an expectant face, took the kettle that was handed to him and poured some out. Then he drank it off, to find it was only lukewarm tea.

'Oh, it's tea,' he said disappointed.

'Is it cold ? ' asked Tarobei.

'Yes, it's cold,' said Kita. 'Would you mind giving me some from the bottle.'

'I'm sorry it's finished,' said Tarobei. 'See for yourself,' and he turned the bottle upside down.

'Ha-ha-ha ! ' laughed Yaji. 'What a do ! '

'Botheration,' said Kita in a low voice. 'I've wasted a cake.'

While he was grumbling to himself the music began to play and the clackers to sound to show that the performance was about to begin. Then as the curtain went up, along the Flowery Way came a group of actors, at whom the audience began to jeer.

'Daiko, Daiko,' they called. 'You're all a lot of Daiko.'

'What's this Daiko ? ' asked Kita. 'Is that one of the actors ? '

'Yes, he's a very good actor,' said the man next him.

Kita was very fond of the theatre and he was soon absorbed in the play and quite lost to his surroundings, so that as the performance went on he began to express his approval of the actors by frequent remarks, which he uttered in a loud voice. The result was that those around him, instead of looking at the stage, began to find more amusement in looking at Kita.

'Bravo ! Bravo ! ' called Kita. 'Daiko, Daiko.'

Now 'Daiko,' which means ' radish,' is a term used in the West Country for a bad actor. Kita did not know this, and as he had heard the others calling out ' Daiko ! Daiko ! ' he imitated them. As he went on calling out ' Daiko,' the crowd began to laugh at him and call him ' mōroku.' In the West Country ' mōroku ' means the same as ' orisuké ' in Edo, that is a low sort of fellow. As Kita was dressed in a blue kimono they thought that he was a common labourer.

'Yaji, do you hear that ? ' he asked. 'What queer names the actors have here,—Daiko, Mōroku. Perhaps they aren't their real names.'

'Probably nicknames,' said Yaji.

'Then the actor that's just come out must be Mōroku,' said Kita, and he began calling out, 'Bravo Mōroku ! Well done, Mōroku ! '

By this time all the audience were looking and laughing at Kita and had forgotten all about the play.

' Mōroku ! ' they called.   ' Fool of a mōroku ! '

' What are they calling mōroku for ? ' asked Kita.   ' What does it mean ? '

' Ha-ha-ha ! ' laughed Yaji.   ' It's you they mean.'

' What for ? ' asked Kita.

' It means the same as orisuké,' said Yaji.   ' They're all making fun of you because you're dressed in a blue kimono.'

' Oh, that's it, is it ? ' said Kita.

' Fool, fool, fool ! ' yelled the crowd.

' You're an insolent lot,' shouted Kita.

As Kita spoke very angrily, all the people in the theatre jumped to their feet, shouting ' A fight, a fight,' and the whole theatre was plunged into confusion.   Then four or five of the theatre attendants rushed up and seized hold of Kita.

' What are you doing ? ' said Kita.

' You're stopping the play,' they said.   ' Come along.'

' Turn him out, turn him out,' yelled the crowd.

' What are you jawing about ?' said Kita.

' Come along, come along,' said the attendants.

' What are you going to do with that man ? ' asked Yaji.

' You too,' said the attendants, and they caught hold of both of them and dragged them downstairs, much to their disgust.   But as there was nothing to be done, they had to leave the theatre grumbling.

' What a nuisance ! ' said Kita.   ' Ha-ha-ha ! '

Wandering along they came to the Gion Shrine.   The hall in the middle of the main building is dedicated to Gōdzu Tennō, the chamber to the east to the Eight Princes and that to the west to the Princess Inada.   In the time of the Emperor Shōmu, the Minister Kibi, on his return home from China, ventured respect-fully for the first time to raise a shrine to Gōdzu Tennō on the top of Mount Hiro in Harima Province.   Besides there are sub-shrines and branch shrines too numerous to mention.   Every day there are crowds of worshippers and from the numerous teahouses comes the smell of the Gion cake.   There may be seen the sellers of tooth powder, attracting customers by their swordplay, and the medicine vendors, and those who imitate the moving world around them, and the actors of the Nō interludes, so that altogether the grounds of the Shrine are crowded with people. Here also may be heard all kinds of amusing dialects, but as

Kanwatei in the 'Kyūkwanchō' has written all about them I will cut short my description.

Yaji and Kita, having looked at everything, went out at the Rō Gate in front of the Niken Teahouse, where they make the beancurd. At the gate of the teahouse a number of girls in red aprons were calling to the passers-by.

'Come in and rest, come in and rest,' they cried. 'Won't you come in ? Have a snack, have a snack.'

'Aha ! ' said Yaji. 'Don't you remember the saying that when you embrace a Gion girl she looks as if she was cutting beancurd. Look, Kitahachi. Isn't that interesting ? '

Peeping in they could hear the girls cutting the beancurd.

'That's amusing,' said Kita. 'What do you say to having a drink here. I feel as if I could do with something.'

'Please go right in,' said the maid.

They went into a back room and the maid brought some tea.

'Let's have some beancurd,' said Kita. 'And you might bring some saké.'

'Ay, ay ! ' said the girl.

'When these Kyōto people deal with a man from another province they always put up their prices,' said Yaji. 'We've got to be careful.'

'Yes, yes,' said Kita. 'It's annoying even to pay two or three coppers more than the proper charge.'

The maid brought in the saké and some cooked vegetables in a bowl.

'I'll bring the beancurd in a minute,' she said. 'Please take a cup.'

'All right,' said Yaji. 'By the way, how much is the saké ? '

'Our saké is extra good,' said the maid. 'It's sixty _mommé_.'

'Eh ? ' said Yaji. 'I don't understand that. How much is this dish ? '

'That's five _bun_, your honour,' said the maid.

'Let's have the beancurd as soon as you can,' said Kita.

The maid went away and soon returned with two trays of beancurd, and the rice-box.

'That's funny looking beancurd,' said Yaji.

'That's arrowroot,' said the girl. 'I'll bring the other in a minute.'

'How much is the beancurd ? ' asked Yaji.

'Ha-ha-ha ! ' laughed Kita. 'What a chap you are for asking

the price of everything. There's no need to ask the price of the beancurd, is there? Let's have a drink.'

'That's good saké,' said Yaji after drinking a cup. 'I can't bear watery stuff. Let's have another cup.'

'Don't drink it all yourself while you're grumbling,' said Kita. 'Pass the bottle over.'

'This stuff won't do,' said Yaji. 'We can't eat this stuff with the saké. Bring us something else.'

The maid went and brought in another dish.

'How much is that dish?' asked Yaji.

'That's two *mommé* five *bun*,' said the maid.

'Dear, dear,' said Kita.

'I'll get them,' said Yaji. 'I know a plan that will teach them not to be greedy.'

Of everything the maid brought in he asked the price, and when they had eaten everything up he called for the bill.

The maid brought in the bill and handed it to Yaji.

'Let's see, let's see,' said Yaji. 'Kita, look what they make the total.'

'Oh, oh!' cried Kita. 'Twelve *mommé* five *bun*. What a price! Make 'em cut it down.'

'No, no, it's cheap,' said Yaji. 'There, bring me the change. Now then, Kita, we've got something to carry. We'll take all these things with us.'

He took all the bowls and dishes, wiped them with paper, and began to wrap them up.

'What's that for?' asked Kita.

'We'll take 'em all away with us,' said Yaji.

'Oh, no,' said the maid. 'Dear, dear, what shall I do?'

'I asked you how much this bowl was,' said Yaji, 'and you told me it was five *bun*, didn't you? Then I asked you how much this dish was and you said it was two *mommé* five *bun*, and the vegetable bowl was three *mommé*. Isn't that right? And the plate three *mommé* five *bun*, didn't you say? Altogether twelve *mommé* five *bun*. I've paid you for them so there's no excuse.'

'Ho-ho-ho!' laughed the maid. 'How funny you are.'

'There's no ho-ho-ho about it at all,' said Yaji. 'I'm going to take them with me.'

He went on wrapping up the plates and dishes with quite a serious air, much to the dismay of the maid.

286

'I was telling you the price of the food not of the dishes,' she explained.

'If I'd been asking about the price of the food,' said Yaji, 'I'd have asked you how much the food in the dish was. But I didn't. I asked you how much the dish was and you said two *mommé* five *bun*, didn't you?'

'Yes,' said the maid, 'but then I thought. . . Oh dear, what shall I do?'

'There's nothing to dispute about,' said Yaji.

Then a man in an apron came in from the kitchen and inquired the particulars.

'You're quite right,' he said to Yaji. 'Please take the dishes

as you have paid for them, but you haven't yet paid me for what you have eaten.'

'I see, I see,' said Yaji. 'What we have eaten won't be very dear. How much will it be?'

'That will be seventy-eight *mommé* five *bun*,' said the man.

'Eh?' said Yaji. 'What a price! Do you think I'm blind? Why it's only worth about five or six hundred coppers. What a terrible price to ask.'

'Not at all,' said the man. 'All the food is brought from Ōsaka on foot and it costs a lot to bring it.'

287

'That may be all right for the fish,' said Yaji, 'but the vegetables can't be so dear. How much was that dish of greens?'

'That's seven *mommé* five *bun*,' said the man.

'What? Seven *mommé* five *bun*?' cried Yaji. 'You're too greedy for anything. It's only worth three or four coppers.'

'That may be what you think,' said the man, 'but the greens are a special production of Kyōto and I always pick them over very carefully and throw away the parts eaten by caterpillars, and select the best. And I always sift the dung out of them too.'

'Nonsense!' said Yaji. 'Whoever heard of such a thing? I'll only pay you two *shū* for what we've eaten.'

'No, no,' said the man. 'That won't do. If you think it's dear please return the things you've bought.'

Yaji now saw that he was beaten at his own game of quibbling.

'Here, Yaji,' said Kita. 'Don't let's bother about it any more.'

'You may make as many excuses as you like,' said Yaji, 'but I tell you the bill's unreasonable. I'll forgive you this time, but just you remember in future,' and with a glare at the landlord he walked out.

'Good-bye,' said the maid. 'Please come again soon.'

'Oh, suck it,' said Yaji. 'Ha-ha-ha!'

They left the precincts of the temple and went quickly in the direction of Sanjō to find an inn for the night, catching up as they did so with a number of women who were selling firewood, ladders, pestles, mallets, and other things, all of which they carried on their heads.

'Don't you want a ladder or a pestle?' they asked.

'Look how it makes them wag their tails,' said Yaji. 'Ha-ha-ha!'

'Won't you buy some firewood?' asked another woman.

'Ain't they strong,' said Kita, 'to be able to carry the things on their heads.'

Soon they came to a river bed, where all the women put down their burdens and sat down to have a smoke.

'That's what you might expect in Kyōto,' said Yaji. 'They ain't bad looking. I'll chaff 'em a bit.'

'You'll get into trouble again,' warned Kita.

'Nonsense,' said Yaji, 'it's you who do that.'

He took out his pipe and drew near to the women.

'Sorry to trouble you but could you let me have a light?' he said. 'By the way, how do you manage to carry those things on your heads? Ain't they heavy?'

'Ay, ay,' said one of the women.

'I used to go about with a stone weighing twenty or thirty *kwammé* on my head,' said Kita, 'and think nothing of it.'

'You must have been a miller's man,' said one of the women.

'You be quiet,' said Yaji.

'Won't you buy this pestle, gentlemen,' said another of the women.

'What, a pestle?' said Yaji. 'I would like to, but this one is too thin. I've got one as big as a log. Besides, I like a square one.'

'Ho-ho-ho!' laughed the woman. 'If you had a square pestle you'd want a square mortar.'

'Of course, of course,' said Yaji. 'At my place we make bean sauce in a store house.'

'What a smart gentleman he is!' said the woman. 'If you don't like the pestle, won't you buy a ladder?'

'Ha-ha-ha!' laughed Yaji. 'Fancy me buying a ladder. How much is it?'

'I haven't been able to sell much to-day,' said the woman, 'so I'll let you have it cheap for six hundred coppers.'

'I'll take it if you let me have it for two hundred coppers,' said Yaji.

'Don't make fun of us,' said the woman. 'Won't you give a little more?'

'No, no, said Yaji.

'Won't you make it five hundred?' said the woman.

'No, no,' said Yaji.

'Well, I should get scolded if I took it home,' said the woman. 'I'll let you have it for two hundred.'

'What?' said Yaji. 'You'll sell it so cheap? What a silly thing to do!'

'It is cheap,' said the woman.

'However cheap it is, what should I do with a ladder?' said Yaji. 'I haven't got a place to put it.'

'That doesn't matter,' said the woman. 'Here, catch hold of it.'

'You must excuse me,' said Yaji. 'The truth is we're only travellers and I'm going to Sanjō to look for an inn. I can't carry a ladder about with me.'

'Well, what did you want to make a bid for it then if you didn't want it?' asked the woman.

'I oughtn't to have done it,' said Yaji. 'If it was something I could put in my sleeve or my bosom I wouldn't mind buying it whether I wanted it or not. But a ladder! It's dreadful.'

'You shouldn't come and make fun of people when they're trying to do a bit of business,' said the woman. 'I won't be played with. Here, take the ladder.'

Then four or five women surrounded Yaji and began scolding at the tops of their voices, while a curious crowd collected. Yaji, in the middle, was unable to escape, and although he made all sorts of excuses, they would not listen to him, and as they were women he could not very well get up a fight with them. In the end he was forced to pay the two hundred coppers and shoulder the ladder, whereupon the crowd dispersed laughing.

'Making me look like a fool!' groaned Yaji. 'Just catch hold of the other end, Kita.'

'Not I,' said Kita. 'You can carry it.'

'I've got caught again,' said Yaji. 'Botheration!'

They went along Shijō and down in front of the temple, Yaji grumbling all the time at having to carry the ladder.

'Ain't you got any feeling for me, Kita ? ' he groaned. 'Just carry it for a bit.'

'You don't get me touching it,' said Kita. 'Awfully heavy, isn't it ? Why don't you carry it on your head like those women.'

'That's a good idea,' said Yaji, and he twisted up a towel and put it round his head, and balanced the ladder on top, holding it with his hands.

'Here, look where you're going,' said a passer-by.

'Sorry,' said Yaji. 'I can't see people coming.'

'Are you a fireman ? ' asked the man. 'Shall I bring some water ? Where's the fire ? '

'Look at that chap with the ladder,' said another. 'What a fool ! '

'Shut your jaw, you rascal,' said Yaji.

'Look what a stupid fellow he looks,' said another.

'Where is the fool ? ' said Yaji, and turning round to see who it was he caught the man a crack on the head with the end of the ladder.

'Oh ! Oh ! ' yelled the man. 'What are you doing carrying a thing like that crossways. Such a fool ! See what a bruise you've given me.'

'What's that you're jawing about a fool ? ' said Yaji.

'Well, look at the lump on my forehead if you don't believe me,' said the man. 'Isn't there one there ? '

'I can see you're a fool without looking at your lump,' retorted Yaji.

'You talk big, don't you ? ' said the man. 'I'll soon settle your hash.'

As there seemed likely to be a fight a crowd began to gather round.

'It's our fault, entirely our fault,' said Kita intervening. 'We're very sorry. Here, come along, Yaji. Walk up.'

'Insolent fellow ! ' growled Yaji. 'Here, Kita, I can't carry it any more. Just hold it up at the back on your shoulders.'

'All right,' said Kita. 'You'll make me look as big a fool as yourself.'

'I wish I could get rid of it,' said Yaji.

They went down a side street where they thought there would
be few people and they could leave the troublesome ladder in spite
of the two hundred coppers they had paid for it and run away
without being seen, but there was always someone watching them,
and finally they arrived with the ladder at Sanjō-dōri, where they
met an inn tout.

'Are your honours stopping here?' he asked.

'Yes, yes,' said Yaji.

'Won't you let me conduct you to my place?' said the man.

'Where is it?' asked Kita.

'It's just here,' said the tout. 'Please come this way,' and he
led them across the bridge to the inn.

SECOND PART

THE sun was already sinking in the west and at all the houses the lamps were lit when the inn servant led them across the bridge to the inn.

'Guests have arrived,' he called.

'Welcome, welcome,' cried the landlord rushing out. 'What about your baggage?'

'We've only got this ladder,' said Kita.

'That's strange baggage,' said the landlord. 'Here, Tako, Tako'—calling the maid—'show the guests in.'

The maid showed them to a room and then the landlord came in.

'As I have very few guests to-night,' he said, 'I didn't have the bath heated, but there's a very good bath-house just by the bridge where you can go if you like.'

'I don't want a bath,' said Kita, 'but you'd better go, Yaji. They say that the water in the capital makes your skin quite white.'

'I don't want to get any whiter than I am,' said Yaij.

'By the way,' said the landlord. 'I suppose you live somewhere in the neighbourhood.'

'No, no,' said Kita. 'We come from Edo.'

'I thought that as you were carrying a ladder you lived somewhere near here,' said the landlord. 'How is it you Edo gentlemen come to be carrying a ladder?'

'Well, there's a reason for that,' said Kita. 'It was entrusted to us to bring from Edo.'

'How did you come to be entrusted with such a thing?' asked the landlord.

'I'll tell you,' said Kita. 'You see I and my friend are intimate with a fellow up in Edo who was born in these parts and he got this ladder sent to him by his people down here, for the reason that as they can't read and write, and it makes them ashamed to get letters and not return 'em, they always send him a ladder when they want him to go up to the capital. By the same token, this chap in Edo can't write and read either—don't know a letter of the alphabet, in fact—though he's too proud to own it. So, as I told him that I was coming down to these parts, he said to me what a lucky thing it was and would I mind taking something to his people. So I said I'd take anything along he wanted, and what do you think he sent me? Just listen. A greasy old priest and that ladder. Well, I didn't mind about the ladder, but I told him it would be very troublesome to carry the priest, because, you know, this priest was alive. Well, he said, then take the ladder only and when you get there hire a priest and get him to carry a bell-clapper and the ladder to my people. Well, then I asked him what he wanted us to take the ladder to Kyōto for and he said that as the ladder had come from his people he was sending it back as an answer.'

'Ha-ha-ha!' laughed the landlord. 'I see, I see. The ladder was to show that he was going up to the capital. But what were the priest and the bell-clapper for?'

'The bell-clapper was to show he wanted to go up but that he had no money,' replied Kita.

'I see,' said the landlord, 'but isn't it an enormous distance to carry a ladder. You couldn't pack it in your baggage. You must have had great trouble with it.'

'Oh, no, not at all,' said Kita. 'It's very convenient having a ladder with you when you're on the road. When you want to ride on horseback all you have to do is to put the ladder up against the horse and mount up. It's very easy to get on a horse that way. A ladder's very useful in crossing rivers too, as you don't have to hire a hand-barrow when you're crossing even rivers like the Ōi and the Abé, and you only want two men to carry it instead of four. If you ever go on a journey I should advise you to take a ladder. People don't know how useful it is.'

'No,' said the landlord, 'I don't suppose anyone has ever thought of taking a ladder with them on a journey. Ha-ha-ha! By the way, are you going to hire the priest here?'

'Of course, of course,' said Kita. 'We must hire him.'

'Luckily I know a very good priest,' said the landlord, 'who would just suit you. Shall I call him?'

Here the landlord jumped up to go and call the priest.

'No, no, wait a bit,' said Kita, who felt himself in a bit of a fix. 'We don't want him in such a hurry. We shouldn't like to lose the ladder, it's so useful. Besides, we don't want to drag a priest about with us, eh, Yaji?'

'That's your business,' said Yaji. 'If we're going to get one it would be better to get one quickly.'

'I didn't expect you to say that,' said Kita.

'But if it is as you say,' said the landlord, 'don't you think it would be better to engage a priest at once?'

'Yes,' said Kita, 'but you see. . . .'

'Just leave it to me,' said the landlord.

'Instead of worrying about that,' said Kita, 'you'd better give us something to eat.'

'Supper will be ready immediately,' said the landlord. 'But what about the priest?'

'Oh, hang the priest,' said Kita. 'I'm really too hungry to think about him.'

The landlord went off to the kitchen and soon the maid came in bringing the supper. Many idle jokes were cracked during supper, and after it was cleared away the landlord came in again. As he himself was fond of a joke, he was pretending to believe Kita's story and had brought a priest, a man of about sixty, with a thin and ragged beard.

'Have you finished your supper?' asked the landlord. 'I've brought the priest that I was talking about.'

'Good evening,' said the priest, who had lost his nose. 'My name is Gyantetsu. I was summoned here by the master of the house.' (Only, as he had lost his nose it sounded like—'Good ebedig. By dabe is Gyadtetsu. I was subbod here by the baster of the house.')

'Thank you for coming,' said Yaji. 'Please sit down.'

'Dear me, landlord,' said Kita. 'I am very sorry you should take all this trouble.'

'Not at all,' said the landlord.

'At the same time,' continued Kita, 'I hope you won't think me rude if I tell you that I don't think he'll do. You see I must have a priest who is a bit of an actor of interludes, even if he is only an amateur.'

'What's that for?' asked the landlord.

'Well, you see,' said Kita, 'as I told you before, the answer means not only that he can't go up to the capital unless he has some money, but also that he can't go unless he has three hundred gold pieces. So I want the priest to act the part of Ume-ga-é in the Bell of Mugen.'

'That's all right,' said the landlord. 'This priest used to take women's parts in the temple plays and was called Hennōsuké Bakamura. He's very clever at it. Luckily also my daughter is now learning the Bell of Mugen. Suppose we act a little of it for fun.'

' Come on, let's start,' said Gwantetsu. ' I'll be Ume-ga-é if somebody will be Genta.

' What fun ! ' said Yaji. ' I've never seen an Ume-ga-é without a nose. You'd better be Genta, Kita. You're just right for the part.'

' Don't talk nonsense,' said Kita. ' I don't like such jokes.'

He went on grumbling to himself with a sulky face, while the landlord brought in his little daughter of thirteen or fourteen years old with her samisen, and the mistress of the house and all the maid-servants and scullions gathered in the next room to see the priest act. Yaji was greatly amused.

' Here, Kita,' he said, pulling his sleeve. ' Look how the mistress of the house and all the servants have come to see you. You'll get lots of applause. Just try.'

At this Kita's spirits began to revive.

' We'll see who can do it best,' he said. ' I'll be Genta. But you must let me make up the words as I go on.'

' All right, all right,' said Gwantetsu. ' Now then, Tora, start from the place where Genta comes in.'

' Ha-ha-ha ! ' laughed Yaji. ' Ume-ga-é with a dirty beard, and Genta with an old blue kimono made of flags. What a sight ! '

' Come on, begin, begin,' said Kita.

Then the little girl began chanting the *jōruri.*

Chorus:	And every night great Genta went.
	To see his lady fair,
	And every night she looked at him
	With proud, disdainful air.
	Oh, Genta, now's your chance, for she
	Is dreaming o'er the brazier. See,
	She does not turn her face to thee,
	But smokes her pipe quite silently.
Genta.	How is it you no longer care,
	But meet me with a haughty air,
	I am a lordless man, 'tis true,
	Whose clothes are worn and dirty too.
Chorus:	She waits, she waits, she waits for you.
Ume-ga-é.	Did I not send to let you know
	My duties would not let me go ?
Chorus:	Her eyes are red, but not with hate.
	The tears of love have fallen of late.

'Here, get further away,' said Kita to the priest. 'You stink abominably. I never saw such a smelly Ume-ga-é.'

'And I never saw such a Genta,' said the priest.

'Didn't I tell you not to come near me?' said Kita. 'Here, I'm going to cut this short.

Genta.	Here, shaven-pate. . . No, no, Ume-ga-é,
	Your helmet where is it, I pray?
Ume-ga-é.	I pawned it for three hundred *mé*,
	To drive my sorrows quite away.
Genta.	Pawned it? Your reason tell to me.
Ume-ga-é.	My bones are rotten as rotten can be.
	No medicine will bring respite
	From pains that ache me day and night.
	But still I would my nose restore,
	To be as high as once before.
	Three hundred *mé* I do require
	To make my nose a little higher.
Chorus:	Twice eight are sixteen
	That's the age when love is seen.
	Twice nine are eighteen,
	When the heart for love is keen.
	Twice five are twenty,
	When there's always love a-plenty.
Ume-ga-é.	Ah! What is this? How little you know my mind,
	That you to treat me lightly are inclined.

'Here, wait a minute,' said Yaji.

Without waiting for an answer he rushed into the kitchen and brought the ladder, which he put up against the wall of the room. Then he climbed halfway up it and struck an attitude, while he wound a towel round his head to make himself look like a person of importance.

'I'll play the part of Genta's mother, Anju,' he said. 'Go on, priest.'

> Ume-ga-é. 'Tis said that if one strikes the bell
> Of Mugen all with thee is well.
> On a far journey I must wend,
> And thus, before I reach the end,
> To strike the bell I fain would tend.
> The power of will transcends all thought,
> And thus this basin I have brought.
> Whether of metal or granite flinty
> It shall the bell of Mugen be.

Thereupon Gwantetsu began striking the washbasin with his pipe.

Meanwhile Yaji from the ladder was scattering coppers while he continued to chant :—

> Anju. Three hundred coppers now I shower.
> It is not like the yellow flower
> Whose petals, fallen from mountain-side,
> Lie scattered far and wide.
> Ume-ga-é. Ah, here are three, and here five more.
> I'll pick up all and have a store.

As the priest went on picking up the coppers and stuffing them into his sleeves, Yaji, from the ladder, seized hold of him.

'I'm not giving it to you really,' he said. 'It's mine.'

Gwantetsu, however, would not give back the money, and in the struggle the ladder slipped and Yaji fell on the floor with a thud, while the ladder fell on the top of Gwantetsu and also struck the little girl on the side, causing her to cry out.

'Oh, oh, oh!' yelled Yaji, rubbing his shin.

'Oh, oh!' groaned Gwantetsu.

'What have you done? What have you done?' cried the landlord, and he and his wife started up, upsetting the tobacco-box and the lantern, and plunging the room into darkness, amid the wails of those injured.

The landlord soon brought another light and was horrified to find that his little girl was unconscious.

'What's the matter with my daughter?' he cried. 'The

Ume-ga-é has brought her unhappiness. She is quite unconscious.'

'Oh, oh!' groaned the priest. 'I've had such a shock. It's driven all my outwards inside.'

'That's serious,' said Yaji. 'I say, landlord, his outwards have gone inwards.'

'That's all right,' said Kita. 'I see you advertise some medicine called "money-plaster." If you rub some of that on your head they'll fall down.'

'What are you talking about!' said the landlord. 'How will putting money-plaster on your head cause them to fall?'

'Why, because when copper goes up in price gold falls,' said Kita.

'Eh?' said the landlord. 'What a thing to say!'

'What shall I do? What shall I do?' said Gwantetsu. 'How is the little girl?'

'Somebody must run for the doctor,' cried the landlord's wife.

'I'll go, I'll go,' said the priest, 'and if he isn't there I'll go on to the temple.'

'Eh?' said the landlord. 'What's that you're talking about?'

'It isn't a joking matter at all,' said Kita. 'Where did it hit her?'

'On the side,' replied the landlord. 'It hit her very badly. She's suffering great pain.'

'For a maiden born in the capital to be struck on the side is a dreadful thing,' chanted Yaji. 'A thousand condolences.'

'It's not a thing to make a joke over,—to come into a person's house and injure his daughter,' said the landlord.

'Ha-ha-ha!' laughed Yaji. 'I should be very ashamed to trifle with a person's daughter.'

'It isn't a laughing matter,' said the landlord. 'I think you're a couple of rogues.'

'Rogues, indeed!' said Yaji. 'You'd better mind what you're talking about.'

'Don't be insolent,' said the landlord. 'Look here, I've kept house for a good many years, but this is the first time that I've ever had guests come with a ladder. It's plain to see you don't come from this part of the country, and yet you go about with a ladder. I don't understand it at all. It looks as if you were thieves who got into people's houses from the roof. My wife was grumbling at my taking such strange guests and I think she was quite right.'

The landlord's insinuations in turn excited Yaji, who was always ready to fly into a passion.

'What nonsense you're talking,' he said. 'We're perfectly respectable travellers. I can't allow you to make such remarks.'

'I said you were going about with a ladder. What's there to get angry about in that?' asked the landlord.

'Never mind him,' said the landlord's wife, 'but just come here and look at the girl. She looks worse and worse.' Here she began to cry.

'Look there,' said the landlord, getting more and more excited. 'If my girl dies you'll both be murderers. Remember that.'

'Oh what terrible trouble has come upon us,' cried the wife.

'She's unconscious,' said the landlord. 'Tora! Tora!'

'Daughter! Daughter!' called the wife.

As the girl did not revive in spite of the medicine and other things given her, and her parents were weeping bitterly over her, Yaji began to get alarmed.

'I say, Kita,' he said. 'What shall we do? We can't stop here.'

'Don't die, Tora!' called the landlord. 'Don't die! How is it?'

'Tora! Tora!' called his wife.

'Tora! Tora!' called her husband.

'What a terrible thing!' said Yaji. 'It's more than I can bear.'

In his alarm he could not keep still.

'I can't allow you to leave,' said the landlord.

'No, no,' said Yaji. 'We're not going anywhere. Look here, Kita, it's all your fault. If you hadn't started that yarn all this trouble wouldn't have arisen. It was the nonsense about the Bell of Mugen which began it all. As you introduced it you're the guilty person.'

'What a thing to say!' cried Kita. 'You're the real criminal.'

'Well, look here,' said Yaji. 'Let's play for it, and the one who loses will be the murderer.'

'Nonsense! I don't know anything about it,' declared Kita.

Meanwhile the doctor had come and by means of medicine and all kinds of ministrations the little girl was restored to consciousness and thus the anxiety was relieved. Yaji's spirits rose and he made all sorts of apologies for his conduct, in which Kita joined him, and finally the matter was settled by Yaji signing a written apology, to which Kita also set his seal as witness. The apology, which was meant to be a very serious document, read :—

This is to give notice.

I hereby affirm that while I was playing the part of Anju in the 'jōruri' Hiragana Seisuiki, when Ume-ga-é was striking the bell of Mugen, which bell can be produced in evidence, I was taking some money from my belt and was throwing it to the ground, when the ladder slipped and fell on Gwantetsu, whose outwards were driven inwards, and also your daughter suffered a blow, all of which happened owing to my having placed the said ladder against the said wall, thus arousing your anger, which was appeased by my excuses, for which I am truly thankful. And I hereby solemnly promise that if I am allowed to stop at this inn hereafter, I will not bring a ladder on the premises. This document is for purposes of record.

(Principal) YAJIROBEI.

Dated   (Witness) KITAHACHI.

The little girl having recovered from the blow and the document having been drawn up and signed, various cups of saké were exchanged to celebrate the settlement of the dispute and all retired to rest.

When the morning broke and the people of the house began to stir, Yaji and Kita woke up, and having breakfasted and packed their baggage, prepared to start.

'We're sorry we've given you so much trouble,' said Yaji to the landlord.

'I hope you'll have a pleasant day,' said the landlord.

'What about the ladder ? ' inquired his wife.

'Ah ! ' said Yaji. 'We'd like to leave it here for to-day. We're just going round sight-seeing and we'll be back here to-night.'

'No, no. Please take it with you,' said the landlord. 'To-night I have other engagements which will not allow me to receive you.'

The fact was that the landlord regarded them as two suspicious characters and did not want to have the ladder left in his charge for fear it should bring him into trouble. There being no help for it Yaji shouldered the ladder and they set forth.

'Where are we going to-day ? ' asked Kita.

'We haven't seen Higashiyama yet,' said Yaji. 'Let's go to the Tenjin Temple in Kitano.'

They went along, asking their way here and there, till they got to Horikawa-dōri.

'I've just thought of something,' said Kita. 'You remember that Kyōto man we met at Furuichi, and how he said he lived at Nakadachiura in Semban-dōri. We might call there on our way to the Tenjin temple.'

'Oh, you mean Yotakurō Henguriya,' said Yaji.

'Yes, that's him,' said Kita. 'We might go and call on him. Perhaps he'd give us some saké.'

'What, that stingy chap?' said Yaji. 'Not likely.'

'You wait and see how I'll get round him,' said Kita.

After a few inquiries they found the way to Yotakurō Henguriya's house, and putting the ladder up against the eaves, they opened the lattice door and went in.

'Who's that?' called Yotakurō. 'Oh, this is a surprise! I am glad you have come.'

'Well, you see,' said Yaji, 'we remembered all your kindness to us at Isé.'

'Not at all, not at all,' said Yotakurō. 'Please come this way.'

'It's quite a time since we had the pleasure of meeting,' said Kita.

'Yes, yes,' said Yotakurō. 'Have you any friends with you outside?'

'No, there are only the two of us,' said Kita.

'Then what's that outside?' asked Yotakurō.

'Do you mean the ladder?' asked Yaji.

'What, are you carrying a ladder?' exclaimed Yotakurō. 'How strange!'

'Well, we heard you lived in a high place,' said Kita, 'so we thought a ladder would be useful to get up to it.'

'Ha-ha-ha!' laughed Yotakurō. 'Well done, well done. But dear me, I'm forgetting my manners. Let me offer you something to eat.'

'Well, we had breakfast at the inn,' said Yaji, 'but we haven't had anything since.'

'It would be a pleasure to me to offer you some saké,' said Yotakurō, 'but unfortunately there isn't a saké shop in the neighbourhood.'

'Isn't that a saké shop next door?' asked Kita.

'No, they don't sell it retail there,' answered Yotakurō. 'But, dear me, after all the trouble you two gentlemen have taken in coming to see me, do have a whiff of tobacco.'

'I'll help myself to my own,' said Kita.

'If you two gentlemen were to go just a little further,' said Yotakurō, 'you'd find all sorts of delicious things. There's nothing nicer than the young trout from the River Katsura, either salted or broiled with bean sauce. Or I should be very happy to show you the way to the Ikesu at Shijō. It's quite near, and the eels they serve there, caught from the River Kamo, are quite special and most extraordinarily well-flavoured. And the baked eggs they serve there are nice too. You have no idea how large they are, and they bring them to you heaped up and steaming on a Chinese porcelain plate. They're so delicious you can scarcely swallow them. But you should come in the autumn and taste the mushrooms. This place is celebrated for them, you know. Fresh mushrooms, made into soup, with just a touch of horseradish, are delicious to take with your saké. You never get tired of eating them.'

As he went on talking about all sorts of nice things without offering them any, Kita, unable to endure it any longer, slipped out of the house and went into the saké shop next door to get a drink. Yotakurō was so lost in his recital of the delicious food of Kyōto that he did not notice Kita's departure at the time.

'But where is your friend ? ' he said at last.

'He's gone,' said Yaji.

'Really,' said Yotakurō, 'I didn't see him go. When did he go ? '

'He went away before the mushroom soup was finished,' said Yaji.

'Oh there's lots of other things,' said Yotakurō. 'I haven't mentioned the cakes yet.'

'Well, we haven't had much entertainment,' said Yaji, 'but you've made me feel so hungry that I must go now.'

'No, no, don't go yet,' said Yotakurō. 'I'm so glad you came, because I wanted to speak to you about something. It's about that time we were at Furuichi. You remember the expenses came altogether to one *ryo*, but by a mistake I paid one *bu* two *shu*. And then there were some expenses on the road which I paid, so that altogether when I got home and made up my accounts I found that you each owed me one hundred and twenty-four coppers.

Unless I receive that I can't get my accounts right. It's only a small amount but if you don't mind I'd like to receive two hundred and forty-eight coppers.'

'That's a nice thing to tell a man when he comes to call on you,' said Yaji. 'You'd better let it be. We had some petty expenses too.'

'If it's owing it ought to be paid,' said Yotakurō. 'Accounts are accounts. Suppose we arrange it this way. I'll reduce the amount to two hundred coppers.'

'It's shameful to ask for it now,' said Yaji. 'Why didn't you ask for it then?'

In spite of all Yaji's grumblings and protestations, however, he had to pay the money.

'Ha-ha-ha!' laughed Yotakurō, 'that makes my accounts right. Well, I suppose you're going to the Tenjin temple now. Then you should have a look at the Kinkakuji. It's getting late so you'd better start at once.'

'Thank you for your trouble,' muttered Yaji.

He went out, very much vexed, and met Kita just coming out of the saké shop.

'Well,' said Kita. 'Did he give you a feast?'

'I've had a terrible time with him,' said Yaji. 'Whatever put it into your head to call on him ? He took two hundred coppers from me.'

' Ha-ha-ha ! ' laughed Kita. ' How was that ? Let's leave this bothersome ladder at his house so as to annoy him.'

' How would it annoy him ? ' asked Yaji. ' What pleasure would there be in making a present of it to a fellow like that ? I'd rather carry it than let him have it.'

They went on, asking their way again, and arrived at the temple at Kitano, outside of which was a teahouse, where a girl with a red apron was standing at the door inviting people to go in and taste the special dish of rice and greens served at the house.

' Won't you come in and taste our rice and greens ? ' she said to Yaji.

' We're just going to the Tenjin temple,' said Yaji, ' but we'll call here on our way back. Would you mind our leaving the ladder here in the meantime ? '

' Not at all,' said the girl. ' Please leave it till you come back.'

Yaji stuck the ladder up against the door of the house and they went on.

' There, I've got rid of that,' he said. ' Catch us going back, eh, Kita ? We'll just let it stay there.'

' Ha-ha-ha ! ' laughed Kita. ' What fun ! '

Soon they reached the Ukon racecourse, where they found a large number of people practising riding on horses which they had hired. A great crowd was standing watching them.

' Halloa ! Here's a lot of people ! What are they doing ? ' asked Kita.

They shoved their way through the crowd to have a look.

' Gee-up ! Gee-up ! ' shouted the riders.

' Woa ! Woa ! ' cried the crowd.

' What a clumsy lot they are,' said an onlooker. ' They look as if they were worn out with dissipation. That old chap with the bald head rides well though.'

' Of course he does,' said another. ' He's a jockey.'

' Is he ? ' said the first. ' Look at that fellow over there. Look how he holds the reins. He must be a weaver's assistant. And look at that twelve-year-old apprentice. He handles the reins as though he was fingering a rosary.'

' I should like to have a ride too,' said Kita, ' with that girl over there.'

He pushed his way through the crowd till he came close behind two or three women who were looking on, and there he gently pinched the stern of one of the girls.

'Oh, oh!' cried the girl. 'Who's that? Here, Maru, just come here.'

'What's the matter?' asked Maru.

'Somebody pinched my bottom,' said the girl.

'It must have been a man who was born in a country where there are no women,' said an older woman. 'Don't take any notice of it.'

'Eh, Kita, you're a bad man,' said Yaji.

'I don't know anything about it,' said Kita.

Then, out of spitefulness he tried to pinch the elder woman, but as he was pretending to look the other way he made a mistake and pinched the child that was on her back.

'Oh, oh!' cried the child and started crying.

'What's the matter?' asked the woman. 'Did someone do something bad to you?'

'That man pinched me,' said the child.

'What a hateful fellow!' said the woman.

'You must excuse him,' said Yaji. 'He is really a dreadful man.'

They went off hastily, somewhat disconcerted, and after visiting the Temma Shrine at Kitano and the Hirano Shrine, they came to the Niken teahouse by the River Kamiya. Here feeling hungry, they went into the teahouse and ordered a meal.

'Have you got anything special!' asked Yaji. 'We want something nice to eat and some saké. Just bring the saké quickly, will you?'

They sat down on the edge of the verandah to avoid taking off their sandals, and the maid quickly brought them a saké bottle and cups and some stewed trout.

'I cooked this trout for you with all my liver,' said the girl.

'With all your liver?' said Yaji. 'What do you mean by that?'

'Because they're *river* trout,' said the girl.

'Thank you, thank you,' said Yaji. 'Then let me give you this with all my shin.'

'Ho-ho-ho!' laughed the girl. 'What do you give me this with all your shin for?'

'Because it's *shinger*,' said Yaji.

306

'Ha-ha-ha!' laughed Kita. 'You two are jokers. Bring the other things quick.'

'Ay, ay,' said the maid. Soon she brought in a dish of beancurd and the rice.

While they were enjoying their meal they noticed that there were two men in the room who were eating behind a screen as if they did not wish to be seen. Both were dressed in coarse and rather dirty kimono. They also were eating beancurd, and from their talk it was evident they were priests.

'Where do you get your hair dressed, Yakkai?' asked one.

'You should get your hair dressed where I have mine done, Mokkai,' said the other. 'They do it very well there. I used to have mine done in the dandy's style, but it's gone out of fashion, so I have it done like this now. It's much more comfortable.'

He took off the light blue towel he had over his head and Yaji and Kita saw that although he was dressed in a priest's robe he had his hair done like an actor. There was something very strange about this that excited their curiosity.

'Yes, it's really done very nicely,' said Yakkai. 'I always have my hair dressed by an apprentice but he shaves me so badly that it's always like this.'

He took off the cloth he had on his head, and they saw that his queue was tied at the nape of his neck and all the rest of his head was shaven. Yaji was unable to restrain his curiosity any longer.

'Excuse me,' he said. 'I'm a man from a far province, and I've travelled a long way and seen and heard all sorts of strange things, but I've never seen priests with their hair dressed like that before. Might I ask where you come from?'

'Yes, it's a strange way of dressing the hair, isn't it?' said Yakkai. 'We are priests from the Kuyadō.'

'Oh, yes, I've heard of that,' said Yaji. 'You sell those tea-whisks, don't you?'

'Yes,' said Yakkai. 'In our sect, from ancient times, although we wear priests' robes, we're allowed to dress our hair like laymen.'

'Yes, I've heard of that,' said Yaji. 'But why do you call your sect the Kuyadō?'

'The reason is this,' said Yakkai. 'You see our sect is well known for the great quantity the priests eat. It doesn't matter what it is, we eat enormous quantities. Whether it's at lunch or dinner, we're so accustomed to pressing people to eat by asking

'' Motto kuya dō jai na,'' (Won't you have some more to eat ?)
that people call it the Kuyadō.'

' That's right,' said Mokkai. ' Look here, we just called in here
for a snack and we've eaten three bowls of rice each already.'

' That's a lot,' said Yaji. ' I'm a bit of an eater myself. When
I was in Shinano, living in an eating-house there, when I got up
in the morning they used to bring me my tea and balls of
rice as big as your head, enough to feed fourteen or fifteen
children on. Even when I was not very well I used to eat seventeen or eighteen of them. And then, when breakfast was ready,
the landlord used to say that he didn't like to put his Edo guest
to any inconvenience so he'd made twenty bowls of barley for
me,—bowls as big as mortars. There they were, all arranged in
a line, and the woman of the house used to pile up the barley in
them I can tell you. Even when I was hardly eating anything and
could barely endure my favourite dish of barley, if I sat down I
used to end up by eating five or six without knowing it.'

' Ah ! ' said Yakkai. ' I see you're something of an eater.
Let's have a *meshimori.* '

' Have they got *meshimori* here ? ' asked Yaji.

' Ha-ha-ha ! ' laughed Yakkai. ' You mean the *meshimori* you
pick up when you're travelling. It's not that kind. You know
when boon companions meet together they hold a drinking-bout
which they call a *sakamori.* So when we meet we have eating-
bouts, which we call *meshimori.* Just have a try. Luckily I'm
not full yet.'

' That's amusing,' said Kita. ' What do you do ? '

' You shall see,' said Yakkai. ' Here, waitress, bring another
bowl of rice.'

The girl brought another bowl of rice, and the priest, saying
that he would begin, filled a rice cup with rice and finished it off
at a gulp.

' There,' he said to Yaji. ' It's your turn now. I'll fill the cup
for you.' He piled up the cup with rice and handed it to Yaji.

' Have I got to eat all this ? ' asked Yaji.

' Certainly, certainly,' said Yakkai.

' All right,' said Yaji. ' It's like changing cups when drinking,
isn't it ? '

Yaji managed to get the rice down and then handed the cup
back to the priest.

' That's good,' said the priest. ' Shall we stop there ? '

'No, no,' said Yaji. 'More, more.'

'Well, we'll have another cup,' said the priest. 'Let me help you,' and he filled up the cup with rice.

'It's your turn now,' said Yaji.

He handed the cup of rice to the priest, who managed to get it down in three gulps. 'If it was saké,' said the priest, 'I'd get it down in one gulp, but as it's rice one has to munch it.'

'You've draggled your beard in the cup and made it dirty,' said Yaji. 'And the drippings from your nose have fallen in too.'

'Don't talk nonsense,' said the priest. 'We can't play the game if you talk like that. Eat it up quickly and pass the cup on.'

'I don't want to play this game any more,' said Yaji. 'It's too dirty. You must excuse me.'

'Didn't you say you could eat four or five mortars full of barley,' said Yakkai. 'It isn't fair to get out of it like that. Go on.'

'Well, let's play for it then,' said Yaji.

'All right,' said Mokkai, 'but you mustn't back out if you lose.' He heaped up the bowl with rice.

'The Satsuma game,' he cried. They played, and Yaji lost.

'There you are. Eat it up,' said Mokkai.

As the priest was so pressing, Yaji felt that he must eat the rice, and he managed to get it down with some trouble.

'Let's change cups and have another,' said the priest.

'No, no,' said Yaji. 'You must really excuse me.'

'I've beaten you then,' said the priest. 'You're only a country bumpkin. You can eat tasteless barley, but you can't eat this pure rice.'

'I can only eat the best rice,' said Yaji.

'Well, this is the best,' answered the priest.

'Well, try a bout with your companion for a change,' suggested Yaji.

'All right,' said the priest. 'But I want a bigger bowl than this.'

He took the vegetable dish and emptied it, and piled it up with rice. In two or three gulps it had all disappeared. He handed the bowl to the other priest, who filled it up again and also gulped it down.

'Shall we try again?' he said. 'But this bowl isn't big enough.'

He went on to the verandah and got the hand-bowl and washed it.

'Now,' he said, 'we shall be able to eat. Won't you have a try?'

'No, no,' said Yaji. 'It's too dirty. That's the thing people wash their hands in after they've been to the closet. Whoever could eat out of that?'

'Well, try a teacup then,' said the priest.

'No, no, no,' said Yaji. 'My stomach's bursting. You know when I was eating that last lot something went snap inside my clothes, and when I looked it was the band of my loin-cloth which had burst because my belly is so swollen. You really must excuse me.'

'Ha-ha-ha!' laughed the priest. 'You are a poor eater. It's just as I expected. Here, waitress, bring the bill.'

'Ay, ay,' said the waitress. 'Shall I put it all together?'

'Of course, of course,' said the priest.

'The saké and the beancurd are eighty coppers, your honour,' said the girl, 'and the rice will be five hundred and seventy-two coppers.'

'Ah, that's cheap,' said the priest. 'We'll divide it between us.'

He laid down the money for half the bill.

'Here,' said Yaji, 'that's going a bit too far. You ate all the rice. I and my companion had only a cup or two each. I can't agree to divide the bill.'

'What are you talking about?' said Mokkai. 'We offered you the rice. It's your own fault if you didn't eat it.'

To this argument there appeared to be no answer and Yaji was forced to agree to pay half the bill.

'Ha-ha-ha!' laughed Kita. 'That was fun. Come on, Yaji, let's be going.'

'I've eaten so much I can't walk,' groaned Yaji. 'Just lend a hand and pull me up.'

'You haven't got any spirit in you,' said Kita. 'There, stand up.'

'Pull harder,' said Yaji. 'I feel as if I was going to be sick.'

'How dirty! Come on.' Kita managed to pull Yaji to his feet, and they went into the temple grounds again and walked on without knowing where they were going, till suddenly they came upon the teahouse where they had left the ladder.

'Wait a bit,' said Yaji when he saw the teahouse. 'There's that ladder again. We oughtn't to have come this way. Let's go back.'

'So it is,' said Kita. 'If we try to pass there they'll be bound to see us and ask us to take it away. It's a nuisance going back though. What shall we do?'

While they were standing there considering, one of the horses from the Ukon racecourse, led by a groom, came along.

'I know what we'll do,' said Kita. 'We'll hide behind the horse so that they won't see us from the teahouse when we pass.'

'That's a good idea,' said Yaji.

They waited till the horse came up to them and then got to the other side of it so as to conceal themselves, but unfortunately when the horse came in front of the teahouse it stopped, and they had to wait there behind the horse till it could be induced to go on again.

'Gee-up! Gee-up!' cried the groom. 'What are you stopping here for. It's getting late.'

The horse refused to move, however, and suddenly let out a stream which splashed on to Yaji and Kita and made them all wet.

'Oh! Oh!' said Yaji. 'Now we've got in another mess.'

'What a stink!' said Kita. 'Look out, Yaji, it's all running your way.'

'Look what the beast's done to me,' moaned Yaji.

Just as he was trying to get out of the way, the girl standing at the door of the teahouse, having a quick eye, caught sight of him.

'This is the house,' she called. 'Please come in.'

'There, she's seen us,' cried Kita.

'What a bother!' said Yaji.

Just as they were making a dash for it the landlord came bustling out.

'Hi, hi!' he called. 'You've left your ladder here. Hi, hi!'

Paying no attention to his cries the two ran on in the dark till their breath was gone. At last they came to Semban-dōri, and from there, by asking the way, they got to the Mibu Temple, where, at a little teahouse, they were directed to an inn.

On the next day they saw the sights at Shimabara and crossing the Tambakaidō came to the great bridge across the River Yodo. There they got on a boat going down the river and went to Ōsaka.

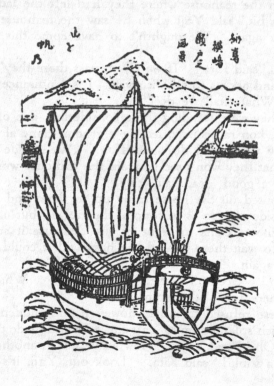

BOOK EIGHT

N the flourishing port of Ōsaka, the like of which is not to be found in the broad seas, lie rows upon rows of ships, from all parts of the country, at anchor at the mouths of the Rivers Kizu and Aji, so prosperous is the city and so many the articles in which it deals. In the spring when the flowers are blooming, there are endless parties being poled up the River Yodo to Mount Tempō or to the Sakura Shrine, or being towed along to the sound of the samisen, while the cup passes from hand to hand. In the summer again, they go to Matsu-ga-saki on the River Yodo, or to the Namba-shinchi-matsu, to hunt fireflies and swell their bellies with bean tea. In autumn they go to the Ukamusé to eat or to the hot baths of Tsuki, and in winter they have the snow-scenes of Tokibunechō. Then at every season there are the unfading flowers of the pleasure-quarter and the gaiety of the theatres in Dōtombōri, where it would seem that special perform-ances are always being given, so great are the crowds.

It was to see such scenes as these that Yajirobei and Kitahachi, round-eyed so that they shouldn't miss anything, arrived at the Hachikenya at Ōsaka by the boat which had brought them from Fushimi. It was already twilight when they landed and knowing nothing of the place they wandered on and on, again and again asking their way to Naga-machi, till at last, at Nihonbashi, they met an inn tout with whom they quickly came to terms and who led them to the Fundōkawachiya in Naga-machi.

' Guests have come,' he called out at the entrance.

' Welcome, welcome,' said the clerk. ' How many of you may there be ? '

' There's forty-seven of us altogether,' said Yaji.

' What ? ' said the clerk. ' Forty-seven ? Here, San, San, there are a lot of people coming. Turn out the room at the back and clean it out thoroughly. Bring some water for the gentlemen to wash their feet. It doesn't matter if it's tepid. Put some cold water in. By the way, these forty-seven people,—are they a long way after you ? '

'They started before us, but they only got as far as Kamakura. We're going to the Amagawaya at Sakai in Senshū.'

'Eh?' said the clerk. 'What's that? Then there are only two of you after all. Here, Tsun, Tsun, there are only two of them. Put them in the small room where the other guest is.'

'Will your honours please come this way?' said Tsun, the maid.

Having washed their feet they followed the maid, and although it was the best inn in the place and contained about seventy or eighty mats, they were shown into a small room, of only six mats. Another person was already in the room.

'I hope you won't mind sharing a room,' apologised the clerk.

'Come in, come in,' said the other guest, who was a Tamba man, and they went in with an apology.

'We're staying here two or three days,' said Yaji to the clerk, 'as we want to see all the sights of the town.'

'Yes, yes,' said the clerk. 'Please make yourselves at home,' and he went off to the kitchen.

'And where be you gentlemen from?' asked the Tamba man.

'Oh, we're from Edo,' said Kita. 'And you?'

'I'm from Sasayama in Tamba,' replied the man, 'and I'm going to Mount Kōya. I'm very pleased to share a room with you.'

'Well, we're all comrades when we're on the road,' said Yaji. 'Very glad to make your acquaintance.'

Then the maid came in with supper and there was more talk, which I will not repeat.

After they had had supper and a bath a blind woman shampooer, heavily pock-marked and of a very unpleasant appearance, came creeping into the room.

'Shall I rub your honours down?' she asked.

'Oh, you're the shampooer, are you?' said Yaji. 'A woman, eh? What do you say, Kita?'

'Just give me a rub,' said Kita.

'You gentlemen are from Edo, aren't you?' said the shampooer. 'I like gentlemen from Edo, they're so honest, and they speak in such a nice way.'

'Can't you see at all?' asked Kita. 'If you could you'd see what handsome fellows are stopping at this house.'

'I'm sure you are,' said the shampooer.

'You should see me,' said Yaji. 'I'm much handsomer than

316

he is. See if you can guess which of us is younger. If you guess right we'll let you shampoo us both.'

'Oh, I can do that easily,' said the shampooer.

'That's interesting,' said Kita. 'How old do you think I am?'

'Wait a minute,' said the shampooer. 'You're about twenty-three or twenty-four.'

'That's smart,' said Kita. 'And ain't I a handsome fellow?'

'Oh, yes,' said the shampooer. 'You've got some features.'

'It would be rather awkward if I hadn't,' said Kita.

'Your eyes are very bright,' said the woman, 'and your nose. . .'

'Is it high or a snub?' asked Kita.

'I hope you won't mind my saying that it's like the nose on a lion's mask.'

'Ha-ha-ha!' laughed the Tamba man. 'That's good, that's good.'

'Well, what about me?' asked Yaji.

'Oh, you're much older,' said the woman. 'I should think you're about forty, and your complexion is very dark and your nose is very flat, and your face is covered with whiskers.'

'Wonderful, wonderful!' cried Kita.

'And you're as fat as a pig,' added the woman.

'No, no,' said Yaji. 'I'm really a very distinguished-looking fellow.'

'It ain't true,' said Kita. 'Here, she's won. Let her rub you down.'

'Well, we made an agreement, so we've got to stick to it,' said Yaji. 'Come along.'

'Ho-ho-ho!' laughed the woman, and she went round behind Yaji and began to shampoo him.

Just then a girl came in selling cakes.

'Good evening,' she said. 'Won't you buy some of my cakes?'

'Halloa!' said Kita. 'Everybody's coming in. They look good. Do you want to sell me some?'

'Yes, yes,' said the girl. 'I wanted to sell you some so much that I ran all the way here.'

'Eh!' said Yaji. 'You're flattering.'

'No, no. We really love you so madly we don't know what to do,' said the girl. 'So please buy some of my cakes. I'll get you some tea.' She put down the boxes of cakes and went off to the kitchen.

'She's a bold-faced chatterer,' said Kita.

While he was talking he winked at Yaji and quietly took five or six cakes out of the box and hid them behind him. Thereupon the shampooer seized hold of them and shoved them into her sleeve without Kita seeing. Yaji also followed Kita's example and took three or four cakes out of the box. Just then he heard a noise from the kitchen, so he quickly closed the box and put it back in the place where it was before, while he hid the cakes behind him. Again the shampooer seized hold of them and shoved them into her sleeve without Yaji knowing anything about it. Then the cake girl came back from the kitchen with some tea.

'Please have some tea,' she said.

'It's very kind of you to take so much trouble,' said Yaji. 'After that we must buy some cakes. How much are these?' He took one out of the box.

'They're four coppers each,' said the girl. 'But those are not so nice. Try some of these.'

Yaji and Kita and the countryman each took some and began to eat.

'Wait a minute,' said Kita. 'We'd better count how many we're eating.'

'That's all right,' said the girl. 'Eat as many as you like. I won't charge you for them, eh, Tako?'

'No, no,' said the shampooer. 'Shall I rub the other gentleman down?'

'What, have you finished me already?' said Yaji.

'Will the other gentleman come and sit here?' said the shampooer.

'There you are,' said Kita. 'Is that all right?'

'Won't you have another cake?' asked the cake girl.

'You've given us quite a feast, Nabé,' said the shampooer. 'They are such kind gentlemen. Just turn the other side will you?'

'What, have you finished that side already?' said Kita. 'You are quick.'

'We've eaten a lot of cakes,' said the countryman. 'How much is it?'

'For the three of you it's two hundred and forty-eight coppers,' said the girl.

'What?' said Yaji. 'It's impossible. How could we have eaten so many? How many have you had, Kita?'

'Let's see, how many was it?' said Kita.

'I've eaten five of those at four coppers,' said the countryman. 'So there's twenty coppers for you.'

'What, do you think we're going to pay for all the others?' said Kita. 'Why it comes to more than the inn bill will.'

'It can't be helped,' said the girl. 'You've eaten them. Ho-ho-ho!'

'There ain't any ho-ho-ho about it at all,' said Yaji. 'I call it disgraceful.'

Yaji went on grumbling, but as there was no help for it, he had to pay the money. By this time the shampooer had finished.

'How much is it?' asked Kita.

'It's a hundred coppers for the two,' said the shampooer.

'What, fifty each?' cried Yaji. 'That's dear.'

But again he had to pay the money, and the woman went away.

'It doesn't do to be off one's guard with these Westcountry girls,' said Yaji, 'but I had that cake girl. If she was a tiger I was Kwōjin. She had a fool of a face anyway. She didn't know I had some of her best cakes hidden here.'

He put his hand behind him to feel for the cakes he had taken, but they were not there. Kita also looked for the cakes he had taken, but they also had gone. Then a girl came in from the kitchen, bringing the teapot and some tea cups.

'Please enjoy yourselves and have a little tea,' she said.

'Those cakes would come in just right now,' said Kita when she had gone. 'I wonder where they are.'

'It was the shampooer,' said the countryman. 'She took them. Ha-ha-ha! But I've got something better here.' He opened his basket and took out a small box. 'It's sugar candy,' he said. 'I got it at a shop in Doshō-machi. Just pass one of those small cups.'

'Thank you, thank you,' said Kita. 'Have some, Yaji. Take a lot.'

'No, no,' said the countryman. 'You mustn't take such a lot. Just pass it over,' and he put it away again very quickly.

Then the maid came in to spread the beds and while she was clearing up another woman looked in at the door and threw the pillows down. Yaji and Kita were surprised to see that it was the shampooer.

'I say,' said Yaji to the maid, 'isn't that woman who came in the blind shampooer?'

'Yes,' said the maid.

'How is it she can see?' asked Kita.

'Well, when guests come,' said the girl, 'she thinks they wouldn't like it if she could see, so the pretends she's blind. But at other times she helps in the kitchen.'

'Then that's how she was able to guess what we looked like,' said Yaji.

'Ah,' said Kita, 'and that accounts for her taking those cakes I sneaked.'

'Ho-ho-ho!' said the girl. 'Those cakes you stole must be those she gave to me,' and she pulled them out of her sleeve to show them and then went off laughing.

'What a joke!' exclaimed Kita.

Laughing over the incident they tumbled into bed and the Tamba man was soon fast asleep and snoring. The other two lay talking for some time longer. They could hear the sound of dogs barking in the fields at the back of the inn and the noise of someone splitting bamboo. Then the drum beat for the hour of midnight.

'What's that rustling sound, Yaji?' asked Kita, lifting his head.

'I couldn't sleep,' said Yaji, 'and I was tumbling about when I found this.'

From the bedclothes he pulled out a small chip box.

'Why, isn't that the box the old chap brought out before?' said Kita. 'The one with the sugar candy in, I mean.'

'Don't speak so loud,' said Yaji. 'It must have dropped out of his wicker-basket. I've had my eye on it for a long time.'

'Let's have a bit,' suggested Kita.

'Wait a minute,' said Yaji. The lantern was so far away he could not see very well, but he took the lid off and put some of the contents into his mouth. 'It's hard,' he said.

'Let's see,' said Kita, snatching the box away. He also put some in his mouth and chewed it.

'Whatever is it?' he said. 'It's like ashes.'

'It's not sugar candy,' said Yaji. 'What a strong smell it has.'

320

Then he began to feel rather sick and to reach, whereupon the Tamba man opened his eyes at the noise and jumped up astounded when he saw what they were doing.

'What are you doing?" he cried. 'What are you eating my wife for?"

'What do you mean by your wife?' asked Yaji.

'What do I mean?' exclaimed the Tamba man. 'It's sacrilege. That is my dear wife. Look on the lid of the box.'

Yaji jumped up and went over to the lantern with the box. There he saw written on the lid 'Shūgetsu Myokwo Shinnyō.' 'Then the box contains the ashes of your wife?' he asked.

'What? The ashes?' cried Kita. 'This is dreadful. That's why I feel so queer.'

'You may feel bad but I feel worse,' said the man. 'I'm carrying those remains from my village to Mount Kōya. It's desecration for you to eat it. You can't be real men. You must be devils or beasts. Whatever shall I do? Whatever shall I do?'

Here he hid his face in his sleeve and began to cry.

'What a terrible thing!' said Yaji, although he was secretly rather amused. 'When you opened your wicker-basket it fell out and got tumbled about without anybody knowing what it was. That was your fault. My fault was in mistaking it for sugar candy. So, as there were faults on both sides there's nothing to quarrel about.'

'No, no,' cried the Tamba man. 'Put it back as it was before. Put it back.'

Thereupon he began to wail and cry again, till Kitahachi managed to soothe him with many excuses and he became appeased.

Then, the matter settled, they sank to sleep again, but not for long, for the dawn came to disturb them in their dreams, and the servant came from the kitchen to awaken them. Rising, the three had breakfast together and then the Tamba man departed for Mount Kōya, and Yaji and Kita, who had decided to stop two or three days, prepared to go out to see the sights of Ōsaka.

'Good morning. What are you going to see to-day?' asked the clerk. 'If you like I could send a guide with you.'

'Ah, we should like that,' said Yaji.

'Very well,' said the clerk, and he called, 'Saheiji, Saheiji, just come here a minute.'

Saheiji came out of the kitchen.

'Would you gentlemen like me to guide you round?'' he asked.

'Yes, and I'd like to get two pairs of straw sandals,' said Kita.

'No, no,' said Yaji. 'One pair's enough. I bought a pair of leather-soled sandals in Kyōto. Those straw sandals make you look as if you were up from the country seeing the sights.'

'It doesn't matter when you're travelling,' said Kita.

'If you gentlemen are ready we'll start now,' said Saheiji.

'Come on, let's go,' said Yaji, and they went off with good wishes for a pleasant day from the clerk and the maid.

'Let's arrange it this way,' said Saheiji. 'You'd better go to the Tennō Temple and the Ikutama Shrine when you go to Sumi-yoshi. To-day we'll look at the sights near here.'

The guide took them along Nagamachi to the shrine at Kōzu. It was at this shrine, in ancient times that the Emperor Nintoku, mounted on the roof, composed an ode. But things have changed since then. Now it is a scene of great prosperity. Inside the temple grounds teahouses abound, and all day long the girls are crying, 'Walk in, walk in. Come in and rest, come in and rest.'

'Now's your time! Now's your time!' called a man at the

entrance to the theatre. 'Come and hear the Shirokiya of Kawaraya Bridge, with Tokubei Kamiya and Han of the Temmaya, followed by the suicide of Benkei. All parts performed by different actors.'

'Come and look,' cried a man with a telescope. 'You can see all the streets of Ōsaka, down to the very ants crawling in the roads. You can see all the people walking on Dōton Bridge and can count the number of priests among them. You can see both young and old and how many pockmarks they've got. You can see all the pretty girls and all the ugly ones too. You can see them buying and eating baked potatoes. You can see them relieving themselves by the rivers. You can see the beggars catching lice and count how many they've got. You can see 'em as wonderful as if you'd got 'em in your hand. You can see all the scenery. You can see Sumiyoshi harbour and the island of Awaji and Hyōgo Point, and Suma, and Akashi. You can see the sailors in the ships and count the bowls of rice they're eating. You can see what they're eating, too. More wonderful still, if you put it to your ear you can hear the actors in the theatres and tell what they're chanting. It's all the same whether you looks or listens. Smell it with your nose and you'll smell the eels they're frying in the next street. Only four coppers for a look through this wonderful glass. Here you are. Ten thousand miles at a glance. Here you are.'

'Can you see famous places like Shinmachi quite near through the glass ? ' asked Yaji.

'Yes, it's just over there,' said the man.

'But you can't see it near,' said Yaji. 'You see it far.'

'What do you mean ? '

'Well, there's only about an inch difference between Kōzu and Shinmachi.'

'That's on the map,' said the man.

'Of course,' said Yaji. 'Ha-ha-ha ! Well, let's see the temple. Aha, it's a fine temple.'

After worshipping there they descended the steps of the temple to Tanimichi-dōri and feeling rather hungry they went into a saké-shop which fortunately stood near by.

'What have you got ? ' asked Yaji.

'We have cockles and whale-flesh,' said the landlord, ' and also rolled herrings.'

' I don't know these Ōsaka dishes,' said Kita. 'Give us anything you've got good.'

' Yes, yes, in a minute,' said the landlord.

' We don't want it in a minute,' said Yaji. 'A bowl will do.'

' Excuse my rudeness,' said Kita, 'but could you tell me where your closet is ? Oh, I see it.'

He went off to the closet, and in the meanwhile the saké and the food were brought.

' Have a cup,' said Yaji to Saheiji.

' After you,' said Saheiji.

Yaji gulped down a cupful and then called to Kita. 'Here, Kita,' he cried, 'it's good saké. Come quickly, or I'll drink it all.'

' Wait a minute. I'm coming,' said Kita from inside the closet. Kita made haste to join them, but when he opened the door of the closet he was surprised to find that the saké shop had disappeared. The reason was that this closet served two houses, the saké shop in front and the house behind, and had two doors, one at the front and another at the back. Kita, in his hurry, had come out of the other door of the closet and was thus bewildered to see an old man engaged in making some light basketware, who stared at him over his spectacles with a puzzled air.

' Who are you ? ' asked the old man.

' I've made a mistake,' said Kita. 'How do you get to the saké shop ? '

' Aha, I see what has happened,' said the old man. 'You were in the saké shop, I suppose. Turn to the left at the end of the verandah and you'll find it.'

' But you can't get any further,' said Kita.

' Open the door,' said the old man.

' What, must I go into the closet again ? ' asked Kita. He tried the door, but a voice called to him inside.

' There's somebody inside,' said Kita, and from inside came Yaji's voice.

' Is that you, Kita ? ' he asked.

' Oh, it's you, Yaji, is it ? ' said Kita. 'I came out of the wrong door. Clear out of there quick.' He tried to open the door, but Yaji had put the catch on.

' Wait a bit,' said Yaji. 'It's bad to strain oneself, so you'll have to wait. It's a bore, isn't it ? I'll give you a song and you might hum the accompaniment.'

'Don't talk nonsense but get out of there quickly,' said Kita. He tried to push the door open but could not succeed. Then Yaji began to sing an ode from the Dōjōji :

> Love's lesson learnt, the faithful wife
> Gives all her heart unto her spouse.
> Her blackened teeth and well rouged lips
> Are records of her vows.

'What a long time you are !' cried Kita. But Yaji went on singing :

> In the end it's all the same.
> You must put your trust in me.
> Was it false the oath you swore ?
> This I ask of thee.

In spite of all Kita's entreaties Yaji refused to move. At last he fell silent, however, and Kita, thinking he had gone, called to him. Thereupon Yaji took up his song again :

> No sign of jealousy disturbs our love.

'What are you doing ?' called Kita.

'I've finished,' said Yaji. 'But let's sing the Yamazukushi before we go.'

At this Kita lost his temper and pushed so hard at the door that the catch broke and he fell inside the closet. Yaji was just opening the other door to go out when Kita fell in, with the result that he was knocked down and both the doors broken.

'Oh ! Oh ! Oh !' yelled Yaji.

'What's the matter ?' cried the landlord, running up. 'You've broken the closet door.'

'It's all your fault,' said Kita. 'You shouldn't have two doors to your closet.'

'Yes, but whoever heard of two persons going to the closet together ?' said the landlord.

'It's my fault,' said Yaji. 'You must excuse me.' Rubbing his knees he went back to the saké shop.

'What's the matter ?' asked Saheiji.

'You said the saké was good here,' said Kita, 'so let's have a drop quick.'

'No, no,' said Yaji. 'Somehow I don't feel at home here. Let's go further on.'

They paid the bill and went off, the landlord looking very black and refusing to return their salutations.

From there they went by Tanimachi-dōri and Andoji-machi to Bamba-no-hara, and at last reached Temma Bridge. Here they found the river full of trading boats passing up and down, some being rowed with sweeps and others being punted up the river to the songs of the boatmen. Then there were also pleasure boats, from which came the music of the samisen and the drum. A crowd had collected on the bridge to watch them.

'Ya, ya!' called a man on the bridge to one of the pleasure boats. 'How are you going to pay the bill-collector when he calls after wasting your money like that? Fool! Fool!'

'What are you talking about?' replied a man in the boat. 'It's you that's the fool.'

'Shut your jaw,' shouted the man on the bridge. 'It's you that's the fool.'

'Like your impudence,' said the man in the boat. 'Do you want to make out who's the biggest fool? We beat you easily.'

'What, give in to you?' said the man on the bridge very angrily. 'We've got the biggest fool here.'

'Yes, everybody knows you're the biggest fool in town,' said his companion, drawing him away. 'Don't mind what they say.'

Then they went off with all the crowd running after them and calling 'Fool, fool, fool!'

Amused at this quarrel, Yaji and Kita went on till they came to the Temma Shrine, where they found a multitude of pilgrims attracted by the divine favours of the god. There they found charming girls in red aprons waiting outside the cookshops and teahouses, and countless booths and archery grounds, with girls calling to the passers-by in shrill voices to soften their hearts. Elsewhere were to be seen monsters of the land or sea, dramatic performances, acrobats, circus-riding,—all within the precincts of the temple.

Thus they went the round of the shrines, not refraining from casting sidelong glances at the white faces of the girls who performed the sacred dances. Passing the corner of the Koyamaya they came to Tenjin-bashi-dōri. Here the thong of one of Yaji's sandals broke.

'There!' said Yaji. 'These Kyōto things are no good. They told me it would never break. What a nuisance!'

Just then a rag-and-bone man passed, calling 'Dei! Dei!'

This is the cry of the rag-and-bone men in Ōsaka, but in Edo it is the cry of the sandal and clog menders, and Yaji did not know this.

'Here,' he called. 'Just look at this sandal.'

'Ay, ay,' said the man. 'But one sandal's no good. What's the good of one sandal? And the thong's broken too. Let's have the one you've got on.'

'It's only just broken,' said Yaji. 'How much for the two?'

The rag-and-bone man, who thought Yaji wanted him to buy them, turned them over and over.

'These would be very cheap,' he said.

'Yes, yes,' said Yaji. 'They must be cheap.'

'Well then, forty-eight coppers for the two,' said the man. 'How's that?'

'No, no,' said Yaji. 'That's too dear. Twenty-four coppers is enough.'

'Eh, you're joking with me,' said the man.

'No, no,' said Yaji. 'You must make it twenty-four coppers.'

As Yaji kept on thrusting the sandals under his nose and insisting upon his having them, the rag-and-bone man, astonished and half amused at the seller (as he thought) wishing to beat down the price, at last pulled out the money.

'All right,' he said, 'I'll lower the price to twenty-four coppers.' He put the money in Yaji's hand, and flinging the sandals into his box, began to move off.

'Here, wait a minute,' said Yaji. 'What do you want to give me the money for? What are you going to do with those sandals?'

'Haven't I bought 'em?' said the man.

'Nonsense,' said Yaji. 'I wanted you to mend the thong that's broken.'

'What, did you think I was a clog-mender?' said the man. 'I'm a rag-and-bone man, I am. None of your dirty outcasts.'

'Well, what do you want to go about shouting " Dei, Dei " for then?' asked Yaji.

As Yaji was beginning to get angry, Saheiji, the guide, intervened.

'I see, I see,' he said. 'It's our mistake. I thought there was something wrong. In Edo the clog-menders call out " Dei,

dei " as they go along, but in these parts the rag-and-bone men use that cry. It's our mistake, but we didn't know, so you must excuse us.'

' A nice thing, making a fool of a man like that,' said the man.

' Well, it's a mistake,' said Kita. ' You must give back the sandals.'

' Taking me for a clog-mender,' grumbled the man. ' Destroying my reputation like that ! '

Kita and Saheiji soothed the man and at last he gave back the sandals, whereupon Yaji hung them at his waist and put on a pair of straw sandals.

They crossed Tenjin Bridge and went along Yokobori-dōri. Here they encountered a crowd of people. At first they thought it was a fight, as everybody was talking and shouting at once, and there was a great uproar. They made their way through the crowd and while they were doing so they noticed a little package lying at their feet. Yaji stooped down and picked it up, not thinking it was anything of value, and on opening it found it was a wooden ticket marked with the number eighty-eight. Although there are no such things nowadays, the temples at that time used to hold lotteries, and apparently one of the persons in the crowd they had just passed had dropped his lottery ticket.

' That must be a lottery ticket you just picked up,' said Saheiji.

' I suppose so,' said Yaji. ' It's number eighty-eight.'

' It's the lottery at the Zama temple,' explained Saheiji, ' and it's going to be drawn to-day. I expect it's already drawn.'

' That would be it,' said Yaji. ' I expect it's a number that failed. It's no good.'

He threw it away, but Kita, who was following close behind him, picked it up again and thrust it into his bosom. Soon they reached the Zama Temple.

Now it happened that that day was the day for the drawing of the lottery and apparently it had just been drawn, for a great crowd had collected in front of the temple and it was impossible for them to push their way through.

' What a pity I didn't buy eighty-eight,' they heard someone in the crowd say. ' If I'd bought that I should have won the first prize of a hundred pieces of gold.'

This gave Yaji quite a shock.

328

'Did you hear that?' he said. 'What a pity we threw away that ticket. What shall we do? Do you think we'd find it if we turned back?'

'You don't suppose it would be there still, do you?' said Kita.

'It's very unfortunate I threw it away,' answered Yaji, and he kept on looking back as he walked.

As the lottery had been drawn the numbers of the winners were being written up one by one in front of the temple, and they saw that the number of the first prize was eighty-eight.

'Oh, oh!' groaned Yaji. 'I'm going to turn priest. My luck's out entirely.'

'Ha-ha-ha!' laughed Kita. 'Don't let your spirits go down. I'm going to get that hundred gold pieces, and I don't mind letting you have four or five out of them. Look at this.'

He pulled out of his bosom the ticket that Yaji had thrown away and held it up before him.

'What?' exclaimed Yaji. 'Did you pick it up? Well done, well done. Hand it over.'

'Oh no,' said Kita. 'None of that. You threw it away and I picked it up, so it's mine now.'

'No, no,' said Yaji. 'I saw it first and picked it up and so it's mine by right although you did pick it up again.'

'Yes, but didn't you throw it away?' said Kita.

'That doesn't matter,' said Yaji. 'You just pass it over.'

He tried to snatch it away from Kita, but Kita held it fast. Then Saheiji intervened.

'Be quiet,' he said. 'If you talk so loud the man who dropped it will hear you and he'll want it back. Let me settle the matter for you. As you've both picked it up, what you must do is to halve the prize, and while you're about it you might give me a share.'

'Of course, I'm quite willing to do that,' said Kita. 'But we'd better enjoy the good things while we have them. We ought to get the money at once. Where do they pay?'

'Over there,' said Saheiji, 'where that man's sitting.'

They went over to the lottery office, but there they saw a notice that owing to the confusion the winner in the lottery would not be paid till the next day. Thus seeing that there was nothing to be got that day, they continued their round of the shrines.

'Suppose the chap that lost the ticket goes and gets the money,' said Kita.

'Oh, don't worry about that,' said Saheiji. 'They won't pay the money till they get the ticket back, no matter how many witnesses he has.'

'Hooray!' cried Yaji. 'I feel quite happy now.'

'We'll get the hundred gold pieces to-morrow,' said Kita. 'It seems a long time to wait.'

'What's a long time?' asked Yaji. 'Ain't we going to get it all right?'

Thus rejoicing over their luck, they forthwith entered a tea-house and called for some saké in honour of the event.

SECOND PART

THUS Yajirobei and Kitahachi, having picked up the winning number in a lottery, by which they thought to get one hundred pieces of gold, and having thus suddenly become full of life and spirits, left the grounds of the Zama Temple and entered a teahouse, where they drank saké till they seemed to themselves to be floating along in a land of pleasant dreams. Then their guide Saheiji took them to the shrine of the Emperor Nintoku, which is called the Inari of Bakuro-chō.

'Come in, come in,' cried the girls at the teahouse at the gate. 'Try our hot baked beancurd with bean sauce.'

'What silly things they say,' said Kita. 'Who'd eat it if it was cold.'

'Come in, come in,' cried the man at the door of the theatre. 'The Bell of Mugen from the Seisuiki is just going to begin.'

'We don't want to hear any more about the Bell of Mugen,' said Yaji. 'We've got a hundred pieces of gold. Isn't it wonderful? I say, Kita, let's go to Shinmachi and buy a courtesan. What do you think, Saheiji?'

'That's a good idea,' said Saheiji, 'but I hope you won't mind my telling you that it's no use your going like you are now. It would be all right for low-class courtesans, but not for those in the front. It would be better to wait till to-morrow evening and put on a better appearance.'

'Yes, yes,' said Yaji. 'You're quite right. We must wait till we've got the hundred pieces of gold. Then we can get the best.'

'How proud he's grown!' said Kita.

'Of course,' said Saheiji. 'I'll go with you whenever you like. By the way here is the Daimaru store. Isn't a fine place?'

'Here you are! Here you are!' cried a man at the door. 'Walk in, walk in.'

'I say, Kita,' said Yaji. 'Suppose we go in and order some clothes.'

'Ha-ha-ha!' laughed Saheiji. 'What a hurry you're in. You'd better wait till to-morrow morning.'

'Yes, yes,' said Kita. 'We mustn't be in too great a hurry. Let's go on.'

'Well, we must leave it till to-morrow then,' said Yaji. 'But I say, Kita, what are you going to get?'

'Clothes, do you mean?' said Kita. 'Well, I'm going to get three fashionable silk dresses and a fine-patterned, rustling silk cloak, so as to make myself look as rich as possible.'

'You'll look like a shopman,' said Yaji. 'If you wear a dress like that people will call after you in the street, "How much did you make yesterday? You told 'em it was the best quality and it was only the common. You did make a lot of profit, didn't you?" That's the sort of thing they'd say. I shall have a black cloak of striped silk and wear a long sword like a judge. That would make everybody stare. An underdress edged with scarlet and above a Yūki silk kimono and a cloak to match. Wouldn't that be stylish? Hachijo silk is out of fashion and *tozan* silk makes you look like an old man. Nambujima silk also is so common that you'd be ashamed to undress in a public bathroom.'

'That's so,' said Kita. 'When you come to think of it there's really nothing to wear.'

'Nothing to wear, eh?' said a man walking behind him. 'With a great big crest on your back and a kimono made out of old flags, eh? Ha-ha-ha!'

'Here, what are you talking about?' asked Kita.

'It's none of your business,' said the man and walked off.

'Impudent rascal!' said Kita. 'He doesn't know how we're going to dress to-morrow.'

'Ha-ha-ha!' laughed Saheiji. 'Excuse my rudeness, but it's funny to hear you two gentlemen talking about wearing all kinds of silk clothes. Well, let's get along to the Amida Lake and the Izumiya at Sunaba.'

'Look here,' said Yaji. 'I'm tired of temples and such. Can't we go somewhere amusing so that it won't seem so long waiting till to-morrow?'

'Well then, I'll tell you what to do,' said Saheiji. 'I'll hire some kimono for you and then you'll be able to go to Shinmachi to-night. You can pay me for them afterwards. I know the keeper of the Ageya teahouse, and as you're going to get a hundred gold pieces to-morrow morning that will be all right. What do you think?'

'Yes, yes,' said Kita. 'That's a good idea.'

332

'Then let's go back to the inn at once,' said Yaji, 'and we'll get you to carry out your plan.'

Delighted with the idea, they hurried along Shinsaibashi-suji till they reached Dōtombori, which is the busiest part of the city, as it is situated between Shimanouchi and Sakamachi and beautiful courtesans and singing girls there abound. It was already four o'clock and from the theatres and wrestling halls came the noisy clamour of the people. Pushing their way through the sightseers, slipping along quickly like thieves, not stopping to look at the announcements in front of the theatres, snatching themselves from the detaining hands of the waitresses outside the teahouses, jostled by the kago carriers and the postboys, the three returned quickly to Nagamachi.

'Here we are,' said Saheiji.

'Welcome back,' cried the maid.

'Thank you, thank you,' said Kita. 'Well, what about that plan ? '

'Certainly,' said Saheiji. 'I'll go and see about it at once.'

'Let's be quick,' said Kita.

He and Yaji went to their room to wait for Saheiji, and soon the maid came in.

'Would your honours like to take a bath now,' she inquired, ' or would you like to have supper first ? '

'We can't eat any supper,' said Yaji. 'We're in a hurry. But I'll just get into the bath.'

'It'll make us late,' said Kita. 'What do you want with a bath ? '

'Well, I'll just wash my face then,' said Yaji.

'Get out ! ' said Kita. 'Ha-ha-ha ! '

Yaji went off to the bath and in a little time Saheiji came back with the hired clothes tied up in a bundle.

'Sorry to have kept you waiting,' he said. He undid the bundle and Kita turned over the clothes.

'They're all very plain,' he said.

'Yes, but they're quite the latest style,' said Saheiji. 'You'd look very well in that black one.'

'What a terrible crest it has on it, and it's too long and the sleeves are too big,' said Kita. 'I should look like an octopus in it. What's that striped one there ? '

'It's of silk,' said Saheiji.

'Well, this speckled one's all right,' said Kita.

But when he spread it out he found it was a woman's kimono.

'Ha-ha-ha!' laughed Saheiji. 'I thought it was a man's. Never mind, put it on.'

'I'll tell you what I'll do,' said Kita. 'As it's got short sleeves I'll put it on underneath and wear the other on top.'

He put the two kimono on, one over the other, and was just tying the girdle when Yaji came back from the bath.

'Halloa, you've got back, Saheiji,' said Yaji. 'Kita's got his clothes on too. He looks so fine that everybody will know they're hired.'

'Don't stand there trying to be funny,' said Kita, 'but get your clothes on at once.'

'This black one will do for me,' said Yaji. 'I'd look like a lord in that if I had a long sword.'

'Look here,' said Kita, 'are you going to get dressed or are you going out bare with only a long sword on. You're not going to feel Kiyomori's pulse so you'd better put your clothes on.'

'What about a cloak?' asked Yaji.

'Wear this one with the crest,' said Saheiji.

'What a short cloak!' said Kita. 'It makes you look like a beggar.'

'Well, you needn't talk,' replied Yaji. 'You look like a quack-doctor's assistant.'

'If you're ready now we'll go,' said Saheiji.

'But I haven't been to the bath yet,' said Kita.

'Don't talk nonsense,' said Yaji. 'Come on, let's go.'

Thus they started off. Saheiji thought that as the two had won a prize in the lottery he would be able to get a share of it, so he had persuaded the clerk at the inn to give him a letter of introduction to a teahouse in Shinmachi, and it was there that he was going to take them.

Thus the three went along Nagamachi, their heads in the clouds, and through Sakai-suji, till they quickly reached Junkei-machi. This place is famous for its night-market. On each side of the road were booths, with not an inch to spare between them, all brightly lit by lanterns. Here were displayed clothes, furniture, bags, combs, coral, agate, and on the next stall, tubs, kegs, rice-boxes, pestles, dippers. Here were persons looking for shrines to which they could make offerings, or for a figure of the Buddha or Kwannon, and running off without paying the full price for them. Here were persons in clogs buying hats and there persons in straw-sandals selling rush-sandals. Here were persons in the exchange-shops jingling money in the scales, there ironmongers whose mouths were as sharp as the swords they sold. Here were the fishmongers bawling their rotten goods.

'Here's your fine bream,' they called.

Then there was the cry of the sweet potato man : 'Hokkori ! Hokkori !. Eat 'em while they're hot. Hokkori ! '

'Here's your tasty boiled herring,' called another.

Then there was the *sushi* seller. 'Here you are,' he called. 'Try our famous mackerel and cockles.'

'I say, Yaji,' said Kita. 'Look there. There are some of those nice rice-cakes we had at Kyōto. Let's buy some. We didn't have any supper to-night and I'm getting awfully hungry.'

'So there is,' said Yaji, and he asked the man the price.

'Ay, ay,' said the man. 'These here are four coppers, and those there are six coppers.'

'They're fine,' said Yaji as he gobbled one down. 'Just wrap us up some.'

The man wrapped some up in a bamboo leaf and Yaji went along eating them.

'Here, give us some,' said Kita.

'I'll give you the leaf when I've finished them,' said Yaji.

'None of that,' said Kita. 'Just pass them over.'

While they were arguing about the cakes a dog suddenly jumped up and snatched them.

'Oh, oh ! ' said Yaji.

'What's the matter ? ' asked Kita.

'Some dog jumped up and got 'em,' said Yaji.

'Bow-wow ! ' barked the dog.

'Oh, it's you, is it ? ' said Yaji. 'I'll teach you.' But when he tried to kick the dog it ran away, and when Yaji ran after it he stumbled over the edge of a well that was in the middle of the road and fell.

'Oh ! Oh ! ' he yelled. 'What do they want to stick a well there for, right in the middle of the cross-roads ? '

'This is called the cross-roads well,' explained Saheiji.

'It serves you right for not giving me any,' said Kita.

As they went along, pushing their way through the crowd, they saw a fortune-teller in a large hat, which completely covered his face, calling to the people to come and have their fortunes told.

335

'Come along,' he cried. 'Don't be afraid. Come and have your fortune told. Show me a letter and I can tell by the colour of the ink whether it is light or dark. If you have lost anything I can tell you where it isn't. I can tell you in what you can't put your trust. I can tell you whether a person will be late when they don't come to an appointment, or early when they do. Whether I'm right or wrong it's all the same charge, sixteen coppers. That's the only thing in which I make no mistake. Come along. Come along.'

'I say, Kita,' said Yaji. 'Let's see whether he knows we're going to get a hundred gold pieces to-morrow.'

'Ah, that would be fun,' replied Kita.

'Just tell us our fortunes, will you?' said Yaji, and he held out sixteen coppers.

The fortune-teller looked at Yaji out of the corner of his eye as he took the money and laid out the sticks on the divining board.

'Aha!' he said, after he had studied them for a while. 'I see you will be extraordinarily lucky.'

'That's right,' said Yaji. 'You've got it just right.'

'Ain't I right?' said the fortune-teller. '*Ke* is *kon*, and *kon* is *konkwai*, and *konkwai* in the vulgar language is fox. That is you will have a fox's luck. Truly I see that unexpected fortune awaits you.'

'Bravo!' said Kita. 'You've got it just right.'

'Nevertheless,' continued the fortune-teller, 'a change of fortune is Heaven's decree, and bodings of Heaven's decree are mystical. For if the fortune of Earth and the fortune of Heaven are joined together, then, as the Book tells us, between Heaven and Earth everything escapes and there is nothing left. When there is no bullet the gun is empty. In everything great care is demanded.'

'That's not right,' exclaimed Yaji. 'There's no truth in that. My fortune's as safe as if I'd got it in my hand. You're telling us bad luck.'

'It's all the same price,' said the fortune-teller, 'whether I'm right or wrong.'

'Come along, Yaji,' said Kita. 'It's sixteen coppers clean thrown away.'

Grumbling they went along over Shinmachi Bridge to Hyōtan-machi. This quarter was first licensed in the Kwanei era and from ancient times it has been very popular. Peeping into the gaily decorated houses as they went along, they passed through Echigo-machi, where they chaffed the common courtesans who caught hold of their sleeves, and came at last to Kuken-machi.

'This large building is the Ageya,' said Saheiji.

'Aha! It's quite a big affair,' said Kita.

'This is where we go in,' directed Saheiji. 'Please wait a minute.'

He left them at the entrance and himself went into the kitchen. The landlord of the Kawachiya, the inn in Nagamachi where they were staying, sometimes gave his guests introductions to the quarter, so when Saheiji handed in the introduction, the landlord of the teahouse bustled out to meet them in his best clothes.

'Welcome, welcome,' he said. 'Here, waitress, show these gentlemen to a room. Please follow her.'

'Excuse me,' said Yaji. 'Here, Kita, aren't you coming? What are you standing at the door for like the willow-tree outside a gardener's shop?'

'Ha-ha-ha!' laughed Saheiji. 'Bravo!'

They were conducted along the passage, past room after room, till they came to a very luxurious room at the back. Saheiji, who treated them both very politely, followed them in and took a seat near the door, while a waitress brought tea and the tobacco-box. Then the landlord appeared.

'Thank you very much for giving me your custom,' he said.

'Are you the landlord?' said Yaji. 'Well, look here. I've come up from Edo on business, and this is the first time I have been in your city. As I hope to patronise you many times during my stay here, I would ask your best attention. I may tell you that I am not one to spare money when I begin spending and don't mind how much it is. But as I'm a trader by nature and this is the first time I've visited you, I should like you to let us have everything very cheap this evening, just for a start. Eh, Saheiji?'

'Yes, yes,' said Saheiji. 'Let's arrange it this way. As you've only just arrived no doubt you're very tired, so I think it would be better for you just to have a little saké and then go home to bed. You can come back again to-morrow night.'

He said this because he thought it was rather unsafe to let them run up a large bill before they had got the hundred pieces of gold, which, after all, there might be some mistake about. He remembered what the fortune-teller had said and was not very easy in his mind in consequence, and he had therefore decided not to leave them there but to wait till they had had a few drinks and take them back to the inn again.

'Anything will do for me,' said Yaji.

'Well then, waitress,' said Saheiji, 'we'll only have a look at the girls.'

Meanwhile saké and comestibles were brought in and the waitresses helped each of the guests. There was a great noise going on in the next room, where a guest, who appeard to be a Westcountry samurai, had summoned a buffoon and a crowd of dancing girls, all of whom were laughing and joking. Through the cracks in the sliding doors Yaji and Kita peeped in to see what was going on. Soon the girls began to sing.

> He's only got three hairs
>> On the top of his head,
> But he rattles out the money,
>> Since he's a rattlehead.
> Gompachi's all right,
>> But he's changed his name you see.
> Now you must swear by Tegetsu.
> Come, take the oath with me.

'That's a song about the southern Gompachi, isn't it?' said the buffoon, whose name was Sōhachi.

'Yes,' replied one of the singing girls. 'Tōnan showed us the dance to that song.'

'Come on,' said the samurai. 'I'll give you a dance. Play up.'

He stood up and tied a towel round his head, so that both his ears stuck out, and then, putting his cloak over one shoulder, he took a fan in his hand and began to dance and sing while the girls played the samisen:

> Kamé of Suyama,
>> Oh an old fox is she!
> Kamé of Suyama,
>> She's well known to me.
> Yoriya aikori!
> Yo aikori yo!
>
> Come a little nearer
> And I shall show you where
> Behind here is a little hut.
>> Oh, Kamé lives there.

> Yoriya aikori !
> Yo aikori yo !
>
> There she sleeps at night,
>   A pumpkin 'neath her head.
> Come along with me
>   And you shall share her bed.

'Bravo ! Bravo !' they all cried when he had finished.

'Oh, Oh !' groaned the samurai. 'I am tired. I shall be scolded by my girl for getting drunk like this. Terrible, terrible !'

'Ho-ho-ho !' laughed all the girls. 'What things you say ! We don't know what you mean.'

'Why ? Why ?' asked the samurai.

'Oh, you horrid man,' cried the girls. 'Look at his face. Look what strange eyes he makes. How bright and glaring they are !'

'You are insulting,' cried the samurai, in a sudden burst of anger. 'Look at your own faces instead of mine. What hateful faces they are, all swollen up like the globe-fish or the cormorant. There's nothing pleasing about them. I'm going home.'

He stood up, but the waitresses caught hold of him. 'There, there,' they said. 'There's nothing for you to get angry about.'

'Don't be rude, Shimé,' said the buffoon. 'I'll tell you what we'll do. We're getting rather bored, so to liven thing up, let's be as jolly as if we were in a steam-bath.'

'A steam-bath is an empty bath,' said the samurai. 'He takes me for a dunderhead. I've a good mind to beat him for his rudeness.'

Apparently the samurai was a man who got angry in his cups. He swore he was going and they were all trying to detain him, when in the middle of the dispute Hikifuné, a courtesan, accompanied by a little girl, came in.

'There, she's come,' cried the waitresses.

'Oh, I am tired,' said Hikifuné. 'What's the matter ?'

'He's awfully angry,' said a waitress. 'He says he's going.'

'Didn't I tell you I was going to Suhama's house and you had to wait ?' said Hikifuné. 'And now you say you're going away. If you don't like being here go away, please.'

'No, no,' said thé samurai. 'I'm not really angry. Only the people here are so rude. But never mind, never mind.'

339

'Then there's nothing to make a noise about. Come along.'

Conducted by the crowd of girls, they went away to another room.

By this time some ten courtesans had gathered in the next room. Then a waitress came in carrying a saké bottle and cup and another with a book and a writing box.

'Ogiya-no-Orikoto,' called the waitress. 'Please come here.'

Orikoto came in, took the cup, pretended to drink and put it down again. Then she looked at the waitress's face, tittered, and went out.

'Tsuchiya-no-Hinamatsu,' called the waitress. 'Please come here.'

Thus each courtesan like the first, took the cup and pretended to drink, while Yaji and Kita looked on, attracted by the strangeness of the scene, and made idle remarks which I will not repeat.

'Which one would you like?' asked the waitress.

'I'd like them all,' said Kita. 'What was the name of the third one?'

The waitress looked in her book. 'That was Nishi-no-Ogiya-no-Azumaji,' she said.

'Well, we only came to-night to have a look' said Saheiji. 'You can come to-morrow night and stay as long as you like.'

'Why not to-night?' asked Yaji.

'I think it would be better to do as I suggest,' said Saheiji, who was longing to get them away. Yaji, however, felt great reluctance to leave.

'Let's have some more saké at any rate,' he said.

'Shall I call in some singing-girls?' asked the waitress.

'No, no,' said Saheiji. 'There isn't time really.'

'We didn't come here only to drink saké,' said Kita. 'We ought to spend more for the good of the house.'

'Yes, please don't go yet,' said the waitress. 'Let me take off your cloaks.'

Several of the girls jumped up to help them take off their cloaks, and while they were folding them up they began to titter at what they saw on the lining.

'There's a great big ten marked on them,' whispered one of the girls. 'They must have hired them somewhere,' and they all began whispering to each other and laughing. It appeared that all the clothes let out were marked on the lining with a big 'ten' done in white cotton, and as all the girls knew this they were laughing at them. Saheiji heard them laughing and guessed what they were laughing at, but Yaji and Kita were quite unconscious of the joke.

'How many courtesans are there in this quarter?' asked Yaji. 'It would be fun to call them all.'

'I'd like to give 'em all a kimono of the same pattern while I'm stopping here,' said Kita. 'Eh, Yaji?'

'They would be very pleased,' said the waitress.

'Has your cloak got the number ten inside?' asked one of the girls of Kita.

'Hush!' said another girl, pulling her by the sleeve. 'Don't ask such questions.'

Then they both started laughing, but Yaji and Kita were still quite ignorant of what they were laughing at.

'Eh?' said Kita. 'Number ten inside? That's some trick, eh? I know your little ways. You've got a sweetheart, haven't you? a handsome fellow! Here, let's have another drink.'

'Ho-ho-ho!' laughed the girls. 'What silly things you say. Here, Master Ten, I'll give you a drink.'

'What's that? said Kita. 'I'm Number Ten, eh? Thank you.'

Quite unconscious that he was being laughed at Kita took the cup that she offered him, but while the girl was filling it with saké he pinched her leg a little, causing her to give a little scream and a jump, which made her spill all the saké in the bottle on Kita's knee, so that his kimono was soaked with it.

'Oh dear, I'm so sorry,' she said.

'Look what you've done,' said another girl. 'Why don't you take care? It'll leave a stain on his kimono. Saké's a dreadful thing to stain. Shall I wash it for you?'

'Yes,' said the first girl. 'That will be best. I'll rinse it out for you. Just take it off.'

She started up to take off Kita's kimono, but Kita remembered that he had a woman's kimono on underneath and thought they would laugh at him.

'Never mind, never mind,' he said. 'Don't trouble about washing it. It's only an old kimono.'

'No trouble at all,' said the girl. 'Do take it off.'

Why she and the other girls really wanted Kita to take off his kimono was to see whether it was marked Number Ten like his cloak, and they began to try and take it off by force. This made Kita angry.

'Let 'em take it off, Kita,' said Yaji. 'It's all right. If there's a stain on it. . . You know. Let 'em wash it a bit. You can easily dry it at the brazier.'

He was afraid there would be trouble about the stain on the kimono when they took it back, and he looked meaningly at Kita to try and made him understand.

Kita was puzzled what to do. 'It was only a drop or two of saké,' he said.

'Even a little leaves a stain,' said Yaji, 'and we don't want a stain on them. Sorry to trouble you, waitress, but if you wouldn't mind washing it a bit.'

'Ay, ay,' said the girl. 'Please take it off.'

'What a nuisance you are,' said Kita. 'Didn't I say it was all right?'

In spite of all his excuses, however, the girls persisted in undoing his girdle and finally took off his kimono. As he had got a woman's kimono on underneath the sleeves were very short, and feeling ashamed he tried to hide his hands.

'Halloa!' said Yaji surprised. 'Have you got a woman's kimono on?'

'Nonsense,' said Kita. 'I feel cold without my kimono,' and he drew himself back as far as he could.

'You must be cold,' said the waitress. 'Let me offer you another cup of saké.'

'Yaji,' said Kita, 'take the cup for me.'

'What's the matter?' asked Yaji. 'Can't you stretch out your hand? There it is. You can take it.'

'Are you making fun of me also?' grumbled Kita.

The waitress soon washed the stain out of the kimono and dried it and brought it back.

'There you are, Master Ten,' she said. 'It's all right now. Ho-ho-ho! Please come a little forward. Ho-ho-ho!'

Her continued laughter annoyed Kita. 'What are you always talking about Number Ten for?' he asked. 'I came here to amuse myself, not to hear about Number Ten.'

Kita's anger sobered the girl a little and she asked his pardon if she had offended him.

'I won't forgive you,' said Kita, 'until you tell me what you mean by Number Ten.'

342

'Don't get cross,' said Saheiji, 'like that samurai did just now. It isn't nice.'

'Never mind whether it's nice or nasty, let's hear what she means by Number Ten,' said Kita.

Yaji and Saheiji tried to pacify him, but as he had drunk a good deal of saké he refused to listen to reason, and persisted that he would not forgive the girl until she told him what she meant by Number Ten. At last Saheiji, finding the matter getting troublesome, spoke to the girl himself.

'You have no right to use such an expression,' he said. 'You don't know whether it's true.'

'Yes,' said the girl, 'but . . .'

'Out with it,' said Kita.

'If I tell you you'll get angry again,' said the girl.

'Never mind that,' said Yaji. 'Just tell us plainly what you mean. I want to hear too.'

'Well, I'll tell you then,' said the girl. 'The Number Ten is here.'

She turned over the cloaks they had taken off and showed them the Ten marked on the inside.

'Oh, the cloaks are marked Number Ten, are they?' said Yaji.

'Ha-ha-ha!' laughed Saheiji. 'Now I see. You know they're both travellers and hadn't any other clothes, so they borrowed some to come in.'

'What are you talking about?' said Kita. 'See me going about in hired clothes! How absurd!'

'It's no use talking like that,' said Saheiji. 'All the clothes hired out in Nagamachi have Number Ten marked inside. Everybody knows that, so it's no use trying to conceal it.'

Now that everybody had found out about their hired clothes Yaji and Kita felt so humiliated that they decided to leave, and they finally slunk out of the house amid the winks and titters of all the waitresses, who gathered at the door to see them off.

THIRD PART

THUS the three, having gone to Shinmachi to enjoy themselves and having been unexpectedly humiliated, left the quarter laughing at their discomfiture. It was already past midnight and the night-stalls were gone from Junkei-machi and the street deserted. Hastening their steps they quickly returned to Nagamachi. In the morning they were to receive a hundred pieces of gold. That was enough to wash away that evening's disgrace, but somehow when they lay down in their room they felt dissatisfied and did not sleep much. At last the early cock began to crow and slowly dawn came. Soon it was daylight and the travellers stopping in the inn began to get up and talk. Yaji and Kita rose, and Saheiji came in rubbing his eyes to tell them to be quick.

After a hasty breakfast they put on the hired clothes they had worn the night before and set off hurriedly for the temple, where they soon found the place where the prizes in the lottery were to be distributed.

'Here's the place,' said Kita. 'Go in, Yaji.'

'You go first,' said Yaji.

'What are you bashful about?' said Kita, and he went in.

'Excuse me,' he said. 'I've won the first prize in yesterday's lottery. Will you please pay me?'

The man in the room came hurriedly forward. 'Dear me,' he said. 'Please come in.'

He led them into the hall, where he left them for a time. Soon he returned.

'We'll pay you the money,' he said. 'Please come this way.'

He led them into a large room at the back where they all sat down. The room was a very fine one, with a magnificent alcove and shelves, and not a crack or a stain to mar it. Soon a handsome boy of about thirteen or fourteen, dressed in black silk, came in with tea and a tobacco-box, and afterwards returned with a saké bottle and some cups and some soup.

'I'll let you have the money directly,' said the priest, 'but just have a glass of saké first, won't you?'

'Thank you, thank you,' said Yaji. 'It's really very good of you,' and he giggled with pleasure.

'What's there to giggle about?' asked Kita. 'You needn't make a fuss about it but just take what's given you.'

'You were very lucky to win the first prize,' said the priest. 'Allow me to drink a cup of saké with you in congratulation.'

'Delighted with the honour,' said Yaji.

'The honour is mine,' said the priest.

'Thank you for your hospitality,' said Kita, and he began gulping down the saké.

When you want to grow corn and reap the grain you have to prepare the ground, and so the priests gave the two as much saké as they wanted and put all sorts of appetising dishes before them. As the priests all took turns in drinking with them they were half drunk when at last the saké was removed and the dinner was brought in.

'Dear me,' said Kita. 'This is beyond our expectations.'

'Please don't put yourselves out for us,' said Yaji. 'Ha-ha-ha! It's so amusing I can't help laughing.'

When they had eaten as much as they could the dishes were removed and a person who seemed to be the chief priest of the temple came in, accompanied by two or three other priests bearing trays on which the gold pieces were piled up. At sight of them Yaji and Kita felt a thrill of rapture and could hardly refrain from laughing for joy.

'I am the head of this temple,' said the chief priest. 'Allow me to offer you my greetings and congratulate you on your good fortune.'

'Ay, ay,' said Yaji.

'Shall I present you with the money?' asked the chief priest.

'Yes, yes,' said Kita.

'But first I have a request to make,' said the chief priest. 'As you will have seen, this temple is in a great state of dilapidation, and as the lottery is arranged for the benefit of the temple we always make a request to the winner for a contribution of ten pieces out of every hundred. Will you be willing to make this donation?'

'Ay, ay,' said Yaji.

'I have another request to make,' said the priest. 'It's a thing that is always done, and that is to make a donation of five pieces to the manager of the lottery. Will you be willing to do that?'

'Ay, ay, ay,' said Kita.

'There is one thing more,' said the priest, 'and that is that you buy a ticket for the next lottery.'

'Ay, ay, ay,' said Yaji.

'Then I'll deduct twenty pieces from the hundred and hand you the remainder,' said the priest. 'Will that be correct?'

'Yes, yes,' said Yaji. 'Whatever you like.'

'Then if you'll hand me the ticket,' said the priest, 'I'll give you the money.'

'Here it is,' said Kita, and he pulled the ticket out of his bosom.

The priest took it and looked at it with a surprised air. 'Is this the only ticket you have?' he asked.

'Yes, that's all,' said Kita.

'Then there has been a mistake,' said the priest.

'What's the mistake?' said Kita. 'Isn't the winning number eighty-eight?'

'Yes, certainly,' said the priest; 'number eighty-eight.'

'Then what mistake can there be?' asked Kita.

'This is not the right ticket,' said the priest. 'The mark on it is wrong. All the tickets issued by this temple have a special mark on them. The winning ticket was 88 *ne*. This one you have is marked 88 *i*.'

All the tickets were marked on the back with one of the twelve signs of the zodiac, so that there were twelve tickets each bearing the same number but with a different zodiacal sign. Kita had known nothing about this and had paid no attention to the mark. That was how the mistake had come about. At once all their hopes were dashed to the ground and they sat there crushed with despair.

'Then it ain't any good, ain't it?' said Kita. 'What shall we do, Yaji?'

'Oh, oh!' groaned Yaji! 'I can't bear it. Really I . . .'

'Don't cry,' said Kita. 'It makes you look such a fool.'

'It was very foolish of you not to examine the ticket,' said another priest, 'excessively stupid.'

'They're frauds,' said the chief priest. 'You'd better be off.'

'Get out,' cried all the priests.

'All right, all right,' said Yaji. 'We've had a good feed anyhow, although it wasn't what we came for. I think you might as well give us the money. A mark or two on the ticket don't make much difference.'

'Don't talk nonsense,' said the priest. 'You're a couple of rascals.'

'Everybody makes mistakes,' said Kita. 'Don't talk so foolishly.'

'If you get cheeky I'll knock you down,' said another priest. Here Saheiji intervened.

'We're in the wrong,' he said. 'I'm sorry you've entertained us for nothing, but it can't be helped now. Come on, Yaji, we'd better be going. What's the matter with you? Can't you stand up?'

'Oh, oh!' groaned Yaji. 'Just lift me up behind.'

'What's the matter with you?' asked Saheiji.

'I've lost the use of my legs,' said Yaji. 'Oh!'

'What a faint-hearted chap you are,' said Kita. 'Come on, stand up.'

'Don't pull me like that,' said Yaji. 'Oh, oh!'

They pulled him up at last and he staggered along. No one went to the door to see them off. Only the carriers gathered there jeered at them.

'I thought they weren't any good,' growled one of them.

'They only came to get a drink. Daylight robbers, that's what they are.'

'None of your insolence,' said Kita. 'I'll knock your head off.'

At this all the kago carriers started up, but Saheiji intervened.

'There, there,' he said. 'It's our fault, it's our fault.'

He dragged Kita along while holding Yaji up, and thus they went out of the temple grounds like men in a dream.

'Well,' said Kita. 'It's a bad business. There's all the difference between thinking you're going to do a thing and doing it.'

'Everything's gone wrong,' groaned Yaji.

'It's your fault, Saheiji,' said Kita. 'You should really have warned us. We're men from another province and don't know about affairs here. If you'd told us about the special marks on the tickets there wouldn't have been all this disappointment. Botheration! Please remember in future.'

'I never thought of it,' said Saheiji. 'You must come back to the inn because of the clothes.'

Saheiji was thinking of the security he had given for the hire of the clothes, while as for Yaji he had almost made up his mind to throw himself into the water from one of the bridges. In this desperate condition, with all their hopes of making a fortune gone astray, they got back to the inn, where the clerk, who had heard about the lottery ticket, thought they must certainly have brought the hundred gold pieces back with them and came out to greet them.

'Welcome back,' he said. 'Please walk in. Girl, bring some tea. I heard last night that you gentlemen had won a prize in a lottery. Let me congratulate you. Did you get the money?'

'No such luck,' said Yaji. 'We got off with our lives only,' and he staggered along the passage to the room.

'It wasn't any good,' whispered Saheiji to the clerk.

'I suppose the mark on the ticket was wrong,' said the clerk laughing.

'Yes,' said Saheiji. 'We'll have to be careful about that older one. He's clean lost heart. Don't lose sight of him, even when he goes to the closet. I shouldn't be surprised if he hanged himself.'

'That won't do,' said the clerk. 'You must get him out of the inn as soon as possible.'

348

Saheiji then went off to Yaji's room and announced that the man had come for the hired kimonos.

'All right, he can take 'em back,' said Kita. 'Come on, Yaji, take off yours.'

They took off the kimonos reluctantly and put on their old clothes.

Then Saheiji produced a paper from his sleeve.

'Here's the bill for the clothes,' he said.

Kita took it and looked at it. 'What's this?' he cried. 'One *kwan* eight hundred *mon*? How dear! Just beg him to cut it down.'

Just as he was handing the bill back to Saheiji a woman came in from the kitchen.

'A man's come from the teahouse with the bill,' she said and she handed it to Yaji.

'What?' he said. 'Fifteen *momme* for the room, three *momme* for refreshments, one *momme* five *bun* for soup, ten *momme* three *bun* for comestibles, two *momme* five *bun* for cake, six *momme* eight *bun* six *rin* for saké, one *momme* two *bun* four *rin* for candles, altogether forty-one *momme* four *bun*. Terrible! Terrible!'

'Look here, Saheiji,' said Kita. 'You think because we are strangers you can make fools of us. What did we have last night to cost all this money? All these Westcountry people are so grasping. Everybody knows they're rascals.'

'It's you that are stingy,' said Saheiji. 'Pay for what you've had. I never heard of such rudeness.'

'What do you mean by calling me stingy?' cried Kita. 'Fool!'

'Then pay up,' said Saheiji.

'Look here, Saheiji,' said Yaji. 'No matter what you say this bill's wrong.'

'What's wrong with it?' asked Saheiji.

'Well, it's got the wrong sign of the zodiac on it,' said Yaji. 'It's marked with the character for *i* when it should be marked with the character for *ne*.'

'Don't talk nonsense,' said Saheiji, 'but just pay up.'

'What an obstinate beggar he is,' said Kita, and he jumped up. But Saheiji was not to be frightened, and they were just about to go for each other when the landlord came in and scolded

Saheiji and soothed Kita, while he inquired into the particulars of the trouble. As the landlord seemed to be a good-natured man the two opened their hearts to him, telling him of their penniless condition, and the difficulties they were in. The landlord was an open-minded man and understood at once.

'Well, well,' he said. 'Even rich people are known to fall short of money when they are travelling. We have to take our guests as they come and if they haven't got any money to pay, well they haven't and there's an end of it. How long do you wish to stay?'

'Thank you, thank you,' said Yaji. 'We want to shorten our stay as much as possible, so we'll start to-morrow morning.'

'Dear me!' said the landlord. 'That seems early after you've come all this way. Take your time and have a look at the city. You haven't seen Sumiyoshi yet. Luckily I'm going to Sumiyoshi myself to-day so you can come along with me. But as I'm going by boat and have to call at Shinden on business on the way, you'd better walk to Tennoji and wait for me at the Sammonji teahouse. Eh, Saheiji? Make it up and go with them. It's past ten now, so you'd better start at once.'

This made the two travellers happy again and they readily agreed to the proposal. Mutual apologies were made by them and Saheiji, and everything being ready the landlord went off by boat and the two travellers started to walk to Tennoji with Saheiji as their guide. As they went by Takatsu Shinchi they soon got to the Ikudama Temple.

This temple is dedicated to Ikudama-no-Mikoto, who was incarnated as a precious jewel, and is visited by crowds of pilgrims. In the precincts are to be found rows and rows of teahouses, where they sell the famous baked beancurd, many shops where they sell tooth-powder, women ballad-reciters, actors like Seichi Azumasei, and many other things. The famous mallets for pounding millet cakes were first made here. A man with a towel tied round his head stood with a mallet raised and cried:

'Here you are! Here you are! Here's the original millet-mallet as shown on the signboard of the Ikudamaya. It will pound anything. It will pound this and it will pound that. It will pound anything—millet, wheat or rice. The servant pounds the master and the young fellow the widow. The old man with the lantern pounds the rice. The courtesan pounds the guest, and the singing girls pound with their feet. Here you are. The cripples' nuts are covered with sand. Yoi ! Yoi ! Sassa ! Here you are ! Here you are ! '

' So much pounding makes me tired,' said Yaji.

Passing out of the precincts of the temple they reached Baba-saki-dōri, where there is a small pleasure-quarter and beautiful courtesans and singing girls make the streets very gay.

' There's a place just off the road I want to call at,' said Saheiji. ' If you go straight on you'll come to Tennoji. I'll catch you up very soon.'

' All right,' said Yaji. ' We'll go on ahead.'

Separating from Saheiji the two went on, conversing as they went, till they came to a place where another road turned off and they felt doubtful which road to take. An old scavenger was going on in front, with two buckets slung across his shoulders, so they called to him, ' Which is the way to Tennoji ? '

' I'm going there,' said the scavenger. ' Ye'd better follow me.'

' I'd rather not,' said Kita. ' What a stink ! ' He began to lag behind, but the scavenger turned round.

' I live near Tennoji,' he said, ' and I'll take you right there. Come along. Come along. Where d'ye come from ? '

' We're Edo folk,' said Yaji.

' Aha ! ' said the scavenger. ' Edo's a fine place. What do they give for two buckets of it up there ? '

' I don't know,' said Yaji.

' I say, Yaji,' said Kita, pulling his sleeve, ' let's fall back a bit.' To let the old man get well ahead Kita relieved himself.

' What a nuisance he is ! ' said Yaji. ' He expected me to know the price of that filth. He's an idiot.'

Thinking the old man must have got a long distance ahead they walked on briskly, when they again came upon the old man waiting for them.

' Eh,' said Kita. ' How annoying ! There's that old man waiting for us.'

' Come on ! Come on ! ' cried the old man. ' You know you don't know the road. I saw one of ye just now doing something for himself. All ye Edo folk are wasteful like that. What a pity ! How many times a day do ye gentlemen do it ? '

' Well sometimes we do it three times a day, and other times we do it four or five,' said Yaji. ' It's not fixed.'

' Does it come out thick or thin ? ' asked the old man.

'You want to know all sorts of things, don't you?' said Yaji.
'I'm no good, but this other fellow is like a waterfall.'

'I wish I'd known before,' said the old man. 'It's all wasted
now.'

'Get on a bit faster, Kita,' scolded Yaji. 'What are you
doing?'

But Kita secretly tweaked Yaji by the sleeve. 'Look inside his
bucket,' said Kita. 'You can see the head of a gold hairpin.'

While Yaji went on talking to the old man, Kita behind picked
up two pieces of bamboo and using them as pinchers tried to pick
the hairpin out of the bucket. Just then, however, the old man
shifted the buckets to the other shoulder and the pieces of bamboo

were knocked out of Kita's hand and a splash of the contents of
the buckets fell on his clothes. With an exclamation of disgust
Kita rubbed it off with a piece of paper, while the old man, who in
changing had shifted the back bucket to the front, discovered the
hairpin.

'What's this?' he asked. He caught hold of the head of the
pin and pulled it out and found it was apparently a valuable pin.

'I suppose it must have fallen in the privy,' said the old man.
'It'll be a fine present for my grand-daughter. I'm going on in
front. Come along after me.'

He went off briskly without troubling any more about them.

'How vexatious!' said Kita.

'You never can do anything right,' said Yaji. 'It must be because you're body's rotten. You should have gone with that stinking old man.'

While he was scolding him they arrived at the west gate of the Tennoji, where they met Saheiji.

'I am tired,' he said. 'I've been pursuing you all the way. Look at that stone gateway. Ono-no-dōfu wrote those letters on the stone.'

'I've heard of that,' said Yaji, 'but I don't know what it means.'

This temple was founded by Shōtoku Taishi and truly it is sacred ground for all Japanese.

The grounds of the temple are very extensive, and there is much to see, but I will not describe it here. From there they went along the Abekaidō, where they heard a man singing in the field at his work:

> Oh come most reverend sir, says he,
> And take a little drop with me.

'Hallo, daddy,' called Yaji. 'You're hard at it. What time is it?'

'Same time as it was yesterday at this time, I expect,' answered the old man.

'Get out with your stale jokes,' said Yaji. 'Here, Kita, just strike us a light.'

'There's a beggar smoking over there,' said Kita. 'Get a light off her.'

'No, no,' said Yaji. 'She's too dirty.'

'Nonsense,' said Kita. 'It's your own pipe you use, ain't it? I'll get a light from her. Here, just give us a light.'

'Ay, ay,' said the girl, who was about twenty-one or twenty-two. 'My pipe's gone out. I'll strike a light for you.'

'Never mind,' said Kita. 'We can strike one.'

'Then strike one for me,' said the girl.

'What a thing to ask!' said Kita. 'Never mind, I'll give you one, as it's you. Look, Yaji, she ain't bad-looking for a beggar is she?'

'A lively girl,' said Yaji. 'Have you got a husband?'

'No, I lost my husband last year,' said the girl.

'Don't you want to get married again?' asked Yaji.

'Yes,' said the girl. 'The other day someone was going to

353

get me a husband,—such a good husband, one of those who go
about with nothing on crying " Ten-ten-ten " all day. Such a
clever begger he is, they say. He's been a beggar all his life and
quite able to keep a wife. They asked him if he wouldn't like
a wife, but he said that he hadn't got a house and as I wouldn't
live with him without a house I didn't go.'

' I'll find you a good husband,' said Yaji. ' How would this
chap do ? '

' Ho-ho-ho ! ' laughed the girl. ' I'd like to live with him.'

' Like to come to my house ? ' said Kita. ' They're repairing
it now. I'll call you when it's finished.'

' Where is your house ? ' asked the girl.

' I don't know what the place is called,' said Kita, ' but if you
go back along this road there's a bridge just being built. When
it's finished we'll have the wedding ceremony underneath.'

' Oh then it'll be made of new mats,' said the girl. ' I hope
it'll be made nicely.'

' Yes, and I'll make you a wedding present of one copper,'
said Kita. ' Ha-ha-ha ! Fancy me a beggar with you for my
wife. Ugh ! '

' Ain't you one of us ? ' asked the girl.

' Of course not,' said Kita. ' We're quite respectable city
people.'

' You're so dirty and ragged I thought you must belong to
us,' said the girl.

' Eh ? Don't talk nonsense,' said Kita.

' Ha-ha-ha ! ' laughed Saheiji. ' She's a clever girl. Come
along.'

The three then went along and soon got into the road leading
to Sumiyoshi. Great crowds of people, of all classes and all ages,
were passing along the road to worship at the temple, and among
them they noticed a man, apparently of good position, accompanied by a crowd of followers. At the door of a dumpling shop
they all stopped and each, one by one, demanded a dumpling on
a skewer, which they stuck into their mouths as they filed out
of the shop. The name of the leader of the band was Kawatarō.

' Here, old lady,' said Kawatarō to the woman in the shop, ' I
want to buy something else besides dumplings. Won't you sell
me something else ? '

' Ay, ay,' said that old woman. ' Whatever your honour
pleases.'

'Well, just sell me one of your doors here,' said Kawatarō.
'I'll give you this for it.'

He took a *bu* out of his bag and gave it to her, and while the old woman was standing there lost in astonishment he lifted one of the doors from its grooves and walked off with it. The jesters accompanying him all looked astounded.

'But master,' they cried, 'what do you want with that broken old door. 'It's not worth a *bu*. What's master's idea?'

'Walking in the sun gives me a headache,' said Kawatarō. 'Here, Kyusuké, just carry the door. I'll give you another *bu* when we get there, so just carry it crossways till we get to Sumi-yoshi. That's it, that's it.'

The man carried the door crossways and Kawatarō walked under it in the shade, for a joke. This Kawatarō, who once lived at Ōsaka, is still remembered for his practical jokes. Kita and Yaji looked on in astonishment.

'What fun!' said Yaji.

'These Westcountry people are not all fools,' said Kita. 'Some of them can joke. Fine, fine!'

They followed after the party, but they had not gone far before Master Kawatarō had changed his mind.

'It's gloomy under the door,' he said.

'Shall I open it for a little,' asked Kyusuké, 'so that you can see the garden and the pond, and Awaji, and the hills? It's very beautiful.'

'No, throw it away,' said Kawatarō.

'Don't you want it any more?' asked Kyusuké.

'No, no, throw it down,' commanded Kawatarō, and Kyusuké threw it down by the side of the road.

'Shall we pick it up, Yaji?' asked Kita.

'No, no,' said Yaji. 'Remember the trouble we had with the ladder in Kyōto.'

'We could carry it by turns,' said Kita. 'I'd like to walk in its shade. It would be a joke.'

'Ah!' said Yaji. 'Kitahachi, it's very hot to-day and walking in the sun gives me a headache. Just carry it, will you?'

'We'll take it in turns,' said Kita.

'All right,' replied Yaji. 'Ah, that's delightful.'

With Kita carrying the door and Yaji walking in its shade they arrived at Tengachaya, where they met a crowd of people returning from the capital.

'Heave her up! Heave her up!' they cried. 'Ha-ha-ha! What an umbrella! Look at the face of the man under it, and what a fool the man looks who's carrying it. Ha-ha-ha!'

'Get out you rascals,' said Kita. 'What are you jawing about?'

'Eh?' said one of them. 'Who are you talking to? I'll make you cry on the other side of your face in a minute.'

'We're Edo folk,' said Kita. 'I'll take you all on.' He turned the door round and round menacingly.

Then a fat old red-faced fellow in the crowd, named Gonshichi of Imamiya Shinké, caught hold of Kita. 'What do you mean by taking this door?' he demanded. 'It's mine.'

'Don't be a fool,' said Kita. 'How can it be yours?'

'Are you blind that you can't see what's written there in such big letters?' said the old man. 'Look, Zenzai-mochi, Sango Dango, Imamiya Shinké, Saikachiya. I wrote it myself. I went out with this company this morning to go to Sumiyoshi for the monthly prayer-meeting. You must have stolen it from my old woman at home while I was out.'

'What are you talking about?' said Kita. 'Do you think I'm a thief, you old rascal? I picked it up by the side of the road.'

'Don't talk nonsense,' said the old man. 'Who'd throw away a door like that? Don't tell such foolish lies.'

'Look here,' interrupted Saheiji, 'I'll tell you what happened. It was like this. Somebody bought that door at your shop and threw it away on the road, and my friends here picked it up. That's how it happened.'

'Don't talk foolishness,' said the old man. 'Look what's written on it. It's my sign-board. It's not for sale.'

'Well, I saw a man pay a *bu* for it,' said Kita. 'So there.'

'Listen to him,' said the old man. 'Who'd pay that for an old door? Most likely you've been eating dumplings at my shop and took the door away when you left. You've got to take it back anyway. Come along.'

'You must excuse us,' said Saheiji. 'If it's your door, you can take it back yourself.'

While they were pushing the door from one to the other and arguing over it, a postboy came along leading a horse. 'Here, what's this?' he said. 'Clear the road, will you?'

He was trying to push his way through the crowd when the

door, which was being shoved this way and that, struck the horse on the nose, causing it to rear up and kick the postboy, who fell sprawling.

'Oh, oh, oh !' he groaned.

'What's the matter ?' asked Saheiji. 'Have you hurt yourself ?'

'Oh, oh, oh !' groaned the man again. 'My nuts have dropped off. Just look and see if you can see them there.'

'What ?' said the old man. 'Your nuts ? I can't see them.'

'Then where can they be' said the postboy.

'Perhaps you've got 'em in your sleeve,' suggested Saheiji.

'They can't be,' said the postboy. 'For why, I haven't got any pockets in my sleeves.'

'Then you can't have brought them with you,' said Saheiji. 'Didn't you leave them at home ?'

'Nonsense !' said the postboy. 'Specially as they're sick and swollen. I had 'em in this bag round my neck.'

'Shake the bag and see if they're there still,' said the old man.

'Aha ! I've got 'em. I've got 'em,' said the postboy. 'It gave me quite a shock. They've got strung up. I must see if I can get 'em out. There, they're out, they're out.'

'Ha-ha-ha!' laughed Kita. 'I see they're swollen.'

'It's like the offertory-bag at a temple,' said Yaji. 'It gets full against the will of those who fill it.'

'Well, they're all right, at any rate,' said the postboy. 'It's only my knee that got scraped. What did you want to hit my horse with that door for?'

'I don't know anything about it?' said Saheiji.

'That's all very fine,' said the postboy, 'but whose door is it?'

'It belongs to my shop,' said the old man.

'Look how I've bruised myself,' went on the postboy. 'It's too bad. What's this written on the door? Imamiya Shinké. Saikachiya. That's important evidence. Come on! Come on! I shall have to look into this very seriously.'

He dragged the door away from the old man, tied it on his horse and led the animal away without taking any notice of the others.

'Here, here!' cried the old man. 'Where are you going with that door? Wait, wait!'

He ran off after the postboy, with all the crowd following and shouting to him to encourage him, 'Manzairakuja! Manzairakuja!'

Going on their way the three soon arrived at Sumiyoshi Shinké, which is a very celebrated place of worship. On each side of the streets are rows of fine teahouses, at the doors of which stand red-aproned girls calling, 'Walk in! Walk in! What can we serve you with? Try our clam soup. Bream and flat fish served here. Walk in! Walk in!'

'What fine teahouses,' said Yaji. 'And what a lot of them.'

This place is famous for its goldfish, pickled clams, biscuits, hot pepper, seaweed, stilts and netted work, which are sold in all the houses. Among the teahouses are the Sammonjiya, Itamiya, Fundoya, and Ebisuya, where there is a constant stream of guests. In fact the popularity of the place is beyond description.

'Here is the Sammonjiya,' said Saheiji. 'Just wait a minute.'

He peeped in at the door of the teahouse and saw that the landlord of the Kawachiya had already arrived.

'Halloa, Saheiji!' he called. 'You've got here early.'

'We've just arrived,' said Yaji. 'We're going to see the temple.'

The god of this temple appeared in the divine age at Awaji-ga-hara to Oto-no-Tachibana of Hiuga province. The main shrine is said to have been founded in the eleventh year of the reign of the Empress Jingo, in the fourth month and the twenty-seventh day. It is divided into four, the Sokotsutsu-ono-mikoto, the Nakatsutsu-ono-mikoto, the Uatsutsu-ono-mikoto, and the Jingo Kwogo. With the branch shrines and others there are thirty-four buildings, all of great elegance. Well may one worship there and say,

> God's silence broods upon the deep,
> And peaceful pines their slumbers keep.

After wandering round the inside, admiring its enormous size, they went to look at the lanterns on the seashore and then turned back to the Sammonjiya, where a maid came bustling out.

'Welcome,' she said. 'Please come this way.'

She led them to a room at the back, where they found Kawashiro, as the landlord of the Kawachiya was called.

'Oh, how hungry I am!' cried Kita.

'Have a drink then,' said Kawashiro and he offered him a saké cup.

'Excuse me, Yaji,' said Kita.

'Pass it along when you've done,' said Yaji.

'Do you want a drink too?' said Kita.

'What would you like to eat?' asked Saheiji.

'Let's have something that will fill the stomach,' said Kita.

'What an unmannerly fellow he is,' cried Yaji.

'What about your own manners?' said Kita,—'taking something to eat before you've been offered the saké cup.'

'Dear me,' said Saheiji. 'How polite you've grown.'

'When I taste the nice things that our landlord's giving us,' said Yaji 'I feel sorrowful to think that I'm only a poor penniless traveller.'

This coming from Yaji, who was always boasting and never admitted being beaten, struck Saheiji as funny, but he hid his amusement.

'You'll have to become a resident of Ōsaka,' he said.

'It would be all right if I had any occupation,' said Kita. 'But I can't earn my living, so it's all the same where we go.'

'Well, I've found something,' said Kawashiro. 'I've found something that one of you can do.'

'What's that?' asked Yaji.

'It's a position as man-mistress,' said the landlord. 'What do you say to that?'

'Really?' said Yaji. 'That would just suit me,' and he grinned with pleasure and began to look his old self again.

'Excuse me,' said Kita, thrusting himself forward. 'Don't you think I'd do better for the position?'

'Ha-ha-ha!' laughed Yaji. 'You wouldn't do at all. But look here, you'll excuse me asking—I've known you such a short time,—but does she really want me? Is there no mistake? If it's true, of course. . . .'

'No, no, I swear there's no mistake about it,' said Kawashiro. 'Moreover the widow's very beautiful, only twenty-three or twenty-four years old. Quite well off, too. I'm very friendly with her head clerk. I saw him just now and had a talk with him about it. He says she spends all her money buying actors, and that it would be better for her to have a respectable man-mistress upon whom she could rely. I shall be glad to recommend you. Would you like to see her?'

'What for?' said Kita. 'It wouldn't matter to him if her eyes were crooked and her nose gone. He'd have her all the same.'

'She's in the next room with her head clerk,' said Kawashiro. 'I'll just go and inquire.'

Kawashiro jumped up with great readiness and went into the next room.

'I'm going through with this, Kita,' said Yaji after the landlord had gone.

'How brave you are!' said Kita. 'Fancy you becoming a man-mistress with that face. Have you ever looked at yourself in the glass?'

'Nonsense!' said Yaji. 'It doesn't matter about a man's looks. I'm better looking than you anyhow.'

'Better looking, indeed!' said Kita. 'What do you say, Saheiji? If you were a woman which would you fall in love with, Yaji or me?'

'I'd rather not fall in love with either of you,' said Saheiji, laughing. 'But when a person's in love they always think they're better looking than other people.'

'We'll call it equal for looks, then,' said Kita, 'but I think I ought to get her as I am the younger.'

'You must give way to your seniors,' said Yaji.

360

'I'll tell you what,' said Saheiji. 'You'd better draw lots. I'll hold the spills and whoever draws the long one shall have her.'

'All right,' said Kita. 'Oh, great god of Sumiyoshi,' he prayed, 'grant unto me that I may draw the long one.'

'There,' said Saheiji. 'Now draw.'

'I've got the long one,' cried Yaji. 'I've won.'

In the midst of Yaji's rejoicing Kawashiro came back. 'It's all right,' he said. 'I've just been consulting with her head clerk. She'll make you an allowance of as much as you like and pay for all the burdock and eggs you can eat, besides providing you with silk clothes all the year round. But you'll have to take Sanzo and Koshiyoshi pills.'

'In Edo, at the Santōkyōden,' said Yaji, 'they have some pills called Tokushō, and without joking they give you enormous energy. I'll get some of those and take them.'

'That's a good idea,' said Kawashiro. 'By the way, she's coming here.'

'What, here?' cried Yaji. 'Now? How awful! In my present condition too. I say, Saheiji, is there a hairdresser in the neighbourhood?'

'Get out,' said Kita. 'You can't make a crow white even if you wash it for a year, and you can't alter a man's disposition, either. You can't follow a trade with your eyes shut, so to speak. If she sees you she's bound to call it off.'

'There's a fine-looking woman coming out of that room over there,' said Saheiji.

'That's her, that's her,' said Kawashiro. 'She's probably coming here.'

'How awful,' said Yaji, and he hurriedly arranged his collar and put on a solemn look.

The widow was a fine-looking woman, with a skin as white as snow and an attractive manner. She was accompanied by her head clerk. Kawashiro rose to greet her.

'This is a pleasure,' he said. 'Please come in.'

'Excuse me,' said the widow, and she tittered as she entered.

'Good day to all,' said the head clerk. 'They're all ladies in the other room and I had nobody to drink with. Luckily Kawashiro came in and invited us to join you.'

'Sit down, sit down,' said Kawashiro. 'Excuse my boldness, but let me press you to have a cup of saké.'

He handed a saké cup to the widow, who took it with a smile.

'I've already drunk too much,' she said, 'so I'll only take a drop.'

She drank a little and then held out the cup to Kawashiro.

'Won't you drink with me in return ? ' she asked.

'I've been drinking a lot already,' said Kawashiro. 'Won't you offer it to somebody else ? '

'Then if you don't mind,' said the widow, and she held out the cup to Yaji.

Yaji, who had been sitting as one in a dream, lost in contemplation of the widow's beauty, woke to life with a start on finding himself thus addressed.

'Yes, yes,' he said, all in a flurry, and he seized hold of what he thought was a saké cup.

'Here, what are you doing ? ' said Saheiji. 'That's not a saké cup you're holding. It's the tobacco-box.'

'Ah, so it is,' said Yaji. 'Ten thousand excuses. Kita, pour for me.'

'It's none of my business,' said Kita sulkily. 'Pour for yourself.'

'What an unmannerly chap he is ! ' said Yaji.

The waitress filled his cup and he tossed it off. Then he offered the cup to the head clerk.

'No, no,' said the head clerk. 'You're an expert at drinking I can see. Have another on top of it.'

'Well,' said Yaji, 'usually when I drink saké I get whiter and whiter till I'm as white as silk. But to-day, somehow, it's made me go all red.'

'Allow me to offer a drink to your companion,' said the widow.

'Yes, yes,' said Yaji. 'Here, Kitahachi, the lady wants to offer you a drink.'

'Mind your own business,' said Kita.

'Ha-ha-ha ! ' laughed Yaji. 'Let me offer you one instead,' he said to the widow.

The widow took the cup with a smirk and drank.

'Dear me,' said Kawashiro. 'You two passing the saké cup to each other makes it look just like a wedding.'

'He-he-he ! ' tittered the widow. 'How funny ! '

'Ha-ha-ha ! ' laughed Yaji in turn.

'Don't laugh so loud,' said Kita. 'You're laughing right into the food.'

'Never mind,' said Yaji. 'You be quiet. I can never do

362

anything to please this chap,' he went on. 'If I just sing a bit of a song to the guitar and get all the girls praising me and saying how clever I am, he gets so jealous I don't know what to do.'

'Dear me,' said the widow. 'What a funny gentleman you are really.'

At this Yaji's heart bounded in his bosom, for he thought he had captured her and that all his bad luck had vanished. Then the widow's maid came in.

'Excuse me for interrupting you,' she said, 'but I thought you would like to know that Master Arakichi has come and is waiting for you in the other room.'

'Has Arakichi come?' cried the widow. 'Thank you, thank you. Excuse me everybody. Good-bye,' and she bowed hastily to them and hurried off, followed by her head clerk.

Yaji was overwhelmed with astonishment. 'What's the matter?' he asked. 'Who's this Arakichi?'

'That's Saburo Arakichi,' said Kawashiro. 'He's all the craze, —young and good-looking,—the leading actor in Ōsaka.'

'Ah, that's why she rushed off in such a hurry,' said Yaji. 'Looks to me as if she was in love with him.'

'It does look that way,' admitted Kawashiro.

'Well, you mustn't let your courage go down, Yaji,' said Saheiji.

'Ha-ha-ha!' laughed Kita. 'What a joke! I say Yaji, when we were coming along I saw a barber's shop just near here. You'd better go and get your head shaved.'

'You're always envious,' grumbled Yaji.

While Yaji was grumbling to himself the head clerk came back.

'You see what anxiety she gives me, Master Kawashiro,' he said. 'She's got a passion for that Arakichi and they's going off somewhere by boat together. I've got to walk. I always get the worst of it. So all our talk comes to nothing. Well, I must leave you now. Excuse me everybody.'

He hurried off into the garden, where they saw the widow starting off with Arakichi and a maid, talking and laughing and looking very delighted.

'That chap Arakichi is a fine-looking fellow,' said Saheiji.

'What's there fine-looking about him?' said Yaji. 'Look at his sickly look. Seems as if he'd never been out in the sun.'

'You may say what you like,' said the waitress, 'but if he isn't a fine-looking man I never saw one. Why, there isn't a woman in Ōsaka that isn't in love with him.'

'Look there, Yaji,' said Kita. 'She's whispering something in his ear and pointing over here and laughing. She's probably talking about you.'

'Botheration!' said Yaji. 'Well, Master Kawashiro, it's very regrettable, very.'

Meanwhile the widow went away talking and laughing without paying the least attention to any of them, and this made Yaji feel so unhappy that he spoke of going back to the inn.

'I've got a good idea,' said Kawashiro. 'I've got a boat waiting. Let's go in it and interrupt their love making.'

'That's a good idea,' said Yaji. 'Come on. Let's go.'

'Wait a bit,' said Saheiji. 'It's beginning to rain.'

'It doesn't matter if it rains cats and dogs,' said Yaji. 'Come along.'

He jumped up and was going out, when all at once there was a tremendous peal of thunder right over his head,—goro-goro-goro.

'It's useless, it's useless,' they all cried, and Yaji ran back, almost stunned by the noise.

Now the rain began to come down in torrents, the lightning flashed and the thunder roared, and the people rushed about the house, pulling out the shutters to keep out the rain. All the women in the house came into the room, frightened out of their wits.

'That's finished you off,' said Kita. 'Wouldn't you like to be Arakichi now? They're in the boat, both wet through, and the widow's telling him how frightened she is and clinging to him.'

'Yes,' said Kawashiro. 'She was in love with him before, but after this storm she'll never let him go.'

'That's so,' said Kita. 'She'll never be able to say no, eh, Yaji?'

'Don't talk to me,' said Yaji. 'I'm praying.'

'There's another flash,' said Saheiji, and the thunder went goro-goro-goro-goro.

'Oh, I'm so frightened,' said Kita, and he threw himself into Yaji's arms pretending that he was the widow. Yaji went flying.

'Oh, oh, oh!' he groaned. 'What did you want to do that for? Oh, oh, oh!'

'Where does it hurt?' asked Kita.

'It's the devil's nose in the wrapper,' said Yaji. 'Oh, it does hurt.'

'Ha-ha-ha!' laughed Kita. 'That's it, is it?'

'The rain's beginning to stop,' said Saheiji. 'Shall we go in the boat now?'

'Come on,' said Yaji. 'Come on quickly.'

He jumped up impatiently, but just as he got to the door there was a great flash of lightning and such a rattle of thunder over his head—goro-goro-goro-goro—that he fell down with a shriek.

'Oh, oh!' he groaned, his face wrinkled in pain.

'What have you done now?' asked Saheiji.

'What have I done now!' said Yaji. 'I've broken it. I've broken it.'

'What have you broken?' asked Kita.

'When it went pss-bang just now,' said Yaji, 'I got such an alarm that I slipped and fell on the bridge of the devil's nose. Oh! it does hurt.'

He kept hold of the devil's nose as he spoke whereupon they all burst into laughter.

In a little time the rain stopped, the thunder got further and further away and the sky began to clear.

'Come, it's getting fine now,' said Kawashiro. 'Let's have another cup before we go.'

So some more saké was brought in and they each drank their fill to the accompaniment of many jests and much laughter.

Afterwards Kawashiro took Yajirobei and Kitahachi back to his inn and there they stayed a long time till they had seen all the sights of the city. Then, both of them being stout-hearted Edo folk, able to bear all kinds of hardships and pass them off with a jest, they determined to set forth on their travels again. The landlord, impressed by their courage, presented them with new clothes and money for their travelling expenses, and thus they started off in search of new adventures.

APPENDIX

APPENDIX

IKKU'S "AFTERTHOUGHT" INTRODUCTION

[This so-called introduction to 'Hizakurigé' was written as an afterthought when the travels of the two heroes had been completed, and the details given in it are inconsistent in some particulars with those given in the travels themselves. Although in modern Japanese editions of 'Hizakurigé' it is used as an introduction to the work, it has been thought best in this translation to add it as an appendix.]

ON the plain of Musashi, says the poem, the flowering grasses melt into the white clouds on the horizon. That was long long ago, when they used to delight in the swift flight of snipe in the twilight from the marshes behind the reed huts. But then, of course, they didn't know what the pleasure-quarter looks like when it is lit up in the evening.

Nowadays the water that flows along the conduits into the wells is full of trout, and there are rows and rows of white-washed store-houses, and the pickle-tubs, empty sacks and broken umbrellas are so many that the landlords want to charge rent for the ground they take. Edo, in fact, is so prosperous that the country people think the streets must be paved with silver and gold, and they come up in their countless thousands and tens of thousands to pick it up.

Among those who thus came to Edo was Yajirobei Tochimenya, who hailed from Fuchū in the province of Sunshū. He had been left fairly well off by his father,—able to lay his hands on a couple of hundred gold pieces at any time without any trouble; but he fell into such dissipated ways and, moreover, was so wrapped up in a boy called Hananosuké, the apprentice of Tarashirō Hanamizu, a strolling player, that, keeping to this path as strictly as though it were the path of filial duty, and as happy as a man who has dug up a pot of gold, by means of all sorts of foolish pranks he managed to make a tremendous hole in his property, and was finally compelled to hoist sail and fly with the boy from the town of Fuchū.

> When your debts pile up to Fuji's height
> That is the time to fly by night.

Thus spitting out their silly jokes they went up to Edo and took a small house in Hatchō-bōri, Kanda. The small amount of money that Yajirobei had left was soon spent in eating the good things of Edo, and in drinking saké, the empty barrels of which in his kitchen were enough to supply all the wash-tubs needed for a tenement house. At last, when they had drunk up all their money, they decided that they would have to change their course of life. So Hananosuké coming of age, his name was changed to Kitahachi, and he was apprenticed at a respectable shop, where, being by nature a smart lad, he soon won the good will of his master and was entrusted with the handling of the petty cash. As for Yajirobei, he got some small jobs of painting, a trade which he had learnt in the country, and was thus able to make enough to buy rice and *natto* and shell-fish from the street-hawkers when they came round, which he did without even taking the trouble to move from his seat. But he never had a spare penny to bless himself with, and his wadded garment, which he had worn continuously ever since he came up from the country, was torn at the sleeves and the wadding all coming out. As for washing his clothes, it was never done because he had no one to do it for him.

Seeing his way of life.one of his friends in the neighbourhood —one who had helped him to spend his money—proposed that he should marry a woman, somewhat older than himself, who had worked as a servant in the friend's house for a number of years, so that the cracked pot might have a new lid to keep it together, and the rents in his clothes, gaping like the mouths of wolves, should be sewn up. In fact that he should have someone to look after him.

With a hard-working woman to take care of him and see that he went to bed early, Yajirobei passed his life in contentment, twenty years slipping away before he was aware of it. But as mountain potatoes, however long they grow, will never become eels, so Yajirobei remained poor. This did not trouble him, however. He still cracked his empty jokes, and his house was the haunt of all the lazy fellows in the neighbourhood, who kept the kitchen filled with empty saké bottles and made it impossible to take the lid off the bean-paste for fear it should go sour with their discordant thrumming on the samisen.

One day, when Yajirobei was absent and Futsu, his wife, was engaged in the kitchen in making preparations for the morrow,

Chōma, the woman who lived in the house at the back of the alley, peeped out of her backdoor.

'Excuse me, Mrs. Futsu,' she said, 'but I should be glad if you could lend me a little sauce. Oh dear! Oh dear! How we did keep it up last night! There's my old sot of a husband, he hasn't come home yet. The other night, when he came home late, the landlord's wife complained that he knocked at the gate at the head of the alley as if he was going to break it. But there, she's always exaggerating and scolding about something. She ain't got any right to call him stupid even if he is. She's too bad, really, ain't she? What if the rent ain't paid for a year or two? It ain't as if we didn't mean to pay it some time. When it comes to that if she's so strict why don't she mend the gutter where it's all gone rotten? Making us clean up the dogs' dirt, too, in front of our houses. What does she think we are, eh, Mrs. Kun?'

The woman whom she thus drew into the conversation was suckling a baby in the house opposite. She now came down to the gate.

'Don't speak so loud,' she said. 'Kentsu's doing a little job for herself in the yard and you know what a chatterbox she is and how she likes to toady up to the landlord's wife by telling her all the bad things we say about her. Look here, what do you think I heard? You know that girl that came to that house the other day, that they said was the wife's younger sister. Well, she didn't go out to service as they said. I found out all about it. It was an awful surprise to me. The day before yesterday she went to a mansion in Shitaya all dressed up to see if she'd suit an old man who wants a young mistress. They say he paid seven ryō as advance money. Fancy a girl with a face like that going out as a mistress. What impudence! If I wasn't so bald and the wen by my ear was a little smaller I'd go out as somebody's mistress myself and make some money. He-he-he! Hasn't your husband come home yet, Mrs. Futsu? Dear me! Whisper about someone and you see his shadow. There he is, just come back.'

At the sight of Yajirobei all the women went into their houses.

'That brute of a woman doesn't care if I sleep on the doorstep,' said Yaji. 'Here, Futsu, is the tea made?'

'Dear, dear!' said Futsu. 'You do nothing but drink. I suppose you haven't had anything to eat yet?'

'Of course not,' replied Yaji. 'I was too busy at the grog shop to go to the prog shop.'

'Well, Kitahachi's been sending someone here to ask for you ever so many times.'

'He wants me to lend him some money.'

'Lend him some money?' cried Futsu. 'What nonsense! What's it about?'

'That fellow's got himself into a mess by taking some of his master's money,' said Yaji. 'Of course he'll be dismissed if it's found out, but it would be very hard on him if he were dismissed just now. The head clerk got an attack of colic in the head the other day and his head got so hard that he died. Then the master, like all these old fools, he must go and take a young wife, and she's worn him out. He won't last more than a day or two, that's certain. So all Kitahachi's got to do is to stop where he is and take the widow. It'll be like digging up a pot of gold for him, and it won't be so bad for me either. But what we've got to do is to keep him from being dismissed. Well, let's have something to eat. What have you got?'

As it was now getting late they lit the lamp, and Yaji was just about to begin his supper when a samurai, about fifty years of age, in travelling dress, appeared at the door.

'Excuse my intrusion,' he cried, 'but does Yajirobei of Fuchū in Suruga live here?'

'This is his residence,' said Futsu. 'May I ask where you come from?'

'Aha!' said the samurai. 'I have a little business with him.'

The samurai forthwith led in a young woman of about thirty. Yajirobei started at him in astonishment from where he sat.

'What, Hyōtazaemon?' he said. 'Why have you come to the capital with your young sister?'

'Why have I come?' asked the samurai. 'Truly not for pleasure. I have come to bring this young sister of mine to you. Perhaps you won't understand unless I explain to you. When you were in the country you seduced my young sister Tako, and although I was very angry when I heard of it, yet as she is my sister I thought I must get her married. As she says that she won't marry anybody else but you, although I think it is very regretable, I have restrained my own feelings and have brought her here in order that you may be married. For this reason I would ask you to receive her kindly. Come, bring out the wine and the cups and let us get it over quickly.'

'Dear, dear!' said Futsu. 'I don't know who you are, but I suppose it's the usual thing everywhere for men to deceive women by promising to remain true to them for two or three lives. It seems to me to be very foolish to have come all the way from Suruga to marry this man on a promise like that. For myself it can't be helped, but look at his dark skin and his three-cornered eyes, and his large mouth, and his hairy body. He's covered with lice too, and his legs are all spotty. Then he's got such a foul breath when he's asleep.'

'Here, here!' said Yaji. 'You mustn't talk about your master like that.'

'He-he-he!' laughed Futsu. 'Then he's a terrible man for women. Even if they've only got one eye and have lost part of their nose he'll run after him. He's intimate with a fair number of them but he's not very popular among them, and I never heard of anyone running after him except you. Besides if he brings two or three wives into this house the landlord will say the floor won't stand the weight and he'll turn us out. You'd better take her away before anybody knows anything about it.'

'Eh?' said the samurai. 'This servant appears to think she has the right to chatter about everything. Who is she?'

'I?' said Futsu. 'Why, of course, I am his wife.'

'His wife?' cried the samurai. 'Impossible! Here, Yajirobei, have you got a wife? Ah! Then there's no help for it. I must tie you up and take you back with me.'

With that he pulled a piece of rope out of his bosom and stood up.

'What?' cried Yaji excitedly. 'Tie me up? What right have you got to tie me up? Is it any reason you should tie me up because I've got a wife? It's outrageous. I'm not to be frightened by those two fish-cutters you've got stuck in your sash.'

'Ha!' said the samurai. 'You talk very big. Now just listen to this. It is by command of the Council of Ministers that I have brought my young sister to the capital. Rikinda Yokosuka, an official, wished to marry her, and as it was an advantageous offer I immediately agreed, and went so far as to exchange wedding presents with him. Then I heard that as my sister had plighted her troth to you she refused to marry anyone else.

Judge of my astonishment ! There was nothing to be done but to send a messenger to Rikinda to tell him that my sister had been seduced by a man named Yajirobei, quite without my knowledge, and that, as I had accepted the wedding presents and my sister would only marry the man of her choice, there was nothing to be done in reparation of the insult but to cut off her head and send it to him. He replied that my sister's head was of no use to him, but that, as he had informed all his relatives and friends that he was going to marry my sister and had been put to shame, he was forced to challenge me to a duel. He therefore asked me to meet him in the bed of the Abé river the following evening to decide the matter. But before I could accept the challenge as a proper solution of the difficulty the Council of Ministers sent for both of us and warned us that it would be disloyal to our Lord, on whose bounty we had lived for so many years, to fight a duel on a personal matter. As I had not known that my sister's affections were engaged when I arranged to marry her to Rikinda, therefore, the Council decided, he had not been wronged ; and as the marriage had not taken place there was no loss of honour to either of us. The Council therefore told us to show our loyalty to our Lord by laying aside all feelings of hatred. I was also ordered to take the girl to Edo and marry her to the man of her choice, as it was a virtuous resolve on her part to marry only him. I received their commands gratefully and brought her here, but as you have a wife already there is nothing for my sister to do but to bear her disappointment and go back again. But can Hyōtazaemon, the samurai, return to his country thus shamed ? Never. If you marry my sister, well and good ; if not you must be tied up and taken back and everything explained to the Council. Unless you are handed over to Rikinda the honour of Hyōtazaemon will be tarnished. Come, allow yourself to be tied up or otherwise I must use force.'

' Ah ! ' said Yaji, ' now I understand the position. But it seems to me that your conduct is presumptuous. Do you suppose I would put away my patient, long-suffering wife to marry your sister ? Not even if you cut me into little bits and salted me. Do with me what you will, it can't be helped.'

Thus saying he put his hands behind his back and the samurai had already begun to tie him up when Futsu threw herself at his feet.

'Stop, stop,' she cried. 'I understand the position now and I see that you are right. It would be a grief to me for you to bind up my husband and put him to shame all the way back to his native country, where, moreover, his life might be endangered, and although I appreciate very much his vow that do what you may he will never desert his patient, long-suffering wife, I want to ask him to let me go. If he was intimate with your sister in Suruga, then it was before he knew me, and what you say is quite right. If he will not let me go, rather than he should fall into your hands I will die.'

With that, weeping the while, she went into the kitchen and got the kitchen knife. But while she was whirling it about preparatory to stabbing herself Yaji got hold of her.

'Here,' he said. 'What are you doing? Be quiet, you fool.'

'No, no,' she cried. 'Let me go or I will . . .'

'Well, well,' said Yaji. 'If you're so set on it it can't be helped. You'd better take a little holiday and go to your father's. I never dreamt I should have to get rid of my dear wife. It's all my fault that we've got to part.'

So saying Yajirobei, feeling sorry for his wife, took her aside and cajoled and consoled her with promises of seeing her again. Then he got out the writing-box and wrote the three and a half lines of divorce and gave it to her. Poor people have no trouble in gathering their things together, and she had only her comb-box and a bundle to carry as she sadly left the house with the tears rolling down her cheeks.

Directly she had gone the samurai cast aside the two swords he was wearing.

'There,' he said. 'Now I can get rid of those heavy things. What do you think of that, Yaji? Didn't I play my part well?'

'I was astonished at your Suruga dialect,' replied Yaji. 'You were the country samurai to the life. I'm sure any country pawnbroker's widow would have taken you for a hundred-*koku* samurai. What a pity you are only Imoshichi, the street hawker. Then Tako, too, she did wonderfully as the country maiden. You'd never have thought she was an attendant at an archery ground. Well, my plan to get the old girl out of the house has been quite successful, thanks to you two. I was tired of the old thing in any case, and then I must have fifteen ryō immediately, and Imoshichi has fortunately shown me how I can get it. There's an old grandfather who's been up to tricks with the maidservant and has altered her shape. So before his daughter and her husband found out he dismissed the girl openly, but privately arranged that she should stop at the house of the person who had recommended her till he had found someone who would take her and the baby too, with the sum of fifteen ryō thrown in as a dowry. This just suited me but the difficulty was that I had a wife already. Still, I thought to myself, if I can only get hold of that fifteen ryō I don't mind if the girl has a devil in her womb, and as I was thoroughly tired of my old wife I arranged this little trick and got you to come and help me carry it out, which you really did very cleverly. But I say, how about the dowry ? Will it come at once ? What do you think ? '

'Of course, of course,' said Imoshichi. 'You said you wanted the money at once and as the baby is likely to be born any minute the sooner the better. I've arranged that she shall come here quietly this evening in a kago. You must get a little saké or something. Have you got any in the house ? '

'Eh, eh ? ' said Yaji. 'Will she come this evening ? That's early. If I'd only known I'd have gone to the barber's and had my hair done. At any rate I'll go and have a shave.'

'Here, here ! ' said Imoshichi. 'Where do you suppose you'd find a barber's shop open at this time of night ? Instead of doing that you'd much better get out the saké. What are you fidgetting about for now ? '

'Nothing, nothing,' said Yaji. 'I thought I'd just cut my nails.'

'Nonsense,' said Imoshichi. 'Don't worry about such trifles.'

'I wasn't going to cut them all,' said Yaji. 'Just two of them . . .'

'Ha-ha-ha ! ' laughed Imoshichi. 'Get out with your foolishness. You make me laugh.'

They cleared away the supper things, kindled the charcoal in the brazier, and got the saké bottle out of the cupboard. Then, as it would have been strange to receive the bride with white faces, they had just sat down, nose to nose, to have a drink, when they heard the clash of the bearers' sticks at the entrance.

'Halloa ! ' said Imoshichi. 'It seems as if she had come.'

Jumping up he opened the door.

'This is the place,' he cried. 'Thanks for your trouble, my men. Here's something for you to have a drink with.'

Thus quickly dismissing the kago bearers with what small change he happened to have on him, he led the woman they had brought into the house.

'There, the bride's come,' he cried. 'Where's the saké cup?'

'It's really very kind of you,' said Yaji.

'There, Mrs. Tsubo, sit down there,' went on Imoshichi. 'Drink a cup and then pass it to your husband. Fill it up, Tako. Now I ought to sing, "On the four seas there is peace," but I don't know how to sing odes. I'll come to-morrow and give you a ballad.'

While they were passing the saké cup backwards and forwards it began to grow late.

'I'm afraid I must go now, Mr. Imoshichi,' said Tako.

'Yes, yes,' said Imoshichi. 'We mustn't incommode you any longer. Well, Mrs. Tsubo, I wish you good night. I hope I shall have the pleasure of seeing you again in the morning.'

Thus saying farewell he went out with Tako. Yaji, pretending that he was going to see them off, went as far as the entrance with them.

'I say, Imoshichi,' he whispered, 'nothing's been said about the money. What shall I do?'

'You leave that to me,' said Imoshichi. 'I asked her just as she was getting out of the kago and she said the old chap would send it to-morrow at noon. There won't be any mistake, I guarantee. Don't worry, but just enjoy yourself this evening.'

Slapping Yaji on the back he went off, and Yaji shut the door.

'It's cold to-night,' he said. 'Would you like something to eat?'

'No, thank you,' said Tsubo.

'Well then, shall we go to bed?' asked Yaji.

'Shall I get out the bedding?' asked Tsubo.

'No, I'll do it,' said Yaji.

He was getting the torn bedding and the bedclothes out of the cupboard when there came a knock at the door,—ton-ton-ton-ton.

'Who can it be at this time of night?' thought Yaji. 'Suppose it's my wife,—suppose she's smelt a rat and come back to make a row. Or perhaps it's her father come to make a complaint. It would be a bother if I were found out.'

He called softly to his wife.

'Here,' he said. 'It's a bit awkward, but in this tenement it's the regular thing when a bride comes to live here for the young

377

men to come and play jokes on her. I wonder how they found out you'd come. But it's them right enough. In your present condition perhaps I'd better tell them you haven't come, eh? What do you think?'

'Dear, dear!' said Tsubo. 'I don't want to see anybody, especially if they're going to play jokes.'

'Then you'd better hide,' said Yaji. 'You can't go upstairs because there isn't any. Let's see. Oh, I know. It's rather a tight fit but it's only for a little time.'

It was a trunk which fortunately still remained to Yaji out of all the things he had sold. Opening the lid he got Tsubo to get in and then shut it up again. Then he went and opened the door. What was his surprise when Kitahachi came panting in.

'Eh? Kitahachi?' cried Yaji. 'What is it you want at this hour?'

'I couldn't rest,' said Kita. 'It's about that fifteen ryō I asked you for the other day. They're going to have a stock-taking to-morrow and unless I can fill up that hole I've made in the cash by to-morrow morning it's all up with me. I shall be like the priest who preached for a hundred days and then spoilt it all by breaking wind. You said you had a plan for getting it and I've been waiting patiently, but I never heard from you and I got so anxious that at last I crept out of bed and came to ask. You will be able to get that money, won't you?'

'Of course I shall,' said Yaji. 'You'll have it by noon to-morrow certain. I'm a man of my word, and however humbly I live, when I say I'll get ten or fifteen ryō or some such trifling sum as that, I do it. There won't be any mistake. You may be certain of that.'

'Thank you, thank you,' said Kita. 'I'll pay you back a hundredfold. As I told you the other day the head clerk is dead and the master's going the same road, and when I get the widow in my hands I shall be the master. I'm like the villain in a play. *This time there shall be no mistake.* It's very very secret, but I'm just on the point of winning her and now is a very important time. If I fail to get that fifteen ryō I shan't be able to get a thing. So do try and get it.'

'I'm not thinking of you only,' said Yaji. 'I'm thinking of myself too. It's for our mutual advantage that I should get it, and I tell you that at noon to-morrow you'll see those fifteen ryō all laid out edge to edge ready for you.'

Just then Tsubo pushed up the lid of the box and called to them.

'Oh, oh!' she cried. 'Help me. I have such a pain that I'm afraid the baby's going to be born. Oh, oh!'

Her groans greatly alarmed Yaji.

'Eh?' he said. 'What on earth am I to do? Here, Kitahachi, have you ever helped a woman in childbirth?'

'What an absurd thing to ask,' replied Kita. 'When did your wife get in the family way? I never heard anything about it. You'd better wake up the woman next door.'

'No, no,' said Yaji. 'We mustn't let them know. It's a secret. Do you think you could heat some water?'

'I can do that right enough,' said Kita. 'But why do you keep your wife in that small box? Here, I'll help her out.'

He took hold of Tsubo's hands and pulled her out of the box, whereupon she looked at him in surprise.

'Oh!' she cried, embracing him, 'is it you? Oh, how glad I am! Did you get anxious about me now my time's so near and come to ask how I was?'

Kita's startled expression aroused Yaji's suspicions.

'Here, Kita,' he said, 'is this woman your friend?'

'Yes, yes,' said Tsubo. 'I was a servant in the same house with Kitahachi and he persuaded me against my will to go with him till I got like I am now and had to leave. My father is so strict that he wouldn't take me home again, and so Kitahachi took me under his protection and put me in lodgings. Then he proposed that he should give me a dowry of fifteen ryō and find me another husband. I didn't want to leave him, especially in my present condition, but he told me it was for my good so I reluctantly agreed and came here against my will as a bride.'

She told her story half crying with the pain. Yaji's anger broke out.

'Eh!' he cried. 'Then you never took fifteen ryō of your master's, and you never had to pay it back, and you were never in debt, and the fifteen ryō was to enable you to marry this woman off to another man?'

'That's it,' said Kita.

'Get out with you,' cried Yaji. 'You rascal, you've put me in an awful position.'

'What position have I put you in?' asked Kita. 'If it's the money, you needn't borrow that now, you know. That will be all right.'

'All right?' stormed Yaji. 'What do you mean by all right? Haven't I kicked out my wife in order to get that money, so that now I shall have to sleep alone?'

'Well, haven't I given you a young wife in her place?' said Kita. 'What have you got to grumble about in that?'

'Don't talk nonsense,' said Yaji. 'Who'd look twice at a woman with a face like that? You abominable rogue!'

Then his face became black with anger and unable to control himself any longer he seized hold of Kita and commenced to beat him. Kita also, losing his temper, returned the blows.

Meanwhile Tsubo was in the pangs of child-birth and was continually groaning. But her groans were unheard by Yaji and Kita, who, through the heat of their anger, were quite lost to their surroundings.

Soon the dawn began to break, and Imoshichi, the match-maker, on the way to buy his day's supplies, called at the house. He was surprised to hear the sound of something being beaten, intermingled with the groans of a woman. He tried the door, but it was fast; he knocked, but no one came. Finally he burst the door open and went in.

'Ah!' cried Yaji, immediately he saw him, 'it's Imoshichi. Here's the rascal who plotted against me. Here's the man who deceived me. But I won't stand it. It's unbearable.'

'What are you talking about being deceived?' asked Imoshichi,

'What am I talking about?' cried Yaji. 'I'm in a terrible position, you insolent rascal.'

Then Imoshichi got angry and commenced to fight, and as he was a little stronger than Yaji he got him down, in spite of Kita's attempts to soothe him. Then there was a terrible scene. The tobacco box was trampled to pieces, and the tea was all spilt from the teapot. At the sound of their wild cries all the neighbours came running to separate them.

Meanwhile Tsubo, who had been rocking herself to and fro in her pain, suddenly fell down unconscious.

'Oh, oh!' cried Kita. 'Tsubo, Tsubo, what's the matter? Here, Imo. Come here. Poor thing! What's the matter with her?'

'She's turned up her eyes,' said Imoshichi. 'Here! Water water.'

'Tsubo! Tsubo!' called Kita.

Then the old gentleman from next door spoke up.

'Who is Mrs. Tsubo?' he asked. 'Is she the good lady of the house?'

'Yes, yes,' said Imoshichi. 'This is her with her eyes turned up.'

'Aha!' said the old gentleman. 'Is this your wife Master Yaji?'

'Well, she is my wife and she ain't my wife, if you can understand me,' replied Yaji.

'Ha-ha!' said the old gentleman. 'I see. Then she must be your wife, Master Kitahachi?'

'Well, she is my wife and she ain't my wife,' replied Kita.

'Well,' said the old gentleman. 'Whosever wife you are—yai, yai.'

'Halloa!' said Imoshichi. 'She's getting cold. It's no use.'

'Eh?' said Kita. 'What a melancholy thing. Yaji, just run for the doctor.'

'Shall I call Mr. Gentaku?' said a neighbour.

'And by the way you might call at the temple,' said Yaji.

The doctor was called, the moxa was applied, and every means was tried by those present to bring Tsubo back to life, but the unlucky Tsubo had breathed her last and lay there motionless with her white face. Kitahachi involuntarily burst into tears.

'Poor thing!' he said. 'It must have been her condition. The row made the blood go to her head. Well, it can't be helped. By the way, Yaji, you'd better forgive everything and not be angry any more. Let bygones by bygones.'

'I've been through some awful experiences,' said Yaji.

'However much he may have disowned her,' said Kita, 'I suppose we'd better let her father know how things have turned out. Is there anybody we could send?'

'Shall I go?' said Imoshichi. 'I don't exactly understand what's happened. I was asked to find a husband for the mistress of an old gentleman who had put her to lodge at the fishmonger's in Shinmichi, and I made a match for her at this house. Now I find she's your wife. How's that?'

'Never mind,' said Kita, 'You'll understand afterwards. That fishmonger used to serve my master's house and the person who lodged her there was me. But never mind. What you've got to do now is to let her father know quickly. You'd better let that fishmonger know and get him to let the father know.'

'Well, I'll go then,' said Imoshichi.

He went off, and the neighbours, after they had helped to clear up the place and expressed their condolences, went away for a time.

'I'd better go along,' said Kita, 'as I came out last night without letting anybody know. Do everything you can.'

He took out his purse and gave two *bu* to Yaji, and was just going off when his shop-mate Yokuhachi came in.

'Is Master Kitahachi here?' he asked. 'The master died this morning at last.'

'I knew he would,' said Kita.

'So the mistress has decided to dismiss Kitahachi,' Yokuhachi went on. '"He's a nasty-minded fellow," she said, "and now that the master's dead he probably won't mind what I tell him and do something bad. You go quickly and tell the man that recommended him that I don't want him any more." I tried to say what I could for you but it seems as if you had done something to offend her. "He's a brazen-faced fellow, and I can't bear to see him about the place." That's what she said. She doesn't want you within ten miles of her, she said. It can't be helped. Are you Master Yajirobei? Please note that my mistress doesn't want Kitahachi any more and so we return him to you.'

'Certainly,' said Yaji. 'Here, Kita, is that all right?'

'Well, it'll be all the same whether it's right or wrong,' said Kita. 'But I didn't mean things to turn out this way.'

'Everything goes to show what a disgraceful rascal you are,' said Yaji. 'I've a good mind to reveal all your misconduct.'

'Here, here,' said Kita. 'I've apologised. Don't, I implore you.'

'Well,' said Yokuhachi, 'I'll plead for you again when I get a chance. I must go now, as we're all in confusion at the shop.'

He went off with a hurried salutation, and at the same time Imoshichi came back.

'I've let the father know,' he announced. 'I must go and buy what's necessary now.'

'Thank you, thank you,' said Kita. 'If you don't mind I'll come with you.'

So saying he took from Yaji the two *bu* that he had given him and went off to buy the coffin and the other articles necessary for the funeral.

'There,' said Yaji, when they returned. 'You've forgotten something. You might have bought the saké while you were about it.'

'Do you think I'd forget it,' said Kita. With that he took a bottle of saké and some raw fish out of the coffin.

As soon as they had begun to drink the other people in the tenement gradually began to come in, and by-and-by it grew into a big feast, more and more saké being bought, till at last they were all half drunk and began to get thick in their speech.

'Now we feel so good,' said Imoshichi, 'we'd better dump the departed into the coffin. By the way, where's your temple ? '

'Fool ! ' said Yaji. 'Do you think I'm likely to have a temple ? '

'What an idea ! ' said Kita.

'What does it matter ? ' said Yaji. 'If we get it out of the house there's sure to be a temple somewhere.'

'All we have to do,' said Kita, 'is to put it on our shoulders and cry it in Temple Street. There are sure to be some buyers.'

'That's a good idea,' said Imoshichi. 'I'm always selling things in Temple Street, and the street cries are different there to other parts. With these kind of goods we ought to cry "Shinda ko, shinda ko ! Yurensō ya ! yurensō ya ! Bakegi ya ! Sotoba no himono ni seki-to no tachi-uri ! " Those sort of things sell well, so we're sure to find a purchaser. Ha-ha-ha ! '

'Poor thing ! ' said Kita. 'It's not a joking matter really. Come, let's get ready.'

Thus uttering their shameless jests, the crowd of them, half drunk, put the body in the coffin, and offered incense and flowers before it. Just then Tsubo's father came in crying.

'Excuse me,' he said. 'I'm the father of Tsubo.'

'I'm glad to see you,' said Kita. 'Please come in.'

'Dear dear ! ' said the old man, 'what sad things have happened. I'm only an old countryman and perhaps it was cruel of me to turn her out, but I never thought things would happen like this. Eh, eh ! Where is she ? If I could get a look at her face . . . Just let me see.'

'You should have come a little earlier,' said Yaji. 'We've slung her into the coffin, haven't we, Imoshichi ? '

'Yes,' said Imoshichi, 'but it's natural her father should want to see her. Quite natural, very natural. As natural as the reason why the child behaved like a fox. Ha-ha-ha! Shall we open it?'

They untied the rope they had put round the coffin and opened the lid. The old man put on his spectacles and gazed earnestly inside.

'There's some mistake,' he said.

'Mistake?' cried Yaji. 'What's the mistake?'

'The departed is different,' said the father. 'This departed has no head. And my daughter was a woman. This seems like the dead body of a man. It's got hair on its chest.'

'What? No head?' said Imoshichi. 'Where? Where? Neither it has. What have you been doing, Yaji?'

'How should I know?' said Yaji. 'Perhaps it's fallen off somewhere.'

'Oh dear! Oh dear!' said the old man. 'These folk are a strange lot. Come, what have you done with my daughter? It's all lies that she's dead or anything happened to her. Give me my daughter.'

'Give you your daughter?' said Yaji. 'We haven't got any other one than this. What an extraordinary old man!'

'Oh, oh, oh!' said the old man. 'I won't put up with it.'

'Look here,' said Kita. 'He's quite right. There ought to be a head.'

'Yes, yes,' went on the old man, 'I may be a countryman, but I'm the headman among the farmers, and if the landlord hears of it he'll be very angry.'

The people standing by tried to soothe the old man, but he would not be appeased and went on talking louder and louder until the landlord hastened over to hear what it was all about.

'Well, well, well!' he said. 'This is really a terrible thing. A dead person without any head. What have you been doing?'

Here he took a peep into the coffin.

'No, no, no,' he cried out. 'It's all right. Don't you worry, grandfather. It's got a head all right.'

'Got a head? Where is it then?' asked the old man.

'Look, they've put the departed in upside down,' said the landlord. 'Ha-ha-ha!'

'Oh then I'm quite satisfied,' said the old man. 'I'm sorry I've given you all so much trouble.'

So in the evening they conducted the funeral ceremony very respectfully.

Then as Kitahachi had been turned out of the shop in which he had served so long and had again become a hanger-on of Yaji, and as both were tired of their way of living and were anxious to mend their luck, they decided to leave Edo. Thus it was that, having borrowed some money for the journey, they started in the middle of February along the East Sea route to welcome what they hoped would prove a lucky spring by making a pilgrimage to the Grand Shrine of Isé.

> We to Naniwa take our way ;
> For good or bad 'tis hard to say ;
> But whether we start or whether we stay
> The day we start is the luckiest day.

NOTES

Page 23.—The pine trees at the gate.

Referring to the small pine-trees planted at the gates of houses as part of the New Year decorations. They are supposed to bring the protection of the gods.

Page 23.—the hair of the head.

The people moving along the roads in single file are compared to the hairs of the head.

Page 23.—Cock-crowing Adzuma.

'Cock-crowing' ('tori-ga-naku') is the pillow-word or conventional epithet applied to Adzuma, a poetical name given to the eastern provinces. In this context practically standing for Edo.

Page 23.—Thousand swift-brandishing.

'Chihayaburu,' a pillow-word generally applied to 'kami' (god). It may also be translated 'thousand rock-smashing.' The significance and meaning of these pillow-words is often very vague, their use being more for ornament than elucidation.

Page 23.—dappled like the flesh of a clam.

This effect is produced by tying up small pieces of the cloth here and there before it is dyed, so that the dye works unevenly.

Page 23.—'Footworn Yamato.'

A pillow-word applied to Yamato. Yamato is properly only applicable to central Japan, that is the portion of Japan where the Japanese dynasty was first established, but it is now used poetically for the whole of Japan.

Page 23.—Grand Shrine of Isé.

This is the Shintō Shrine dedicated to the ancestors of the Imperial Family and therefore the most sacred shrine in Japan. It is visited by thousands of pilgrims every year, and Ministers of State are also supposed to worship there when they are appointed and on other special occasions.

Page 23.—Naniwa.

The ancient poetical name for Ōsaka.

Page 23.—A hundred coppers.

This is the copper coin called the 'mon.' It had a hole in the centre so that it could be strung on a string, which was the usual way of carrying a quantity. The purchasing value of the 'mon' was about equal to the modern 'sen,' or one farthing in English money.

Page 24.—To pass the barriers.

From ancient times barriers had been erected on the main roads, with guardhouses attached, to examine all travellers passing through. The penalty for going round the barriers was very severe.

Page 24.—Stone weight.

Weight put on top of the pickles to keep them pressed down in the pickling liquor.

Page 24.—Saké.

The national drink, distilled from rice and generally drunk warm.

Page 24.—It is not right.

This is written in imitation of a Chinese comic poem and is thus quite irregular if read as Japanese. Chinese being a monosyllabic language each character corresponds to a syllable. Each line in the original has thus seven characters, corresponding to seven syllables. Read in the Japanese style Chinese poetry loses all its rhythm and rime.

Page 24.—Suzu-ga-mori.

This was the execution ground of Edo.

Page 24.—Mannenya.

A teahouse.

Page 24.—Two trays.

Meals for two people.

Page 25.—Daimyō's procession.

The daimyōs (rulers of the provinces) had to make annual visits to Edo, where they resided for six months in the year. As a further precaution their wives and children were made to reside altogether in Edo as hostages for their good behaviour. Consequently they had to maintain vast establishments in Edo, which added greatly to the wealth and prosperity of the city. The daimyōs travelled in considerable state. Lord Redesdale (formerly Mr. A. B. Mitford) in his book 'The Garter Mission to Japan' gives a description of a daimyō's procession:—

'First came the swaggering leaders with their hoarse cry of 'Shita ni iro! Shita ni iro!' Be down! Be down! for as the great man passes every man, woman and child must grovel with head bowed in the dust. . . . Then followed a number of swashbucklers, putting on airs of preternatural fierceness; a whole army of coolies carrying luggage in baskets swung to bamboo poles; more men-at-arms, armed with great spears fringed with horsehair tufts below the blade; others with halberds which were really swords on spear handles, all putting on the most bloodcurdling expression. To them succeeded by himself the wrestler or fencing-master, and immediately after him the "norimono" or palanquin in which the great man was carried by eight bearers. After him the master of the procession on horseback; then the physician in ordinary, with shaven head, like a priest, ready to prescribe, apply moxa, or perform acupuncture according to the most orthodox methods of

388

the Chinese school. . . . After them the daimyō's horse, richly caparisoned, with saddle cloth of rare fur; then more men-at-arms, more coolies, more baggage, luncheon box of gold lacquer, clothes, stores of all kinds, and finally a few more guards.' Lord Redesdale's impressions of the procession were inspired, however, by the sight of a sham one in Tokyo, and the real thing does not seem to have been so dramatic, at any rate when it was travelling between the stages. The 'swaggering leaders' he speaks of are presumably the 'saki-barai,' here translated as 'running footmen' but literally 'front-sweepers.' Judging from the description given in Ikku's time they were generally inn servants, replaced from stage to stage. Sir Rutherford Alcock, the first British Minister to Japan, in his 'The Capital of the Tycoon,' describes the 'saki-barai' in his journey overland from Hyōgo to Edo as "a couple of little ragged urchins, dragging their brooms after them, and shouting as they went, as an advertisement to all whom they might meet, the magic word which brings every Japanese to his knees, 'Shitaniro !' or rather this was the word that should have been articulated; but in their mouths it was transmuted into a sort of monotonous cry or howl.'

Page 25.—Those with the head covered.
People who wished to escape observation either because they had not paid their debts or for other reasons, concealed their faces, either by wrapping their heads in a towel, with only their eyes uncovered, or by wearing a kind of inverted basket, with two holes for the eyes. These are still used by pilgrims and also in the prisons to conceal a prisoner's identity when he is being conveyed through some public place.

Page 25.—because he said off with them.
In the original the joke turns upon the similarity in sound of 'tōru,' to pass along, and 'toru,' to take off.

Page 25.—postboy.
Literally 'horse-boy,' i.e. groom. The word 'groom' having now taken another significance, however, it has been thought best to revive the word 'postboy.' They travelled backwards and forwards between the stages, leading the horses at a footpace.

Page 25.—Kumonryō.
Said to be the name of a very tall man in the famous Chinese novel of 'Suikōden' (Japanese pronunciation). Atago is a hill in Tōkyō.

Page 25.—Yoshichō.
The courtesans' quarter in Edo.

Page 26.—Bōshū.
This is the 'short' form for Awa Province. The termination 'shū' means province, and the shortening consists in taking one character of the name of the province and adding 'shū' to it.

Page 27.—Rice-cake.
This is the famous 'mochi,' made from a specially glutinous rice, which is cooked and pounded into a paste, and then formed into cakes.

Page 28.—Awa and Kazusa.
The names of provinces on the other side of Tōkyō Bay. Now portions of Chiba Prefecture.

Page 28.—Ōshū.
This was the name given to all north-eastern Japan.

Page 28.—Horser.
'Umauemon' in the original.

Page 29.—the decoys.
These are the girls sent out from the inns to induce travellers to stop. They were usually called 'tomé-onna,' stop-girls.

Page 29.—Katabira.
The name given to a summer garment made of hemp.

Page 29.—Musashiya.
Name of an inn. The 'ya' at the end of the names of inns and teahouses signifies 'house.'

Page 30.—six or seven cups of rice and soup.
Three cups of rice and one, or perhaps two, bowls of soup are what etiquette allows.

Page 31.—All the inns have notices up.
That is notices that the accommodation contained in them has been engaged, presumably by some daimyō's train. The daimyōs themselves were accommodated at special rest-houses.

Page 31.—hot water.
To wash their feet with. Footgear is removed on entering a Japanese house.

Page 32.—Comestibles.
To eat with the saké. Such comestibles are called 'sakana,' now the usual word for 'fish,' though one may suspect that it was originally associated with all kinds of food eaten with saké.

Page 33.—seized a teacup.
The saké cup is very tiny and hardly holds a mouthful.

Page 33.—kamaboko.
Made of fish pounded to a paste. The white kind is only steamed; the red kind is both steamed and baked. The best kind of 'kamaboko' is made of bream and flatfish; the cheap kind of shark.

Page 33.—shiso berries.
'Shiso' is the 'perilla nankinensis.'

Page 33.—saké cup.
It is the Japanese custom to use only one saké cup and pass it from one to another.

Page 33.—drained the cup of saké.
Kita's idea was that the maid would give the cup back to him as a signal of her agreement to his desires. Hence his anger when she gives it to Yaji.

Page 34.—brought in the rice.
This is the real meal, to which the saké drinking is but the preliminary, though often the rice stage is never reached.

Page 34.—divine favour of the thousand-handed Kwannon.
Kwannon is the goddess of mercy, who in one form is represented as having a thousand hands. The name is therefore appropriately used for lice, a pest which seems to have been very common in feudal times.

Page 34.—In the bamboo.
Sparrows among bamboos was the crest of the Daimyō of Sendai, and it was from this crest that the song originated.

Page 34.—Over Hakoné.
The climb of twenty miles across the Hakoné range was one of the noted parts of the journey between the two capitals. There is a well known poem which reads.

> Hakoné hachi ri uma demo kosu ga
> Kosu ni kosarenu Ōi-gawa,

which means that it is possible to cross the Hakoné range even on horseback, but it is not always possible to cross the River Ōi.

Page 35.—a ballad-singer.
'Chongaré-bōzu.' The more usual name now for these ballads is 'Naniwabushi.' While resembling 'jōruri' they appeal to the less educated and are supposed to be of use in keeping alive the martial spirit. A Minister of State once drew attention to the moral value of 'Naniwabushi' and was consequently nicknamed 'Chongaré-daijin' (Minister). We must imagine the ballad-singer chanting his requests to Yaji and Kita.

Page 35.—loin cloths.
In the original 'Etchū fundoshi.' The original loincloth took six feet of material, but the lord of the Province of Etchū devised a loin cloth which only required half this length. This was called the Etchū 'fundoshi.'

Page 36.—Torii.
These are the arches, formed of two uprights and a cross piece, either in stone or wood, which are erected outside Shintō shrines.

Page 36.—Jizō.
The Buddhist deity who is supposed to help those in trouble.

Page 36.—Hetanasu.
This is a comic name, something like 'Spotty-face.'

Page 36.—Kusatsu.
A celebrated mineral spring in Gumma Prefecture.

Page 36.—Daifukuchō, etc.
These names are all invented by Kita and Yaji. 'Chō' means both street or town and account book. 'Daifukuchō' is thus literally 'ledger;' 'Tozachō,' current account book; 'Hantorichō,' receipt book; 'Tanachinchō,' rent book; 'jidai' is ground rent, and 'soroban' is the abacus.

Page 37.—Take a kago.
'Kago' is literally 'basket.' Here it is used in the sense of a wicker chair in which travellers were carried. The 'kago' was slung on a stout pole and carried by two men, the traveller having to squat down inside. Kago are still in use in Japan in places where other means of travelling are not available.

Page 38.—The master's rather hard.
The word translated 'hard' suggests both heavy and hard in a metaphorical sense,—hard with his cash. The answer of the other carrier also suggests in the original that Yaji is not very free with his cash.

Page 38.—guide-book.
'Dochu-ki,' travel-diary. Japan in feudal times had probably the best guidebooks in the world.

Page 38.—Yoshitsuné.
The celebrated brother of Yoritomo, the first of the Kamakura Shōguns (1147-1199). Yoshitsuné helped to establish his brother in his position of Shōgun, but his ability was so great that his brother feared him as a possible rival and encompassed his death. There are many superstitions connected with Yoshitsuné.

Page 38.—Saigyō.
Died 1198. Described as an eccentric monk and a famous poet.

Page 38.—Mongaku Shōnin.
This is the Buddhist name of Endō Moritō, cousin of Kesa Gozen. Kesa Gozen was a beautiful woman who was already married to another when her cousin fell in love with her and tried to persuade her mother to give her to him. Kesa Gozen, fearing for the safety of her mother, whom her cousin threatened to kill if she did not consent to his desires, pretended to agree to his wishes but laid down the condition that he must first kill her husband. At the time arranged for the assassination she took the place of her husband and was killed by the cousin, who was so horrified at what he had done that he forsook the world and became a monk under the name of Mongaku Shōnin.

Page 39.—Because we're good-goers—geegees.
In the original the answer is 'Dō-dō da kara.' 'Do-do' is the Japanese equivalent for 'gee-up' and also means 'going together.'

Page 39.—Because there are two of us.
This is a punning answer. Kitahachi answers 'Buta ni nagara kyan to,' which means 'Two pigs and ten dogs,' but also resembles in sound 'Futari nagara Kwanto,' which means 'Two from the Kwanto,' the name given to the eastern provinces.

Page 39.—lover who undoes his girdle, etc.
This joke turns upon the word 'toku,' which means both 'to undo' and 'to solve.'

Page 40.—Because you undo it when you hang it up, etc.
The joke here turns not only upon the two meanings of 'toku,' but also on two meanings of 'kaké,' to hang up and to answer a riddle.

Page 40.—One room of ten mats.
The sizes of Japanese rooms are conveniently described by the number of mats that can be put on the floor, the mats being standardised at (about) six feet long and three feet wide.

Page 40.—Jōdō sect.
One of the Buddhist sects.

Page 41.—What time's the funeral ?
Buddhist temples are associated in Yaji's mind with funerals, these presumably being the chief occasions when he had visited temples.

Page 41.—Uirō.
This is a kind of medicine sold at Odawara and also of a kind of rice-cake sold in Edo.

Page 41.—their hats.
Their hats are described as 'sando-gasa,' specially designed to prevent travellers hurting their noses should they fall from their horses. The pace of the horses was so slow that travellers were in constant danger of falling asleep in the saddle and losing their balance.

Page 42.—the place in the tobacco-box made to hold it.
This is an earthenware jar filled with ashes in which a live piece of charcoal is placed.

Page 42.—boiled rice.
The joke is lost in the translation. Boiled rice is 'meshi,' which is also used in the sense of 'meal.' Yaji uses it in the sense of 'meal.' Kita takes it literally as boiled rice.

Page 42.—if the bath's hot.
In the original, 'If the hot water is heated.' The Japanese language has separate words for hot water and cold water and the word for hot water is commonly used to designate a hot bath. Yaji's correction reads literally, 'If the cold water has been heated to become hot water I'll go in.'

Page 42.—Goemon bath.

Goemon was a celebrated robber who lived in the time of Hideyoshi (1536–1598). He was caught and condemned to death with his son, and was executed by being boiled alive in oil in a large cauldron in the bed of the river at Kyōto. Goemon is regarded as a sort of Robin Hood, who robbed the rich but succoured the poor. It is recorded that he charged Hideyoshi with being a greater thief than he, since Hideyoshi had taken the whole country, whereas he had only despoiled a few Japanese, and that he evinced his spirit by holding his son out of the boiling oil as long as his strength lasted. The Goemon bath in its proper form is simply a large iron cauldren which is heated from underneath. The one in which Kita met with his accident was an attempt to imitate it.

Page 43.—Her tears fell like dew.

Yaji is chanting from a 'jōruri' or 'jewel song,' a kind of ballad which has now been replaced by the 'Naniwabushi.' Since the beginning of the nineteenth century it is stated that the writing of jōruri has almost altogether ceased.

Page 44.—Do you not feel sorry for Ishidōmaru ?

Kita is singing a line from a 'jōruri.' Ishidōmaru was the son of a samurai who had left his home before his son was born and had become a monk in the famous monastery on Mt. Kōya. The boy and his mother go to find the father, but as women were then not allowed to climb the mountain she had to wait at the foot while her son ascends the mountain alone. He meets a kindly priest whom he instinctively knows to be his father, but the priest is bound by his vows not to reveal himself, and the boy returns down the mountain alone to find his mother dead.

Page 45.—If we had gone to Yoshi-chō.

Yoshi-chō is here used as a general term for the pleasure quarter. Yaji's joke turns on the phrase ' to empty the boiler (or cauldron),' a slang expression for homo-sexual relations.

Page 48.—Gongen.

Properly the term used to describe the incarnations of Buddha, especially Ieyasu, the founder of the Tokugawa dynasty, but here actually used as the name of a temple.

Page 48.—Everywhere I look I see rustic faces.

Kitahachi is here quoting from a jōruri.

Page 48.—Sai-no-Kawara.

The Buddhist Styx. The name is given to several places in Japan. It means literally the river-bed of souls.

Page 51.—Chōmei.

Kamo-no-Chōmei, the supposed writer of a sort of guide-book to the Tōkaidō, although others give the authorship to Tosa Mitsuyuki. The Tōkaidō is also spoken of as the Azumakaidō, Azuma being the poetic name for the Eastern provinces.

Page 51.—Here we have, etc.
The passage is in imitation of the Nō drama, where a description of the scene and the circumstances is given in the form of an opening recitative.

Page 51.—Kumano.
This is in Kishū. The Atago Shrine referred to lower down is in Kyōto.

Page 51.—Hamamatsu in Enshū.
There is a saying about Hamamatsu that although it looks large it is really small ('hiroi yō de semai'). Yaji is apparently punning on this by turning it into 'kuroi yō de amai,' the blacker the sweeter.

Page 51.—The smoke goes up into the sky.
Fuji, it has to be remembered, was an active volcano as late as 1708.

Page 52.—a robber.
In the original 'hattsuké,' a contraction of 'hari-tsuké,' crucified.

Page 52.—Helmet-stone.
' Kabuto-ishi,' a stone shaped like a helmet. The removal of the helmet was an acknowledgement of defeat.

Page 53.—Red-bear.
' Aka-kuma,' here used as a nickname.

Page 54.—Ashikaga.
The line of Shōguns who ruled from the 14th to the 16th centuries.

Page 54.—Turtle.
This is the snapping turtle.

Page 55.—Ama kembiki.
The street cry of the blind shampooers. 'Kembiki' means the art of shampooing.

Page 55.—spirit.
This is 'shōchu,' much stronger than saké.

Page 56.—Senshū.
Now a part of Osaka-fu.

Page 56.—Gihei of the Amagawa.
This and the other names given by the travellers are taken from the famous drama 'Chūshingura,' which is founded upon a real vendetta which took place in 1703. The story is told in Mitford's 'Tales of Old Japan' and in the last volume of Murdoch's 'History of Japan,' under the title of 'The Forty-seven Rōnin.' A translation of the 'Chūshingura' was made by the late Mr. Frederick V. Dickins. Gihei was not one of the Forty-seven Rōnin who avenged their lord's death, but a retainer of the clan who secretly helped them to get armour. Yoichibei was the father-in-law of Haya-no Kampei, who was originally one of the rōnin but who committed suicide before the revenge was

accomplished, in the belief that he had killed his father-in-law. Karu was Yoichibei's daughter and Kampei's wife. Tanuki-no-Kakubei and Meppo Yahachi are two hunters who appear in the drama. The wild boar figures as the cause of the death of Yoichibei's murderer, who is shot by Kampei in mistake for the boar. The constant references to 'Chūshingura' in Hizakurigé show how popular the drama was.

Page 56.—Tentsuru.
This is in imitation of the sound made by the samisen.

Page 56.—Tandon.
The 'don' is the title of address. 'Tan' is a corruption of 'San.' The joke turns on the similarity in sound of 'Tandon' and 'tadon,' a charcoal ball, suggesting that the girl was swarthy.

Page 56.—white goods.
Courtesans. The Kisokaidō is the road from Gifu to Nagano.

Page 57.—Just about ordinary.
The Japanese expression is 'jū-nin mae,' ten people before. Kita wilfully mishears the expression as meaning 'enough for ten.'

Page 58.—same age as the moon.
This refers to the popular children's song,

> Tsuki sama ikutsu
> Jū-san nanatsu

'How old is the moon? Thirteen and seven.'

Page 62.—Sorry my eye.
'O ki no doku no Hitomaro sama da.'
The sentence properly ends at 'hito,' the 'maro sama' being attached to form an expression of contempt. Kakino-moto no Hitomaro was a poet who lived in the eighth century. In the original Yaji in his excitement goes on to change 'Hitomaro' into 'shitodaru,' a four-measure tub, and finally demands that the landlord should produce this 'shitodaru.'

Page 62.—Fuchū.
Now called Shizuoka.

Page 63.—letter-carriers.
Carrying dispatches for the Shōgun's Government.

Page 63.—Idaten.
A strong and handsome youth in the Buddhist Pantheon.

Page 63.—Ei-sassa.
These are the cries used by the carriers to bring their efforts into unison.

Page 65.—stuck by a prig.

Kita uses the word 'goma-no-hai' for thief. The samurai does not understand this word, whereupon Kita uses the commoner word 'dorobō.' Again the samurai does not understand, and it is only when Kita uses a Sinico-Japanese word that he catches the meaning. Ikku was laughing at the high-flown expressions used by the samurai.

Page 65.—a leather purse.

In Japanese 'Inden no kinchaku,' explained as a purse from India, or one made of Indian leather.

Page 66.—precipice at Kiyomizu temple.

This temple, which is in Kyōto, overhangs a precipice, and it is supposed that those who have full faith in Buddha can jump from the precipice without being hurt.

Page 66.—Sawamura Sōjurō.

A celebrated actor of the time.

Page 67.—Hot water.

This is the hot water in which the macaroni is boiled and which therefore contains some of its flavour and strength.

Page 68.—konnyaku.

Made from the root of the Amorphophallus rivieri.

Page 68.—rōnin.

A wandering samurai, that is one not attached to any lord.

Page 68.—Come let us eat and drink our fill.

This is in imitation of the odes sung by the chorus in the 'Nō' drama.

Page 68.—Kwannon.

The priest is supposed to be reciting from the Sutra of the Lotus of the Pure Law, of which this is a parody.

Page 68.—the empty hole beneath the nose.

The hole beneath the nose is, of course, the mouth. Ikku is laughing at the priests who go round collecting contributions towards the building of some alleged temple or shrine.

Page 69.—name on earth.

After death the dead person receives new earthly and heavenly names.

Page 70.—Soga brothers.

Two youths named Soga, whose father had been killed by another man, resolved to avenge themselves when they grew up. They succeeded, but one was killed in the fighting that ensued and the other was executed (1193).

Page 71.—Hostel.

For the accommodation of daimyō when they were travelling. Usually the mansion of a wealthy man.

Page 72.—cheap lodging-house.
For pilgrims and beggars.

Page 72.—Sushi.
Cooked rice made up into cakes with fish or vegetables. May be described as rice-sandwiches.

Page 72.—a pilgrim and two palmers.
'Rokubu' (here translated 'pilgrim') is a contraction of 'rokujū-rokubu,' literally 'sixty-six volumes,' especially of the 'Hokkekyō,' the great Lotus Sutra. 'Rokubu' have now almost entirely disappeared. Both sexes participated. They carried small Buddhist images on their backs and chanted as they went 'Nammai-dabu! Nammai-dabu!' a corruption of 'Namu Amida Butsu' (Praise be to the Amitabha Buddha). 'Junrei' (translated 'palmer') is especially one who visits the thirty-three holy places in the Kwansai district where Kwannon is enshrined. Such palmers wear a cloak to which the seals of the temples visited are affixed.

Page 73.—three ' go.'
About a pint.

Page 74.—large number of cats.
The skin of the cat is used as parchment for the drum of the samisen.

Page 76.—Minobu.
This is the headquarters of the Nichiren sect of Buddhism and is situated at the foot of Mount Fuji. Minobu is really the name of the village where the temple is situated but is used for the name of the temple.

Page 78.—gidayu.
A kind of ballad chanted to the accompaniment of the samisen. They are named after Gidayu Takemoto, a reciter of 'jōruri' or ballads who lived in the 17th century and gave performances in Osaka. He chiefly recited the 'jōruri' of the famous Japanese dramatist Chikamatsu and became so popular that the ballads came to be called by his name. The samisen used in the accompaniment of 'gidayu' has a thicker and heavier stem than the ordinary samisen so as to give a deeper tone.

Page 78.—futozao.
Means literally 'thick stick,' and is used in speaking of the 'gidayu' samisen.

Page 79.—light packhorse.
The packhorses were divided into two classes, those which could carry two hundred pounds and those which could only carry half that weight.

Page 81.—Abekawa-chō.
This is where the pleasure quarters are situated.

Page 81.—Miroku.
The Buddhist Messiah, whose advent is expected to take place five thousand years after Buddha's entry into Nirvana.

Page 82.—Sengen.
The goddess of Mount Fuji. She is also called Asama or Kono-Hana-Saku-ya-Himé, that is 'the princess who makes the flowers of the trees to bloom.' There is a temple dedicated to her at Shizuoka.

Page 82.—Kajiwara's horse.
Kajiwara Genta Kagesué was a follower of Yoritomo and fought at the battle of the River Uji, where he and another contended which could cross the river first. His horse was a celebrated one given him by Yoritomo.

Page 82.—some of them are one 'bu.'
The 'bu' was a gold coin, in value a quarter of a 'ryō,' which was the largest gold coin. The 'bu' was divided into four 'shū' or ten 'mommé.'

Page 84.—Nitten.
The god of the sun in the Indian pantheon. Not to be confused with the Japanese Sun goddess.

Page 85.—Ten Shōkō Daijingu.
Amaterasu O Mikami, the Sun goddess.

Page 86.—Katsuyama.
A girl's name. Nakadaya is the name of a teahouse.

Page 95.—Mount Oé.
This is Mount Oé, near Fukuchiyama, a town on the road to Maizuru celebrated on account of the ogres said to have lived there. The encounter between Shūten Doji, their chief, and the warriors Raiko and Tsuna at the Rashō Gate at Kyōto, is a favourite art motive.

Page 95.—Sekison.
This is a name given to Mount Ōyama in Sagami province. Apparently it was the name of the Buddhist deity formerly worshipped there, but now replaced by Shintō deities.

Page 95.—Hainai of Kumé.
Hainai of Kumé was a 'rōnin' noted for his valour, who made a vow to behead a thousand persons but later repented, and in order to atone for his wickedness carved images of himself and got people to trample on them. The inscription 'Here lodges Kumé Hainai' is still used as a means of driving away epidemic diseases.

Page 97.—Bungo-bushi.
A kind of chant.

Page 98.—like that dog of Jirō and Tarō.
This is a reference to the children's song beginning
> Tsuki sama ikutsu
> Jū-san nanatsu

already referred to. The song is as inconsequential as an English nursery rhyme, but it tells in one part of the upsetting of a dish of fat and how all the dogs ran to lick it up :—

> Tarō-don no inu to
> Jirō-don no inu to
> Mina namete shimatta

Tarō and Jirō are common boys' names.

Page 99.—Echigo or Niigata.
Northern provinces, where, it may be supposed, prices were higher.

Page 100.—Minoya Shirōtoshi.
Said to have fought at the Battle of Dannoura with a broken sword.

Page 101.—Kumano.
Another name for the province of Kii.

Page 102.—We are not willow trees.
The willow tree was planted in front of shops as a trade sign.

Page 103.—the ants' walk.
The perineum.

Page 103.—Tamachi.
A district of Edo.

Page 104.—Witches.
Women able to summon persons from the dead.

Page 104.—call upon Bonten.
Bonten and Taishaku were the two Buddhist gods whom warriors invoked before going into battle. Taishaku was introduced into Japan as the guardian of Buddhism. Ama-no-Iwato is the cave in which Amaterasu Omikami, the Sun Goddess, hid herself. Kokuzo, the god of the ten thousand good fortunes, is enshrined on Asama-ga-také in Mié Prefecture.

Page 104.—Great Shrine of Izumo.
This ranks next in sanctity to the Great Shrine of Isé. It is situated in Shimané Prefecture.

Page 106.—twanged her bow.
Witches seem to have carried small bows which they pretended to shoot with to drive off evil spirits.

Page 109.—By stealth I entered.
The translator has here yielded to the temptation of a very obvious pun. In the original the pun is on Kitahachi's name.

Page 110.—The dried up mother-in-law.
'Hata' means a dry field and 'ta' a wet field for growing rice. 'Shūto' means mother-in-law.

Page 110.—play for it.
This is a method of drawing lots called 'ken.' It is done with the hands. Flattened the hand represents a piece of paper, folded a stone, and with two fingers extended, a pair of scissors. Scissors beat paper because they can cut it, but lose to stone because they cannot; stone for the same reason beats scissors but loses to paper because it can be wrapped in paper; and paper loses to scissors and beats stone. In another form of the game called Satsuma 'ken,' the hands held up to the ears represent a fox, placed on the knees the master, and placed in position for holding a gun, a gun. The gun beats the fox, the fox beats the master, and the master beats the gun. Satsuma is a province in Kyūshū.

Page 114.—persons who get drunk on tea.
The translator has here had to deviate from the original to bring out the joke. In the original the word Kitahachi repeats is 'cha,' the Japanese for 'tea.'

Page 119.—one 'sho' two 'go.'
Ten 'shaku' equal one 'go,' and ten 'go' one 'sho.' The 'go' is equal to a third of a pint.

Page 120.—hundredth day after.
The hundredth day after the funeral, when a ceremony in memory of the dead person is held.

Page 121.—I see you're not blind.
The calling of shampooer is confined to the blind as a rule.

Page 125.—the kites here must be teetotallers.
That is fond of sweet things.

Page 131.—Era of Genroku.
The period from 1688 to 1704.

Page 131.—My heart is as black.
This bridge is supposed to have decayed so quickly that travellers to Kyōto found it gone when they made the return journey.

Page 133.—I'll give a fist.
The carriers and postboys had special slang expressions for the fares they received.

Page 134.—Deep in the hills.
This is a well known poem by Sarumaru. The carrier pretends he believes it to be Kitahachi's own composition, but later slyly tells his mates that Master Sarumaru has invited them to take a drink.

Page 135.—hakama.
A kind of divided skirt worn over the kimono.

Page 135.—they're all Fukusuké.
Fukusuké was a dwarf performer who gave his name to entertainers of this class. The cushions they sat on were piled up to bring them on a level with the audience, who sat upon the floor.

Page 137.—the priest game.

The baggage changes hands every time a priest is met. The game is still played, but priests being rarer than in feudal times, persons wearing spectacles are substituted.

Page 139.—Yoshitsuné.

The brother of Yoritomo (1192–1199), the first of the Kamakura Shōguns. After defeating his brother's enemies he was himself attacked and slain by order of his brother, who feared his ability and popularity. Since then he has become a traditional hero and many stories and superstitions are connected with his name. The names mentioned are persons with whom he is associated. The Lady Shidzuka was his mistress, and Benkei was a robber-priest who allied himself with Yoshitsuné's fortunes and figures as the Friar Tuck of Japan.

Page 140.—Tenjin Sama.

This is the name under which is apotheosised the great Minister and scholar Sugawara-no-Michizané, who was charged with having spoken disrespectfully of the Emperor and was banished to Kyūshū (901 A.D.).

Page 140.—Emma at the Chōraku Temple.

Emma is the Regent of the Buddhist Hell. The Chōraku Temple is presumably that at Higashiyama, Kyōto.

Page 141-2.—wicked old fox.

The fox is credited with the power to change itself into the human shape to deceive people, only its tail remaining as evidence that it is a fox. Yaji later shows that he is on his guard against the kind of tricks foxes are supposed to play. Dogs are supposed to be able to see through the fox's disguise.

Page 146.—On the four seas.

This is Aston's translation of the ode from the Nō drama of 'Takasago,' which is always sung at weddings.

Page 151.—Her hair was rather disordered.

Disordered hair in woman is regarded as a sign of madness.

Page 153.—Did you say high-priced trout ?

In the original the joke turns upon his pretending to hear her say that the fish was pickled in vinegar,—a way in which they were never prepared apparently.

Page 156.—straw sandals.

These are 'waraji,' sandals made of coarse straw-rope, tied on to the feet. They were used when travelling. The other kind of sandal is held on by a thong which goes between the toes. Horses were also fitted with straw sandals, the use of iron being extremely limited in Japan in feudal times. Fukuzawa in his autobiography records that the thing that excited the greatest astonishment among the Japanese who first visited western countries was the great use made of iron.

Page 157.—game of chess.

Curiously enough in Japan chess is the game of the lower classes. 'Go' (commonly called 'checkers' by foreigners) is now the game of the intellectuals.

Page 158.—gold and silver.

The names of two of the pieces used in Japanese chess.

Page 159.—Onbako.

At Atsuta, near Nagoya, there is said to be a stone statue of an old woman in a sitting position which is dedicated to this god. Tradition relates that in the Era of Eiroku (1558–1570) a priest named Kwojun was drowned in crossing the River Shojin, and that a covetous old woman who stole the dead priests's robes was punished by this god.

Page 165.—a fire-blower.

This is a bamboo tube through which the charcoal in the brazier is blown to a glow.

Page 181.—Namada.

This is from the Sanskrit 'namo,' honour. Kitahachi wilfully mis-interprets it as the Japanese 'nama,' raw, and suggests that the 'tako' (octopus) is not eaten boiled but raw.

Page 182.—to go to heaven by sneezing.

Yaji is joking on the saying 'Shama kara chōro,' from an acolyte to a patriarch—('You must learn to creep before you walk'),—but he substitutes 'kushami' (sneeze) for 'shami.'

Page 183.—Kompira.

Kompira is a highly popular divinity, especially with seamen and travellers, and many shrines are erected throughout the country to his honour. Some pilgrims confine their devotions entirely to these shrines. Kompira is the Sanskrit 'Kumbhira,' but has been claimed as a Shintō god.

Page 188.—The gear for carrying two people.

This was a kind of cradle that was placed across the horse's back, the two riders balancing each other on either side.

Page 191.—Kampei and O Karu.

Two characters in the Chūshingura, as already noted. The inscriptions on the targets are in the form of riddles, and the answer to the riddle is given should the shooter hit the target with his dart. The reference lower down to Yoichibei being out for the sake of his child on a dark night is also taken from the Chūshingura. Yoichibei was returning home with the money for which his daughter O Karu had sold herself for the sake of enabling her husband to contribute to the funds for carrying out the revenge, when he was set upon by a robber and murdered. Afterwards his son-in-law Kampei came along and shot at a wild boar, missing the boar but killing the murderer of his father-in-law. He finds the money on the man and takes it home, but later learns that his father-in-law has been killed and robbed. Thinking that he has himself killed his father-in-law, he commits suicide. Yaji expects that the answer to the riddle on the target would be the wild boar, but it is the Giant Mikoshi, a kind of ghost, with a long neck, which is supposed to appear on dark nights.

Page 193.—Shunman Shosando.
This is the name of a writer of comic poems of the time. His real name was Kubo Shunman, but he also called himself 'Nandaka Shiran,' which is equivalent to the English locution 'Whatshisname.'

Page 193.—Hizakurigé.
Ikku is recorded to have made a pilgrimage in November 1805.

Page 198.—Senshuan.
A writer of comic poems who died in 1814. His real name was Akamatsu Masatsuné. He was also known as 'Sandara Bōshi.'

Page 198.—Shakuyakutei Ushi.
A writer of comic poems who lived in Edo and died in 1845. His real name was Tsugawara Jiroemon. He was also known as 'Chōkon.'

Page 199.—Koikawa Harumachi.
Novelist and artist of Edo who died in 1789.

Page 199.—What's that phrase ('san') written above it?
The questions and answers are a series of puns on the numerals, 'ni' (two), 'san' (three), 'shi' (four), 'go' (five), 'roku' (six), 'shichi' (seven). Gomajiru always goes one higher than Kita.

Page 199.—Takuan.
A Buddhist priest of the Zen sect, born 1573, died 1645. His real name was Sohō Heiji, but he wrote under the name of Takuan. He is famous for his writings and poems, but still more, perhaps, for having introduced from China methods of pickling vegetables. Pickled radish is still called 'takuan' after him.

Page 200.—Is it in Toba?
This and the answer are quotations from the Chūshingura.

Page 206.—Miyazono and Kunidaiyu.
These are the names of tunes or chants, so styled after the names of the composers.

Page 208.—tambourine-chamber at the Chizukaya.
Presumably a room where the principal decorations are representations of tambourines.

Page 209.—Kawasaki Ondo.
This is the Isé Dance, which was originally performed at a place near Furuichi called Kawasaki.

Page 209.—Shintō priest.
These are not properly priests, but persons who look after the pilgrims and conduct them to lodgings, etc.

Page 209.—Are you beggars then?

That is people who go about reciting 'jōruri' in the street for a living.

Page 209.—doing some business for themselves.

There is a double meaning attached to this phrase.

Page 213.—It will pay at least for the oranges.

There is a pun here which it is impossible to produce in a translation.

Page 213.—Fujiya.

'Fuji' is the wistaria, which was perhaps where Yaji got his idea of something hanging down.

Page 216.—Chikuma pot.

In the village of Irié in the district of Sakata, in Omi Province (Shiga Prefecture) there is a religious festival held every year on the 1st of April which is called the festival of the Chikuma pot. In ancient times the women received an earthenware pot for each time that they had been married, and these they had to carry in the festival procession every year. Those who had been married more than once and were ashamed to own it were supposed to incur the wrath of the god and to become ill if they did not carry the right number of pots. Nowadays the festival is celebrated in September, when eight maidens carry vessels shaped like pots in the procession. Apparently the vessels were carried on the head.

Page 221.—Benten.

One of the seven gods of luck.

Page 225.—Feather-robe pine-tree.

There is a tradition that an angel descended at Matsubara in the Province of Suruga and left its robe of feathers on a tree. A Nō drama is founded on this tradition.

Page 225.—the spearmen of a daimyō's procession.

On entering a town it was the custom of the spearmen who accompanied the Daimyos' processions to throw their spears into the air and catch them again.

Page 226.—Sugi and Tama.

Tradition has it that two beggar girls started this game at Ai-no-yama. Later many others took it up till the authorities interfered and restricted it. It is still to be seen at Isé.

Page 228.—the net has eyes.

The joke in the original turns on the similarity in sound of 'kané' and 'kazé.' There is a Japanese proverb reading 'Ami (net) no mé (meshes) ni kazé (wind) tamarazu (does not collect),' the wind does not collect in the meshes of a net. Ikku inverts the proverb and substitutes 'kané' (money) for 'kazé' (wind), making the proverb read 'Money stops in the meshes of a net.'

Page 228.—the Holy Mirror and the Holy Sword.

These are part of the Imperial Regalia. The Mirror is the emblem of the Sun Goddess Amaterasu, to whom the Shrine is dedicated.

Page 229.—Gekū Temple.

This is the Outer Temple. Ikku has confused Kunitokotachi with Toyoukebimé, who is the goddess of food. They are two separate deities. The shrine was formerly dedicated to the former but is now dedicated to the latter.

Page 232.—a duck of a spoon.

In the original the joke turns upon the material of which the spoon is made,—that is bamboo. In Japanese a bamboo-grove doctor is a quack doctor.

Page 232.—Dōjō temple.

A well-known temple south of Wakayama in Kii Province. Its bell is famous in legend in connection with the story of the monk Anchin, who sought secape from a woman to whom he had made a love vow by hiding under the bell. The woman changed herself into a dragon and by lashing the bell with her tail made it redhot, so that Anchin was scorched to death. Here, as in the other cases, the picture of the temple has a punning connection with the medicine. Cinnamon is 'keishi' in Japanese and Keishi was the name of a well-known actor in the Dōjō theatre.

Page 232.—Emma.

Emma is the god of the infernal regions and is called 'Daio,' great king, which is also the word for 'rhubarb.'

Page 232.—Dog on fire.

Dried orange-peel is 'chimpi,' which represents 'chim' (or 'chin') dog, and 'hi' (changed to 'pi' after m or n) fire.

Page 232.—jasmine root.

Jasmine root is 'sanjishi,' where 'san' is childbirth and 'jishi' or 'shishi,' the sound in making water.

Page 232.—lizard tail.

This is 'hangé' (Saururus loureiri), read as 'han,' stamp or seal, and 'ge' or 'ke' hair.

Page 232.—aegle.

This is 'kikoku' (Aegle sepiaria), where 'ki' represents devil and 'koku,' breaking wind.

Page 232.—hayamé.

Medicine for easing the pains of labour.

Page 234.—the three countries.

Japan, China and India specifically, but used in the sense of the world,—the only world known to feudal Japan.

Page 237.—the book of Izumo.

The Shrine of Izumo, which ranks next in importance to the Grand Shrine of Isé, is dedicated to the god Ōnamuji, who is supposed to keep a record of all marriages. The temporary connections formed on the road while travelling, however, are not recorded in the Book of Izumo.

Page 237.—Satsuma sweet-potato.

The sweet-potato was first introduced into the rest of Japan from Satsuma Province and is still called the Satsuma-potato.

Page 238.—Chujō Island.

This was a pleasure quarter near Fushimi.

Page 238.—Dōtombōri.

This is still the entertainment quarter of Osaka.

Page 239.—Okesa and Matsuzaka.

The names of two tunes or chants.

Page 240.—'The roll is mine.'

This refers to an alleged incident in the life of Yoshitsuné, when he sought to get access to a manuscript dealing with the art of war and only succeeded by dint of making love to the owner's daughter and getting her to steal it.

Page 243.—Shirokoi.

'Shiruko' is a food prepared from peas, and the joke here is that the like-sounding 'Shirokoi' stands for 'Shiro, come,' 'shiro' (white) being the name given to white dogs.

Page 243.—a new pot.

In Japanese 'shibin,' urinal.

Page 246.—a hovel in the river bed.

Owing to the steepness of their fall a large number of the rivers in Japan are dry for many months of the year. The dry beds were greatly resorted to by beggars, who built their hovels under the bridges.

Page 251.—the day of the rat.

Years, days and hours were all counted in feudal Japan as belonging to one of the twelve signs of the zodiac, the order of which is :— Rat (né), bull (ushi), tiger (tora), hare (u), dragon (tatsu), serpent (mi), horse (uma), goat (hitsuji), monkey (saru), cock (tori), dog (inu), boar (i). These were combined with ten 'celestial signs' borrowed from China, thus making cycles of sixty days or years.

Page 252.—Saburo Yoshihidé.

Kita means that he would not stop even if he were the lowest of retainers, such as Saburo Yoshihidé.

Page 255.—getting through the holes.

Those able to get through the holes are supposed to obtain easy entrance into paradise.

Page 256.—Ya-en-sa.
Meaningless cries of encouragement.

Page 262.—Namu Amida Butsu.
This is the prayer of many of the Buddhist sects. 'Namu' is from the Sanskrit, a word meaning 'reverence,' 'honour.' The whole prayer is practically equivalent to 'Save me Amida Buddha.' Amida is the Sanskrit Amitabha. The Great Buddha at Kamakura is a representation of Amida.

Page 263.—Atsumori's burial place.
Atsumori was a youth of seventeen who fought on the side of the Heiké in the great clan struggle between them and the Genji. After the Heiké were routed at Ichi-no-tani at Suma he was making his way to a ship when a Genji warrior challenged him. He turned back to fight and was defeated and slain.

Page 268.—'Kachin.'
'Kachin' is a dialect word for 'mochi,' rice-cake; 'yachin,' with which Yaji rimes it, means 'rent.'

Page 272.—Praying to Kompira.
This is a favourite deity originally Buddhist but later taken over as a Shintō god.

Page 273.—Namu Kimyō Chōrai.
'Namu' and 'Kimyō' are practically synonymous, with the meaning already given. 'Chōrai' means humble ceremony, here prostration at the feet of the god. This prayer is used for all Buddhist divinities.

Page 273.—cold water penance.
This is a favourite penance among all Buddhist devotees.

Page 277.—the famous saké of Kamogawa.
This and the other names mentioned in this paragraph are mostly names of places. But Kamamoto is the name of a maker of face-powder and the Teikinōrai is the name of a book.

Page 277.—stolen journey.
Stolen because they had run away without paying their bills.

Page 277.—Gojo Bridge, where of old Ushiwakamaru fought with Benkei.
Ushiwakamaru was the name of Yoshitsuné in his boyhood. Benkei was a robber priest who was trying to collect a thousand swords and lay in wait on the bridge to rob people of their swords. He met his match in Ushiwakamaru, however, and after a fierce fight was driven off. On the following day there was another encounter, when Benkei owned himself defeated and vowed allegiance to the youth who had defeated him. He remained faithful to Yoshitsuné through all his fortunes till he died fighting for him.

Page 277.—Kadodé Hachiman.
A shrine dedicated to Hachiman, the god of war.

Page 278.—kappa.
An imaginary animal supposed to live in the rivers.

Page 280.—purple hoods on their heads.
Miyagawachō was a pleasure quarter. One suggestion is that the men were actors who took women's parts.

Page 281.—the famous Sangoro.
A well known actor of the time. Also Arakichi and Tomokichi.

Page 281.—box-opener.
The boxes in the Japanese theatre are squares separated by a very low rail. The audience sit on cushions on the floor.

Page 281.—Uji.
Uji, near Nara, is famous for its tea.

Page 283.—Flowery-way.
This is the 'hana-michi,' a raised gangway running from the stage to the back of the theatre, along which the actors sometimes make their entrance.

Page 289.—We make bean-sauce in a storehouse.
The storehouse ('anagura') is a pit dug in the ground to keep provisions in.

Page 294.—the ladder was to show that he was going up to the capital.
The Japanese also speak of going up to the capital.

Page 294.—that he had no money.
Both 'money' and 'bell' are 'kané' in Japanese, and both the bell-clapper and the beggar-priest were to intimate that the son had no 'kané,' money.

Page 295.—interludes.
These are comic pieces enacted between the Nō dramas.

Page 295.—Mugen.
Mugen is a temple dedicated to Kwannon at Nishiyama in Tōtōmi Province. He who strikes the bell of Mugen is supposed to get rich in this life but to be doomed to eternal punishment in the next. In the theatres a washbasin is introduced instead of a bell.

Page 295.—Ume-ga-é (plum-branch).
This is the name of a girl in the pleasure quarter with whom Genta is in love. Genta is Kajiwara Genta Kagesué, who fought at the battle of the Uji River, contending with one of his comrades who should cross the river first.

Page 299.—when copper goes up in price.
Copper here stands for the smaller coins of copper. On exchange, when the value of the copper coins goes up, gold falls. Here the joke turns on the popular name for the male organs,—golden spheres.

Page 299.—go on to the temple.
To arrange for the funeral, funerals being always carried out under Buddhist rites in those times.

Page 299.—For a maiden born in the capital.
Yaji is parodying a poem.

Page 306.—I cooked this trout for you with all my liver.
The puns in the original are as silly as those substituted and are hardly worth explaining.

Page 307.—Kuyadō.
The priest's account of the origin of the name is a joke. The order, which is a branch of the Jōdō sect of Buddhism, was founded by Kuya Shōnin. The priests were not required to shave their heads, could marry, and could wear laymen's dress. They went about selling tea-whisks. Ikku, however, represents them as dressed in priests' robes.

Page 308.—a 'meshimori.'
Yaji takes this word in the meaning of maid at an inn, i.e. girl who serves the rice ('meshi'). The 'sakamori' was a saké feast.

Page 309.—the Satsuma game.
See previous note.

Page 312.—Tambakaidō.
The road to Tamba Province.

Page 315.—forty-seven people.
This is another reference to the Forty-seven Rōnin. The Amagawaya at Sakai was where there lived a retainer of the nobleman whose death the rōnin were determined to avenge. The retainer assisted the rōnin in getting armour. 'Amagawa' means the Milky Way and 'ya' is house. The Milky Way House was the sign of the shop kept by the retainer.

Page 316.—Mount Kōya.
A celebrated mountain in Kishū on which a monastery was founded by Kōbō Daishi, the great Buddhist preacher who lived in the ninth century. Mount Kōya is a favourite place for burials.

Page 317.—nose on a lion's mask.
That is anything but a high nose.

Page 321.—Shūgetsu Myōkwō Shinnyō.
This is the Buddhist name given to the wife after she was dead.

Page 322.—Emperor Nintoku.
The Emperor Nintoku reigned from 313 to 399.

Page 323.—Come and hear the Shirokiya.
Ikku has mixed up the names of the jōruri which the man is calling out. Benkei did not commit suicide, but fell in battle.

Page 325.—An ode from the Dōjōji.
The Dōjōji is here the name of a 'jōruri' concerning the temple.

Page 325.—blackened teeth.
The married women blackened their teeth in feudal times.

Page 325.—Yamazukushi.
A song made up of the names of celebrated mountains, beginning with Mount Fuji.

Page 329.—I'm going to turn priest.
That is renounce the world.

Page 332.—Yūki silk kimono.
Yūki is the name of a place in Shimosa Province where the silk is made. Hachijō is one of the islands of the Bōnin group. 'Tōzan' is the name of a design originally hailing from China.

Page 334.—to feel Kiyomori's pulse.
This is stated to be an expression taken from a song. Kiyomori was the great statesman of the twelfth century.

Page 336.—sticks on the divining board.
There are fifty sticks and six divining boards. Half of the latter have indentations and represent the negative or female principle, and the other three are unmarked and represent the positive or male principle.

Page 336.—the Book tells us.
This is the fortune-teller's bible,—the Eki-kyō.

Page 336.—Kwanei Era.
From 1624 to 1644.

Page 338.—southern Gompachi.
Gompachi is the name given to buffoons, but it seems here to be used with reference to the celebrated robber Shirai Gompachi, whose story is told in Mitford's 'Tales of Old Japan.'

Page 338.—Yoriya aikori yo aikori yo.
This is a meaningless chorus, like ' Hi-tiddlety-hi-ty.'

Page 350.—the old man with the lantern pounds the rice.
Pounding the rice has here apparently the meaning of sitting down on the ground by accident.

Page 353.—Shōtoku Taishi.
Described as the Constantine of Japanese Buddhism. He founded the temple about the year 600.

Page 355.—lifted one of the doors from its grooves.
The door would be a framework covered with paper and sliding in grooves, with the name of the shop and an advertisement of the goods sold painted on the paper. 'Zenzai-mochi' is a kind of rice-cake and 'Sango-dango' a kind of dumpling.

Page 358.—Manzairakuja.
A meaningless expression.

Page 361.—I'll hold the spills.
It is customary to use paper rolled into spills in drawing lots in this way.

Page 361.—burdock and eggs.
These are considered aphrodisiacs; also Sanzo and Koshiyoshi pills.

Page 364.—pulling out the shutters to keep out the rain.
The shutters slide in grooves and are slid into a sort of box in the daytime and pulled out at night or when there is a violent rainstorm, so as to prevent the paper windows from getting wet.

Page 369.—Musashi.
The name of the province in which Edo stood.

Page 369.—says the poem.
The poem appears in the 'Zoku Kokinshiu,' a continuation of the ' Kokinshiu,' the anthology compiled by Ki-no-Tsurayaki, the author of the ' Tosa Nikki.'

Page 369.—flowering grasses.
Specifically the ' obana,' tail flower (Miscanthus sinensis).

Page 369.—pleasure quarter.
Specifically Nakano-chō, a street in the Yoshiwara district.

Page 369.—Edo.
Edo was founded by Ieyasu and became the capital of the Tokugawas when they attained the Shogunate.

Page 369.—Tochimenya.
Ikku's names all have a humorous tinge. 'Tochimenya' means ' acornface,' and lower down ' Hanamizu' is ' nose water.'

Page 369.—Fuchū.
The old name for Shizuoka, the capital of Suruga Province, the ' short' form for which is Sunshū. Mount Fuji is in Suruga Province.

Page 370.—thus spitting out.
In the original ' Kaku Ashikubo no cha naru koto wo haki-chirashi.' The commentators explain that Ashikubo is the centre of the tea-producing district of Shizuoka prefecture, which is famous for its tea. The joke seems to lie in the use of the word ' cha ' (tea) as a term of contempt.

Page 370.—Kanda.
This is one of the wards of the city.

Page 370.—coming of age.
This was the ceremony of cutting the hair and shaving the head which signified the attainment of manhood. A change of name was very common at that time

Page 370.—natto.
Made from soya beans.

Page 370.—mountain potatoes.
The yam (Discorea japonica).

Page 372.—grog shop.
Yaji coins a punning word for an eating house on the analogy of a drinking house.

Page 372.—What have you got.
In the original Yaji here makes a pun. Futsu says she has some soup made of the meat of shell-fish ('mukimi'). Yaji wilfully mishears this as 'nukimi,' which means a drawn sword, and asks how he can eat that. Then he continues the joke by hearing 'karajiru' (shell soup) as 'kirazu,' not able to cut, and concludes that if the sword will not cut there is no danger.

Page 373.—bring out the wine.
The drinking of saké by the bride and bridegroom is part of the Japanese marriage ceremony.

Page 373.—two or three lives.
That is to say each vows to become man and wife again when they are reincarnated.

Page 373.—two fish-cutters.
Samurai above a certain rank wore two swords.

Page 373.—Council of Ministers.
Each daimyō had a Ministry resembling that of the Shōgun.

Page 373.—wedding presents.
The wedding presents exchanged between the families of the bride and the bridegroom are a guarantee that the contract will be carried out.

Page 375.—three and a half lines of divorce.
The legal formula for divorce occupies three and a half lines of Japanese writing. This is divorce by mutual consent, though too often the wife's consent is taken for granted.

Page 375.—hundred 'koku' samurai.
Each samurai was allowed so much rice according to his position. A samurai who received two hundred 'koku' of rice would be of high rank. A 'koku' is equal to about five bushels.

Page 376.—to receive the bride with white faces.
Under the influence of saké the Japanese get very flushed.

Page 376.—the clash of the bearers' sticks.
The sticks of the kago bearers, used to support the kago pole on when changing shoulders.

Page 378.—this time there shall be no mistake.
Kita is here quoting from some ' jōruri.'

Page 381.—yai, yai.
The Japanese think a person can be restored to consciousness by shouting at them.

Page 383.—Shinda ko, etc.
These are all imitations of common street-cries. ' Shinda ko,' meaning ' dead child,' is put for ' shin daiko,' new radishes; ' yurensō,' (' yurei,' ghost) is for ' hōrensō,' spinach; ' bakegiya ' (' baké,' ghost) is for ' wakegi,' onion ; ' sotoba no himono ' is literally ' dried fish tablets,' ' sotoba ' being the wooden tables set up in commemoration of the dead ; ' sekitō ' is tombstone, and ' tachi-uri ' means that the buyer can purchase any quantity he requires.

Page 384.—the child behaved like a fox.
Imoshichi is quoting from a ' jōruri,' which tells of a fox which changed itself into a woman and was married and had a child. It was through the child's behaviour in eating rats and so on that the real nature of the mother was discovered.

Page 385.—Naniwa.
The ancient poetical name for Osaka.

IKKU'S LAST POEM

Kono yo woba

    Dorya o itoma ni

Senko to

    Tomo ni tsui ni wa

    Hai sayonara

Come leave this world thou dost

not think to make a longer stay

The funeral incense turns to dust

thou forbear to say farewell to day